Accession no.
36238359

WITHDRAWN

Contemporary French cinema

D1362836

MANCHESTER
1824

Manchester University Press

For Joanne, Joseph and Patrick

Contemporary French cinema

An introduction

Second edition

GUY AUSTIN

LIS - LIBRARY

Date	Fund
1/7/16	Che-F

Order No.

0275261X

University of Chester

distributed exclusively in the USA by Palgrave Macmillan

MANCHESTER UNIVERSITY PRESS Manchester and New York

Copyright © Guy Austin 1996, 2008

The right of Guy Austin to be identified as the author of this work has been asserted
by him in accordance with the Copyright, Designs and Patents Act 1988

This edition published 2008 by Manchester University Press
Oxford Road, Manchester M13 9NR, UK
and Room 400, 175 Fifth Avenue, New York, NY 10010, USA
www.manchesteruniversitypress.co.uk

Distributed exclusively in the USA by
Palgrave Macmillan, 175 Fifth Avenue, New York,
NY 10010, USA

Distributed exclusively in Canada by
UBC Press, University of British Columbia, 2029 West Mall,
Vancouver, BC, Canada V6T 1Z2

British Library Cataloguing-in-Publication Data
A catalogue record for this book is available from the British Library

ISBN 978 0 7190 7829 3

Library of Congress Cataloging-in-Publication Data applied for

This edition first published 2008

18 17 16 15 14 13 12 11 10   10 9 8 7 6 5 4 3 2

Typeset in Photina with Frutiger
by Koinonia, Manchester
Printed in Great Britain
by Bell & Bain Ltd, Glasgow

Contents

Illustrations

All illustrations courtesy of BFI Stills, Posters and Designs

Every effort has been made to obtain permission to reproduce the images in this book. If any proper acknowledgement is lacking, copyright holders are invited to contact the publisher.

Preface

This book is written for students and fans of modern French cinema, and is intended to provide an introduction to French film studies. I have concentrated mainly, though not exclusively, on films which have had either a theatrical or video release in Britain, or which are available on video or DVD from France. It seems important to me that the films analysed here be fairly readily available to the readers of this book, and there are other books which bring the attention of an Anglophone audience to more obscure or neglected French films.

For ease of understanding I have provided my own translations of the French comments cited in the text, although all film titles remain in the original.

Acknowledgements

Thanks to my wife Joanne and my brother Thomas, for everything.

To the staff and students at Sheffield University French Department, especially to Julia Dobson, for their valuable suggestions. Also to Graeme Hayes and Martin O'Shaugnessy at Nottingham Trent University for their insight, to the staff at the BFI Stills Department for their help, and to my editor Matthew Frost for his support and patience.

Finally to Arrow, Artificial Eye, Electric, Gala, Metro, Nouvelles éditions de films and President Films for granting permission to publish stills.

French cinema from 1895 to 1968, a brief survey

1

The birth of cinema

The year 1995 saw France celebrating the centenary of cinema as a national achievement, a celebration enhanced by the recent victory over the United States regarding the exemption of films from the GATT free-trade agreement. Numerous film exhibitions and retrospectives were organised, including a showing of the entire catalogue of 1,400 short films made by the pioneering Lumière brothers. A hundred years after the Lumières' break-through in 1895, the film industry remained the barometer by which the French measured the cultural state of their nation.

The pioneers of moving pictures

The development of moving pictures was a piece-meal process, dependent on experimentation and advancement in the recording, reproduction and projection of photographic images. The first steps in this process were the invention of the magic lantern in the seventeenth century, and of photography and various moving-image toys – such as Jacob Plateau's *phénakistiscope* – in the 1830s. By 1895, developments were coming to a head on both sides of the Atlantic. In the States, Eadweard Muybridge had made his photographic studies of people and animals in motion, and Thomas Edison had patented and exported his kinetoscope, whereby a single spectator could watch a tiny image on film. The first kinetoscope parlour in France opened in late 1893, and Parisians could also watch the animated cartoons of Émile Reynaud's *Théâtre optique.* But the first truly collective film show, and hence the birth of cinema, took place on 28 December 1895, when the Lumière brothers' *cinématographe* was watched by an audience paying one franc each at the Grand Café, boulevard des Capucines in Paris. The *cinématographe*, a combined motion-picture camera, projector and printer, had first been patented by the photographers and inventors Auguste and Louis Lumière in February 1895.

Whereas Edison's early films had to be shot in the studio, the *ciné-matographe* was light enough to be used for filming in the street, and the Lumières captured such unstaged events as a baby playing or workers leaving a factory. Their famous short film of 1895, *L'Arrivée d'un train en gare de La Ciotat*, 'is said to have made the unprepared audiences scatter in alarm as the locomotive seemed to approach them' (Robinson 1994: 9), while *L'Arroseur arrosé* of the same year, the world's first (albeit brief) fiction film, established the visual gag as the basis for film comedy. Besides initiating what later became the documentary and comedy genres, the Lumières also developed film techniques which were to prove fundamental to the grammar of cinema. Their series *Les Pompiers de Lyon* (1895) linked together various shots taken from different angles in a pioneering example of editing; a year later one of their agents developed the tracking shot while shooting from a gondola in Venice (Sadoul 1962: 7).

If the Lumières pioneered the recording of action on film, and the techniques of open-air filming and montage (editing), their contemporary Georges Méliès used *mise en scène* (staging) to create artful and fantastical tableaux. The two strands of cinema that they inaugurated can be traced throughout film history, the Lumières influencing documentary, neo-realist and *nouvelle vague* film, Méliès the fantasy film, literary adaptation, historical reconstruction and *la tradition de qualité* (see below). A professional magician, Méliès built the precursor of the film studio in 1897, a glasshouse with a central stage, which was filmed from a point of view identical to that of the spectator watching a play. This concern with filmed theatre even led Méliès to move the titles of his films up the screen in imitation of the curtain going up on a stage play. Spurning camera movement for static tableaux and close-ups for a wide composition showing all the stage, Méliès had to exaggerate the size of important objects, hence the enormous key in *Barbe-Bleue* (1901). As already noted, the genres established by Méliès were numerous, but he was most famous for his fantasy films, either fairy-tales and legends like *Cendrillon* (1899) or science-fiction films adapted from the novels of Jules Vernes, like *20 000 lieues sous les mers* (1907). He prefigured the heritage film's obsession with authenticity (see chapter 7) in his careful researching of recent events for films like *L'Affaire Dreyfus* (1899). His tight control over all aspects of staging and filming – including the introduction of innovative effects like the double exposure and the dissolve – and his idiosyncratic style also make Méliès the first *auteur* in French cinema (see below). He seems to have recognised this himself when declaring that the success of film as a medium was due not to its inventors the Lumières, but to those who used it to record their own personal productions (Sadoul 1962: 8).

Early French cinema as a global force

Following Méliès' lead, the cinema entrepreneurs Charles Pathé and Léon Gaumont built studios in Paris in the early years of the twentieth century. Both men also headed powerful French companies, Pathé Frères originally specialising in the phonograph, L. Gaumont et Compagnie in photography. Between them, they established the French film industry as a commercial force of such global influence that in the years 1908 to 1910 the majority of films distributed in the world were French (Billard 1994: 56). Commercialising the new medium far more rapidly than their American counterparts, Pathé and Gaumont were responsible not only for developing technical hardware, but also for producing and distributing films, and for setting up chains of cinemas in France and in England.

While Méliès, having failed to adapt his rigid film style, ceased independent production in 1909, the directors employed by Pathé and Gaumont ensured that innovation continued, particularly by launching new and extremely popular genres. At Pathé, for example, Ferdinand Zecca introduced the crime film and the use of seedy, realistic settings with *L'Histoire d'un crime* (1901) and *Les Victimes de l'alcoolisme* (1902). In the ensuing years, the melodramas, crime stories and comedies of Zecca and his colleagues at Pathé were distributed with great success through a series of agencies in Europe, Japan and America, and in 1908 Pathé sold twice as many films to the United States as all the American production companies combined (Sadoul 1962: 12). Meanwhile Léon Gaumont, who had given up directing in 1900, turned to his secretary Alice Guy, who thus became the first woman film-maker. Guy directed numerous films before setting up a branch of Gaumont in New York in 1907. After Guy's departure, her co-director on *La Vie du Christ* (1906), Victorien Jasset, launched the detective film with the *Nick Carter* series, filmed between 1908 and 1910 for the third major production company, Éclair. The immediate popularity of the genre led Louis Feuillade, Guy's replacement at Gaumont, to emulate and indeed surpass Jasset's success, by filming the *Fantômas* novels written by Pierre Souvestre and Marcel Alain. If Nick Carter was the world's first film detective, Feuillade's Fantômas, star of a cycle of adventures shot in 1913 and 1914, was its first arch-villain, known as 'the emperor of crime'. Set in realistic urban surroundings, and combining a documentary attention to the streets of pre-war Paris with an evocation of mystery and lyricism, the *Fantômas* series was to prove a major influence on surrealism (see below). It also ensured, along with Jasset's *Nick Carter* films, French dominance in popular cinema before World War One. The formula employed by Jasset and Feuillade was imitated across the world, by the *Homunculus* series in Germany, *Ultus* in Britain, *Tigris* in Italy and *The Perils of Pauline* (filmed for Pathé by a French director) in the United States.

France was pre-eminent in the field of the art film. Founded in 1908 and reliant first on Pathé and later on Éclair for production and distribution, the *Film d'Art* company brought the 'high' culture of the theatre into the realm of cinema. Using stage actors from the Comédie Française and prestigious writers from the Académie, the company achieved its greatest success with Charles Le Bargy's film *L'Assassinat du duc de Guise* (1908), followed by literary adaptations from Victor Hugo, Eugène Sue, and others. Like the work of Méliès, the *film d'art* is a major precursor of *la tradition de qualité* and the heritage film. But in pre-war cinema, it was overshadowed by popular genres, notably the crime story and also the Pathé comedies starring the first international film star, Max Linder.

French dominance of world cinema was curtailed by the outbreak of the First World War in 1914. The Russian and eastern European markets were lost immediately, while the threat to Paris from the German army halted film production for a year, and subsequent French production included nationalistic propaganda films which were far less successful than the pre-war offerings. Moreover, as was to happen in 1940, a number of French technicians and directors left the country to work elsewhere. Coincidentally, American cinema was beginning to compete successfully both in the United States and in Europe. In return for exporting French productions, Pathé, Éclair and Gaumont imported American films into France, notably the popular comedies of Mack Sennett and Charlie Chaplin. Aware that France was on the point of losing its Anglophone markets in Britain and the United States, Charles Pathé decided in 1918 to pull out of film financing and production, and to concentrate on distribution. Emerging from the war victorious but damaged, France found that in terms of cinema, the United States was now the dominant force. By 1919, only 10 per cent of films on French screens were home-produced, and an unprecedented 50 per cent were American (Billard 1994: 57).

The first and second avant-gardes

In the aftermath of World War One, not only was French cinema commercially in decline, it was also aesthetically stagnant. While Germany, the United States, Britain and Sweden all boasted emergent national film movements of considerable artistic importance – the most influential being German expressionism – French productions were still in the pre-war vein. Yet within ten years, France had provided cinema with its first avant-garde movement – impressionism – and with surrealist film, known as 'the second avant-garde'.

Impressionism

The prime mover behind impressionism was Louis Delluc, a journalist and director who is often credited with inventing film criticism. Having established the first *ciné-club* in 1920 to promote alternative films, the following year Delluc launched the review *Cinéa*, in which he declared: 'Que le Cinéma français soit du cinéma, que le Cinéma français soit français' [Let French Cinema be true cinema, let French Cinema be truly French] (Sadoul 1962: 24). Reacting against the literary adaptations of the *film d'art* – although far from commending the popular genres of comedy and crime story – Delluc asserted that cinema was an artistic medium in its own right, distinct from theatre or literature. Influenced by D. W. Griffith's *Broken Blossoms* (1919), Delluc sought in his own films to convey, through editing, the motions of human psychology, and to this end developed the flashback technique in *La Femme de nulle part* (1922). Similar aims were held by the film-makers associated with Delluc and forming the impressionist avant-garde. Germaine Dulac, who had directed *La Fête espagnole* from Delluc's scenario in 1919, summarised impressionist practice in assessing her film *La Mort du soleil* (1920): 'I used, in addition to facial expressions, [...] objects, lights and shadows, and I gave these elements a visual value equivalent in intensity and cadence to the physical and mental condition of the character' (Williams 1993: 101). The innovations in film technique which resulted from the impressionists' desire to evoke human subjectivity included close-ups, camera movements, rapid editing, flashbacks and subjective point-of-view shots. Marcel L'Herbier's *El Dorado* (1921) featured 'semi-subjective' sequences to express a character's psychological state: 'The most famous of these is set in a cabaret where a dancer [...] distractedly sits with other women, thinking about her sick young son. She is out of focus, the other characters perfectly in focus' (Williams 1993: 105). Rhythmic cutting to express a drunken or unstable state of mind, first evident in Abel Gance's *La Roue* (1922) and subsequently in Jean Epstein's *Cœur fidèle* (1923), was perhaps the technique most closely linked with the movement. In *Napoléon vu par Abel Gance* (1927), the most famous and idiosyncratic member of the group combined a commercial, conventional subject – the historical epic – with radical new forms. His use of three screens for the projection of the film predated Hollywood's Cinerama by over twenty years, while the subjective camera was employed in a number of startling new ways, all facilitated by the portable movie cameras available in France at the time. For chase scenes, Gance attached a camera to a horse; when Napoléon dived into the sea, a camera was thrown off a cliff to record his point of view; at the staging of the siege of Toulon, a tiny camera in a football evoked the experience of a soldier blown into the air.

With the exception of Gance's *Napoléon* and L'Herbier's *L'Argent* (1928) – neither of which was purely impressionist – no major productions came out of the movement after 1923. Out of favour with the large production companies and the public, impressionism had nevertheless established film in France as a complex artistic medium supported by a critical discourse and an alternative screening and debating network, the *ciné-clubs*. It was this network, and in particular the avant-garde Parisian cinemas, Studio des Ursulines and Studio 28, which provided the second avant-garde – surrealism – with an audience.

Surrealism

Born out of the pacifist and absurdist Dada group, surrealism developed as a major artistic movement in Paris during the 1920s, under the authoritarian leadership of André Breton. The year 1924 saw the publication of Breton's first surrealist manifesto, and the group proceeded to demand a revolution in the arts and indeed in lifestyle, subverting received norms of expression in many fields including literature, painting, photography and cinema, and aiming to liberate the unconscious from codes of civilised behaviour. The first surrealist film was the ironically titled *Le Retour à la raison* (1923), a short collection of animated photos by the American photographer Man Ray. The film's première, a Dadaist evening, in fact degenerated into a riot. The riot produced a schism out of which the surrealist group was formed. The following year René Clair, a young film-maker not directly associated with either group, was asked by the Dadaist painter Francis Picabia to direct his short scenario. The result, *Entr'acte* (1924), was an absurdist 'rewriting of a pre-war chase movie' (Williams 1993: 144), in which a coffin chased by mourners zoomed about the streets of Paris. Clair's subsequent success as a director of comedies such as *Un chapeau de paille d'Italie* (1927) was however dependent on the very narrative structures subverted in *Entr'acte*. In a 1924 review of Jean Epstein's *Cœur fidèle*, Clair compared impressionism's gratuitous optical effects unfavourably with 'American film technique, which is completely at the service of the progression of the story' (Williams 1993: 134), and in the 1940s he was to work in Hollywood as part of that classical narrative tradition.

Another director from outside the group who nonetheless created a seminal surrealist work was the former impressionist Germaine Dulac. Her adaptation of a scenario by Antonin Artaud, *La Coquille et le clergyman* (1928), used optical effects and clever editing to convey the repression of unconscious desires. Premièred at the Studio des Ursulines, the film was not well received by the generally misogynistic surrealists who accused Dulac of 'feminising' Artaud's scenario (Williams 1993: 148). In contrast, Salvador Dali and Luis Buñuel's *Un chien andalou* of the same year was immediately hailed by Breton as a surrealist masterpiece. Although only twenty minutes long, the film managed to disrupt the codes of cinematic representation (time, space, character definition, narrative structure – even silent titles are all subverted), and to create disturbing dream-like episodes dynamised by violent desires. The infamous opening scene, showing a woman's eyeball sliced in half with a razor, was both a deliberate shock tactic and a warning that, in the words of the surrealist-inspired young director, Jean Vigo, 'dans ce film, il s'agira de voir d'un autre œil que de coutume' [in this film, one will have to see things with a different eye than usual] (Prédal 1972: 194). Contrary to Dali and Buñuel's intentions, *Un chien andalou* was a success with middle-class audiences, running for nine months at the Studio des Ursulines. Two years later, Buñuel's feature-length sound film *L'Age d'or* (1930) attempted to put this right by launching a violent attack on the bourgeoisie, parodying the Church, the police, and all manner of Establishment conventions, presented as so many obstacles to the consummation of a couple's sexual desire. Again, the Dali-inspired images were startling – a cow in a luxury bedroom, a burning giraffe being thrown out of a window – but were also more determinedly sacrilegious, as in the concluding sequence which portrayed Christ as a libertine from the Marquis de Sade's *Cent vingt journées de Sodome*. Unsurprisingly, the right wing took offence, and the film was prohibited by the *préfet de police* after a fascist mob destroyed the Studio 28 cinema during a screening in December 1930. Buñuel went on to have a long and brilliant career, making numerous films in France, Spain and Mexico, and carrying his own brand of surrealism into the 1970s (see chapter 3). But most avant-garde film-makers, including Germaine Dulac, were unable to continue in the 1930s, faced with the technical demands and high production costs of the sound film.

Sound cinema and poetic realism

The late 1920s and early 1930s saw French cinema in crisis. Production became increasingly dependent on foreign input, either in the form of technology or finance, usually of American origin. In 1924 Gaumont in France merged with MGM, and in 1927 Pathé joined George Eastman's production company to form Kodak-Pathé. In terms of overall production, 1929 marked a nadir, with only fifty-two feature-length films made in France, as compared with hundreds annually before World War One (Prédal 1972: 114). The crisis was compounded in 1927 when *The Jazz Singer*, made in Hollywood for Warner, inaugurated the era of the 'talkie'.

The coming of sound and the crisis of the early 1930s

The Jazz Singer was premièred in France in February 1929. By that time, French film studios and cinemas alike had begun to re-equip for the new medium of sound cinema, an expensive process requiring American technology. For the studios in particular, the coming of sound was ill timed. Dating mostly from the early 1920s or the pre-war period, French film studios had only just finished modification to accommodate electricity. The first French sound studio at Épinay was ready in February 1929, but the earliest French 'talkies' were actually shot in Britain or Germany, while other films, like L'Herbier's *L' Argent* (1929), were partly sonorised half way through production (Crisp 1993: 104). Many French cinemas, meanwhile, were not equipped to screen sound films until 1934, and when they did so, relied on the American Vitaphone system rather than Gaumont's own underdeveloped Cinéphone (Crisp 1993: 100).

The technical problems associated with the advent of sound were compounded by the purist attitude of many leading French film-makers – including Abel Gance and initially René Clair – who deemed it fit only for musicals and vaudeville. To turn 'silent' films into 'talkies' would be to 'produce talking films that were restricted to a specific-language community' and to lose the 'universality' of the original medium (Crisp 1993: 97). Such a stance only weakened

French cinema further in the face of Anglophone dominance. Ironically, it was René Clair, one of the vociferous opponents of sound, who directed the first great French sound film, *Sous les toits de Paris*, at the Épinay studio in 1930. Although the film did manifest an adventurous use of sound – privileging songs while reducing dialogue to a minimum, and including some counterpoint experiments, in which sound and image were not synchronised – it was most notable for Lazare Meerson's set design, which evoked a realistic yet lyrical picture of working-class Paris. At first ignored by the French public, *Sous les toits de Paris* became an enormous world-wide success, fêted in Berlin, London, New York and Tokyo (Sadoul 1962: 317). By late 1934, however, Clair had left France for England and subsequently Hollywood, after the commercial failure of *Le Dernier Milliardaire* (1934). The same year saw the death of Jean Vigo, whose *Zéro de conduite* (1933) and *L'Atalante* (1934) had suggested a fruitful integration of surrealist imagery into realistic narrative cinema. French film production also entered a crisis in 1934 to rival that of 1929. Exacerbated by the Depression, which struck France later than it did Britain or the United States, and above all by the financial collapse of both Gaumont and Pathé, film production fell from 158 features the previous year to only 126 in 1934, and 115 in 1935 (Prédal 1972: 114). But although production remained at this level for the rest of the decade, the industry was to be revitalised in aesthetic terms by poetic realism, the key genre of classic French cinema.

Poetic realism

In general terms, the evolution of sound cinema shifted film-making from location shooting to studio production and from modernism to realism (Crisp 1993: 104). The coming of sound was a particular catalyst in the development of poetic realism: for technical and economic reasons, sound film was best shot in the studio, hence the increased importance of set design. Poetic realism, a naturalistic but lyrical genre shot almost exclusively on carefully designed studio sets, was given its characteristic atmosphere by art directors like Lazare Meerson and Alexandre Trauner. As Colin Crisp has noted, 'The set decorators' contribution to this style was crucial, and [...] helps to clarify a "movement" which is notoriously difficult to define' (Crisp 1993: 367). Like poetic realism as a genre, the set design which served it was a stylisation of reality, in which the guiding principle was realism, simplified, exaggerated and rendered symbolic. Whether in historical farce (Meerson's reconstruction of seventeenth-century Flanders for Jacques Feyder's *La Kermesse héroique* (1935)) or contemporary tragedy (Trauner's urban sets for Marcel Carné's *Quai des brumes* (1938) and *Le Jour se lève* (1939)) set design established the tone of the film. As Trauner said, it was essential to isolate and emphasise the principal details of the setting (Crisp 1993: 372). In a similar way, characterisation was based in reality but was also larger than life, with certain types representative of social class or position, the most prevalent and famous example of which is Jean Gabin's iconic status as the working-class hero. Gabin's roles in particular tended to be tragic heroes trapped by fate. Fatalism – which was also found in the slightly later American genre of the *film noir* (see chapter 5) – was manifest, indeed often personified, in a number of films written by Jacques Prévert and directed by Marcel Carné. Their first great film of the period, *Quai des brumes*, featured Gabin in a fog-bound Le Havre as a deserter driven by love to murder, while in *Le Jour se lève*, a year later, Gabin was again the doomed working-class hero, this time trapped in a house by the police and recalling his past love and his motives for murder. With Gabin's tragic hero, Trauner's realistic yet symbolic sets, and the theme of fate – here personified by a blind man – *Le Jour se lève* epitomises the poetic realism of the 1930s. But the reception of Carné and Prévert's *Les Portes de la nuit* (1946) proved that the genre was out of place after the harsh realities of World War Two and the German occupation of France.

While poetic realism was at its height, Jean Renoir – the most important film-maker of the era, a talismanic figure in post-war film and arguably the greatest ever French director – was faced with a generally lukewarm reception from critics and audiences. Renoir had met popular success with his version of Emile Zola's *Nana* in 1926, but in the ensuing decade his work was not well received despite encompassing a variety of genres from the comedy of *Boudu sauvé des eaux* (1932) to the political propaganda of *La Vie est à nous* (1936). In 1937 the pacifist *La Grande Illusion* was a success, but the cool reception of *La Règle du jeu* two years later, combined with the outbreak of war, led Renoir to leave France for Hollywood. It was only in the 1950s, thanks largely to *la politique des auteurs* (see below), that his importance was recognised. Often cited as an exemplary director of actors, Renoir also displayed a technical mastery of the medium. Throughout the diversity of setting and tone, his films are characterised by fluid camera movements (particularly tracking shots), by deep focus photography, and by a careful *mise en scène* which contrasts foreground and background. These techniques allowed him to develop a humanist concern for the place of the individual in society, filmed with a realism far less stylised than that of his contemporaries. He has proved a major influence not only on the *nouvelle vague* cinema of the 1950s and 1960s (see below), but also on the heritage genre of the 1980s (see chapter 7).

Wartime cinema and *la tradition de qualité*

In 1940, France suffered a humiliating defeat at the hands of the German army. The resultant period of occupation – in which the country was initially divided into a northern zone administered by the invaders and a 'free' southern zone governed by Marshal Petain's neofascist Vichy regime – was to prove one of the most traumatic eras of French history. While responses varied from active collaboration with the Germans to flight or underground resistance, most of the population struggled to continue living as before. Cinema-going increased, and, ironically, the German occupation actually saw a flowering of classical French cinema.

Film during the Occupation

Naturally enough, 1940 saw French film production reduced to an unprecedented low of thirty-nine films (Prédal 1972: 115). Many film personnel were lost to the industry. A few (such as composer Maurice Jaubert) were killed in action, but most simply fled the country. Directors Jean Renoir, René Clair and Max Ophüls began new careers in Hollywood, while Alexandre Trauner and a number of other Jewish technicians sought the temporary safety of the south (the 'free' zone was later invaded by Germany). Although many personnel resettled in Nice or Marseilles, production facilities and capital remained in Paris. As a result, 'Almost the only producer in a position to work on a film was Marcel Pagnol, who had his studio, actors, technicians, and bank accounts all in the Marseilles region' (Williams 1993: 248). Pagnol was thus able to follow his popular comedies and melodramas of the thirties with *La Fille du puisatier* in 1940.

Thanks largely to German finance and also to an influx of filmmakers replacing those who had departed, after 1940 French film production began to increase, more than doubling in quantity by 1943 (Prédal 1972: 115). During the 1930s the German companies Tobis and U.F.A. had produced many French films, and they were now joined by Continental. With imports from America and Britain banned, the French film industry, censored and to some extent controlled by the Germans, could monopolise its captive audience. Many German and some Italian films were also screened, but French-produced cinema claimed 85 per cent of box-office receipts during the Occupation (Sadoul 1962: 89). Moreover, despite the desire of Joseph Goebbels, the German Propaganda Minister, that the French public should be fed a diet of empty and stupid films (Prédal 1972: 91), a vibrant French film industry was a useful tool to placate the population and thus to deter resistance. The result was indeed a highly successful era for French cinema, albeit one characterised by escapism and fantasy, and shot almost entirely in a closed studio environment (Crisp 1993: 375). Constrained by censorship but also reflecting a national desire for an escape from the present, Occupation cinema has been characterised as a cinema of isolation and immobility, dominated by historical subjects, lyrical fantasies and remote settings (Williams 1993). Thus Christian-Jacques' *L'Assassinat du Père Noël* (1941) took place in a snowed-in mountain village and Jacques Becker's *Goupi Mains-Rouges* (1943) in a remote inn, while the major successes at Parisian cinemas – Marcel L'Herbier's *La Nuit fantastique* (1941), Marcel Carné's *Les Visiteurs du soir* (1942) and *Les Enfants du paradis* (1945), and Jean Delannoy's *L'Éternel Retour* (1943) – were either fantastical or historical subjects or both at once. Even Henri-Georges Clouzot's controversial thriller *Le Corbeau* (1943) was set in a small provincial town isolated from the outside world. None the less, the contemporary setting and bleak plot of *Le Corbeau* – in which poison-pen letters ultimately provoke murder – did spark a critical debate about the film's relation to the realities of the Occupation. Although the film could be interpreted as a comment on the neuroses and betrayals of life in occupied France, as resistance intensified and the Occupation was lifted, Clouzot was subjected to attacks from the Comité de Libération du Cinéma, which contrasted the defeatist pessimism of *Le Corbeau* with the spirited optimism of Jean Gremillon's aviation story *Le Ciel est à vous* (1944). With the Liberation of Paris in 1944, Clouzot was driven out of the film industry. But after three years he returned, just as the themes and styles of Occupation cinema were to return in the immediate post-war period.

Post-war 'quality' production

In the decade following the Liberation, the French film industry exploited to commercial success the trends established by the cinema of the Occupation. Literary screenplays, historical or nationalistic subjects, and an increasing attention to production values were predominant in the post-war era, resulting in what came to be known as *la tradition de qualité*. This was a period of consolidation and of competition with the Hollywood films which, banned under the Occupation, flooded post-war France. The Blum-Byrnes agreement of 1946 had reduced the industry's protectionism against American imports and this decision, combined with the appeal of high-quality Hollywood studio productions fronted by famous stars, appeared to jeopardise the commercial viability of French cinema. But the domestic industry was aided in its efforts by two institutions originally set up by the Vichy regime during the war. The Comité d'Organisation de l'Industrie or COIC, established in 1940 to revitalise French production and distribution, was continued in a modified form as the Centre National de la Cinématographie (CNC) after 1946. In addition, the national film school IDHEC (Institut des hautes études cinématographiques), which dated from 1943, was given government support (as was the pre-war film archive, the Cinémathèque française). In a policy which was to be echoed by government aid for the prestigious heritage genre in the 1980s (see chapter 7), from 1949 a CNC committee 'began to select projects deemed worthy of *primes de la qualité* or "bonuses for quality"', including literary adaptations of classics by Zola, Stendhal and Maupassant (Williams 1993: 278). European co-productions, especially with Italy, were also encouraged, and the average film budget rose from 50 million old francs in 1950 to 100 million five years later (Sadoul 1962: 103). Such tactics proved invaluable in the competition with Hollywood: whereas in 1948 American films accounted for 51 per cent of French box-office receipts and home product only 32 per cent, by 1957 the situation had been reversed (Sadoul 1962: 145).

Among the literary adaptations central to the success of the *tradition de qualité* were Christian-Jacques' *La Chartreuse de Parme* (1948) and Claude Autant-Lara's *Le Rouge et le Noir* (1954), both taken from nineteenth-century novels by Stendhal. Both films also featured the actor Gérard Philipe who, along with Martine Carol, played in numerous films of the period and epitomised the new French star system. The acting style of the 1930s, in which characters embodied a given social class and gave an 'extrovert expressiveness' to poetic realist film, was now superseded by the 'anguished interiority' of literary adaptations in which the psychology of the individual characters was paramount (Crisp 1993: 365). The decline of poetic realism was most clearly marked in the hostile reception of Marcel Carné and Jacques Prévert's *Les Portes de la nuit* (1946). Although the film was set in post-war Paris, the fantastical plot and Alexandre Trauner's stylised sets 'already seemed dated, belonging to a past era' (Crisp 1993: 375). After the commercial and critical failure of *Les Portes de la nuit*, Carné's fantasy film *Juliette ou la clé des songes* (1951) met a similar fate, as did Jean Cocteau's cryptic fantasy *Orphée* (1950). If the historical drama flourished in the 1950s, the fantasy genre entered an almost terminal decline, not arrested until the coming of the *cinéma du look* in the 1980s (see chapter 6).

For all the popularity of the costume drama – and in particular of films set at the turn of the century, such as Jacques Becker's *Casque d'or* (1952) or Jean Renoir's *French Cancan* (1954) – French post-war cinema included a number of more contemporary dramas. As under the Occupation, the thriller genre allowed a cynical and pessimistic portrayal of society, witness Yves Allegret's *Une Si Jolie Petite Plage* (1948) and Henri-Georges Clouzot's *Les Diaboliques* (1954). A more documentary-style realism was provided by René Clément's depiction of the war, *La Bataille du rail* (1945). Although Clément went on to film typical 'quality' projects, such as the Zola adaptation *Gervaise* (1955), *La Bataille du rail* belonged to the realist style of post-war European cinema, as did Robert Bresson's *Le Journal d'un curé de campagne* (1950), *Un condamné à mort s'est échappé* (1956) and *Pickpocket* (1959). Bresson's films, although stylised to an extent, used real locations and amateur actors, as did the most important realist movement of the period, Italian neo-realism. And although such examples were relatively rare in French cinema during the 1940s and 1950s, they prefigured the emergence of *la nouvelle vague*, a style of film-making which sought to destroy the high production values and orthodox format of *la tradition de qualité*.

Cahiers du cinéma and la nouvelle vague

In the decade after the Liberation, a fresh conception of cinema evolved in parallel with the development of *la tradition de qualité*, but in strident opposition to the values embodied by 'quality' productions. First formulated by young critics in the magazine *Cahiers du cinéma*, the new film theories were put into practice in the late 1950s and early 1960s by many of those same critics who, as directors, became known as *la nouvelle vague.*

La politique des auteurs

Cahiers du cinéma was launched in April 1951 by Jacques Doniol-Valcroze, Lo Duca and André Bazin. As editor, Bazin became the mentor to the young critics who contributed to the magazine, including François Truffaut, Jean-Luc Godard, Claude Chabrol and Eric Rohmer. These critics tended to praise the work of idiosyncratic French directors such as the comic actor and director Jacques Tati, along with many Hollywood productions, especially the film noir and the B-movie thriller (see chapter 5), but they reserved contempt for the French offerings of *la tradition de qualité.* This position was most strongly stated in François Truffaut's polemical article 'Une certaine tendance du cinéma français', published in *Cahiers* on New Year's Day, 1954. Targeting the scriptwriters Jean Aurenche and Pierre Bost, who had worked on numerous 'quality' films for various directors since the war, Truffaut contrasted the 'abject characters' they created with the more personalised creations of Jean Renoir, Robert Bresson, Jean Cocteau and Jacques Tati, all of them '*authors* ["*des auteurs*"] who often write their own dialogue and in some cases themselves invent their own stories, which they then go on to direct' (Crisp 1993: 234). Truffaut went on to write: 'I cannot see any possibility of peaceful coexistence between the *Quality Tradition* and an *auteur cinema*' (Crisp 1993: 234–5).

La politique des auteurs, or in other words, the conception of 'an *auteur cinema*' in which the film-maker, like an author or an artist, uses the medium (including not just the direction but the screenplay and even the production) to express a personal view of the world, was not invented by Truffaut in 1954. The idea of cinema as art had been first propounded in 1908 by the *film d'art* group (see above). More recently, an article by Alexandre Astruc for *L'Écran français* in 1948, had suggested the concept of 'la caméra-stylo' – the movie-camera used like a pen – by declaring: 'After having been successively a fairground attraction, an amusement analogous to boulevard theatre, or a means of preserving the images of an era, [cinema] is gradually becoming a language [...] by which an artist can express his thoughts' (Williams 1993: 306). Nevertheless, it was the *Cahiers* group who popularised the concept during the 1950s. Most significantly, they applied the term to almost all of their favourite film-makers, irrespective of nationality or cultural status. Among French directors, Jean Renoir was considered the classic *auteur*, writing, directing and even starring in his own films. The first special issue of *Cahiers* was devoted to him in January 1952. The reappraisal of Renoir was facilitated by the re-release of *La Grande Illusion* (1937) in 1946, and the first showing of the unfinished *Une partie de campagne* (1936) the same year. These films, along with post-war Hollywood productions, were watched by the *Cahiers* critics at the Cinémathèque française. But the subsequent veneration of popular Hollywood directors like Alfred Hitchcock, Howard Hawks and Sam Fuller proved controversial: 'Part of the scandal created by the *politique* was caused by its application to popular American cinema, generally thought of as mass entertainment reproducing·dominant ideology and incompatible with the interests of art' (Cook 1985: 126). Ironically, whereas in the 1950s *la politique des auteurs* attacked *la tradition de qualité* while granting Hollywood directors like Hitchcock serious critical attention for the first time (see chapter 5), since the 1970s auteurist criticism in France has been used to defend 'quality' French art cinema against the very notion of anonymous Hollywood product which the *politique* originally challenged.

La nouvelle vague

In 1957 François Truffaut acted on his auteurist convictions and founded his own production company, Les Films du Carrosse, which was to produce nearly all his work from his second short, *Les Mistons* (1957) to his final feature *Vivement dimanche!* (1983). One year later, in June 1958, a new wave of French cinema – *la nouvelle vague* – was launched, with the preview at the Cinémathèque française of Claude Chabrol's first feature, *Le Beau Serge*. Set in a small rural community and shot with a rigorous realist style in bleak locations, the film was not a popular success. But it was followed in 1959 by three films which gave *la nouvelle vague* a commercial as well as an aesthetic impact: Chabrol's *Les Cousins*, Truffaut's *Les 400 coups* and Godard's *A bout de souffle.* While the latter was a fine example of collaboration within *la nouvelle vague* – conceived by Truffaut, it was scripted and directed by Godard, with Chabrol as artistic supervisor – *Les 400 Coups* was a personal triumph for its director. Banned from the 1958 Cannes film festival for his outspoken views as a critic, Truffaut won the best director award at Cannes a year later for *Les 400 Coups*, his first feature film. This 'instant critical and commercial success not only afforded Truffaut considerable artistic independence [...], but also made it much easier for other *Cahiers* critics turned film-makers to finance their own projects' (Monaco 1976: 13). While *Les Cousins* and *A bout de souffle* owed a particular debt to the Hollywood thriller, *la nouvelle vague* as a whole brought a fresh sensibility and a radical style of filming to French cinema, indeed arguably to world cinema. Godard's *A bout de souffle* startled audiences with the systematic use of jump-cuts, and Truffaut's *Les 400 Coups* ended in stunning fashion with a freeze-frame. In contrast with *la tradition de qualité*, 'the aesthetic of New Wave cinema was improvisational (unscripted), and its photography and editing· were far less mannered than its predecessors' (Cook 1985: 40). Working with low budgets, using the new cheaper and lighter equipment, able to film in real locations and at night if required, influenced by television practices like hand-held shooting and the interview straight to camera, the *nouvelle vague* film-

Contemporary French cinema

makers paradoxically achieved a vibrant and graphic realism while at the same time experimenting self-consciously with the medium of film.

La nouvelle vague is usually taken to encompass five principal directors: François Truffaut, Jean-Luc Godard, Claude Chabrol, Eric Rohmer and Jacques Rivette, all of whom wrote for *Cahiers du cinéma* in the 1950s (Monaco 1976). However, this canonical list, and indeed the dating of the movement as beginning in 1958/9, should be qualified. Agnès Varda, a major omission from some accounts of the movement, predated Chabrol, Truffaut and Godard by shooting her first feature, *La Pointe courte*, in 1954. Shot independently on a very small budget, the film alternated between realism and symbolism, as does much of Varda's subsequent work (see chapter 4). Everyday life in a fishing village provided a graphic background to a young couple's rather literary discussions about their struggling relationship. *La Pointe courte* was given a limited release in 1956, the year which saw another important precursor of *la nouvelle vague*, Roger Vadim's *Et Dieu créa la femme*, prove a great commercial success. Despite its low budget, Vadim's film benefited from the presence of Brigitte Bardot in her first screen role, and its performance at the box office encouraged production companies to finance projects by unknown directors, a policy which was instrumental in the evolution of *la nouvelle vague*. Contrary to the rhetoric of cinematic revolution which surrounds *la nouvelle vague*, the emergence of the movement was thus prepared not only by technical factors, allowing more flexible filming techniques, but also by the commercial significance of *Et Dieu créa la femme*, and even by the post-war system of state subsidy, which saw Chabrol's *Le Beau Serge* gain a *prime de la qualité* alongside the 'quality' productions more readily associated with this prestige bonus (see above). One might conclude that, for all its stylistic innovations, 'the New Wave does not represent a sharp break with past practices, but the culmination of a development which had been apparent [...] ever since the war' (Crisp 1993: 376).

Among the forms explored by *la nouvelle vague* and related filmmakers were fantasy genres hitherto neglected in France: science fiction in Chris Marker's *La Jetée* (1963), Godard's *Alphaville* (1964) and Truffaut's *Fahrenheit 451* (1966); the musical in Godard's *Une femme est une femme* (1961) and Jacques Demy's *Les Parapluies* de *Cherbourg* (1964) and *Les Demoiselles de Rochefort* (1966). The New Wave also tended to mix previously distinct genres, thus making use of generic structures while submitting them to a personal, auteurist vision. Truffaut's *Tirez sur le pianiste* (1960), for example, although an adaptation of an American crime novel by David Goodis, added comic and fairy-tale elements to the basic thriller narrative. By the middle of the decade, however, Truffaut had become much more conservative in terms of both narrative structure and genre, a development which resulted in his becoming the most commercially successful film-maker to come out of *la nouvelle vague*. Meanwhile, Chabrol had started to work consistently within the thriller genre (see chapter 5), but both Eric Rohmer and Jacques Rivette did not break through commercially until the late 1960s and early 1970s (see chapter 3). If the mid-sixties marked the dissipation of the movement, it did not see any diminution in the formal innovations carried out by the most radical of the group, Jean-Luc Godard. While Truffaut and Chabrol had become *auteurs* in a fairly conventional mould, Godard remained at the cutting edge of both cinema and politics. Experimenting with colour in *Le Mépris* (1963) and *Pierrot le fou* (1965), he also challenged the traditional identification between audience and characters through his use of interview techniques in *Masculin-Féminin* (1966) and *Week-End* (1967). The latter, with its violent attack on the bourgeoisie and depiction of counter-culture terrorists, has been interpreted in retrospect as heralding the social unrest which shook France in May 1968 (see chapter 2). Godard's political activism was also evident in his collaboration with a group of film-makers including Agnès Varda, Alain Resnais and Chris Marker, on the protest film *Loin du Vietnam* (1967).

For all its artistic influence – manifest not just in Europe but in the work of American directors such as Arthur Penn and Martin Scorsese – *la nouvelle vague* was not a major commercial form. The French box office of the 1960s was dominated by the popular genres of the thriller and the comedy. Although cinema-going in France declined over the decade, from 355 million spectators in 1958 to 185 million in 1970 (Prédal 1991: 212), there were notable hits, including Yves Robert's childhood comedy *La Guerre des boutons* (1962) with 9.6 million spectators, and Gerard Oury's Resistance comedy *La Grande Vadrouille* (1966) with over 17 million (Prédal 1991: 404). The late 1960s also saw increasing numbers of pornographic films being made in France, a trend which was to culminate in the mid-seventies with the temporary acceptance of pornography into mainstream French cinema (see chapter 3).

References

Billard, P. (1994), France-États-Unis: Une guerre de cents ans, Paris, *Le Point*, 1163, 56-8.

Cook, P. (1985) (ed.), *The Cinema Book*, London, BFI.

Crisp, C. (1993), *The Classical French Cinema 1930–1960*, Bloomington and Indianapolis, Indiana University Press.

Monaco, J. (1976), *The New Wave*, New York, Oxford University Press.

Prédal, R. (1972). *La Societé française (1914–1945) à travers le cinéma*, Paris, Armand Colin.

Prédal, R. (1991), *Le Cinéma français depuis 1945*, Paris, Nathan.

Robinson, D. (1994), *The Chronicle of Cinema, 1: The Beginnings*, London, Sight and Sound/BFI.

Sadoul, G. (1962), *Le Cinéma français (1890–1962)*, Paris, Flammarion.

Williams, A. (1993), *Republic of Images: A History of French Filmmaking*, Cambridge, Massachusetts and London, Harvard University Press.

The Occupation, colonial conflicts, and national identity

2

May 1968 and political cinema

In May 1968 French students, workers and professionals united briefly in a wave of demonstrations, strikes and sit-ins – known as 'the events of May '68' – which challenged the institutions of President Charles de Gaulle's Fifth Republic and the ideals of the consumer society. The official reporting of the violent clashes between protestors and police throughout May 1968 revealed the extent to which the complicit French television system functioned as an apparatus of the State. The response of independent film-makers and collectives was to report the struggle from a viewpoint outside state control. Already in February of 1968 film-makers had been mobilised against government control of the media by the sacking of Henri Langlois as secretary of the national film archive, the Cinémathèque française. In May came the establishment of the States-General of the Cinema, with the declaration that 'free speech does not exist in either cinemas or television in this country, as a very small minority of writers and technicians control both production and the means of expression'. As the States-General reported later, eyewitness films were made during the 'events' and distributed from mid-June onwards (Fisera 1978: 303, 304). Despite the continuation of de Gaulle's presidency until 1969, and a general return to the political *status quo*, in terms of film culture the 'events' had a profound effect, facilitating the development of politicised and collective film-making, and contributing to the rise of gay film and women's cinema in the decade that followed. Above all, and naturally enough, it was documentary film-making which was most directly influenced by what happened in May 1968.

Documentary film-making in France in the 1960s had been dominated by *cinéma-vérité* – the recording of everyday life and events – as in Jean Rouch's *Chronique d'un été* (1961) and Chris Marker's *Le Joli Mai* (1963). This style was gradually supplanted by more formally experimental and politically-motivated forms of documentary from the late sixties onwards. The anti-war film *Loin du Vietnam* (1967), a group venture including Marker, Jean-Luc Godard, Agnès Varda and Alain Resnais, prefigured 'the collective production' and 'interventionist role [...] which was characteristic of political and documentary film making after 1968' (Forbes 1992: 15). Moreover, after May '68 the very distinction between documentary and fiction was questioned, nowhere more so than in Jean-Luc Godard and Jean-Pierre Gorin's *Tout va bien* (1972).

Tout va bien: new subjects, new forms

Godard's attacks on the consumer society in *Week-End* and *La Chinoise* (both 1967) seem in retrospect to have heralded the upheavals of May 1968. In the years that followed he worked with Jean-Pierre Gorin on a number of political projects outside mainstream cinema, usually financed by foreign television companies. In an explicit break with his career as a key *auteur* in *la nouvelle vague* (see chapter 1), Godard no longer worked under his own name but in collaboration with Gorin as the Dziga-Vertov Group, named after a revolutionary Soviet filmmaker. The primary aim of the group was to 'faire politiquement des films politiques' [make political films politically], and more precisely to situate themselves 'historically' in regard to May '68 and contemporary political struggles (Godard 1991: 116–17). *Tout va bien*, filmed in 1972 with Yves Montand and Jane Fonda, was an attempt to consider the legacy of 1968 from within mainstream cinema, a strategy facilitated by the box-office power of the two stars. The film that resulted has been described as 'perhaps the single best cinematic description of France in the aftermath of '68' (MacCabe 1992: 20).

Interviewed about *Tout va bien* in April 1972, Godard and Gorin rejected the *cinéma-vérité* style of documentary associated with Rouch as unable to answer the questions raised by May '68 (see Godard 1991: 127). The only response was to marry new subjects to new forms, breaking down what Gorin called the 'bourgeois' distinction between fiction and documentary in order to create 'materialist fictions' (Godard 1991: 131, 133). In other words, both form and content were to be politicised, in what Godard had already termed in 1967, with regard to *La Chinoise*, a 'struggle on two fronts' (Godard 1991: 10–58). The political, yet not documentary, nature of *Tout va bien*, its status as a 'materialist fiction', is best illustrated by the images in the film of demonstrations and clashes with the police. Although alluding explicitly to situations from 1968, and particularly to the death of student Gilles Tautin while fleeing from police dispersing a demonstration at the Flins Renault factory in June of that year, these sequences are clearly not documentary footage but staged versions of what took place. The fictionalising of events characteristic of May 1968 also provides the film with its central narrative, the story of a factory occupation set in May 1972, during which the characters played by Montand and Fonda are locked in with the boss by striking workers. Accusing the strikers of being 'contaminated' by May '68, the boss renders explicit the political symbolism of the factory occu-pation, after which the protagonists, like France itself, appear to return to the *status quo*. The strike is not filmed, however, as docu-mentary nor even as realism. The non-realistic use of colour, the cross-sectional staging interpreted by tracking shots, and the playing of several scenes as farce all distance the factory sequences from the ostensibly 'truthful' forms of documentary and naturalism, and place the fictional nature of cinema in the foreground. (The use of a 'low' cinematic form, such as farce, supposedly inappropriate to serious referential content is raised again by Godard in the context of Holo-caust representation (see below).) If *Tout va bien* does propose any final truth, it is in the male and female voice-overs which conclude the film, stating of the protagonists that 'ils ont commencé à se penser hi-stor-ique-ment' [they have begun to think of themselves hi-stor-ic-ally], and proposing that 'chacun sera son propre historien, [...] moi ... toi ... lui ... elle ... nous ... vous!' [everyone will be their own historian, me ... you ... him ... her ... us ... you!]. This proposed fragmenting of history into personalised narratives perhaps predicts Godard's retreat into non-commercial video projects in the mid-seventies. It also subverts the dominant historical discourse of the period, the Gaullist myth that France had been united (in resistance) during the Second World War and ever since. This view of history was to be readdressed in the representations of the Occupation and the Holocaust which began to proliferate in the aftermath of 1968.

Holocaust documentary

The extent of French collaboration with Nazi Germany during the Second World War, and most crucially the role of the Vichy govern-ment in the deportation of French Jews, were taboo subjects in the 1950s and 1960s. But they were addressed with increasing urgency during the 1970s and 1980s. This concern was ultimately mani-fested in the trials of the collaborator Paul Touvier and 'the Butcher of Lyons', Klaus Barbie, in the investigation surrounding Vichy police chief René Bousquet, and the debate over the wartime actions of the Catholic Church and of François Mitterrand. It was also evident in French cinema, both in documentary and fiction form. Documentary images of the Holocaust were first seen in French cinemas during 1945, with footage of the concentration camps shown in the Actu-alités Françaises newsreel, *Les Camps de la mort* (Colombat 1993: 14). The major Holocaust documentaries are Alain Resnais's *Nuit et brouil-lard* (*Night and Fog*, 1955), Marcel Ophüls's *Le Chagrin et la pitié* (*The Sorrow and the Pity*, 1971) and Claude Lanzmann's *Shoah* (1985). Each of these seminal films marks a new stage in Holocaust represen-tation, and raises distinct questions: '"What exactly happened?" "How could we allow the Holocaust to take place?" and "What memory of these horrifying events should be kept alive for future generations?"' (Colombat 1993: xiv).

Nuit et brouillard and the myth of *le résistancialisme*

The Gaullist myth of a united France was based on *le résistancialisme*, the theory that during the Occupation the French nation had supported Charles de Gaulle and the Resistance rather than collaborating (see Rousso 1991). Established initially by de Gaulle's speech on the liberation of Paris in 1944, the myth was perpetuated during the Fourth Republic that followed, and cemented with the founding of the Fifth Republic by de Gaulle in 1958. In the determinedly forward-looking context of the 1950s, Resnais's *Nuit et brouillard* was a warning not to forget the atrocities of the past. Following a commission by the Comité d'Histoire de la Deuxième Guerre Mondiale, Resnais worked with the writer and Holocaust survivor Jean Cayrol to produce a short, stylised film of great poetic resonance. (They were to work together again on the fiction film *Muriel* (1963) which, like much of Resnais's work, presents a world akin to the enclosed, traumatic world of the concentration camp (see below).) *Nuit et brouillard* establishes the classic photographic dichotomy of the Holocaust film, according to which the past is seen in black and white and the present in colour. The aesthetic quality of the film stems from the inter-relation of Cayrol's text and Eisler's music with Resnais's editing, which juxtaposes colour images of the ruins of the death camps with black and white archive footage of the camps and their victims during the war. Resnais thus excavates the horrors lying beneath the deceptively banal landscapes of the present day, landscapes which like those in Lanzmann's *Shoah* are at times startlingly beautiful with blue or pink skies and orange trees. It has even been remarked that these colours are too bright, like open wounds or 'draining blood' (Ward Jouve 1994). The disembodied and anonymous narration in *Nuit et brouillard*, the universalized themes, and the absence of any precise reference to the extermination of the Jews (the film just speaks of 'victims') might be seen as conforming to the myth of *le résistancialisme*. Although a specifically French context is given by brief allusions to the camps at Pithiviers and Compiègne, and to the deportations from the Vélodrome d'Hiver in Paris, the image which most explicitly challenged the Gaullist myth – a French policeman surveying the camp at Pithiviers – was censored (Colombat 1993: 27). Cinema was not to demythologise the official version of French history during the Occupation until after 1968. Nevertheless, *Nuit et brouillard* remains a powerful call to awareness, particularly via the archive images of the dead and dying, and in the concluding voice-over which warns of 'the coming of new executioners' whose faces are not 'really different from ours'. It is notable that in May 1990, after anti-Semitic attacks on Carpentras and other Jewish cemeteries, all five French state television channels simultaneously broke their programming to broadcast Resnais's film.

History on trial: from *Le Chagrin et la pitié* to *Hôtel Terminus*

Faced with Hitler's rise to power, the young Marcel Ophüls and his family fled from Germany to France in 1933, only to leave for the United States eight years later in order to escape the Occupation. After the war, Marcel worked as assistant on his father Max's last film, *Lola Montès* (1955), before embarking on a career as a director of fiction films and ultimately documentaries. In 1967, working with André Harris and Alain Sedouy for French state television – the ORTF (Office de radio et télévision française) – he made *Munich*, the first third of a projected documentary series on the Second World War. In the aftermath of May '68, and following the resignation of the three film-makers from the ORTF, the series ended. In 1969 Ophüls began filming *Le Chagrin et la pitié* (1971) for German and Swiss television, with Harris and Sedouy as executive producers. It was this film above all others that was to shatter the illusions of the Gaullist Resistance myth, to end the period of 'repression' that myth entailed, and to allow the genera- tion of May '68 to look into what Rousso terms 'the broken mirror'. This process was not immediate, however. The ORTF subjected the completed film to what Ophüls called 'censorship by inertia' (Insdorf 1983: 242), and it was not broadcast on French television until after the Socialists came to power in 1981. Its cinema presentation in 1971 was however a success, attracting a large, predominantly young audi- ence. Subtitled 'Chronicle of a French town under the Occupation', the film focuses on the choice between collaboration and resistance for the people of Clermont-Ferrand. Black and white throughout, it includes interviews with French, German and British witnesses, news- reel footage and propaganda films of the period. It has been noted that throughout *Le Chagrin et la pitié*, and especially in the interview with Madame Solange, resistance is portrayed as masculine and collabora- tion as feminine (Reynolds 1990). It was some years before a more complex portrayal of women's experience under the Occupation was given in Claude Chabrol's 1988 fiction film *Une affaire de femmes* (see below).

In contrast with the impersonal quality of Resnais's *Nuit et brouil- lard*, Ophüls favours a personalised filmic style. Although not as strong an authorial presence as in his later work, Ophüls does exercise his political commitment and strong sense of irony throughout *Le Chagrin et la pitié*, most notably through the editing and a frequent disjuncture between sound and image, as in the parodic 'tourist guide' introduc- tion to the town of Clermont-Ferrand, which is undermined by solemn images of a war memorial. As in Lanzmann's *Shoah*, the staging func- tions to symbolise the role of each witness: hence the SS volunteer Christian de la Mazière is interviewed in the German castle of Sigmar- ingen, and a British pilot in the cockpit of a Lancaster bomber. In a sequence which prefigures Abraham Bomba's testimony in *Shoah*, the right-wing hairdresser Madame Solange is filmed in a hairdresser's, her interview ironically preceded by images of *l'épuration* – the post-war purges – showing women suspected of collaboration having their heads shaved. The politician and war veteran Pierre Mendès-France is privileged as a surrogate narrator, complementing the unidentified narrative voice-over which punctuates the film, adding a political discourse and raising in particular the spectres of anti-Semitism, Anglophobia and anti-Communism as factors in the collaboration with Germany. The testimony of Mendès-France is addressed from the beginning at younger generations, that is, directly at the film's principal audience.

The reception of *Le Chagrin et la pitié* was determined by the debate over Gaullism initiated in 1968. Although de Gaulle himself had died in 1970, President Pompidou continued the Gaullist regime. From such a perspective, Ophüls's portrayal of de Gaulle was startlingly negative. Not only was the latter rarely mentioned in his mythical role as leader of the Free French, when he was referred to it was as much in relation to his loss of power after the 1969 referendum defeat as to his wartime activity. The film also drew an unmistakable visual parallel between de Gaulle and Marshal Pétain, the head of the collaborationist Vichy government. Part one ended with an image of Pétain and part two with a shot of de Gaulle. This parallel was to be drawn even more strongly in Harris and Sedouy's *Français si vous saviez* (1973), the poster for which shows statues of de Gaulle and Pétain side by side, the one being constructed out of the other. *Le Chagrin et la pitié* also caused controversy over the glaring rift it presented between German and French interpretations of events 'at a time when the Franco-German Collaboration was the key-stone' of Gaullist European policy (Colombat 1993: 182). Ironically, the film was also unpopular with militant film-makers like Godard and Gorin, who judged it to be empty of political analysis and hence 'revolting' (Godard 1991: 139). Certain critics have subsequently attacked *Le Chagrin et la pitié* as 'politically vacuous', and for ignoring the role of the Catholic Church within Vichy (see Avisar 1988: 19). Nevertheless, the film does engage with the internal conflicts of the Resistance, illustrating the rupture between Catholic and Communist elements in the juxtaposed testimonies of the interviewees Du Jonchay and Duclos. It was this even-handed portrayal of the 'popular struggle', and the revelation that collaborators were mostly ordinary people rather than ideologues, which saw the film condemned by some on the left – along with Louis Malle's controversial fiction film *Lacombe, Lucien* (1974) – for epitomising *rétro* cinema (see below). Ophüls followed *Le Chagrin et la pitié* with a film on Northern Ireland, *A Sense of Loss* (1972), and *The Memory of Justice* (1976), a documentary on the Nuremberg trials which also considers the wars in Algeria and Vietnam. *Hôtel Terminus* (1987) was filmed in tandem with the development of the trial of the Nazi war criminal Klaus Barbie, 'the Butcher of Lyons', who was eventually sentenced to life imprisonment for crimes against humanity. Barbie is in fact an absence rather than a presence in the film – he was not present at the trial until the verdict – while Ophüls establishes a running contradiction between the testimonies of Barbie's colleagues, both in Germany and the Americas, and of his victims. Partly because it concerned war crimes committed by a German Nazi rather than French collaborators, *Hôtel Terminus* proved less controversial than *Le Chagrin et la pitié*. It was also overshadowed by the release two years earlier of the mammoth Holocaust documentary *Shoah*, whose director Claude Lanzmann may have been right when he said of the Barbie trial: 'All of this will be forgotten while *Shoah* will not be forgotten' (Colombat 1993: 108).

Shoah: reliving the Holocaust

Ophüls has described Claude Lanzmann's *Shoah* (1985) as 'the greatest documentary about contemporary history ever made, bar none, and by far the greatest film I've ever seen about the Holocaust' (Insdorf 1983: 254). Lanzmann had fought with the French Resistance as a youth before travelling to Israel after the war and making the film *Pourquoi Israël*. But his major achievement is undeniably *Shoah*, a project which took eleven years to make – from 1974 to 1985 – the first six years recording testimony in fourteen different countries, the next five years editing the film from 350 hours of footage into the 9½ hour result. 'Shoah' is Hebrew for 'annihilation', and Lanzmann's film challenges the conscious and unconscious annihilation of the Holocaust as a lived experience. The film is therefore about the so-called Final Solution in its terrible specificity, evoking the very logistics of a genocide that exterminated six million European Jews. In this regard, the historian Raul Hilberg is a key influence on Lanzmann, both via his book *The Destruction of the European Jews*, and via his presence in the film as a commentator, much like Pierre Mendès-France in Ophüls's *Le Chagrin et la pitié*. It is Hilberg who stresses the importance of asking small questions about the details of 'the bureaucratic destruction process', rather than attempting to address the Holocaust as an abstract concept. Following this line of enquiry, Lanzmann elicits testimony from his interviewees about the actual process of extermination in camps which functioned as what the SS guard, Franz Suchomel, calls 'a primitive but effective production line of death'. The Final Solution demanded of its perpetrators, as Hilberg notes in the film, 'Do these things, do not describe them'. In *Shoah*, Lanzmann records at length a testimony which, shot in long takes, expressed in a diversity of languages, delayed while it is translated into French and punctuated with silences, presents an agonised description of the indescribable.

Shoah was made and released during an extended period of debate and controversy surrounding the Holocaust. In France the late seventies and early eighties saw a rise in anti-Semitic terrorism, the arrest of Klaus Barbie, the beginnings of new proceedings against Touvier and other collaborators, and also the emergence and eventual trial, in 1983, of the revisionist historian Robert Faurisson (Colombat 1993: 99). Faurisson's stance is epitomised by his claim in 1979 that: 'I have tried in vain to find a single former deportee capable of proving to me that he had really seen, with his own eyes, a gas chamber' (Felman 1992: 215). In such a context, Lanzmann's filming of the gas chambers and the sites of the death camps, and above all his recording of testimony from numerous Jewish survivors, Polish onlookers and Nazi perpetrators, assumes an even more urgent relevance. The essential difference between *Shoah* and other Holocaust documentaries, in particular *Nuit et brouillard* and *Le Chagrin et la pitié*, is that Lanzmann avoids using archive footage, and that consequently no photographic distinction is set up between the past and the present. All of the material in *Shoah* is shot in the present and practically all of it in colour, partly because Lanzmann felt that archive film of the death camps was losing its impact upon audiences, and also to establish the continuity between past and present which is fundamental to the film. If there is a structural dichotomy in *Shoah* it is between sound and image, establishing 'an absolute contrast between the beauty of the landscape and the horror of what is said' (Lanzmann 1993). Thus the first images in the film are of a beautiful green Polish landscape, through which Simon Srebnik, one of only two survivors from the Chelmno death camp, travels slowly by boat. Srebnik comments that 'It was always this peaceful here', even when the Germans were burning two thousand Jews a day. Srebnik's return to Chelmno forms the introduction to the film, which is structured in two halves. *The First Era* and *The Second Era* correspond to the development of the extermination process in the death camps of Treblinka, Auschwitz, Belzec, Chelmno and Sobibor. Although *Shoah* is characterised by repetition in terms of both testimony and image, it presents a loose narrative development, whereby the eyewitness accounts, like Lanzmann's camera, slowly approach and ultimately enter the camps. Certain images recur throughout the film: green Polish forests, trains and railtracks, the stones commemorating the dead, and a long, slow dolly shot of Auschwitz for which Lanzmann himself pushed the dolly. The two halves are both introduced by a witness singing: in the first case, Srebnik sings precisely as he used to while under SS guard on the river at Chelmno; in the second, the former SS man Suchomel sings the song the worker Jews at Treblinka were forced to learn, a song which he alone knows, since the Jews were all killed. In a further irony, it is the blurred, monochrome images of Suchomel (and of the other Nazis filmed secretly with hidden cameras) which are closest to the images of death captured in the black-and-white archive footage of traditional Holocaust documentary.

Shoah has often been described as not just a historical documentary but also the director's personal obsession. Lanzmann himself has called it a crime film and a Western, in which he (and survivors like Srebnik) 'come back to the scene of the crime' (Felman 1992: 256, n. 34). As he told *Cahiers du cinéma*, the film is a 'fiction of reality', with the witnesses turned into 'actors' in order to 'relive' and 'transmit' their experiences (Colombat 1993: 312–13). Hence the importance in *Shoah* not just of montage – as in the cross-cutting between Hilberg citing Czerniakow's diary and Grassler denying the atrocities in the Warsaw ghetto – but of the traditionally fictional strategies of *mise en scène*. Most notably in the case of Abraham Bomba, a survivor who had to cut the hair of those about to be gassed, it is the staging of the interview – in a Tel Aviv barbershop – as much as Lanzmann's relentless questioning, which results in a 'transmission' of intense personal suffering from the interviewee to the film spectator, as Bomba breaks down on what Lanzmann terms 'the border of the unspeakable' (Colombat 1993: 343). Like the barbershop, the locomotive driven towards Treblinka by Henrik Gakowski was rented by the director in order to bring the past more graphically to life for witness and spectator. Such 'reactivation' turns the film into what Lanzmann calls 'an incarnation, a resurrection' (Felman 1992: 214). This is evident not only in the celebrated sequence wherein Srebnik, returning to the church at Chelmno, is confronted with the rekindled anti-Semitism of the villagers, but also in the clandestine filming of Suchomel which presents the secrecy of the Holocaust even as the SS guard testifies to the camouflaging and invisibility of the death camps. The 'reactivation' throughout *Shoah* also conforms to a widespread perception that traumatic events such as the Holocaust are not fixed in history and time: 'trauma refuses to be represented *as past*, but is perpetually reexperienced in a [...] traumatic present' (Leys 2000: 2).

The concluding hour or more of *Shoah* – the interviews with Karski, Grassler and Rottem, and Hilberg's readings from Czerniakow's diary – concerns the acknowledgement of the Holocaust as an event which, however secret, must be told. The precise focus is the Warsaw ghetto, the site of a physical struggle and also the subject of a struggle over the reality of the Holocaust. The testimony of Jan Karski in particular, edited by Lanzmann from eight hours of footage into forty minutes, enacts the movement from ignorance to awareness and then to 'reactivation' of the past which is crucial to the film and to the spectator's response. As the former courier to the Polish government in exile, a man whose mission was to report what he saw in Warsaw and elsewhere to the Allies and to plead for action, Karski stands on the threshold between the 'inside' of the Holocaust and the outside world. His position thus parallels that of the spectator of Holocaust film, and of *Shoah* especially: 'I never saw such things, I never ... nobody wrote about this kind of reality. I never saw any theatre, I never saw any movie ... this was not the world.' Karski's struggle to comprehend what he saw, to be believed, and also to speak to Lanzmann of something he has not mentioned for twenty-six years, is followed in the film by the Nazi administrator, Grassler's, revisionist account of the ghetto against which Lanzmann himself fights, telling Grassler 'I'll help you to remember'. The interview with Karski is also subject to Lanzmann's most dramatic and unexpected use of imagery: while in voice-over Karski recounts his own anguished visits to the ghetto and the urgent pleas he was to give the Allied leaders, we see serene blue skies over American skyscrapers and German factories. The impassive symbols of American wealth and democracy – the New York skyline, the White House – and of German industrial strength – the Ruhr – implicitly give the response to Karski's messages, and also suggest a collective guilt shared by the Allies and the Germans. Lanzmann's editing and camerawork then link the present to the past explicitly, as an image of a German factory flame gives way to a slow pan down a bare tree to the debris of Auschwitz and close-ups of the piles of shoes and brushes taken from the dead. The last interviewee in *Shoah*, the ghetto fighter Rottem, describes himself alone in the Warsaw ghetto as 'the last Jew'. This has been compared to Srebnik's comment early in the film that if he survived the camps, he would become 'the only one left in the world'. Asked about this apparently cyclical conclusion, Lanzmann has responded that the Holocaust 'still goes on' and that therefore 'I decided that the last image of the film would be a rolling train, an endlessly rolling ... train' (Felman 1992: 242). As with the shot of the Saurer lorry – the same make as the gas vans – in motion at the end of *The First Era*, the 'continuous, incomplete motion' of the train 'reminds us that there is no end to *Shoah*' or to the Holocaust (Colombat 1993: 338). The trauma refuses to remain in the past.

La Guerre sans nom: breaking the silence on the Algerian War

The films of Ophüls and Lanzmann established documentary film as a means of breaking taboos on political or historical subjects. The influence of Ophüls in particular is manifest in the work of Bertrand Tavernier, who appeared in *Hôtel Terminus* before in turn producing Ophüls's film on the war in Bosnia, *Veillées d'armes* (1994). Ophüls's *The Memory of Justice* had included testimony about the torture practised by the French army during the Algerian War. Tavernier and Patrick Rotman's four-hour documentary *La Guerre sans nom* (*The Undeclared War*, 1992) considers in much greater depth this forgotten period of French history which, as Tavernier's narration makes clear, has never been officially acknowledged as a war, but euphemistically termed an operation to keep law and order. Tavernier had already explored the wounds left by the First World War in his 1989 fiction film *La Vie et rien d'autre* (see chapter 7). He felt *La Guerre sans nom* to be, in a sense, a continuation of this work (Tavernier 1993: 267). The documentary also makes a brief allusion to Tavernier's jazz movie *Autour de minuit* (1986), in the closing interview with a traumatised veteran. Indeed, music is used very effectively throughout, whether it be live – the final scene in which the jazz-loving veteran plays 'The Girl from Ipanema' on the piano – or added to the sound-track, in the form of the sixties pop songs which punctuate the film. Recordings of gunfire and of the radio messages sent by troops to their families are also employed to revivify the events described in the interviews. *La Guerre sans nom*, like Ophüls's *Le Chagrin et la pitié*, has a specific geographical focus: the film begins in Grenoble, with evocations of a protest against conscription to fight in Algeria. When the film was due to be shown on French television (it also received a cinema release), Tavernier was asked by the station concerned, Canal Plus, to cut the demonstration sequence. He refused, 'because it anchors the film within a precise French context, one that has never been shown before' (Tavernier 1993: 257). In Tavernier's words, the aim of the film was 'to give a voice to people who had been silent, who had been excluded from history; to bring back to life a forgotten memory'. To this end, the film-makers interviewed former conscripts and 'recalled' soldiers, none of them ranked higher than lieutenant, from the Grenoble area: 'No volunteers, no professional soldiers or senior officers [...]. And we've left out any archive or newsreel footage, anything "official". We have only used amateur photographs taken by our witnesses' (Tavernier 1993: 267). The decision to rely solely on present testimony recalls Lanzmann's strategy in *Shoah*, while the numerous witnesses are in many cases breaking thirty years of silence to talk about their experiences in Algeria. The tension of their hesitation on what Lanzmann calls 'the border of the unspeakable', a tension ultimately released by the cathartic power of music in the final scene, conveys not only the horrors of the Algerian War but also the suffering involved in breaking the taboo which has surrounded it.

Nonetheless the fact remains that the film conforms to certain reactionary and quasi-colonial constructions of Algeria, most notably through the absence of the indigenous population. In this regard, Benjamin Stora quotes the Algerian newspaper *El Watan*: the film, like so many others before it, and despite its apparent intentions, presents 'l'Algérie, sans les Algériens. Le vieux rêve colonial, enfin réalisé' [Algeria without Algerians: the old colonial dream, realized at last] (Jurt 1997: 118). This remark seems especially pertinent to the colour sequences which show Algeria as a deserted land, an empty landscape. As the camera pans slowly across these huge spaces, they are appropriated through memory and, via the sound-track, through the words of the popular song 'Un jour tu verras', on behalf of the French soldiers who fought there and who are the sole focus of the film. To this extent, *La Guerre sans nom* continues the French mythologizing of Algeria, critiqued by Resnais forty years earlier in *Muriel*, where Alphonse declares that Algeria is simply a beautiful country of sun and blue skies. We later learn that the character has never been there and is peddling a fantasy of Algeria. This is a tendency that not even Tavernier and Rotman's well-meaning documentary can entirely escape.

Representing Resistance under the Gaullist myth: *La Ligne de démarcation* and *Fahrenheit 451*

On 19 December 1964, the ashes of Jean Moulin, Resistance hero, were transferred to the Panthéon in Paris for burial, in a state ceremony that marked the apotheosis of the *résistancialiste* myth. De Gaulle seized the opportunity 'to draw together nation, people, and state in a shared identification in Resistance heroism' (Atack 1999: 108). With

Gaullism at its height, the Resistance became the subject not just of national commemoration but of representation in literature, television, and even in historical research. Meanwhile, in a decade or more characterized by the repression of troubling memories, the difficult questions about France's wartime past – anti-Semitism, collaboration, Vichy, French involvement in the Holocaust – were left well alone (see Conan and Rousso 1996: 32–3). Amnesty laws passed in the early fifties had ensured that collaborators were no longer pursued. State censorship in the sixties similarly ensured that taboo subjects were kept off-screen. It is in this context that the formulaic war film *La Ligne de démarcation* (1966) has been termed the 'perfect codification' of the Resistance myth (Lindeperg 1997: 341). Written by Resistance veteran Colonel Rémy and directed by Claude Chabrol during his wilderness years, the film is set among a remote community in the Jura region who come together to smuggle a wounded French airman past the inept German occupiers. Resistance is portrayed as a shared activity which unites schoolteacher and priest, old and young, the nobility and the workers, while collaboration is limited to one isolated and ineffectual individual. The German occupiers are alternately stupid (the ordinary soldiers) or sinister (the Gestapo). Pierre, the wounded French officer (Maurice Ronet) turns from resigned defeatism to a final heroic gesture, while his wife Mary (Jean Seberg), named after the Holy Virgin, functions as a Resistance saint. Because the film is set just inside the German-administered northern zone, moreover, it bizarrely manages to celebrate Resistance while also representing Vichy France as a land of freedom across the river. Notwithstanding such anomalies and a characterization so schematic as to be laughable, on its release *La Ligne de démarcation* was commended to the younger generation by the film critic of *L'Aurore* as a true record of France under the Occupation. In truth, it was a prime example of the way that myth functions to abolish the complexity of human actions and to restore instead a world without ambivalence or contradictions (see Barthes 1957).

That same year one of Chabrol's *nouvelle vague* colleagues, François Truffaut, had shown an entirely different approach to representing the Occupation, and in particular its forgetting. His futuristic fairy-tale *Fahrenheit 451* (1966), although adapted from an American science-fiction source (the novel by Ray Bradbury), and filmed in London and Welwyn Garden City with an English-speaking cast, offers a cogent and carefully drawn allegory of France under Vichy – and since. Its dual function as both a tale of the future and a tale about the past is best expressed as follows:

The whole point of allegory is that it does not need to be read exegetically; it often has a literal level that makes good enough sense all by itself. [...] We must avoid the notion that all people must see a double meaning for the work to be rightly called allegory. At least one branch of allegory [...] serves political and social purposes by the very fact that a reigning authority (as in a police state) does not see the secondary meaning. (Fletcher 1964: 7–8).

The same could be said of the censors of the *résistancialiste* period when confronted with *Fahrenheit 451*, and their blindness to the political allegory has continued in the film's critical reception. Very few writers on Truffaut have warmed to the film, quite possibly because it seems unsatisfactory to them on the literal level and because they do not identify the allegory at work. Moreover, the film's linguistic and generic status may also have mitigated against it. If there is a clear precursor to *Fahrenheit 451*, it is another English-language film by a classic French director: Jean Renoir's *This Land Is Mine* (1942), a propaganda piece shot in the United States and designed to persuade the American public of the legitimacy of the French Resistance. Like Truffaut's allegory, Renoir's film is set in an unnamed country that we can identity as France, and celebrates the power of literature as a form of resistance against fascism. What distinguishes *Fahrenheit 451* is that, alongside the representations of fascism (the black-shirted firemen burning books), of a Pétain-like cult of personality (the captain handing out images of himself) and of resistance (the underground or *maquis* hiding out in the woods), there is also an engagement with the politics of memory. In this futuristic version of Gaullist France, books are forbidden and television is controlled by the state. When Montag (Oskar Werner) confronts his wife and her friends, he finds them unable to even mention the ongoing war (a direct allusion to the undeclared war in Algeria) or to address the fact that at least one of their husbands has been killed in action. Brandishing Dickens's *David Copperfield* – a personal history that also stands in for the absent national history – Montag declares that he for one will uncover the past hidden behind the official mythologies and euphemisms: 'I've got to catch up with the remembrance of the past...'. With hindsight this seems a very prescient line, predicting the revelations about France's wartime history that were to be made over the next decade or so.

La mode rétro

As already noted, although Charles de Gaulle died in 1970, Gaullist policy was continued by his chosen successor as President, Georges Pompidou. It is thus 1974, the year of Pompidou's death in office and the election of Valéry Giscard d'Estaing, that marks the end of the Gaullist dominance of post-war France. Hence François Nourrisier's comment in an article of the time: 'Le Père est mort, on fait l'inventaire de l'héritage' [The Father is dead, time to take stock of the inheritance] (see Morris 1992: 105). The death of Gaullism coincided with a wave of re-interpretations of the Occupation on the part of writers and filmmakers who had been children during the war. In literature, this trend began with Patrick Modiano's 1968 novel *La Place de l'étoile*, while in cinema it was Ophüls's *Le Chagrin et la pitié* (1971) which set the tone. Despite the positive reception of such works by the public, the critical response – from both Gaullists and the Left – was often to denigrate them as stylised and apolitical revisions of French history, in short, as inaugurating *la mode rétro*. This critique was fundamentally a response to the revision of Gaullist history taking place across French culture and society, exemplified by Giscard d'Estaing's decision in 1975 to replace the 8 May celebrations of Germany's defeat with a festival of Europe.

Those who attacked *la mode rétro* saw themselves as guardians of a historical truth under threat; hence *Le Chagrin et la pitié*, intended according to Ophüls and Harris to 'eliminate mythology' and challenge *le résistancialisme* by addressing French collaboration, was rejected by the director-general of the ORTF because it destroyed myths which the French people still needed (Morris 1992: 43–4). Subsequent critiques of *la mode rétro* were launched in Ganier-Raymond's 1975 history of anti-Semitism during the war, *Une certaine France*, and by *Cahiers du cinéma* in the summer of 1974 under the heading 'Anti-rétro'. Apart from *Le Chagrin et la pitié*, two fiction films bore the brunt of these attacks: Louis Malle's *Lacombe, Lucien* (1974, co-written by Modiano) and an Italian film of the same year, Lilianna Cavanni's *The Night Porter*. All three films generated controversy by representing collaborators or Nazis rather than Resistance fighters, a choice of subject compounded in *Lacombe, Lucien* and *The Night Porter* by an attractive *mise en scène* and elements of eroticism. Since the visual style of *la mode rétro* did not extend to any disruption of form, contesting the myth of Gaullism via content and ironic tone instead, it elicited criticism from avant-garde film-makers like Godard and Gorin (Godard 1991: 139). *Cahiers du cinéma* succinctly defined *rétro* cinema as a snobbish fetishising of old costumes and décors combined with a contempt for history, while in an interview for the magazine, Michel Foucault epitomised the anger of the Left faced with the demythologising of the struggle against Occupation, observing with dismay that if a 'positive' film were made in 1974 about the Resistance, it would be either ignored or laughed at by the audience (Bonitzer and Toubiana 1974: 5, 8). Foucault was right to say that if the Gaullist myth of *le résistancialisme* (all of the French were Resistance fighters) was not accurate, then neither was the new myth of *la mode rétro* (all of the French were collaborators), and that the historical truth lay in a gradual movement during the war years from collaboration to resistance. In French cinema after *la mode rétro*, however, this movement was not always perceived as purely 'positive' or ideological, but also – in response to the ongoing scandals about the wartime past of François Mitterrand and René Bousquet, among others – as contaminated by a cynical opportunism and leading to the horrors of *l'épuration*, the post-war purges against anyone suspected of collaboration (see below).

Lacombe, Lucien: the collaborator not as monster but as 'youth of today'

Although belonging to the same generation as the film-makers of the *nouvelle vague* (see chapter 1), Louis Malle is a classical rather than an experimental director. His career has comprised fiction and documentary films, the latter including *Calcutta* (1969) and *Place*

1

Pierre Blaise in *Lacombe, Lucien*

de la République (1974). Despite his liberal sympathies, even before
the making of *Lacombe, Lucien* in 1974 Malle had been faced with
suggestions of right-wing allegiance for working with Roger Nimier
on *Ascenseur pour l'échafaud* (1957) and for basing *Le Feu follet* (1963)
on a novel by Drieu La Rochelle (Colombat 1993: 77). The project that
was to become *Lacombe, Lucien* was always intended as a portrayal
of collaboration: it was first to be about Algerian *harkis* (Algerians
who fought with the French and against the FLN – the Algerian independence movement) helping the French maintain control of their
country, before Malle settled on the subject of France during the Occupation. This subject would have proved taboo in the 1960s by Malle's
own admission, but by the early seventies he felt that *Le Chagrin et
la pitié* had 'prepared the ground by forcing Frenchmen to question themselves on this matter' (Morris 1992: 105). Consequently
shocked at the *furor* surrounding his film, Malle stressed in interviews
that the characters in *Lacombe, Lucien* – including the incongruous
figure of the black Gestapo foot-soldier – were in fact based closely on
historical research, while comparing the 'objective' stance of the film
to his documentary work, an assertion supported by the use of non-
professional leads and by the (false) authentication of the narrative as
historical fact in the final caption. He later declared that 'What they
teach French school-children about the Occupation period is a bunch
of lies' (Insdorf 1983: 123), and that to conform to the prevalent
mythology a collaborator should have been presented as a club-footed
monster to be exterminated rather than understood (Morris 1992:
58). Far from demonising Lucien in this way, the film portrayed him –
according to the press release – as 'un jeune d'aujourd'hui' [a youth
of today] (Bonitzer 1974: 44).

The film is set in 1944 as the Allied advance begins. Lucien (Pierre Blaise) is a peasant youth living in the rural south-west. Having been rejected by the Resistance as too young, he stumbles into the local Gestapo headquarters by accident after his bike gets a puncture. While drunk he betrays the Resistance contact who refused him, before being given a machine gun and kitted out in fashionable clothes as the newest member of the Gestapo. Meeting a Jewish tailor and his family, Lucien begins an affair with the daughter, France (Aurore Clément). After the tailor has been taken into custody by the authorities, Lucien sees France and her grandmother being deported, and rescues them. The trio then flee into the backwoods. A caption at the film's close asserts that Lucien was tried and shot for collaboration. Significantly, the narrative is generated by chance – and by Lucien's apolitical and often petty motivations – rather than by ideology. The same is true of Cavanni's *The Night Porter*, where 'by chance' the former Nazi Max comes across Lucia, his 'favourite victim' from the camps, in post-war Vienna (Daney 1974: 30). It was this absence of ideology – in the representation of the most crucial period of ideological choice in recent French history – which proved so controversial. As an uneducated peasant who ignores the radio broadcasts of both sides, who loves a Jewish woman and who uses Pétain's image for target practice, Lucien is as apolitical as an active collaborator can be. His responsibility for the fates of the *résistant* schoolteacher and France's father is carefully qualified. Even during his apparently 'good' act of rescuing France and her grandmother from deportation, Lucien kills the guard merely in order to reclaim a watch he considers his. The closing sequence in the woods places Lucien and France as young lovers outside the realm of history and politics in a pastoral idyll into which the war makes only a perfunctory return in the final freeze-frame and caption.

The erotic and pastoral aspects of the film, strongest in the closing reel, were particularly confusing to the Left, as noted in *Cahiers* (Bonitzer and Toubiana 1974: 15). Foucault claimed that the eroticism functioned to rehabilitate the anti-hero Lucien (Bonitzer and Toubiana 1974: 10), while Jean Delmas writing in *Jeune cinéma* in 1974 described the film as 'la récupération sentimentale d'un salaud' [the sentimental rehabilitation of a swine] (Prédal 1989: 116). It is in fact typical of Malle to be more interested in sex, psychology and adolescence than in history or politics – witness *Au revoir les enfants* (1987) and *Le Souffle au cœur* (1971) (see below) – and thus Foucault and Delmas misread *Lacombe, Lucien* as a film on history with sexuality added, instead of the reverse. Of course, war films are traditionally concerned with male psychology and sexuality, and *Lacombe, Lucien* conforms to this trend. In Malle's portrayal of masculinity, Lucien is defined as a man through the power he exercises as a member of the Gestapo. This power is symbolised in his machine gun (which replaces the rifle of his absent father) and is exercised over women, principally France but also those queuing in the street for food. When Lucien confronts other men he seeks to emasculate them, remarking to France's tailor father that only women sew, or humiliating a *résistant* prisoner by gagging him with a piece of tape on which he draws a mouth in lipstick. Reviewing the film for *Cahiers*, Pascal Bonitzer observed that in the latter sequence the prisoner, like the audience, expects Lucien to enter history either as a *résistant* or as a *collabo*. In fact Lucien neither frees the prisoner nor tortures him, side-stepping these ideological choices first by asking why the prisoner addresses him as *tu*, and second by gagging him. As Bonitzer observes, the act of gagging, thus emptied of any ideological meaning, epitomises Lucien's function throughout the film as a political cipher (Bonitzer 1974: 44). It is however in terms of sound rather than image that *Lacombe, Lucien* most clearly exhibits the *rétro* sensibility of privileging style over history. While historical discourse, contained in the radio broadcasts which punctuate the film, remains a barely audible background presence, the sound-track is dominated by jazz tunes of the 1940s carefully chosen by the director to evoke the style of the period.

In the wake of *la mode rétro*, the Occupation became the premise for one superbly unsettling exploration of fascism and the scapegoating of Jewish identity, Joseph Losey's *Monsieur Klein* (1976), alongside several much less impressive comedies and sex films, two tendencies combined in Francis Girod's *René la canne* (1977). With *Emmanuelle* star Sylvia Kristel the female lead, and Gérard Depardieu and Michel Piccoli as a pair of rogues, *René la canne* relies on comic stereotypes. Depardieu's thief and Piccoli's policeman team up to fight the Germans and both survive the war unscathed: the challenging of *le résistancialisme* inherent to *la mode rétro* is thus absent while only a stylised *mise en scène* remains; the Citroën cars, berets and ragtime music all derived directly from *Lacombe, Lucien*. In playing the Occupation for farce, however, the film prefigures Bertrand Blier's much more thoughtful parodying of the war movie in *Merci la vie* (1991) (see below).

The Occupation in fiction films of the 1980s and 1990s

By the 1980s Foucault's judgement that a 'positive' portrayal of the Resistance was impossible no longer held true. *Le Dernier Métro* (1980), François Truffaut's rather facile representation of Resistance – effortlessly embodied by the two leading stars of the day, Catherine Deneuve and Gérard Depardieu – attracted over three million spectators and proved Truffaut's most popular film ever in France. And after a decade in the United States following the reception of *Lacombe, Lucien*, Louis Malle made a triumphant return to French cinema and to the war period with *Au revoir les enfants* (*Goodbye Children*, 1987), a world-wide success which gained an Oscar nomination and seven Césars, and was watched by two million French spectators. More melancholic and less controversial than *Lacombe, Lucien*, the film has an understated narrative, a subdued *mise en scène* and a bleak music track. With the exception of the secondary character, Joseph, who is a reprise of Lucien, this is a positive portrayal of the French during the Occupation, especially of the priests who – in contrast with the complicity of the Catholic Church in the Vichy regime – shelter Jewish boys in their school. The narrative functions as a mystery story about the true identity of new boy Jean Bonnet/Kippelstein, and is viewed through the eyes of the young schoolboy Julien. The historical reality of the Holocaust is thus present for the spectator and for Jean, but not for Julien: it lies hidden behind the enigma of Jean's identity. *Au revoir les enfants* is also an evocation of boyhood, with constant echoes of Jean Vigo's *Zéro de conduite* (1933). The lengthy forest scene is exemplary in combining Julien's innocent exhilaration with the historical apprehension shared by Jean and the audience. Ultimately, Julien inadvertently betrays Jean to the Germans, and here as throughout, the narrative is authorised by Julien's point of view, the final image switching from Jean's exit to a reaction shot of Julien. As at the end of *Lacombe, Lucien*, history intrudes upon innocence, here in the form of a voice-over declaring that Jean, the other Jewish boys and the priest who sheltered them, all died in the camps. Yet despite this conclusion, the film remains essentially a childhood buddy movie rendered poignant by its historical resonance, just as *Lacombe, Lucien* is a love story complicated by the Occupation and *Le Souffle au cœur* (1971) an incest narrative set against the war in Indo-China (see below).

Gender in the war film: *Une affaire de femmes*

With rare exceptions – such as Diane Kurys' *Coup de foudre* (1983) (see chapter 4) – French representations of the Occupation and the Holocaust concentrate on male experience, as do war films in general (see Selig 1993). This masculine discourse, epitomised by Pétain's speeches in Claude Chabrol's compilation of Vichy newsreels, *L'Œil de Vichy* (1993), is challenged by Chabrol's fiction film on female experience, *Une affaire de femmes* (1988). Co-written by Colo Tavernier O'Hagan, and based on a true story, the film follows the efforts of Marie Latour (Isabelle Huppert) to bring up her two children in Cherbourg during the Occupation. As a favour to a friend, Marie carries out an abortion, and gradually begins to make money through this illegal activity. Her husband, Paul (François Cluzet), a prisoner of war, is released and returns to Cherbourg. It is he who finally betrays Marie to the police. Tried in Paris for crimes against the state, she is found guilty and guillotined in July 1943.

Chabrol films this story in a bleakly realist style, using music sparingly and shooting in brown tones which evoke deprivation and poverty. Marie's activity as an abortionist is a double threat to the official policy of collaboration, first by depriving the Germans of potential French workers, and second by contradicting the Vichy dogma of family and motherhood, inscribed in the motto *travail, famille, patrie* and in the celebration of *la fête des mères*. Chabrol portrays the process of abortion with the neutral, unspectacular realism which characterises the film, but ultimately turns to the structures of melodrama to realise Marie's personal tragedy. Hence she rises highest in her creative ambition – to be a singer – at the moment of her impending downfall and arrest. A plot-line typical of the 'woman's film' thus dramatises the female war experience. In *Une affaire de femmes* the Occupation is an experience that women have come to terms with and one which in a sense does not concern men, who are largely absent. Marie rents out a room to her prostitute friend Lulu as a deal 'between women'; she cryptically tells Paul that she does 'women's favours' for her friends and neighbours; her tarot reading makes no mention of men, but suggests she will have many women in her life; throughout the film she enjoys female companionship with her Jewish friend Rachel, with Lulu and with the prisoners who share her cell in Paris. This iterative stress on the common concerns and responses of women in wartime sidelines the masculine arena of combat, as it sidelines Paul within the narrative. He eventually takes his revenge for this – and for Marie's affair with a young spiv – by denouncing his wife to the (male) authorities. Marie's response to her sentence is emblematic of the film as a whole and subverts the claims of the conventional war movie: 'Qu'est-ce que tu veux qu'ils comprennent, les hommes?' [What do you expect men to know about it?]. Enduring and ameliorating the conditions of war is here a woman's business, condemned and punished by the patriarchal Vichy state.

Docteur Petiot: the Holocaust as horror film

The question of cinematic form is a particularly fraught one for films on the Holocaust and the Occupation; these subjects are conventionally considered susceptible either to a documentary approach or to classical realism. Culturally 'low' genres like horror, fantasy and farce seem inappropriate and are therefore rare. The enormity of the Holocaust as a historical event may determine not only the choice of genre, but also of monochrome rather than colour, as for example in *Schindler's List* (Spielberg, 1993). Such delineations of what is considered appropriate have been challenged in the nineties by films which run counter to the classical realist tradition of French cinema and of the war movie: Christian de Chalonge's *Docteur Petiot* (1990), Bertrand Blier's *Merci la vie* (1991, see below), and Jeunet and Caro's *Delicatessen* (1990, see chapter 6).

Despite being based on the actual case of a serial killer operating in Paris during the Occupation, *Docteur Petiot* rejects historical realism for something altogether more unexpected, the horror genre. The plot concerns Petiot's double life. Ostensibly a respectable doctor and family man, he takes on a vampiric persona at night, secretly promising Jews fleeing from the Nazis safe passage out of France before murdering them and stealing their possessions. Thus there is a truly horrific referent behind the generic horror style. Petiot's efficient and systematic murder of Jews – whose bodies are subsequently burned in his enormous basement stove – is clearly analogous to the horrors of

2

Michel Serrault as Docteur Petiot

the Holocaust. The stereotypical portrayal of some of the Jewish characters notwithstanding, the film thus engages effectively not just with the Occupation but with the Holocaust. By representing the casual and banal logistics of Petiot's murders, albeit distanced by the fantastical and at times farcical style, Christian de Chalonge comes close to making what Godard has defined as the intolerable but necessary film which has yet to be made about the camps: 'The only real film to be made about them [...] would be if a camp were filmed from the point of view of the torturers and their daily routine. [...] The really horrible thing about such scenes would be not their horror but their very ordinary everydayness' (Godard 1986: 198). In this regard, de Chalonge's choice of genre has two consequences. By choosing a fantasy genre which has a monster as its usual protagonist, he is able to show what Godard calls 'the torturer's daily routine' without departing from a popular and accessible generic format. (In other words, the horror film naturally allows the representation of horrors which would be unrepresentable in a purely realistic mode.) Second, by juxtaposing Petiot's grotesque appearance as an archetypal vampire with the 'everydayness' of his efficient, murderous routine, the director asks where the real horror lies: in the style of Petiot's behaviour or the specific (anti-Semitic) content of his actions.

The opening sequence of the film suggests what is to come by submitting historical images to a sense of theatrical spectacle, with black-and-white newsreel footage of Paris in 1942 framed by the red curtain of a movie theatre. The newsreel (history) is then succeeded by 'Hangman's Castle', a German monochrome horror film in the style of Murnau's expressionist masterpiece *Nosferatu* (1922). The sequence which follows is an exemplary piece of self-conscious cinema: finding the vampire movie ridiculous and clumsy, Docteur Petiot himself emerges from the audience to remonstrate at the film, at which point his shadow appears on the screen opposite the figure of the vampire. While Petiot's words thus cast him as more realistic and less ridiculous than the generic vampire on the screen, the image – which is then frozen for the opening credits – equates the two as similarly horrific and fantastical. After the credits, the stilled image moves again and Petiot tears through the screen to enter the horror film, stirring cauldrons as a black-and-white version of his 'historical' self. This invasion of the horror space situates *Docteur Petiot* within the genre both explicitly – via the monochrome photography, shadowy expressionist *mise en scène* and eerie music – and implicitly, since the self-referential motif of crossing the screen that separates cinematic fantasy from the 'real world' is a staple of the horror film from *King Kong* (1933) onwards (Clover 1992: 195). As Petiot goes on his rounds, the black-and-white photography fades to situate the action once more in Paris, 1942, shot in colour and with some realism. Generic horror elements remain throughout the film, however, in the suspenseful music and moaning sound effects which accompany Petiot's nocturnal movements, in the gloomy expressionism of the *mise en scène*, and above all in the person of Petiot himself (Michel Serrault), whose theatrical gestures, black cape and pale make-up continue to characterise him as a vampire. There are realistic glimpses of poverty and deprivation under the Occupation, such as the shot of Parisians catching pigeons to eat. Until the final reel, however, horror overrides history, with Petiot laughing maniacally as he cycles through the dusk, hiding under the bedclothes when dawn light comes through the shutters, or described as 'le vampire' in newsreels after his crimes come to light.

After the police discover the scene of Petiot's crimes, the doctor goes into hiding before reappearing during the Liberation of Paris with a false identity as Captain Valéry, a Resistance war hero. As the film nears its close, Petiot's new disguise and eager involvement in anti-collaboration purges – *l'épuration* – render him no longer a personification of war crimes against the Jews, but of French postwar manoeuvrings and myth-making. The myth of *le résistancialisme* and the controversial conduct of public figures such as René Bousquet and François Mitterrand is addressed through Petiot's seemingly effortless metamorphosis from murderer to hero. In 1990, the year *Docteur Petiot* was released, the role of former Vichy police chief René Bousquet in the deportation of Jews, and the friendship between Bousquet and Mitterrand, were under great scrutiny. Bousquet's trial was delayed by the French judiciary. Finally, in April 1991 he was indicted for crimes against humanity, only to be assassinated in 1993. Moreover, in May 1990, the desecration of a Jewish cemetery at Carpentras, and the revisionist theories of Bernard Notin, contributed to a picture of 'une France sur la défensive, inquiète dans son identité' [France on the defensive, unsure of its identity] (Jeambar 1990). This is the very situation personified by Petiot's change of identity at the close of the film, a change complemented by a transformation of genre, from the horror film to the thriller. In a reprise of the opening sequence, and an ironic allusion to the escapist function of cinema during the war period (see chapter 1), Petiot again crosses the screen, this time in order to evade capture by the police. His attempt to enter the thriller he is watching fails, however, and he is arrested behind the screen. Nevertheless, this scene clearly signals the shift in genre which has taken place: no longer coded as horror, the narrative concludes both as a thriller – the pursuit and capture of the suspect – and also as historical realism. The return of history is realised in the form of a voice-over which explains that Petiot was found guilty of twenty-seven murders, and guillotined on 24 May 1946. The image track meanwhile shows a lingering slow pan on the fifty-three suitcases full of possessions recovered after Petiot's trial, an image which recalls the discovery of personal belongings hoarded in the death camps, and more precisely, Lanzmann's filming of the piles of brushes and shoes in the documentary *Shoah* (1985). The closing images of *Docteur Petiot* thus confirm this horror film's urgent relation to the historical enormity of the Holocaust.

Merci la vie: parodying the French war movie

Bertrand Blier's *Merci la vie* (1991) is a mix of genres, part buddy movie, part sex comedy and part war film. Blier had already worked consistently within the first two genres, but this interest in history was novel. The narrative of the film shifts throughout between the present and the past, allowing Blier to explore two crises: the trauma of the Occupation and the threat of Aids. The two are equated metaphorically, rather as disease and occupying powers were conflated in the wartime epithet 'la peste brune' [the brown plague] and in Albert Camus's post-war novel *La Peste*. Blier's protagonists, Joëlle (Anouk Grinberg) and Camille (Charlotte Gainsbourg), pursue sexual adventures in much the same fashion as their male counterparts in his first film, *Les Valseuses* (1974). They find themselves caught up, however, in the fantasies of two male film directors, the second of whom is shooting a movie set during the Occupation. This allows Blier to parody not only the conventional representation of women in film (see chapter 3), but also conventional modes of filming the Occupation.

While Blier's films are often characterised by farce and black comedy, a wartime subject might appear to preclude such a treatment. Jean-Luc Godard was attacked in 1963 for combining newsreel footage with what he called 'improvised farce' in his war film *Les Carabiniers* (Godard 1986: 198). In *The Holocaust and the Literary Imagination*, however, Langer asserts that rather than verisimilitude (so often the recourse of films on the Occupation and the Holocaust), the farcical, the fantastic and the grotesque are best suited to the representation of 'the unimaginable' (see Avisar 1988: 1–2). These elements are of course used to great effect in Christian de Chalonge's *Docteur Petiot* and Jeunet and Caro's *Delicatessen* (both 1990). For his part, Blier combines

3　　　　　Michel Blanc, Anouk Grinberg, Charlotte Gainsbourg
　　　　　　　　and Gérard Depardieu in *Merci la vie*

the comic and the grotesque, reducing the torture of Raymond (Jean Carmet) to a farce, and revealing the artifice of the war film when the Blier-lookalike film director asks if he is being shot by fake or real bullets. The functioning of monochrome and colour in the Holocaust documentary, epitomised by Resnais's *Nuit et brouillard* (1955), is also kept in the foreground throughout *Merci la vie*. Michel Drach had reversed the conventional dichotomy – black and white for the past, colour for the present – in *Les Violons du bal* (1973), but Blier's alternation of colour and monochrome is completely random, divorced from the chronology of the narrative. The director has compared *Merci la vie* to channel-zapping between six different movies, including a black-and-white film by Jean Renoir and a colour fantasy film by Joe Dante (Mény 1991). The list might also include the recent French war films parodied through Blier's *mise en scène*, such as Malle's *Lacombe, Lucien* (1974), Girod's *René la canne* (1977), Truffaut's *Le Dernier Métro* (1980) and Jean-Marie Poiré's *Papy fait de la Résistance* (1983). The latter – a comedy in which the policy of Franco-German collaboration degenerates into a farcical cohabitation – is a clear precursor for *Merci la vie*, parodying as it does previous war films, including Jean-Pierre Melville's *Le Silence de la mer* (1949) and *L'Armée des ombres* (1969). Blier and Poiré also share a close relation to the *café-théâtre* of the 1970s. This style of comedy, based at the Café de la Gare and le Splendid in Paris, produced such actors as Michel Blanc, Miou-Miou, Thierry Lhermitte and Christian Clavier, and first made an impact on French cinema in 1974 with Blier's own *Les Valseuses* (see chapter 3).

Blier worked frequently in the next two decades with actors from the Café de la Gare – Miou-Miou, Depardieu, Patrick Dewaere – and also with Josiane Balasko and Michel Blanc from le Splendid. Poiré's films remain more genuinely popular – and populist – than Blier's: *Papy fait de la Résistance*, a product of le Splendid starring Clavier, Blanc, Balasko and Lhermitte, attracted nearly four million spectators in 1983, while a decade later, Poiré and Clavier were responsible for the hugely popular comic fantasy *Les Visiteurs* (see chapter 8).

No more heroes: *Un héros très discret* and the end of the Mitterrand era

In 1994 the wartime past of President François Mitterrand was under intense scrutiny. Pierre Péan's book *Une jeunesse française* revealed the close ties the president had established with the Vichy government before belatedly joining the Resistance. On the cover was a photo of Mitterrand meeting Marshal Pétain, the architect of collaboration, on 15 October 1942. The tarnishing of Mitterrand's public image was not helped by his persistence in laying a wreath on Pétain's grave, his refusal to apologise for the role of the French state in the Holocaust, and his defence of his friendship with the suspected war criminal René Bousquet. Such is the context of suspicion and doubt behind Jacques Audiard's spoof docu-drama about the Resistance, *Un héros très discret* (*A Self-Made Hero*, 1996). Released the year after Mitterrand left office under a cloud, and just weeks after his death in January 1996, *Un héros* can be interpreted as a playful celebration of the capacity for reinvention that allowed public figures like Mitterrand to achieve high office despite their murky wartime activities. The film has also been read as an allegory of the career of government minister and war criminal Maurice Papon (see Seal 2001). The parallel with Mitterrand seems more persuasive, however, particularly if we bear in mind that he, like the film's fictional hero Albert Dehousse, was never engaged in or accused of war crimes, and that the central issue in both the real-life debate and the film is the gulf between image and reality. In this respect both Mitterrand and Dehousse reflect the national anxieties about the Occupation that were at their height in the mid nineties: 'The interest of the Mitterrand affair lies less in the fact that he was president than in the fact that he embodied all the ambiguities and complexities of the period' (Duhamel 1998: 228).

Fundamental to both Mitterrand and Dehousse is the redefinition of the self through history. Indeed, General Alain de Boisseau (de Gaulle's son-in law) might have been describing Dehousse when he declared: 'some people are attempting to use the Resistance to pass off M. François Mitterrand as a great resistance fighter. He took from anyone who would give, and he behaved throughout this period of his career like a calculating man on the make' (Rousso 1991: 181). In *Un héros* Dehousse (Mathieu Kassovitz) experiences moments of drama, comedy and excruciating embarrassment during his rise from obscurity to the status of Resistance hero. Where doubt was cast in some minds as to the ideological purity of those who joined the Resistance late (the so-called *résistants de la dernière heure*), there is no doubt at all regarding Dehousse. He is entirely an opportunist, a young man whom the war passed by completely and yet who joins the Resistance, as the voice-over makes clear, nine months after the Liberation. In other words, he is reborn as a fantastical embodiment of post-war France. And so well does he personify the spirit of the times that hardly anyone spots the deception. Having used a mixture of manipulation and memory to bluff his way into veterans' meetings, Dehousse is welcomed into the charmed circle only too eagerly, and is eventually appointed Lieutenant Colonel in the French army occupying Berlin after the end of the war. The truth only comes out when he confesses to his invented history after having had to make a decision regarding the lives of French volunteers found fighting for the German SS. In this scene Dehousse is confronted by the fact that his invented persona now makes decisions which have grave consequences in the real world, that are literally a matter of life and death. His response is to reassert his assumed identity for the last time (stating his name and rank while his face is shown in close up) before ordering the SS men to be shot 'in action' so as to save them, and France, from a controversial trial. The colour then disappears from the scene as the dead bodies are shown in the monochrome of history. In reality, the issue of French SS volunteers was not quite so easily dealt with, not quite so black and white. As Audiard will surely have known, in June 1944 SS troops destroyed the French village of Oradour, killing all 642 inhabitants. In June 1994, just before the film was shot, President Mitterrand attended a ceremony to commemorate the fiftieth anniversary of the massacre. But in between times, French MPs had voted in 1953 to grant an amnesty to the thirteen French SS soldiers who had been among the largely German perpetrators of the atrocity. For years afterwards these MPs had been *persona non grata* in Oradour, among them one François Mitterrand.

This crucial sequence also points to a ludic interest in film form which characterises *Un héros*, particularly in the spoof documentary sequences where we see talking heads contradicting each other as to Dehousse's authenticity, in a growing cacophony of testimony which eventually becomes an incomprehensible babble. Eyewitness accounts are not the only sources presented as fallible: several archive photographs are infiltrated by Dehousse, so that the spectator begins to doubt the veracity of photography as a transparent record of historical truth. Moreover, whenever the sound-track becomes noticeably moving or dynamic, Audiard suddenly shows the musicians playing the non-diegetic score, again undercutting the realism of the drama. However, despite these self-conscious moments, Kassovitz's performance and the often poignant voice-over supplied by the elderly Dehousse (Jean-Louis Trintignant) maintain a sense of identification with the protagonist and prevent the film from collapsing into self-reflexivity. *Un héros* is less a deconstruction of film form than a playful investigation of the two parallel narratives identified by historian Henri Rousso: 'Alongside the history of Vichy, another history took shape: the history of the *memory* of Vichy, of Vichy's remnants and fate *after* 1944' (Rousso 1991: 1).

From the Vichy syndrome to *la fracture coloniale*

By the late nineties, French history under the Occupation seemed to have been exhausted, and the Vichy syndrome was at an end. In cinema, contradictory voices still explored both sides of the past: hence in *Seul contre tous* (Noé, 1998), the introductory voice-over could describe France off-handedly as 'le pays du fromage et du collabo' [the land of cheese and collaborators], while at the same time the resuscitation of heroic Resistance was expressed in the form of the populist heritage drama *Lucie Aubrac* (Berri, 1997). But certain political events of the mid-nineties had already neutralized the Occupation as a subject of national controversy. Three months after he was elected as Mitterrand's successor, President Jacques Chirac made a speech on 16 July 1995 at the monument to the victims of the 1942 deportations known as the Vel' d'Hiv, in which he spoke of collective guilt and recognized the responsibility of the French state. This was a gesture that neither de Gaulle nor Mitterrand had been able to make. It laid the ghost of Vichy to a certain extent, and six months later Mitterrand himself was dead. But there was another trauma from the past ready to replace the Occupation as a national obsession: Algeria. The new millennium saw a flood of memoirs, investigations and documentaries on the subject of the Algerian War which had been fought forty years previously. Among these memoirs was Paul Aussaresse's *Services spéciaux*, 'a catalogue of "necessary" misdeeds which led to its author's conviction, in December 2001, for complicity in the justification of war crimes' (Tomlinson 2004: 358). The fascination with the Algerian conflict continued with the rerelease of the legendary Italian-Algerian film *The Battle of Algiers* (Pontecorvo, 1965) in 2004. A year later the controversial law of 23 February 2005 required French schools to stress the positive aspects of the colonial project, but this revisionist tendency was severely challenged by the publication of a wide-ranging study of the after-effects of colonial conflicts on French society, *La Fracture coloniale* (Blanchard et al, 2005). The same year also saw the release of Haneke's postcolonial thriller *Caché*. Both the book and the film reveal the *banlieue* as a quasi-colonial space, and colonial conflicts like the Algerian War as the source of traumas that are still being experienced in France today (see below).

The Indochinese and Algerian Wars in fiction film

On 7 May 1954, the French army in Indochina was heavily defeated by the Vietminh at Dien Bien Phu. The fall of Dien Bien Phu was a turning point not just in Indochina but in French colonial power, heralding the futile conflict in Algeria (1954–62), decolonisation, and the decline of the French empire. Moreover, 'Psychologiquement, Dien Bien Phu devient le symbole du désastre' [Psychologically, Dien Bien Phu symbolises disaster] (Accoce and Stavridès 1991: 23). Precisely because the colonial wars fought in Algeria and Indochina proved so traumatic, they remained taboo, practically absent from the French cinema of the period. When films were made which referred to the conflicts they ran the risk of censorship, as with Godard's *Le Petit Soldat* (1960), which was banned until 1963, a year after Algerian independence. The difficulty of representing on screen the Algerian War – and particularly the war crimes associated with it – is addressed in Alain Resnais's *Muriel* (1963). Set in Boulogne in November 1962, the film concerns memories of both the Second World War and the Algerian War. The mysterious Muriel is the personification of the latter conflict. Apparently the fiancée of the male protagonist Bernard, she in fact remains invisible, unrepresentable except via sound in Bernard's recollections and in a tape recording which seems to capture her torture and death at the hands of French soldiers in Algeria. As one of the soldiers later declares, 'Muriel, ça ne se raconte pas' [Muriel's story cannot be told].

The Algerian War was subjected to a direct, naturalistic portrayal in Gillo Pontecorvo's Italian-Algerian co-production, *The Battle of Algiers* (1965). So close was the film to the site of the trauma it represented that Pontecorvo required the ruins of the buildings where the struggle had been fought to be rebuilt in order to record their destruction a second time. In France, however, the colonial wars were still approachable only at a tangent. Those, like René Vautier, who offered a direct record of the atrocities risked arrest and imprisonment. Colonial conflict remained in the background rather than the foreground, as in Jacques Demy's *Les Parapluies de Cherbourg* (1964). In *Le Souffle au cœur* (1971) Louis Malle characteristically used the fall of Dien Bien Phu as historical background for an evocation of adolescent sexuality. Here the conflict in Indochina assumed a function analogous to its place in the work of Malle's collaborator on *Lacombe, Lucien*, Patrick Modiano, for whom wars were merely a chronological index: 'les meilleurs repères, ce sont les guerres' [wars are the best landmarks] (Modiano 1975: 19). Claude Chabrol explored the legacy of the two wars in *Le Boucher* (1969), a thriller about a serial killer at large in a small French town. From the outset, Chabrol makes it plain that the butcher Popaul (Jean Yanne), is an army veteran who has been marked by his experiences in Algeria and Indochina. An uneasy tension is established between the ostensible normality and continuity of provincial life – evoked by the dancing and folk songs during the long wedding sequence – and the hidden traumas arising from the past, realised in iterative shots of the war memorial accompanied by haunting and suspenseful music. The anguish and violence implicit in the symbol of the war memorial is rendered explicit when Popaul, aggressively chopping slabs of meat in his shop, begins to tell his customers about the mutilated bodies he saw as a soldier.

When the local headmistress Hélène (Stéphane Audran) finds the victim of the first murder, she tells Popaul that the body resembles the atrocities he has described. Although from this point on Chabrol moves from psychological concerns to a more generic suspense narrative in the style of Alfred Hitchcock, through the character of Popaul a connection between present violence and past traumas has clearly been made. As with Hollywood representations of the Vietnam War in the 1970s, it is obliquely through the figure of the returning veteran that the conflict itself is addressed. And as with the films on Vietnam, in *Le Boucher* 'the authenticity of [the veteran's] experience and the reconstitution of a masculine identity require the ultimate exclusion of women and female sexuality' (Selig 1993: 10). Popaul's victims are all women, while he makes friends only with the overtly desexualised Hélène, who has been celibate for ten years. At the film's close, he tells Hélène that it was only in her company that he was free from the visions of blood which have haunted him since his war experiences.

Stimulated both by the reappraisal of history following 1968 and by their increasing distance from the colonial wars, film-makers began to engage directly with Algeria and Indochina during the 1970s. In 1972 Vautier, who had worked with the independence-seeking FLN (Front de libération nationale) during the conflict, directed *Avoir 20 ans dans les Aurès*, credited as 'the first fictional film about the Algerian War' (Tavernier 1993: 289). This was followed swiftly by Yves Boisset's less well-received *R.A.S.* (1973). But the director most consistently concerned with the two wars in question is the veteran Pierre Schoendoerffer.

Hearts of darkness: *Le Crabe-Tambour* and *Dien Bien Phu*

Having volunteered to go to Indochina, Schoendoerffer served as a cameraman with the French army until his capture at Dien Bien Phu. In 1963 he published *La 317e Section*, a novel based on his experiences in Indochina, which he himself filmed the following year. The same pattern over a decade later produced first the novel, then in 1977 the film version, of *Le Crabe-Tambour*. Like Resnais's *Muriel*, the film explores memories of war through an enigmatic central figure – who may or may not be imaginary – and through the juxtaposition of different conflicts.

Willsdorff, nicknamed 'Le Crabe-Tambour' (Jacques Perrin), is a mysterious officer who has served in both Indochina and Algeria. Crucially, he is identified with the traumatic disasters which concluded those conflicts, having been captured at Dien Bien Phu and implicated in the *putsch* of 1961 which sought to prevent de Gaulle granting Algerian independence. Evoked throughout the film by the recollections of Pierre, a naval doctor (Claude Rich), and his skipper (Jean Rochefort), Willsdorff becomes a partly historical, partly mythologised figure, a mixture of Moby Dick, Lawrence of Arabia and Kurtz from Joseph Conrad's *Heart of Darkness*. Schoendoerffer's narrative is, besides, explicitly Conradian. It follows a French naval vessel, the *Jaureguiberry*, heading towards the Arctic in the hope of finding Willsdorff, who is apparently in charge of a boat crewed by veterans of Algeria and Indochina. As the *Jaureguiberry* nears its quarry, the sailors and fishermen encountered tell of Willsdorff's growing isolation and madness. Two years before *Apocalypse Now* (1979), Coppola's celebrated representation of the Vietnam War through the journey towards 'Colonel' Kurtz, Schoendoerffer realises a hellish quest, not through the jungle but through the ice, in search of a personification of colonial history and defeat. During this quest the red décor and lighting on the ship suggest the bloodshed of the past, while the grey emptiness of the ocean functions as a screen upon which both doctor and skipper project memories of Willsdorff as a soldier, an adventurer, an opium junkie and a traitor (he is given twenty years for his part in the *putsch*). The constant cross-cutting between sequences in the Arctic (the present) and in Indochina and Algeria (the past) is complemented by the use of radio and television broadcasts about the Vietnam War. By setting *Le Crabe-Tambour* in 1975 during the fall of Saigon, and by insistent juxtapositions, Schoendoerffer establishes a grim continuity between the conflicts of four decades, as when one character's story about U-boats in the Second World War is interrupted by television images from Vietnam. Ultimately, radio contact is made with Willsdorff, but he remains unseen, present only as the protagonists' obsessive memory/fantasy. In an attempt to exorcise the traumas that Willsdorff represents, the skipper who has relentlessly pursued him simply says 'Adieu' over the radio before turning back for France. It is precisely this evocation and hence exorcism of the past which Schoendoerffer attempts in *Dien Bien Phu* (1992), which he called his farewell to Indochina (Stavridès 1991: 26).

After years of struggling to finance his films, Schoendoerffer was able to spend $25 million on an epic account of the defeat in Indochina. Despite the high production values and the hundreds of extras, however, *Dien Bien Phu* is not quite the sumptuous mythologising of the past suggested by both the press and the producers. Schoendoerffer's prime means of distancing himself from this stance, so typical of the heritage film (see chapter 7), is the ironic use of a theatrical frame for the narrative. The opening sequence shows an orchestra warming up, then the lights going up on a stage set for a concert in Hanoi by French violinist Béatrice Vergnes (Ludmila Mikael) against a backdrop of the tricolour and of Marianne, personification of France. The frame is closed at the end of the film as the concert finishes and the lights dim, implying that the empire, and indeed its filmic representation, is mere spectacle. Framed within this ironic device, however, is Schoendoerffer's personal account of Dien Bien Phu, an autobiographical and realistic portrayal of the confusion and monotony of two months of fighting. The film is shot largely from the point of view of the French soldiers who took part, including an army

LIBRARY · UNIVERSITY OF CHESTER

cameraman who evokes the director himself. But both the images and the sound-track present a tension between the autobiographical and the theatrical: the general realism of the combat scenes is modified by a spectacular *mise en scène* during the nocturnal bombardments, while the battle is at once introduced by an unidentified first-person plural voice-over, and mediated by the melancholic and wordless chorus of Béatrice's violin. The theatrical gives way to the personal in the film's conclusion as, after the narrative frame is closed with Béatrice playing the swan song of the French empire, the screen fades to black and the commentary passes into the present, speaking of the shattering experience of returning to Dien Bien Phu after forty years in order to shoot the film. In its final statement the voice, saying 'I' for the first time, is identifiable as the director's, as the credits immediately confirm. Thus although framing the film as a spectacle about the fall of empire, Schoendoerffer in the final analysis charts a personal journey analogous to the quest undertaken in *Le Crabe-Tambour*.

Caché: hidden camera, hidden trauma

The Freudian concept of the 'return of the repressed' has often been evoked to explain the impact of colonial conflicts after the original events. Hence 'The silence about colonial crimes meant that, according to the law of the return of the repressed, colonial racism would haunt post-imperial France' (Vergès 1998: 90). Similarly but with a stress on the 'inherent latency' of the traumatic experience, trauma theory has suggested that trauma 'is fully evident only in connection with another place and in another time' (Caruth 1995: 8). Most recently, Benjamin Stora has observed that the unresolved traumas of the Algerian War have shifted to France: 'Le refus de l'autre, le métissage, ce sont les questions de l'Algérie coloniale. [...] La mémoire s'est transférée d'une rive à l'autre. Tout ce qui n'a pas été réglé se retrouve donc en France' [The rejection of the other, racial mixing, these are questions from colonial Algeria. Memory has crossed the sea, so that everything that was not resolved is now reappearing in France] (Stora 2003: 12). These questions, in particular colonial memory and the rejection of the ethnic other, constitute the terrain explored by Michael Haneke in his masterful thriller *Caché* (*Hidden*, 2005).

Set in Paris in the present, *Caché* delves into the past of its protagonist Georges (Daniel Auteuil) and, via his memories and fantasies, into the colonial past of the French nation. The supremely tense plot hinges on a series of videotapes sent anonymously to Georges and his wife Anne (Juliette Binoche). Along with the tapes are childlike drawings that represent a traumatic event instigated by Georges at the age of six in 1961, and that concerns an Algerian boy named Majid. The importance of the drawings, of Georges's nightmarish flashbacks, and of Haneke's spatial representation of racial tension has tended to be neglected, however, in the film's reception. Critical and popular reaction – from the film's screening at Cannes onwards – has largely ignored its postcolonial politics in favour of a fascination with film form and the attempt to solve the mystery of who made the tapes. Haneke certainly enjoys asking this question. The camerawork generates a persistent unease throughout *Caché* by throwing doubt on the ontological status of what we see, challenging the audience to ask of almost every sequence whether it is objectively or subjectively filmed. The process begins with the opening sequence, apparently an example of objective camera but later revealed as part of a videotape sent to Georges and Anne by their mystery stalker. It continues to the very end of the film, when Haneke's ambivalent final shot reveals the sons of Majid and Georges in conversation without allowing us to do more than guess their motives.

But one question (who made the tapes?) can hide another, potentially much more uncomfortable: what is Georges (and the contemporary white French bourgeoisie that he embodies) so afraid of? *Caché* posits Georges's personal past as a metaphor for France's continuing fear and hence violence towards the ethnic other, principally the Algerian community. The film brings to light what was supposed to stay hidden from view. The repressed memories that return to haunt Georges concern the events of October 1961, when Majid's parents were killed in the murderous response of the Paris police to an Algerian demonstration supporting independence. The orphaned Majid was then betrayed by Georges and in effect deported by Georges' parents, removed from the heart of France (a farm in *la France profonde*, the site of traditional French values) to the margins (the orphanage, the *banlieue*) where he would no longer be visible. The nightmares that Georges suffers express his own trauma, one of guilt. But the drawings that accompany the tapes, and eventually the suicide of the adult Majid (Maurice Bénichou) represent the latter's trauma, one of suffering. Where the aggressively assertive yet anxious Georges represses, denies, and hides the truth, the mildly spoken Majid tries to make it visible. This is surely the meaning of his suicide – a desperate and shocking attempt to make himself and his suffering visible to Georges. In a sense, this action is a final drawing, a piece of testimony in which trauma is visualised by splashes of blood. As with the videotapes, Haneke never actually reveals who made the drawings. But Georges remarks that they look like the work of a child, and they are strongly reminiscent of the type of paintings made by children traumatized by war, from Spain to Bosnia and beyond. Above all, they recall the images made by Algerian children in the documentary short *J'ai 8 ans* (Le Masson and Poliakoff, 1961). Both films depict childhood trauma related to Algeria via pictures of bleeding bodies, and via disquieting, silent shots of a child's face – the lingering repeated close-ups on the witnesses in *J'ai 8 ans*, Georges's nightmarish memories of the young Majid in *Caché*. The fragmentary nature of these memories again situates *Caché* in the realm of trauma theory, which has often commented on 'the match between the visuality common to traumatic symptoms (flashbacks, hallucinations, dreams) and [...] visual media like cinema' (Kaplan 2005: 69).

The importance of testimony to colonial crimes and to postcolonial suffering has not been sufficiently recognized in the rather formalist critical reaction to *Caché* in France and elsewhere. This is all the more surprising given the film's precise context: just months before its release, the law of 23 February 2005 required that the teaching of French history stress the 'positive role' of the French colonial project, particularly in North Africa. Moreover, *Caché* was released the same year as two other French films about Algeria, Philippe Faucon's *La Trahison* and Alain Tasma's *Nuit noire, octobre 17 1961*. Nonetheless *Positif* magazine, for instance, did not mention Algeria once in its review of *Caché*. This reminds one inevitably of Georges's own position, in utter denial, and of what the editors of *La Fracture coloniale* term 'la difficulté à intégrer l'épisode coloniale dans nos représentations collectives, renvoyant en cela à la difficulté de penser la question de la différence' [the difficulty in including the colonial episode in our collective representations, which is linked to the difficulty in thinking through the question of difference] (Blanchard et al 2005: 24). In the final scene of *Caché* Georges cuts himself off from the unwelcome return of the repressed, taking sleeping pills and closing the curtains on the outside world. The colonial dream of 'Algeria without Algerians' has been replaced by a postcolonial dream of France without Algerians, of Georges without Majid.

Beur cinema

Beur, derived from the word 'Arabe' backwards, 'denotes a second-generation child of North African immigrants who was born in France, or else came to France at an early age', and is usually applied to 'the Algerian, rather than the Moroccan or Tunisian, immigrant community'. Consequently, *beur* cinema has been defined as 'any film directed by a young person of North African origin who was born or who grew up in France, usually featuring *Beur* characters' (Bosséno 1992: 47, 49). Already in the 1960s and early 1970s first generation North-African immigrants in France were making films, mostly documentaries or realistic narratives on social themes such as racism, a choice of subject later termed 'miserabilism'. *Beur* cinema developed in the 1980s, when second-generation Algerians started making commercial feature films with professional actors, linear narratives and themes concerning suburban youth. The realism of the urban settings was at odds with the heritage-film trend which developed at about the same period in white French cinema (see chapter 7), but may have influenced directors such as Beineix and Carax to set films in the Parisian suburbs (Bosséno 1992: 51).

Bosséno claims that *beur* cinema 'displays enough characteristics to be classified as a genre on its own' and that its 'influence on the French cinema is quite out of proportion with the number of films' it comprises (Bosséno 1992: 56). It has often been associated with the *banlieue* film (see Tarr 2005), and might also be considered a sub-genre within the recent trend known as *jeune cinéma* (see chapter 9). The most important *beur* films prior to the rise of the *jeune cinéma* in the mid nineties were Abdelkrim Bahloul's *Le Thé à la menthe* (1984), Mehdi Charef's *Le Thé au harem d'Archimède* (1985), *Camomille* (1987) and *Miss Mona* (1987), Cheikh Djamai's *La Nuit du doute*, Rachid Bouchareb's *Bâton rouge* (1986) and *Cheb* (1991), and Malik Chibane's *Hexagone* (1993). Several enjoyed success at the box office, in particular *Le Thé au harem d'Archimède*, which attracted 100,000 spectators in Paris, played at Cannes and won the Prix Jean Vigo for best first feature. The young characters in *beur* cinema are not solely Maghrebi but also white French, as in the cross-racial friendships of *Le Thé au harem d'Archimède* (1985) and *Bâton rouge* (1986). Since social integration is the main aspiration for these characters, racism tends not to be a central issue here, while comedy and the buddy movie are the principal genres used. Bosséno argues that *beur* cinema is essentially transitional, an 'exorcism' of North-African concerns and identity which precedes and facilitates integration into French society. Hence Charef's first film concentrates on questions of ethnic identity, while his subsequent work considers other marginalised groups, but not in racial terms (Bosséno 1992: 55–6). This tendency has resulted in some critics terming these films an unrealistic and submissive 'harki' cinema. One could respond to this accusation by pointing out the metaphorical representation of *Beurs* through outsider figures such as the transvestite in *Miss Mona*. In 1993 Carrie Tarr reported that 'As yet no *Beur* women have achieved funding to make a feature film' (Tarr 1993: 325). That situation however has changed. Tarr has recently pointed out the renegotiation of images of Maghrebi women in features by female directors, among them Rachida Krim's *Sous les pieds des femmes* (1997) and Yamina Benguigui's *Inch'Allah dimanche* (2001) (see Tarr 2005: 213).

Rites of passage in *Hexagone*

Shot in only twenty-four days, *Hexagone* (1993) is Malik Chibane's début film, financed by a local association which he established in the Parisian suburb of Goussainville. Set and filmed in this deprived urban environment, the film was intended to increase the 'cultural visibility' of Chibane's generation of *Beurs* (Bouquet 1994: 11). With this in mind, Chibane claimed that *Hexagone* was the first French film to have five *Beurs* in lead roles (Bouquet 1994), playing a group of friends: Ali the student (Karim Chakir), Nacera who seeks independence as a *beurette* (Faiza Kaddour), Staf the dandy (Hakim Sarahoui), Samy the drug addict and petty criminal (Farid Abdedou), and his unemployed brother Slimane (Jalil Naciri). It is Slimane who, sparingly, narrates the film: he introduces the setting and characters; later he explains the significance of Eid al-Adha, the Islamic holiday celebrating Abraham's sacrifice of his son; and his voice-over concludes the film.

Particularly in the establishing shots, *Hexagone* is documentary in style, Chibane's handheld camera exploring urban locations with a rawness that would become associated with the *jeune cinéma* (see chapter 9). The director also makes a sparing and effective use of pictorial compositions, such as the shot of Goussainville station, the icon showing Abraham's sacrifice, or the symbolic image of the dead sheep lying on the grass which immediately follows Samy's death, and which evokes the Abraham myth. The absence of sound-track music – apart from during the end credits – and the preponderance of street patois in the dialogue, commingling *verlan* (backwards slang), Parisian slang and Arabic, maintains a realism which is complemented by the naturalistic acting of the non-professional actors. Again, these characteristics link the film to nineties *jeune cinéma*, as do its themes. Unemployment, integration and questions of cultural identity are addressed for the most part directly in the film, while racism is evoked more obliquely in a comic episode wherein Staf pretends to be an Italian called Xavier in order to sleep with a racist white French woman, only revealing to her afterwards in a cryptic message that he is a *Beur*. Chibane adds a more tragic, symbolic strand to his narrative via the religious story of Abraham sacrificing his son to God. This mythical paradigm is applied to Samy's death on the feast of Eid al-Adha. Arrested for shoplifting, Samy is rescued by Slimane, but having escaped from the police he collapses and dies from an overdose. Slimane's concluding voice-over attempts to find some sense of continuity after his brother's death. The rite of passage characteristic of the buddy movie is here given a mythical dimension, as well as being emblematic of the *beur* situation, where a passage to integration is advocated both by Ali in the film, and by Chibane in interview (Bouquet 1994).

France outside, Algeria inside: space and gender in *Samia*

While the masculine buddy movie is a narrative model used in several *beur* and *banlieue* films, such as *Hexagone* and most famously *La Haine* (see chapter 9), there are also a few recent examples of the representation of female adolescence in non-white French communities, among them Fabrice Génestal's *La Squale* (2001) and Philippe Faucon's *Samia* (2000). The latter is the story of a fifteen-year-old girl, one of eight siblings living in a traditional Algerian family in Marseilles. The film follows Samia (Lynda Benahouda) as she rebels constantly against the patriarchal restrictions imposed on her freedom of movement, behaviour and dress by her inherited culture, personified by her older brother Yacine (Mohamed Chaouch). As Yacine tells Amel, Samia's older sister, near the start of the film, 'Dehors, tu es en France, mais à la maison tu es au bled' [outside you're in France, but inside, you're back home in Algeria]. Such statements are backed up with violence as Yacine first attacks Amel for seeing a white boyfriend and later hits Samia with his belt for refusing to do the domestic chores. The aggressive authoritarianism of Yacine's position is in part explained by a crisis of authority within the household, with the father hospitalised, as well as by Yacine's inability to find his place in the wider French society which treats him with suspicion and brutality: he cannot find work and is threatened by the police. Nonetheless, the film also represents Samia's life in the family home as a form of imprisonment (as she herself calls it), and juxtaposes claustrophobic interiors with exterior spaces that signal Samia's rare moments of freedom: dancing at a football match and a concert, roller-skating, swimming. To this extent the film may be seen as conforming to what Deniz Gökturk has called 'narratives of rescue, liberation and Westernization' (cited in Tarr 2005: 112). But *Samia* does embed the cultural tensions in a wider sense of societal racism and suspicion, while presenting in its protagonist a strong and determined character who speaks back to both her brother and the skinheads who abuse her, and who has no need of a white hero to 'rescue' her. Samia, it seems, is 'able to negotiate a provisional space of resistance' (Tarr 2005: 121) where she can assume her own identity. Thus in the final sequence she and her mother leave Yacine behind, to spend the summer in Algeria with the hope of a new family regime for when they return.

For most of the narrative, however, Samia has to negotiate the demarcation of space along gender lines, whether this means eating at a separate table from her father and brothers in the family home, or helping her sisters clean the house while her father plays cards with local men in the café. Both in and out of the home, Yacine attempts to replicate his father's authority by policing space and movement, for example refusing to leave Amel alone with the (white, male) doctor, or bundling Samia into a car to return her to the wedding she has sneaked out of. In the film's most shocking sequence, Yacine and his mother also attempt to police Samia and her sisters' bodies by taking them to have a medical examination to prove that they are still virgins – that their own internal space, and with it family honour, is therefore still intact. Gender imbricates not only with space, but also with national identity: Samia's mother is told that her daughters are bringing shame on the family by behaving as if they are French girls. Their gender means that they are caught between two ways of being: hence Samia and her sisters do not just alternate rapidly between French and Arabic, but also frequently change from Arab to western clothes and back again, whereas their brothers do not have to change appearance like this.

Despite the deliberately realist *mise en scène* (naturalistic lighting, unobtrusive camerawork, no sound-track music until the final credits) Faucon does make use of repeated mirror compositions to emphasise that identity is at stake in the film. We see Samia and her sisters reflected in mirrors as they dance to American music, while her father and aunt are reflected praying. In one striking composition, while visiting her father in hospital, Samia moves aside from her family to stand by a half-open window. Through the glass is an image of escape and peace: a garden with a large tree, framed within the window and placed next to Samia's head, as if she were fantasising a utopian place away from cultural and family conflicts. This dream is at least partially realised when Samia, having seen her mother finally reassert her authority over Yacine, catches the boat for Algeria. The irony remains, however, as Tarr has observed, that the promised change 'can only take place away from the *banlieue*, in the transitional space of a boat that is actually heading for a country where women are perceived as even more oppressed' (Tarr 2005: 116). This ending recalls the representation of national space in another film about a North African family in Marseilles, Karim Dridi's *Bye-Bye* (1995). In *Bye-Bye* it is male rather than female identity which is the main focus of attention, with the attraction and the threat of macho gun culture embodied by Renard, the drug-dealer, who declares 'Ou tu baises, ou c'est toi qu'on baise' [screw or get screwed]. But again it is the return home 'au bled' (in this case, to Tunisia) which offers a fantasy of escape. In neither case, it seems, is the solution to racism, conflicted identity and inter-cultural tension to be found by staying put.

Zidane: national hero, cultural 'miracle'

French cinema has recently seen the rise of (male) *beur* stars such as Jamel Debbouze and Samy Nacéri (see chapter 8). In the wider realm of popular culture the current national hero is also a *Beur*, the footballer Zinedine Zidane. Winner of the World Cup in the multicultural success story of 1998, captain of the national team in the World Cup of 2006, 'Zizou' is for many the face of contemporary France. Even when sent off for violent conduct towards the end of the 2006 World Cup Final (which France lost), Zidane was celebrated rather than pilloried for his actions. He has been honoured by President Chirac, celebrated in songs and video games, and has been the focus of a documentary, *Zidane, un portrait du 21e siècle* (Philippe Parreno and Douglas Gordon, 2006), which films his performance during a single game for Real Madrid with seventeen different cameras. Like Jamel, Zidane thus offers a positive model of the male *Beur* within French society. This becomes problematic however when constructed as an exception to the rule. Figures like Zidane and Jamel from the domain of sport or spectacle, while embodying success and integration, can be read as implying that French North Africans who do not function in the world of performance and celebrity are failures or threats. Zidane was described in 2004 by *L'Express* magazine as a 'miracle' both on and off the pitch. The flipside of such praise is the implicit message that 'la figure de Zidane compose l'image d'une exception – le "miracle!" – renvoyant le reste des "Arabes" à l'échec [the figure of Zidane constructs an image of exception – a 'miracle'! – which condemns all other 'Arabs' to failure] (Deltombe and Regouste 2005: 196). All the more so since the miracle Zidane was celebrated for achieving off the pitch was apparently to make women like football and racists like Arabs! The burden of living up to this impossible ideal thus falls to *Beurs* in general of whom it is expected, via the celebration of Zidane as national hero, that they manage to make themselves acceptable to racists. If stars like Zidane are represented in this way, the danger remains therefore that political, social and economic factors in the fragmentation and prejudice within French society are erased to construct the victims of discrimination as the authors of their own suffering (see Deltombe and Regouste 2005: 197). In the France of *la fracture coloniale*, stardom is not always a sign of acceptance for one's ethnic and cultural community.

References

Accoce, P. and Stavridès, Y. (1991), Retour à Dien Phu, Paris, *L'Express*, 9 May 1991, 24–5.

Atack, M. (1999), *May '68 in French Fiction and Film: Rethinking Society, Rethinking Representation*, Oxford, OUP.

Avisar, I. (1988), *Screening the Holocaust: Cinema's Images of the Unimaginable*, Indianapolis and Bloomington, Indiana University Press.

Barthes, R. (1957), *Mythologies*, Paris, Editions du Seuil.

Blanchard, P., Bancel, N., and Lemaire, S. (2005) (eds.), *La Fracture coloniale: la société française au prisme de l'héritage colonial*, Paris, La Découverte.

Bonitzer, P. (1974), Histoire de sparadrap (Lacombe Lucien), Paris, *Cahiers du cinéma*, 250, 42–7.

Bonitzer, P. and Toubiana, S. (1974), Anti-rétro: Entretien avec Michel Foucault, *Cahiers du cinéma*, 251/2, 5–15.

Bosséno, C. (1992), Immigrant cinema: national cinema – the case of *Beur* film, in R. Dyer and G. Vincendeau (eds), *Popular European Cinema*, London and New York, Routledge, 47–57.

Bouquet, S. (1994), Malik Chibane, Paris, *Cahiers du cinéma*, 476, 11.

Caruth, C. (1995), Trauma and experience: introduction, in C. Caruth (ed.), *Trauma: Explorations in Memory*, Baltimore, Johns Hopkins University Press.

Clover, C. J. (1992), *Men, Women, and Chain Saws: Gender in the Modern Horror Film*, London, BFI.

Colombat, P. A. (1993), *The Holocaust in French Film*, London, Filmmakers, No. 33, The Scarecrow Press.

Conan, E. and Rousso, H. (1996) *Vichy, un passé qui ne passe pas*, Paris, Gallimard.

Daney, S. (1974), Anti-rétro (suite), Fonction critique (fin), Paris, *Cahiers du cinéma*, 253, 30–36.

Deltombe, T. and Regouste, M. (2005), L'ennemi intérieur: la construction médiatique de la figure de l''Arabe', in P. Blanchard, N. Bancel and S. Lemaire (eds.), *La Fracture coloniale: la société française au prisme de l'héritage colonial*, Paris, La Découverte, 191–8.

Duhamel, E. (1998), François Mitterrand between Vichy and resistance, in M. Maclean (ed.), *The Mitterrand Years: Legacy and Evaluation*, Basingstoke, Macmillan, 217–32.

Felman, S. (1992), The return of the voice: Claude Lanzmann's *Shoah*, in S. Felman and D. Laub, *Testimony: Crises of Witnessing in Literature, Psychoanalysis, and History*, London and New York, Routledge, 204–83.

Fisera, V. (1978) (ed.), *Writing on the Wall. May 1968: A Documentary Anthology*, London, Allison and Busby.

Fletcher, A. (1964), *Allegory: Theory of a Symbolic Mode*, Ithaca, NY, Cornell University Press.

Forbes, J. (1992), *The Cinema in France After the New Wave*, London, BFI/Macmillan.

Godard, J.-L. (1986), *Godard on Godard*, ed. by T. Milne, London, Da Capo.

Godard, J.-L. (1991), *Godard par Godard: des années Mao aux années 80*, Paris, Flammarion.

Insdorf, A. (1983), *Indelible Shadows: Film and the Holocaust*, Cambridge and New York, Cambridge University Press.

Jeambar, D. (1990), La Profanation, Paris, *Le Point*, 921, 49.

Jurt, J. (1997) (ed.), *Algérie-France-Islam*, Paris, L'Harmattan.

Kaplan, E. A. (2005), *Trauma Culture: The Politics of Terror and Loss in Media and Culture*, New Brunswick, Rutgers University Press.

Lanzmann, C. (1993), Interview for *Moving Pictures*, BBC Television.

Leys, R. (2000), *Trauma: A Genealogy*, Chicago, University of Chicago Press.

Lindeperg, S. (1997), *Les Ecrans de l'ombre: La Seconde Guerre Mondiale dans le cinéma français 1944–1969*, Paris, CNRS.

MacCabe, C. M. (1992), Jean-Luc Godard: A life in seven episodes (to date), in R. Bellour and L. Bandy (eds), *Jean-Luc Godard: Son + Image 1974–1991*, New York, Museum of Modern Art, 13–21.

Mény, J. (1991), *Making* Merci la vie, FR3 television.

Modiano, P. (1975), *Villa triste*, Paris, Gallimard.

Morris, A. (1992), *Collaboration and Resistance Reviewed: Writers and the Mode Rétro in Post-Gaullist France*, New York and Oxford, Berg.

Prédal, R. (1989), *Louis Malle*, Paris, Edilig.

Reynolds, S. (1990), *The Sorrow and the Pity* revisited, or be careful, one train can hide another, Chalfont St Giles, Bucks., *French Cultural Studies*, 1:2:2, 149–59.

Rousso, H. (1991), *The Vichy Syndrome: History and Memory in France since 1944*, translated by A. Goldhammer, London, Harvard University Press.

Seal, H. (2001), Screening the past: representing resistance in *Un héros très discret*, in L. Mazdon (ed.), *France on Film: Reflections on Popular French cinema*, London, Wallflower.

Selig, M. (1993), Genre, gender, and the discourse of war: the a/historical and Vietnam War films, Glasgow, *Screen*, 34:1, 10–18.

Stavridès, Y. (1991), 'Notre adieu à l'Indochine ...', Paris, *L'Express*, 9 May 1991, 24–8.

Stora, B. (2003), L'absence d'images déréalise l'Algérie, *Cahiers du cinéma*, Hors série: Spécial Algérie, 7–13.

Tarr, C. (1993), Questions of identity in *Beur* cinema: from *Tea in the Harem* to *Cheb*, *Screen*, 34:4, 321–42.

Tarr, C. (2005), *Reframing Difference:* Beur *and* Banlieue *Filmmaking in France*, Manchester, Manchester University Press.

Tavernier, B. (1993), I wake up, dreaming, London, *Projections*, 2, 252–378.

Tomlinson, E. (2004), Rebirth in sorrow: *La Bataille d'Alger*, *French Studies*, LVIII:3, 357–70.

Vergès, F. (1998), Memories and names of Algeria, *Parallax*, 4:2, 89–91.

Ward Jouve, N. (1994), A woman in black and white, London, *Sight and Sound*, July 1994, 29.

Representations of sexuality

3

Porno and after

If 1968 marked a watershed in French cinema's engagement with politics and history (see chapter 2), 1974 did the same for representations of sexuality. In that year, pornography entered mainstream French cinema.

Emmanuelle and the legitimising of the porn film

The gradual relaxation of censorship in the late 1960s had seen a steady increase in the number of erotic films made in France, culminating in Jean Rollin's vampire series. But the increase in sexual candour in films like Bertrand Blier's *Les Valseuses* (1974) still met with controversy and complaint. The watershed came with the enormous success of *Emmanuelle* (1974), which achieved a genuine cross-over from porn to mainstream. Based on a novel by Emmanuelle Arsan, the film starred Sylvia Kristel and was directed by a former fashion photographer called Just Jaeckin. The plot – the sexual initiation of a French woman in Bangkok – was merely a premise for glossy soft-porn photography. Playing to packed houses in cinemas usually given over to mainstream hits, *Emmanuelle* eventually became the best-attended French film of the decade, attracting nearly nine million spectators. Its phenomenal success legitimised the porn film, and was followed by other hits including the hard-core porn of Jean-François Davy's *Exhibition* (1975). If soft-core pornography like *Emmanuelle* is characterised by 'indirection' and 'masquerade', hard-core cinema abides by 'the principle of *maximum visibility*' (Williams 1999: 48, 49). Sex acts are graphic, repetitive, and are actual rather than simulated, displayed as such via genital close-ups. In response to the influx of hard-core into the mainstream, the French government passed a law on 30 December 1975, which greatly increased taxation on the production and exhibition of pornographic films, and subjected them to an X classification. These measures were intended to reduce the porn sector to its previous 10 per cent of the market (see Forbes 1992: 8). But because foreign porn was also targeted, France continued to produce and consume large numbers of X-rated films. The porn vogue peaked at the end of the seventies: 1978 saw 167 X-rated films released in France, but by 1987 production had completely dried up (see Prédal 1991: 434). Porn cinema in the eighties was almost totally dependent on the video market, with most films shot straight on to video. But the explosion of the mid-seventies inscribed explicit sexual representation in French film to such an extent that in the work of certain directors porn became a metaphor for cinema itself.

Post-porn: from *Sauve qui peut (la vie)* to *Je vous salue Marie*

After playing a major role in the *nouvelle vague* of the 1960s (see chapter 1), Jean-Luc Godard retreated into 'research' on the video image before making his return to the cinema in 1979 with *Sauve qui peut (la vie)*. This work also inaugurated a quartet of films – culminating in the controversial *Je vous salue Marie* (1985) – which explore the role of sexuality in cinema. Godard had already used prostitution as a metaphor for the consumer society in *Deux ou trois choses que je sais d'elle* (1966), and the relation between sex and politics in video material such as *Numéro deux* (1975). But *Sauve qui peut (la vie)* is distinguished by the fact that it comes after the porn boom, and after the law of December 1975 which relocated porn outside the realm of mainstream French film. Godard has said of this watershed: 'I think that one of the great defeats for the French cinema was the moment when they passed the law on pornography and when film-makers let them close up pornography by failing to defend it' (Godard 1980: 12).

In *Sauve qui peut* pornography and cinema are brought together again, via a narrative which concerns the inter-relations between Denise (Nathalie Baye), her lover Paul (Jacques Dutronc) and Isabelle, a prostitute (Isabelle Huppert). It is primarily through the stunning use of stop-motion photography that Godard investigates the desires and ordeals of these three characters. (The film's Anglophone title is *Slow Motion*.) Affectionate or erotic embraces in the film are slowed to a point at which the violence underlying them becomes visually apparent: Paul's desire for Denise is translated into an assault; his attempt to kiss his daughter Cécile becomes heavy with an incestuous threat. Although these examples involve Paul, whose death at the close of the film is also filmed in stop-motion, most of the slowed sequences in the film present decompositions of the movements of women. As Godard says of his video experiments, 'when one changes the rhythms, [...] one notices that there are so many different worlds inside the woman's movement. Whereas slowing down the little boy's movements was a lot less interesting' (Penley 1982: 49). In this regard, Godard seems to conform to the voyeurism which has always linked pornography and cinema: 'one intractable direction of cinematic narrative evolution follows the pleasure of seeing previously hidden

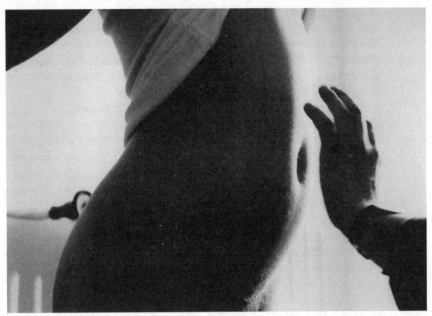

4   Myriam Roussell in *Je vous salue Marie*

parts, or hidden motions, of the woman's body' (Williams 1990: 53). Godard nevertheless uses the 'hidden motions' of the women in *Sauve qui peut*, and of Isabelle in particular, not to uncritically realise pornography, but rather to interrogate it. When Isabelle picks up Paul in a cinema queue, the image slows and freezes on her staring eye, framed by the shadow of Paul's face. The voyeuristic male gaze accommodated by pornography is challenged by this lucid female eye. The subsequent sex scene between Paul and Isabelle evacuates the pornographic image through its submission to an obdurately non-pleasurable sound-track. Godard shoots Isabelle's face in close-up during sex, so that she becomes 'the inevitable icon of the pornographic lovemaking scene, the close-up of the moaning woman's face serving as the guarantee of pleasure' (Penley 1982: 47). This pleasure is undermined, however, first by Isabelle's overacting – Paul has to tell her to stop faking it – and then by Isabelle's own thoughts, which are spoken in voice-over. This interior monologue not only contradicts the visual simulation of sexual pleasure central to the porn film, but does so by introducing Isabelle's most banal plans: to tidy her room, clean the windows, send for a plumber. The deconstruction of pornography is however most evident in the orgy sequence, wherein Isabelle, another prostitute, and a male employee are ordered into certain positions by a businessman. Their choreographed sexual activity resembles the act of filming itself, with the boss/director creating first an image track, then a sound-track: 'l'image ça va, maintenant on va faire le son' [the image is OK, now for the sound]. Moreover, the mechanical slowness of the actions involved recalls Godard's own decomposition of movement throughout the film. Thus *Sauve qui peut* presents pornography – or more precisely, the laborious creation of faked sexual pleasure – as a metaphor for cinema. A similar process, though one informed by pleasure rather than excluding it, can be observed in Alain Tanner's *Une flamme dans mon cœur* (1987), where the sex show becomes the encapsulation of both cinema and theatre.

Just as cinema and porn are analogous in *Sauve qui peut*, Godard also links sex and filming in certain sequences of *Passion* (1982), for instance, when a film technician has sex with a woman while urging her to say her lines. The dialogue also focuses on penetration, openings and closings, a bodily discourse which is continued in *Prénom Carmen* (1983) and *Je vous salue Marie* (1985). The question of representing the female body is crucial to the latter film, which retells the story of the Virgin Birth and thus has to represent the Mother of God. Setting the narrative in contemporary Switzerland, Godard dramatises his/our relation to the body of Marie (Myriem Roussel) through the terrestrial desires of her husband Joseph (Philippe Lacoste). The early sequences of the film are dominated by close-ups of Marie's almost child-like face, reminiscent of both Catholic iconography and of Godard's framing of his wife, Anna Karina, in his sixties films. There are also occasional images of Marie's body, for example in the bath, which tend to be shot from above, from the perspective of God or Godard, and which are not visible to Joseph, who longs to see his prospective wife naked. But although the angle of vision here, and Marie's own voice-over – which offers her body to 'the gaze of He who had become my master forever' – suggest that Godard is ironically identifying both director and spectator with God, it is in fact Joseph's struggle to look at Marie without desire which dynamises the filming of the female body in *Je vous salue Marie*. The key sequence concerns Joseph's efforts to touch Marie's virgin/pregnant stomach. When this contact is finally achieved, it is framed in the first close-up of Marie's body (her naked stomach), and is immediately followed by luminous images of meadows, trees and skies. From this point on, Joseph disappears, and Godard proceeds to explore visually the contradiction within the narrative, the virginity/sexuality of Marie's body. Bridged by Marie's monologue which declares 'Il n'y aura plus de sexualité en moi' [There will be no more sexuality in me], explicit shots of her naked body give way to images of the sun, plants, animals. Marie's divine and yet human body thus belongs not to pornography but to the 'virgin' imagery of natural history. In a similar gesture, Agnès Varda films Jane Birkin's naked body in extreme close-up as a kind of human landscape in *Jane B. par Agnès V.* (1987, see chapter 4).

Identifying in French cinema of the 1980s a turning away from porn and towards the sacred, René Prédal has written that *Je vous salue Marie* is characteristic of 'l'après-porno' in its submission of sexuality to an intellectual approach (Prédal 1991: 435). Such a perspective is shared by the novelist and film-maker Marguerite Duras, who contributed to Godard's *Sauve qui peut (la vie)* between working on her own films (see chapter 4). In the nineties, however, Duras saw her novel *L'Amant* turned into a glossy sex film which seemed to reverse the post-porn trend.

L'Amant: a return to *Emmanuelle*?

Jean-Jacques Annaud is associated with cosmopolitan casts, large budgets and high production values. Having begun his career in advertising, he was responsible for eighty television adverts per year from 1970 to 1975. His first two feature films failed to make a great impact in France, but *La Guerre du feu* (1981) and *Le Nom de la rose* (1986) brought him international success. *L'Ours* (1988) proved the highest-grossing French film of the year, attracting over nine million spectators. *L'Amant* (1992) was originally to be a collaboration between Annaud and Marguerite Duras, the author of the novel. As it turned out, Duras not only pulled out of the project, but responded to the film with her own rewritten version of the story, *L'Amant de la Chine du Nord*. The narrative of both Duras's original novel of 1984 and Annaud's film concerns the relation between an unnamed French girl at boarding-school in 1930s Saigon and a similarly nameless Chinese landowner. Where the film version diverges from the text is not so much in the substance of the narrative as in the exotic style of representation employed. Serge Daney, the former editor of *Cahiers du cinéma*, attacked the film for compiling 'promotional objects, from the virgin car to the designer girl'. This photogenic approach to a sexual narrative runs the risk of steering towards soft porn, of becoming in Daney's terms 'a kind of *Emmanuelle* with a bit of literary gloss' (Daney 1992: 16).

The photography in the film is minutely realistic and yet stylised and fetishistic. The location is Vietnam, there are numerous extras, and yet as Daney remarks, 'How utterly pointless it was for Annaud to have shot the film in the real Vietnam', since the style of the film already precluded any chance of 'his camera accidentally recording a few seconds of unprocessed reality' (Daney 1992: 16). Spectacle over-rides narrative, be it in the sex scenes or the street scenes. Jane Marsh as the young girl is composed from a number of fetishised constit-uent parts – her shoes, the man's hat she wears, her pigtails – and frequently introduced by such itemisation or by the panning of the camera slowly up her body from the feet and legs. Annaud's tendency to avoid the more complex and brutal qualities present in Duras's text is highlighted by the slippage between Jeanne Moreau's frequent voice-over and these images. The gulf is best exemplified during the scene in which the girl loses her virginity to her Chinese lover. While the voice-over, following the text, speaks of the blood which results, and which the lover washes from her body, the image track shows no such image. Annaud's coyness here contrasts with the frank deflow-ering scene from Truffaut's *Les Deux Anglaises* (1971). Truffaut's film is also a literary adaptation, of Henri Roché's novel *Les Deux Anglaises et le continent*, but when the text, and hence the voice-over, declares that 'Il y avait du rouge sur son or' [There was red on her gold], Truffaut actually presents a stunning close-up of the sheet slowly turned red by Muriel's blood. It is perhaps significant that *Les Deux Anglaises* was made before the porno vogue of the mid-seventies, while the decorative sex in *L'Amant* seems like a return to soft porn.

Woman as object

The representation of the female body by means of itemisation and close-up is not confined to porn. As many critics have demonstrated, voyeuristic objectifications of the female body are central to cinema's representations of women, and date back to the very beginnings of cinema at the turn of the century: in early cinema, 'the frequent presence of a voyeur on screen constituted a veritable inscription in the film of a predominantly male audience's relationship to the stripping woman' (Burch 1979). After the decline of the 'voyeur films' of early cinema, voyeuristic desires were no longer explicitly embodied by a character so much as institutionalised in the classical framing of women's bodies by the close-up, the lascivious pan and the point-of-view shot: 'cinema can and does fragment the body [...] the movement up is the appraising sweep of the male gaze fixing the woman for the film [...], film plays on the passage between fragmented body and the image possession of the body whole' (Stephen Heath, cited in Burch 1979; see also Mulvey 1975). Perhaps the most consistent example of this in contemporary French film is the work of François Truffaut, a director acutely influenced by both early cinema and classical models such as Hitchcock and *film noir* (see chapter 5).

Fetishising the female body: from *Domicile conjugal* to *La Lectrice*

The women in Truffaut's films are fragmented and fetishised, with a particular emphasis on images of their legs. Indeed, the archetypal Truffaudian shot could be said to show a woman's legs in close-up as she ascends or descends a stairway, from Madame Doinel in *Les 400 coups* (*The 400 Blows*, 1959) to Marion Steiner in *Le Dernier Métro* (*The Last Metro*, 1980). It is above all from the representation of women in American *film noir* that Truffaut takes his cue: 'The *femme fatale* is characterised by her long lovely legs [...]. In *Double Indemnity* Phyllis' legs [...] dominate Walter's and our own memory of her as the camera follows her descent down the stairs, framing only her spike heels and silk-stockinged calves' (Place 1980: 45). In *La Femme d'à côté* (*The Woman Next Door*, 1981) Truffaut introduces the *femme fatale* Mathilde (Fanny Ardant) by identical means: she descends a staircase into view, her legs the focus of the image. Similarly, *Domicile conjugal* (*Bed and Board*, 1970) begins with a tracking sequence in which Christine (Claude Jade) walks down the street, her legs framed in close-up. *Domicile conjugal* is the fourth and penultimate film – after *Les 400 coups*, *Antoine et Colette* (1962) and *Baisers volés* (1968) – in the Antoine Doinel series concluded by *L'Amour en fuite* (*Love On the*

Run, 1979). In the last two films of the cycle the character of Antoine, played throughout by Jean-Pierre Léaud, is gradually reduced to a series of tics, repeating gestures and lines of dialogue from previous works. Moreover, certain images are duplicated exactly from one film to the next – Antoine and Christine kissing in the cellar in *Baisers volés* and *Domicile conjugal* – and eighteen minutes of footage from the other films of the cycle is uneasily integrated into the narrative of *L'Amour en fuite*. Thus, Truffaut fetishises not just the female body but cinema itself, whether it be his own (the Doinel cycle reprised throughout *L'Amour en fuite*), that of the pioneers (the Lumière brothers' first fiction film pastiched in *Les Mistons* (1957)), or the basic techniques of modern film-making depicted in *La Nuit américaine* (*Day For Night*, 1973). A similar doubling of the fetish is presented in Michel Deville's *La Lectrice* (1988), an erotic and self-conscious adaptation of the novel by Raymond Jean. While Marie (Miou-Miou) reads a suggestive text to the wheelchair-bound Eric, close-ups of her thighs as she crosses her legs alternate with shots of Eric looking at her. Throughout the film, point-of-view shots belonging to Marie's predominantly male clients fragment and objectify her body, concentrating on her legs and breasts. These close-ups and lascivious pans up her body coincide regularly with erotic passages from the books she is reading aloud, such as Maupassant's *La Chevelure* and Duras's *L'Amant*. In *La Lectrice* it is at once the female reader's body and the various texts she reads which are fetishised.

Woman/nature/dirt: *Buffet froid*, *Les Valseuses*

Bertrand Blier, who first came to prominence in 1974 with the contro-versial hit *Les Valseuses*, has consistently presented absurdist varia-tions on sexual themes. His films conform to many archetypes, and transcend or invert many others, but in his early work women tend to function solely as objects. It is not just through fragmentation and framing that women are objectified in cinema. The representation of women in Western culture has tended to reduce them to certain idealisations or metaphors. Woman has for instance become synony-mous with nature. At the end of Blier's *Buffet froid* (1979), a surreal nightmare in which women are either absent, dead, or idealised as Death, the three male protagonists escape from Paris to a country retreat. What might have been a pastoral idyll in another film is here an ordeal, in which nature becomes a feminised threat, embodying the 'female' principles of dampness, fertility and dissolution. The police chief (Bernard Blier, the director's father) complains about the 'hole' they have ended up in, where everything is 'damp.' Blier does not however privilege a 'male' environment over this metaphorical representation of the female body. The 'masculine' urban landscape of *Buffet froid* is sterile, violent and alienating, epitomised by the cold geometry of the Parisian district of La Défense.

Buffet froid became a cult classic in France, without ever making much money. The reception of *Les Valseuses* was the opposite: a

Miou-Miou in *Les Valseuses*

success at the box office, it met with a stiff critical response because of its explicit portrayal of sex. Critics described the film as pornography and, incredibly, as a 'nazi' work (see Haustrate 1988: 19). This is self-evidently not the case; but the representation of women in the film, and especially of the hairdresser Marie-Ange (Miou-Miou), does conform closely to patriarchal codes. These codes include the association of women with nature, but also with dirt: 'the bodies of erotic women, especially proletarian ones, become so much wet dirt' (Theweleit 1987: 421). In *Les Valseuses*, it is not so much Marie-Ange's social status (nearly everyone in the film is also working-class) as her sexually-active behaviour which qualifies her as 'dirty.' After he himself, Pierrot (Patrick Dewaere), and the scrapyard dealer have all slept with Marie-Ange, Jean-Claude (Gérard Depardieu) asks her if he can touch her intimately, since 'it's good luck to touch something dirty, like stepping in shit'. As the incident in the scrapyard shows, Marie-Ange also functions as a commodity, an object of exchange: she is given to the dealer by Jean-Claude and Pierrot as 'payment' for his help. Marie-Ange is also replaceable by other female objects (Jeanne Moreau, Isabelle Huppert). But unlike the 'dirty' woman, Marie-Ange does not experience sexual pleasure, only indifference. Ironically, it is neither Jean-Claude nor Pierrot but the virgin Jacques with whom she first achieves orgasm. Through this twist, and the characterisation of both Pierrot and Jean-Claude as slightly effeminate (see below), Blier thus undercuts the male archetype of the macho stud, while never really challenging the filmic objectification of women.

La Grande Bouffe: the edible woman

Jill Forbes has identified a 'crisis of masculinity' in *Les Valseuses* and other films of the period, including *La Grande Bouffe* (1973), a French/ Italian co-production by the Italian director Marco Ferreri (Forbes 1992: 184). But as well as representing the 'social and sexual malaise' of the male protagonists, Ferreri's film explores the objectification of women, primarily through a combination of woman-as-nature and as commodity. In *La Grande Bouffe*, woman has become food. The plot concerns a collective suicide by four middle-aged men. Philippe the judge (Philippe Noiret), Marcello the pilot (Marcello Mastroianni), Ugo the cook (Ugo Tognazzi) and Michel the television director (Michel Piccoli) shut themselves in a large house and eat themselves to death over a number of weeks. They are joined briefly by a group of prostitutes and then by a primary-school teacher, Andréa (Andréa Ferréol), who promises to marry Philippe but in fact acts as nurse and lover to all four men. One by one the men die, but Andréa survives.

The central metaphor is first introduced by the cook Ugo, who compares a prostitute's behind to a chocolate meringue. But above all it is Andréa who is equated with food. Ugo inscribes her name in sauce, creates 'la tarte Andréa' by having her sit in the dough, and 'tastes' her body as he does his own cooking. After Ugo's death (which identifies sex and food: masturbated by Andréa, he dies on the kitchen table), Andréa turns cook for the last survivor, Philippe. She serves him two cakes in the shape of breasts, a parody of her own maternal body, to which he clings in death. The last scene of the film places Andréa in the garden of the house as a now redundant delivery of meat is hung on the trees and bushes. In this context, Andréa is just one more piece of meat. (A comparable moment from *René la canne* (Girod, 1977) shows Sylvia Kristel carrying sausages wound around her body.) Unlike those who consume her, the woman will not die: she survives as an eternal object, as nature itself. The serene idealisation of Andréa (who eats as much as the men but shows no change) thus only exaggerates the 'crisis of masculinity' in the film, characterised by impotence, repetition and mortality.

The *récit*: misogyny, desire, spectatorship

As we have seen, the framing of the female object of desire is crucial to representations of sexuality, particularly within male-authored heterosexual cinema. Laura Mulvey's celebrated feminist reading of classic narrative cinema explains how women function on the level of spectacle while both narrative drive and spectatorship are construed as 'male' (Mulvey 1975). In some ways this model is analogous to the structure of the French short novel or *récit*. Naomi Segal has defined this literary form as a first-person narrative, 'usually embedded in a frame narrative, in which a male protagonist tells [his] story'. The central object of the narrative is a woman who 'usually ends up dying, while the man lives on to tell "his" tale' (Segal 1988: 9). This pattern is common in French cinema, with male narrator–protagonists recounting the story of their doomed relations with female objects of desire. Patrice Leconte's *Le Mari de la coiffeuse* (1990) and *Tango* (1993), Luis Buñuel's *Cet obscur objet du désir* (1977), Jean Becker's *L'Été meurtrier* (1983) and Jean-Jacques Beineix's *37°2 le matin* (1986) all either conform to or modify the format.

Le Mari de la coiffeuse and *Tango*: the *récit* as misogynistic

Patrice Leconte worked as a cartoonist for the fantasy magazine *Pilote* before turning to film. After directing comedies derived from the *café-théâtre* and concerning the exploits of *les Bronzés* (see chapter 8), he moved into the thriller genre with *Monsieur Hire* (1989, see chapter 5). The plot of *Le Mari de la coiffeuse* (*The Hairdresser's Husband*, 1990) is simple: a young boy, Antoine, develops a fascination for having his hair cut by the maternal hairdresser Madame Schaeffer, to such an extent that he declares it his ambition to marry a hairdresser when he grows up. His youthful fetish is only strengthened when Madame Schaeffer is found dead in her salon. Antoine next appears as a middle-aged man (Jean Rochefort) intent on carrying out his ambition. He encounters a beautiful hairdresser, Mathilde (Anne Galiena), and marries her. They are happy together, and have a lively sex life in the salon, which they rarely leave until one night after making love Mathilde runs off and drowns herself. Antoine is left to sit in the salon and reflect on his story.

The *récit* form is manifest in the framing of this narrative as well as in the plot. Although the opening shot is of the young Antoine dancing to his favoured Arab music, a close-up immediately after the credits of the older self (Jean Rochefort) soon establishes the presence of a narrator, and his thoughts in voice-over cast the film as one long flashback. Moreover, at salient points throughout the film, such as the moment Mathilde accepts his proposal of marriage, the close-up image of Rochefort 'recalling' the events of the narrative (and the melancholy Michael Nyman sound-track which first accompanied it) recurs. 'The connexion with the outside world of the frame narrative, the significance of the story, belong [...] to the hero who speaks, not to the heroine who dies' (Segal 1988: 12). A woman – in this case Mathilde – may form the ostensible focus of the *récit* form, but her story is mediated by the man who tells it: 'If women have pleasure, then men alone have a knowledge of that pleasure which can be spoken' (Segal 1988: 5). The sequence which culminates in Mathilde's suicide equates female sexual pleasure with death in the archetype of the hysterical woman, and leaves the hero alone to muse on the meaning of her actions. This pattern, and the reprise of the opening scene which it entails, is also present in Beineix's *37°2 le Matin* (1986) (see below). Throughout *Le Mari de la coiffeuse* Mathilde is presented by Leconte as generic, just another of her sex/just another hairdresser: first introduced by Antoine's voice-over as 'une coiffeuse', it is some time before she is named. She is identified with her trade/ shop, which she rarely leaves (except to visit her former boss and to commit suicide by drowning), thus proving not so much a discrete individual as a repetition of the first hairdresser of the film, Madame Schaeffer. It is through Mathilde that Antoine restores his youthful obsession with Madame Schaeffer's maternal body: 'the narcissist seeks his own image within the frame of the mother's body' (Segal 1988: 9). Through his marriage to Mathilde, Antoine is freed to return to the pleasures of childhood: not required to work, he sits in the salon where he frequently dances to *raï* music, as did the young Antoine in the opening scene of the film. This is also his response to Mathilde's suicide, in the final scene which repeats the sign of narrative framing (the dancing). But the *récit* model – the male survivor narrates the woman's death – is attenuated by the final silence as Antoine and the customer wait for Mathilde's return. The narrator has lost his voice (-over), and hence the film has moved beyond the narrative frame of the *récit*. No image of Antoine-as-narrator mediates the final sequence, although the melancholy music returns. There is grief and poignancy in this ending. But it is again a repetition, of the moment earlier in the film when Antoine saw Madame Schaeffer's dead body. And just as Mathilde replaced the first hairdresser, so there is the possibility in Antoine's ambiguous last words that Mathilde will be replaced by another hairdresser, thus allowing the narrator to continue to define himself in relation to that maternal body: 'La coiffeuse va venir [The hairdresser will be here soon].'

There is no narrative frame or voice-over in Leconte's subsequent film, *Tango* (1993), but it is his most crudely misogynistic work. The film is characterised by cartoon-like action sequences, brightly coloured photography, fragmented compositions of women's bodies (the framing of Madeleine's torso through the car window, frequent close-ups on legs or breasts) and consistently misogynistic dialogue, declaring that women are either nymphomaniacs or prudes. The prologue concerns a pilot, Vincent (Richard Bohringer), who repays his wife's infidelity by causing her death in a loop-the-loop. The pattern is repeated when, cleared of murder by François (Philippe Noiret), a chauvinistic judge, Vincent is then blackmailed into tracking down Marie (Miou-Miou), the unfaithful wife of the judge's womanising nephew Paul (Thierry Lhermitte), in order to kill her. The main body of the film is hence a buddy movie/road movie in which the three men follow Marie to Africa. Although in the rather facile conclusion, Marie is spared and finally reconciled with Paul, women are for the most part absent, dead, or silent in the film. Indeed the film ends with the judge's 'joke' that even when dead, women continue to 'piss off' men.

It is not Leconte, but Bertrand Blier, who explores the implicit desires of the all-male buddy/road genres (see below). Leconte does not challenge the form, he merely inhabits it, rather like the second-rate Blier of *Calmos* (1976). Perhaps most kindly interpreted as an *hommage* to Blier, although one which repeats Blier's chauvinistic stereotypes without any of his attempts to deconstruct them, *Tango* includes a clear allusion to the episode from *Les Valseuses* in which Jacqueline asks to be deflowered by Jean-Claude and Pierrot. In Leconte's film, a young woman, Madeleine (Judith Godrèche), asks for the buddies to give her a baby, and Vincent obliges. The other major intertext for Leconte is Alfred Hitchcock, long considered the epitome of cinematic voyeurism: the aeroplane sequence in which Vincent terrorises his wife's lover recall *North by North-West* as strongly as the voyeurism of *Monsieur Hire* (1989) recalls *Rear Window* (see chapter 5). *Le Parfum d'Yvonne* (1994), Leconte's film of Patrick Modiano's novel *Villa Triste*, repeats the *récit* structure, beginning with the male protagonist's voice-over, which narrates the story of his relationship with an enigmatic young woman, and punctuated by voyeurism (the narrator uses a cine-camera to film the object of his desire). The only twist concerns the situation of the narrator, whose remembering of the narrative is signalled by facial close-ups lit by flames which come, as we learn in the final scene, from the crashed car in which a man has died.

Interrogating desire: *Cet obscur objet du désir*

Luis Buñuel, although Spanish, directed films in Mexico and France as well as in Spain. The architect of surrealist cinema in the 1920s (see chapter 1), his mature work in the sixties and seventies consisted mainly of French productions, and included explorations of female sexuality – *Belle de jour* (1966), *Tristana* (1970) – and satires of bourgeois society – *Le Charme discret de la bourgeoisie* (1972), *Le Fantôme de la liberté* (1974). His final film, *Cet obscur objet du désir* (*That Obscure Object of Desire*, 1977), was based on Pierre Louÿs's novel *La Femme et le pantin*. This text had been filmed several times before, most notably by Duvivier with Brigitte Bardot, and by Sternberg with Marlene Dietrich. Laura Mulvey has taken Sternberg's framing of Dietrich to embody 'the ultimate fetish' where the image of the woman is 'in direct erotic rapport with the spectator' (Mulvey 1975: 203). What is at stake in Buñuel's film is the rapport between male subject (the narrator, the film-maker and ultimately the 'male' spectator) and female object of desire. But, as the title implies, there is no 'direct erotic rapport': for Buñuel, the transparency of possession is replaced by obscurity, constant deferral and slippage.

Most of the film consists of a flashback, introduced by the narrator–protagonist Mathieu (Fernando Rey), and interrupted at several points by his audience, the passengers who share his train carriage on the journey from Seville to Paris. Mathieu is a wealthy and lecherous man who has just terminated, or so he claims, an erotic obsession with a young Spanish woman called Conchita (played alternately by Carole Bouquet and Angela Molina). The flashback reveals the origins and the development of this obsession, which is characterised by Conchita's infuriating deferral of sexual consummation (infuriating both for Mathieu and, via the narrative structure of his tale and of the film, for the passengers and the spectator) and, even more bizarrely, by

6   Carole Bouquet and Fernando Rey in *Cet obscur objet du désir*

Mathieu's complete ignorance of the fact that Conchita is, in a sense, two women. (The duality of Conchita's identity, which is alternately coolly composed (Carole Bouquet) and provocatively voluptuous (Angela Molina), operates as a visual comment on the generalised expectations that male desires place on women, and also parodies the virgin/harlot stereotype.) When Mathieu's tale is finally ended, the object of it – Conchita – appears on the train and the couple recommence their relationship in Paris.

As is usual with the *récit* form, the female object of desire is absent from the opening scenes which establish the narrative frame. In the absence of Conchita herself, the first representation of her in the film is through objects and clothes belonging to her which are scattered about Mathieu's villa: a shoe, a bloodstained cushion, a pair of knickers. These objects are presented to Mathieu by his servant, Martin, who maintains a misogynistic discourse throughout the film, describing women as 'sacks of shit'. The realisation of misogyny in Buñuel's work is however far from that manifested by Leconte. In *Cet obscur objet*, Martin's chauvinism is ludicrously literalised in the series of sacks carried by various characters in the film, including Mathieu himself. Mathieu's attitudes towards women (and indeed the spectator's own) are submitted to a more complex interrogation. Conchita's appearance in the film (as Mathieu's new maid) does not preclude her representation by synecdoche (parts standing for the whole). Indeed it is only parts of her body, or objects belonging to her, that Conchita will allow Mathieu to possess, always deferring the moment of consum-

7   Fernando Rey and Angela Molina in *Cet obscur objet du désir*

mation when he will, he imagines, have 'all' of her. Hence the grada-
tion of objects which Mathieu is permitted to grasp or consume: first
the handkerchief she drops at the hotel in Lausanne, then the sweet
she feeds him out of a box held suggestively on her lap, eventually
her body itself, but not entire: she remains dressed in a nightgown
or, when that obstacle is overcome, protected by a chastity belt or the
bars of a gate. Like the film's spectator, Mathieu is restricted to visual
pleasures; voyeurism is his only access to Conchita's body as a whole,
whether he is watching her as she dances nude for tourists or, in his
culminating humiliation, staring despite himself as she puts on a
show of sex with her young lover in the very house that he has bought
for her as a preliminary to consummation.

   Mathieu concludes his tale by declaring 'C'est terminé maintenant'
[it's over now]. But unlike the archetypal *récit*, which depends on the
woman's absence, Mathieu's story is interrupted by Conchita's very
real presence: she appears on the train and pours a bucket of water
over his head. In the crucial final scene Mathieu, now reconciled – for
the umpteenth time – with Conchita, pauses to look at some objects
in a shop window and lets her walk out of shot unnoticed. The objects
which grab his attention are a number of nightgowns like those worn
by Conchita earlier in the film, and which have just been taken out of
a sack. He thus desires a return to the synecdochic objectification of
Conchita which characterised his own narrative. The female object of
desire can only exist as an object and can never finally be possessed.
Furthermore this object ('woman') is itself a cultural construct, epitomised for Buñuel by the bourgeois domestic activity of embroidery,

represented in Vermeer's painting *The Lacemaker* which appears in Buñuel's first film, *Un Chien andalou* (1928), and which informs the closing scenes of *Belle de jour* and of *Cet obscur objet du désir*. The final sequence of the latter shows a female window-dresser completing a piece of embroidery (leaning on a bloodstained nightgown, perhaps representative of the forever absent consummation) and Mathieu catching up with Conchita again before a terrorist explosion ends the cycle of desire. The French feminist Luce Irigaray has said of Freud that he 'cracked his head against all that remains irreducibly "obscure" to him in his speculations. Against the non-visible [...] nature of woman's sex and pleasure' (Irigaray 1985: 139). Mathieu, like Freud, has had to rely on the fetishisation of objects to come anywhere near a possession of female sexuality, and to be able to narrate the story of male desire. Buñuel, however, demonstrates in the constant slippage of the film away from the expected moment of possession/closure that female sexuality remains obscure to the male desiring subject.

The gender of genre: 'male' *récit* and 'female' melodrama in *L'Été meurtrier*

Jean Becker, like Jean-Jacques Annaud, found success in the 1980s after making adverts for television. In this case, however, the director had previously made four thrillers in the 1960s, before spending seventeen years in television. His cinematic comeback with *L'Été meurtrier* (*One Deadly Summer*, 1983) was spectacular: attracting four and a half million spectators, the film owed a great deal of this success to its female lead, Isabelle Adjani. The pulling power of Adjani, at its peak in the mid-eighties, was again evident in 1988 with the marketing of *Camille Claudel* (see chapter 7).

It is principally through the fluctuating power/impotence of Éliane, the female protagonist played by Adjani, that *L'Été meurtrier* achieves its tension, and in particular its startling oscillation between the male-narrated *récit* form and melodrama, traditionally gendered as feminine (the 'woman's movie' or 'weepie'). The film has not been fully credited, however, for its exploration of genre and gender. René Prédal's comments are emblematic of the critical response, enjoying the film's opening, in which the 'male' *récit* is toned as sexual comedy, but dismissing the rest of the film as ridiculous and over the top (Prédal 1991: 501). This dismissal of the melodrama which constitutes much of the film is not however surprising. As Linda Williams has noted, melodrama and other 'body genres' are considered culturally inferior because they mobilise coincidence, repetition and non-naturalistic plot strategies, and because they present the spectacle of bodily excess – orgasm in the porn film, terror in the horror/slasher film, and weeping in the melodrama (Williams 1991). (The strategies which characterise the sexual comedy and the *récit*, and which are present in the first reel of *L'Été meurtrier*, are also components in the porn film: a presumed male (active) audience, and a fantasy of seducing/being seduced.) Becker's film initiates a complex interference between gendered genres. The film begins (after a cryptic credit sequence which will only be decodable halfway through the film) with a male voice-over in which Pin-Pon (Alain Souchon) introduces himself, his village, and his first glimpse of Éliane. At this stage, sexuality is comic and unproblematic, exemplified by the scene in which Pin-Pon and the projectionist's wife make love in the aisle of the cinema immediately after a showing. The implication in this choice of location, and in the reaction of Pin-Pon's friends and his brother, who are practically an audience to his actions – they wait outside in a lorry for him to finish – is that the film will reassure spectators about how uncomplicated heterosexuality can be. In this context, the arrival of Éliane in the village is not perceived as a threat, but as an object for conquest/ seduction. In the world of the sex comedy and of the *récit*, Woman (Éliane's nickname is 'Elle') is expected to function as a sexual object. This is an impression which Éliane deliberately cultivates with her flirtatious behaviour and revealing outfits, and in which the camera implicates the spectator, as Adjani's body is shot in close-up from Pin-Pon's point of view, interpreted by his voice-over.

After Éliane and Pin-Pon have gone out on their first date, the narration switches from his voice to hers, and there are the first hints at an ulterior motive for her behaviour. From this point onwards, the film oscillates from one genre, and one voice-over, to the other. Scenes of Éliane's seduction of Pin-Pon, her introduction to his family, and her frequent provocative nakedness alternate with glimpses of Éliane's parents, her crippled father and anguished mother. The crucial relation within the *récit* form, the heterosexual couple, is replaced by the staple of melodrama, the mother-daughter dyad. The bodily excess of the genre is evident not only in Éliane and her mother's tears when they talk to each other, but in the disturbing scene in which Éliane is suckled by her mother. Éliane's narration while she looks at a photograph of Pin-Pon's father and later at the barrel organ stored in the barn mobilises brief flashback sequences relating to her secret, but it is a third switch of narration, to Éliane's mother, which entails a full flashback. While she tells her daughter 'for the hundredth time' what happened, we see how the mother was raped by three men twenty years previously, while her husband was away visiting his sister. The scene is directed as almost unbearably grotesque, with screams, blood, swaying lights, and finally the nightmarish jollity of the barrel organ as the men force Éliane's mother to dance with them in the snow. This is the primal scene which governs Éliane's actions in the film, and which has already been repeated in fragmented flashbacks before it is shown entire. One body spectacle, the daughter as sex object, has been deciphered as a screen for an earlier and excessive body spectacle, the rape of the mother. As Williams suggests, 'melodramatic weepie is the genre that seems to endlessly repeat [...] the loss of origins impossibly hoping to return to an earlier state which is perhaps most fundamentally represented by the body of the mother' (Williams 1991: 10–11).

The central section of *L'Été meurtrier* develops a sense of female solidarity reminiscent of the 'weepie,' with Éliane and Pin-Pon's grandmother becoming friends and allies. The grandmother's narration introduces another version of the flashback scene, and allows Éliane to identify the men she believes responsible. Éliane also makes use of her lesbian former schoolteacher's desire in order to further her plan, which requires the appropriation of the conventionally male/patriarchal role of avenger which her father was apparently too weak to carry out. It is through killing the men who raped her mother that she hopes to restore 'normal' family relations. Yet the twist in the film's conclusion not only reappropriates revenge as a male action but negates both Éliane's mission and therefore her identity. Discovering that her father has in fact already murdered the real perpetrators, Éliane suffers a breakdown in which she regresses to the age of nine (before she realised that she was 'de père inconnu'). The belatedness characteristic of melodrama (Williams 1991: 11) is thus doubled: it is too late now to prevent the rape or to accomplish the revenge. And yet this is also the moment when the film spectacularly reaffirms itself not as melodrama but as *récit*. Having visited Éliane in an asylum (like Zorg visiting Betty in Jean-Jacques Beineix's *37°2 le matin*), Pin-Pon, the original narrator of the film, is left to finish her misconceived revenge. By a stroke of excessive and coincidental plotting, Éliane has left the names of her two suspects (the third, Pin-Pon's father, is long dead) with the schoolteacher. Pin-Pon retrieves the names and retrieves the film as a male-motivated genre by shooting both men. The voice-over of the opening scenes and its cryptic references to terrible decisions and doomed destinies is now identifiable as Pin-Pon's narration from prison awaiting judgement. The final image of the film is of Pin-Pon firing, in slow-motion, at the camera (from the point of view of his second victim), reinscribing the film as his story, not Éliane's. The *récit* again, but placed in a dynamic relation to genre (melodrama) and hence to gender.

37°2 le matin and the female spectator

During the seventies and eighties various shifts took place in theories of film spectatorship, as summarised for instance in Klinger (1988). The dominant theories in film studies had been apparatus theory, epitomised by Mulvey (1975) – wherein an essentially passive spectator is positioned ideologically by the film they watch (for instance, the male spectator posited as desiring a female object) – and the closely-related field of psychoanalytical theory. In the nineties, studies such as Jackie Stacey's *Star Gazing* challenged these canonical views of spectatorship by exploring the patterns of identification and consumption that exist between female spectators and female stars, asking 'What pleasures can [women] gain from the feminine images produced for the male gaze?', and suggesting that 'female spectatorship might be seen as a process of negotiating the dominant meanings of [...] cinema, rather than one of being passively positioned by it' (Stacey 1994: 11–12).

This is particularly relevant to those films within the *récit* sub-genre whose 'dominant meanings' might be negotiable by the spectator to produce something other than a misogynistic objectification of hysterical women. Two key examples are Becker's *L'Été meurtrier* and Beineix's *37°2 le matin*, both popular films featuring female stars, and which owe a great deal of their success at the box office (attracting audiences of four and a half million and two million respectively) to female viewers. The success of *L'Été meurtrier* and *37°2* with female as well as male spectators suggests that the *récit* form, and cinema in general, may draw on a more flexible model of viewer identification than previously assumed, a model which has been identified in the horror genre by Carol Clover (Clover 1992).

37°2 le matin (*Betty Blue*, 1986), by Jean-Jacques Beineix, is closely based on a novel by Philippe Djian. (The version originally released was shorter by an hour than the 'version intégrale', and thus necessarily less faithful to the text.) The opening scene of the film, an extended slow zoom on Betty (Béatrice Dalle) and Zorg (Jean-Hugues Anglade) naked on a couch having sex, is a microcosm or 'a metaphor for the whole film' (Norienko 1991: 194), which concerns the torrid and doomed love affair of this young couple. The first scene also lies 'outside the hero's trajectory' (Norienko 1991: 194), that is, outside the *récit* narrative which frames the film as one long flashback, mobilised by Zorg's voice-over. The frame opens with Zorg alone cooking chilli for himself (prior to Betty's decision to move in with him) and closes with the same situation, and a repetition of the chilli pot image, shot from the same low angle. There are two essential differences: Betty is now truly absent, since Zorg has 'put her out of her misery' (although she maintains a partial, fantasy presence through the cat which 'speaks' to Zorg); and Zorg is truly a writer, involved in writing/ narrating the story we have just seen, a story which has charted what the souvenir booklet in the box-set video describes as 'Betty's decline from "kooky" to crazy' (Constellation 1993: 8).

The film thus appears to conform strongly to the *récit* model. But this is to read the film as essentially 'masculine', monosexual in its appeal to the spectator. This reductive 'masculine' reading of the film as 'one of the ten great bonking movies of all time' (*Empire* magazine, November 1991, cited in Constellation 1993: 11) is indeed the established reaction to *37°2*. Describing the film as 'a male fantasy of the "supreme fuck"', Susan Hayward fails to account for its appeal as a female fantasy, and therefore can only condemn for their false consciousness those female spectators who find pleasure in the film: 'the fact that it is much liked by many young female spectators' is 'a bit worrying' (Hayward 1993: 293). As Jackie Stacey remarks about canonical film theory in general, 'The reluctance to engage with questions of cinema audiences [...] has led to an inability to think about active female desire beyond the limits of masculine positionings' (Stacey 1994: 29). 'Active female desire' is in fact explored throughout *37°2* by means of the various problems and issues in Betty's life, with which the female spectator may strongly identify. This narrative identification with Betty is centred on her desire for Zorg and her desire for children, which results not just in her fantasised pregnancy but also (in a sequence restored in the 'version intégrale') her kidnapping of a small child. Such episodes testify to a more melodramatic element within the narrative, existing alongside the 'male sexual fantasy' which would construct Betty's body as a spectacle. The parallels with Isabelle Adjani's dual functioning (as narrative and as spectacle) in *L'Été meurtrier* are clear. Adjani was of course a star at the height of her fame when she made that film, while Béatrice Dalle was an unknown who was subsequently touted as the new Bardot (see Austin 2003: 108–20). Iconic identification (whereby female spectators identify with the star in terms of appearance) is encouraged by *37°2* as much as by *L'Été meurtrier*. Both films use the image of the female protagonist for their poster design, while the English-language title of Beineix's film is of course *Betty Blue*. Betty is the focus of the film, but not as a silent or objectified premise, like the generic hairdresser Mathilde or the absent wife Marie in Leconte's works. Thus a more 'bisexual' trend of narrative and iconic functioning can be observed: the *récit* form mediated by melodrama, the male fantasy complemented by female desires.

Woman as subject

Writing on Susan Seidelman's *Desperately Seeking Susan* (1985), Jackie Stacey compares the relation between the female protagonists – desiring Roberta and iconic Susan – to that between female spectators and female film stars. The narrative of the film is, she adds, 'propelled structurally by Roberta's desire' (Stacey 1987: 57). It is interesting to note that in interview (Root 1985), Seidelman has acknowledged the debt her own 'playful feminist' film owes to Jacques Rivette's *Céline et Julie vont en bateau* (*Céline and Julie Go Boating*, 1974). Rivette's film – shot in the same year as both *Emmanuelle* and *Les Valseuses* – focuses not on women as sexual objects but as the desiring subjects of the narrative. The two female protagonists do not conform to a male fantasy, rather it is their own fantasies which dynamise and direct the film they inhabit. In this regard it is important to stress that the film is a collaborative effort, co-written by Rivette, Edouardo Gregorio, and its three principal actresses: Juliet Berto, Dominique Labourier and Marie-France Pisier.

Céline et Julie vont en bateau: narrative as female fantasy

Like Godard and Truffaut, Rivette wrote for *Cahiers du cinéma* (see chapter 1) before making his own films. Despite the commercial failure of his first feature film, *Paris nous appartient* (1961) and the censorship of his second, *Suzanne Simonin, la religieuse de Diderot* (1965), he continued to make complex, often improvised films with immense running times, centring on the themes of theatre and fantasy. *Céline et*

Julie was an avowed attempt to attract a larger and more mainstream audience through comedy, and to leave the ghetto of experimental cinema while still reflecting on the nature of the medium itself. For all its length – over three hours – and its low production values – it was shot in 16 mm rather than the usual 35 mm – the film was a success at the box office and remains one of Rivette's most accessible works.

Julie, a librarian (Dominique Labourier), is sitting on a park bench in Paris, reading a book on magic. She tries out a spell and seems to conjure out of nowhere the mysterious Céline (Juliet Berto). Like the white rabbit in Lewis Carroll's *Alice in Wonderland*, Céline runs by, dropping belongings as she goes. Julie follows her, putting on the scarf and sunglasses that she discards, and tracking her to a hotel where she is registered as a magician. This almost silent opening sequence initiates the exploration of fantasy and identification which is essential to the film. By following Céline and donning her garments, Julie is in a sense behaving as a fan does towards a film star. But unlike, say, *Desperately Seeking Susan* (where Roberta puts on Susan's identity along with her jacket) *Céline et Julie* does not present a straightforward narrativisation of the female spectator's identification with an enigmatic icon. Thus the two sequences set in the magic club allow Julie, rather than simply imitating Céline's act, to enact a critique of its deference to the male audience. In Julie's revision of Céline's act, she addresses the male clientele (and also the spectator in the cinema), accusing them of leering at her and calling them (us) a bunch of 'perverted voyeurs' and 'cosmic pimps'. The comic element of her tirade does not detract from the significance of this attack on the male objectifying gaze and its role in constructing the female body as spectacle, be it in cinema, theatre or, indeed, this magic act. This episode is typical of Rivette's achievement in the film, whereby he both entertains the viewer and, with a light and absurdist touch, raises questions about the way that cinema functions.

Once Céline has moved in with Julie, the pair team up to form a female variant – rare in seventies French cinema at least – on the traditionally male buddy movie (see below). The mystery that they set out to solve together centres on an old house from which Céline has recently been ejected. Both women take it in turns to visit the house and investigate, but it is only through sucking on magic sweets that they can overcome their amnesia about what transpires inside the house. Piece by piece, the flashbacks that they 'see' along with the audience begin to unravel the mystery. This plot dynamises a crucial ambivalence, according to which Céline and Julie are at once active subjects whose desires and investigations structure the film and, in a more passive role, spectators watching the flashbacks brought on by the sweets. The parallel between the latter role and the position of the cinema audience is brought to the foreground by the composition of the sequences in which Céline and Julie suck their sweets simultaneously: sitting side by side like spectators in an auditorium, the two women directly face the camera and therefore the actual spectators of the film. This reflection of the audience's experience is compounded when, in response to the lengthy and repetitive nature of the flashbacks, Julie declares that it is time for the interval, during which she wants to smoke a cigarette. The narrative presented and repeated in these fragmentary glimpses concerns a perpetual day lived inside the old house. Whereas in *L'Amour fou* (1969) Rivette had distinguished between 'reality' and the film-within-a-film by shooting each in a different format (35 mm and 16 mm) here it is the décor, costumes and above all the dialogue and style of acting – the indications of genre – which set the theatrical spectacle apart. Based on stories by Henry James, the melodrama in the house concerns the rivalry between two women, Camille and Sophie (Bulle Ogier and Marie-France Pisier), for the love of Olivier, a widower (Barbet Schroeder). Céline and Julie are never purely spectators in this narrative, however, for each plays the part of 'Miss Angèle', nurse to Olivier's young daughter Madlyn. Since their presence in the house implies a change of genre, they too assume a melodramatic delivery as they speak the nurse's lines. Towards the end of the film, however, they enter the house together, both playing the Miss Angèle role. It is during this joint visit that they play upon the theatrical nature of the melodrama – pausing in the wings between 'acts', accepting the applause of a hidden audience – before disrupting the eternal cycle in which Sophie poisons Madlyn. Céline's declaration 'On n'est plus dans le mélo' [we're not in a melodrama any more] heralds their rescue of Madlyn and the return of all three, Céline, Julie and Madlyn, to 'the real world'.

Julie's suggestion to Madlyn – 'On va t'emmener en bateau' [We're going to take you for a ride] – reflects on Rivette's knowing choice of title and introduces a concluding sequence which revises the film's opening. Asleep on a bench, it is Céline who wakes to see Julie hurrying past; when Julie drops her book of spells, Céline picks it up and chases after her. The fantastical cycle closes with the image of a cat staring enigmatically at the camera. By recasting the relation between the bearer and the object of the gaze – is Céline Julie's fantasy or vice versa? – the film's conclusion also asks whether cinema is the fantasy of the director or the viewer. Throughout the film, spectatorship has been associated not with passivity but with active identification – Céline and Julie identifying with Miss Angèle and playing her part in the melodrama that they are watching. The spectator participates in a conjuring trick which allows them to both desire and identify with the protagonists on the screen, to access a realm of fantasy which, as Rivette himself points out, is a child's dream of the cinema (Sadoul 1990: 58). The celebration of game-playing and imagination in *Céline et Julie* led Jean Delmas to call it the most surrealist film ever made (cited in Prédal 1995: 393). Despite having no formal links to the surrealist movement, Rivette certainly displays – both here and elsewhere, as in his later, darker film *Histoire de Marie et Julien* (2003) – a fascination with representing the unconscious, with dreams and fantasies, ghosts and gothic houses. Delmas observes that *Céline et*

Julie also plays with André Breton's notion of *les vases communicants*, where the 'real' and the 'imaginary' act as communicating vessels, allowing multiple transitions between the two planes. This is what Céline and Julie achieve with their visits to the gothic house. Moreover, when Madlyn is rescued it is as if the spirit of childhood (associated in surrealism with dreams, the unconscious, the marvellous) is freed from the stifling confines of bourgeois respectability, of high literary culture (Henry James) and inherited conventions. Finally, in terms of form, the film also exhibits a certain surrealist openness, with its repetitions and detours, with its extreme length, and with the absurd, improvised dialogue (as in the library sequence) recalling the surrealist game of *cadavre exquis*. The film thus shares the surrealists' resistance to the concept of art as a finished product: 'l'intérêt réside dans le travail, pas dans le produit, dans le "work in progress" et nullement dans l'objet achevé [...] d'où cette repugnance à finir' [the interest lies in the process not the product, in the work in progress and not the finished object: hence this reluctance to finish] (Prédal 1995: 389).

Social difference: *4 aventures de Reinette et Mirabelle*

Eric Rohmer, like his *nouvelle vague* colleagues, wrote on cinema for *Cahiers* in the 1950s before shooting his own films (see chapter 1). During the sixties he worked in television as well as beginning the series of films that was to make his name, the six 'Moral tales'. Culminating in the popular trio of *Ma nuit chez Maud* (*My Night with Maud*, 1969), *Le Genou de Claire* (*Claire's Knee*, 1970) and *L'Amour l'après-midi* (*Love in the Afternoon*, 1972), the series was considered by Rohmer to constitute variations on a single theme: in each film, a man pursuing one woman inadvertently comes across another before finally returning to the first. But unlike the *récit* form, the 'Contes moraux' do not present authoritative male narrators. Although based on Rohmer's own first-person, male-narrated texts, the films tend to complicate or qualify the male protagonist's perspective. At the conclusion of *Le Genou de Claire*, for example, Gilles's supposed infidelity, a fact originally 'authenticated' by the camera's collusion in Jérome's point of view as he spies on Gilles through binoculars, and then corroborated as Jérome tells both Claire and Aurora his interpretation, is strongly qualified. Seen from Aurora's perspective, Gilles offers Claire an alternative explanation for his apparent infidelity. She believes him and the two are reconciled. The male point of view has proved false, or at least dubious: while Jérome is the 'titular narrator', he sees what he wants to see; Aurora, the 'real narrator' sees the truth (Rohmer 1980: ix). In the 1980s Rohmer shot a new series of six films, called 'Comédies et proverbes', and then embarked on 'Contes des quatre saisons'. Both collections concentrate on women as desiring subjects, inverting the premise of the 'Contes moraux'. Rohmer's heroines during this period tend to embark on a rather melancholy search for a male object of desire, a search which is ultimately rewarded with a crucial revelation: Delphine's glimpse of the green ray in *Le Rayon vert* (1986), Léa's awakening to her emotions in the forest in *L'Ami de mon amie* (1987), Félicie's rediscovery of her child's lost father in *Conte d'hiver* (1992). Two factors distinguish *4 aventures de Reinette et Mirabelle* (1986) from these films and from most of Rohmer's oeuvre: it stands outside a series and it does not present heterosexual desire, but rather a pairing of two women. The film is mobilised not by sexual difference but by the social difference between two girls, a country mouse and a Parisienne.

The first episode, 'L'Heure bleue', introduces city-girl Mirabelle (Jessica Forde) into the rural milieu inhabited by Reinette (Joëlle Miquel). Reinette tells Mirabelle about the 'blue hour', a moment between night and day when nature is completely silent. This moment, like the sighting of the green ray in *Le Rayon vert*, will render sacred a relationship: there between Delphine and the young man, here between Reinette and Mirabelle. Rohmer's construction of the moment is notable for the dramatisation of the looks which Reinette and Mirabelle offer each other. At once subject and object of the gaze, they are inter-related by Rohmer's editing, which relies on the traditional shot/reverse-shot technique. Five times in succession Rohmer switches from one girl to the other as they face each other in the garden. It is this moment of looking, as much as the silence of the blue hour which surrounds it or the embrace which follows, that inaugurates the friendship between the two.

Mirabelle is also shown Reinette's surreal paintings, which consistently present fetishised views of women's naked bodies. A typical example, shown in close-up, depicts a woman seen from the rear. As the camera dwells on the picture, Reinette explains to Mirabelle that she finds the behind the prettiest part of a woman's body, and therefore likes to place it in the centre of her paintings. Such an objectification of the female body raises questions about the representation of women in Rohmer's cinema, which in fact scrupulously avoids fetishised fragmentation, apart from the express exception of Claire's knee in *Le Genou de Claire*. In Reinette and Mirabelle's fourth and final adventure, 'La Vente du tableau', the spectator's suspicions about the origin of Reinette's paintings are voiced by the gallery owner (Fabrice Luchini), who ascribes them to the fantasies of a mature, indeed old, man rather than to a young girl. This ironic characterisation of Rohmer himself questions the status of fantasy in the film – are the paintings Reinette's fantasies or are they, and Reinette and Mirabelle themselves, the fantasies of a middle-aged director? – and is only partially mitigated by the revelation in the closing credits that the paintings are the work of Joëlle Miquel, the actress who plays Reinette. The question raised by the paintings remains: the female subjects in this film, and indeed in any film by a male director, are necessarily male fantasies. Moreover, the role of woman as object is further brought to the foreground in the closing episode by Reinette's vow of silence. Her mutism in front of the gallery owner parallels the subordination of the (silent) actress to the (verbal) male director, and is particularly pertinent to Rohmer, whose adherence to his own scripts is well known. And yet *4 aventures*, like *Le Rayon vert* and indeed Rivette's *Céline et Julie vont en bateau*, relies to a great extent on dialogue improvised by its principal actresses. It is this quality which allows all three films to authenticate female desiring subjects even as they dramatise the constraints imposed upon those subjects by the cinema as spectacle.

Merci la vie as feminised buddy movie

Bertrand Blier's representations of sexuality often subvert the classic heterosexual *ménage à trois* or the male buddy movie. The latter form, combined with the traditionally macho sub-genre of the road movie, is used to depressingly conventional effect in Patrice Leconte's *Tango* (1992, see above). One year previously, Blier himself had made what is undoubtedly his most complex film, *Merci la vie* (*Thank You, Life*, 1991), in which the assumptions of the buddy movie are challenged by feminising the form. Before the film was shot, Blier expressed a desire to leave behind the staple of the male duo and to build a film around two women (Haustrate 1988: 27), and also to return to the road genre after what he considered to be 'un film trop chic' [a too stylish film], *Trop belle pour toi!* (*Too Beautiful For You*, 1989). The key intertext for *Merci la vie* is Blier's first successful film, *Les Valseuses* (1974), a fairly conventional, if sexually explicit, buddy movie, in which Pierrot and Jean-Claude (Patrick Dewaere and Gérard Depardieu) go in search of sexual adventures (see above). *Les Valseuses* is strongly alluded to in the opening sequence of *Merci la vie*, both by the identical typeface used for the credits, and most obviously via the image of the shopping-trolley, which functions as a quotation from the earlier film: Camille pushes the passed-out Joëlle in a trolley just as Pierrot pushes Jean-Claude in the opening scene of *Les Valseuses*.

Camille (Charlotte Gainsbourg) finds Joëlle (Anouk Grinberg) dumped on the side of the road in a wedding dress. She takes her home to her parents' empty apartment in a deserted seaside resort (a setting familiar from *Les Valseuses*), and the pair begin a series of picaresque adventures, including a serious sub-plot in which Joëlle contracts Aids (see below). The strong characterisation of the two young women belies the accusations of misogyny and chauvinism which have dogged Blier throughout his career. During the early sequences, it appears that the two are as autonomous and carefree as the male buddies of *Les Valseuses*. But this is not simply a role-reversal buddy movie, for Blier is manifestly aware in *Merci la vie* – as Rohmer is in *4 aventures de Reinette et Mirabelle* – that women in cinema risk being submitted to male fantasies. As Joëlle asserts while in the resort, peeping Toms are everywhere. The position of the peeping Tom is occupied not only by two male directors who use the women, particularly Joëlle, in their films-within-the film, but also by Blier himself and by the spectator in the auditorium. In a typical scene, Joëlle, failing a screen test for the first film director encountered by the two women, and bursting into genuine tears, has her grief intruded upon: the

Contemporary French cinema

film crew returns, the director calls for action, and the cameras roll. The primary effect of such self-conscious moments is to qualify the narrative function of Camille and Joëlle as desiring female subjects by exploring their relation to the male film crews and the camera itself. This self-consciously voyeuristic strain in *Merci la vie* culminates with a doctor, Marc-Antoine (Gérard Depardieu), tracked by a film crew, running down a corridor to place an eye, torn from Camille's father Raymond (Jean Carmet), in Joëlle's vagina. The disembodied eye recalls Norman Bates's bulging eye in Hitchcock's *Psycho* (1960) as well as the finale of Georges Bataille's pornographic novel *Histoire de l'œil*. Raymond, from whom the eye is taken, is only the last in a long line of men in *Merci la vie* who have desired Joëlle: he thus takes possession of her visually (scopophilia) before doing so sexually (at the railway station towards the close of the film). The discomfort aroused in the spectator by the eyeball scene, a discomfort not wholly mitigated by its farcical treatment, is redoubled by the climactic deportation sequence. Blier's film alternates between sepia and colour photography, between a contemporary setting and a recreation of the German Occupation (see chapter 2). In one of the sepia sequences, the Nazis deport Joëlle and Raymond. There follows a burst of machine-gun fire and the image of naked bodies falling from the train. Blier's use here of sepia photography, slow motion, and violins on the sound-track dares the viewer to enjoy this spectacle despite its horrific connotations. Blier is not interested in the 'destruction of pleasure' championed by feminist film theory (Mulvey 1975) but in the collusion between the pleasurable and the disconcerting. The deportation having broken up the female buddies, Camille finds herself back in the resort, and in a 'real world' of conventional family relations, with her mother and father and a boyfriend. Heterosexual structures replace the female pairing, and the horrific threats of Nazism and Aids give way to the normalised banalities which are Blier's usual targets.

Masculinities

In *Mensonge romantique et vérité romanesque*, René Girard stated that all desire is triangular in form, and that rivals for a love object are as strongly bound to each other as to their common object. The implications of this theory for 'male bonding' and the buddy movie have been noted by Laura Mulvey (1975) and Naomi Segal (1988: 205). The one French film-maker who has made his name by exploring 'triangular' desire and the implicit homosexuality of the buddy movie is Bertrand Blier.

From *Les Valseuses* to *Tenue de soirée*: the permutations of masculine desire

Even within the rampant heterosexuality of *Les Valseuses* (1974), Blier reveals glimpses of the homoerotic foundation of Jean-Claude and Pierrot's friendship. This is most explicit in the sea-side resort

Patrick Dewaere and Gérard Depardieu in *Les Valseuses*

sequence. With Pierrot (Patrick Dewaere) emasculated by a bullet-wound in the groin, Jean-Claude (Gérard Depardieu) makes advances to him in the intimacy of the deserted villa, washing his hair, drying him, and finally (in an elided scene) raping him. The reading of this situation by both men integrates the rape into the discourse of the conventional buddy movie, with Jean-Claude claiming that 'Entre copains, c'est normal' [It's normal between mates], and Pierrot generalising his humiliation to prove that the world is against him: 'Partout où je vais, je me fais enculer' [I get fucked over wherever I go]. The sequence concludes with the two reconciled, wrestling and 'bonding' on the beach. The representation of gay sex between buddies as explicit and unproblematic rather than implicit and repressed is central to Blier's revision of this straight/macho genre. A less overtly sexualised but equally significant feature of the film is the visual identification of the two men with each other. While the natural comic tensions between the melancholic Dewaere and the more convivial Depardieu are exploited throughout the film, in the pastoral sequence set by the canal the two are equated through identical costumes (white flares, blue vest, straw hat) and synchronised gestures. This visual twinning of buddies is even more pronounced in Blier's Oscar-winning *Préparez vos mouchoirs* (*Get Your Handkerchiefs Out*, 1978), which uses the same actors to great effect. The premise for the buddies to get together is here a shared love object, Solange (Carole Laure). By offering his wife Solange to Stéphane (Dewaere) as a gift, Raoul (Depardieu) initiates a relationship between himself and Stéphane which is fundamental to the narrative and rhythm of the film. Solange is merely the object of an exchange which inaugurates the buddy pairing. As in *Les Valseuses*, the men share not only a woman but also a stock of gestures and clothes, in particular an obsession with Mozart (an invisible buddy, whom they imagine paying them a visit and partaking of their *ménage à trois*) and a taste for identical jumpers knitted by Solange. Early on in the film Raoul shows Stéphane his open-plan apartment, declaring 'J'aime bien casser les cloisons, moi. Pas toi?' [I like breaking down walls, don't you?]. By the end, the barriers have been broken down and Solange herself, the very premise of their relationship, no longer matters as the two men walk off together into the night (see also chapter 8).

Blier's most sustained and remarkable exploration of the permutations of masculine desire is to be found in *Tenue de soirée* (*Evening Dress*, 1986). Initially conceived in response to the homophobic joking between Dewaere and Depardieu on the set of *Préparez vos mouchoirs*, the film was to have starred that pairing again. After Dewaere's suicide Michel Blanc took the role of Antoine, rendering his character more vulnerable to the physical presence of Bob (Gérard Depardieu), and inspiring the celebrated final scene (Haustrate 1988: 81). The third member of the *ménage à trois* is Antoine's wife Monique (Miou-Miou, who played Marie-Ange in *Les Valseuses*). Just as the alienation of 'la zone' [slum belt] provides the setting for sexual adventures in *Les Valseuses*, urban poverty is the context for *Tenue de soirée*. Hence the film's concern with prostitution, and the central metaphor: burglary. Inviting himself into the lives of Antoine and Monique, Bob introduces them to the pleasures of housebreaking, pleasures that are overtly sexualised by his commentary on moistening locks and penetrating inside. Moreover, this activity seems to stimulate sexual desire, whether in the three thieves or in their victims, one of whom proposes an orgy. It is after a break-in that Bob makes his first passes at Antoine, insisting that sex is natural between buddies. The presentation of these intentions as 'burglary' is furthered by the stereotypical attribution of Bob's homosexuality to his years spent in prison. Blier is on less conventional ground, however, as the film proceeds to map out a series of permutations within the *ménage à trois*. One of the trio is excluded in turn by the formation of a couple, at first straight (Antoine and Monique, Bob and Monique) and then gay, after Antoine has succumbed to Bob.

It is above all this pairing of Bob and Antoine which allows Blier to subvert heterosexual models and expectations. Thus Monique's dream of 'a house and kids', and her mother's prediction that one day men would be at her feet, are both cruelly subverted when she finds herself cooking and cleaning for Bob and Antoine, and sleeping on the floor at the foot of their bed while they have sex. Betraying Monique as he earlier did Antoine, Bob sells her to a pimp and then casts Antoine as his 'wife'. This requires Antoine to act as a domestic drudge, and results in another inversion of heterosexual archetypes as he complains that Bob takes him for granted and never notices what he wears. The logical extension of this sequence is realised when Bob, having earlier promised to make Antoine his queen, turns him into a drag queen, buying him a dress and a wig and calling him 'elle' or 'Antoinette'. In an ironic variant on the opening scene (which finds Antoine and Monique at a dancehall) the two then go out dancing as a 'straight' couple. The subterranean sexual identities of the trio are charted further in the toilets under the dancehall, where Bob jilts Antoine for a gay pickup while Antoine, dressed as 'Antoinette', discovers Monique working as a prostitute under the name Dolores. Having stabbed Monique's pimp only to be shot and wounded by her in return, Antoine is framed in a series of mirrors as he picks up the pimp's gun. Once armed with this phallic weapon, he is in a position to impose on Bob a final, startling change of sexual roles. In another composition refracted by mirrors, Antoine forces Bob to put on the wig before shooting at the glass and thus destroying the reflected images of the two men. Feminised by the wig, dominated for the first time by the gun-toting Antoine, Bob too becomes a transvestite. The epilogue (which provided the film's poster, under the slogan 'Putain de film!') shows Monique, Antoine and Bob, all dressed as female prostitutes, working the street. As they enter a café, they begin to talk about Pascal, Antoine and Monique's child, to whom Bob is 'godmother'. But even this heterosexual ideal is subverted: no image of Pascal is offered, and the playground sound-effects seem to confirm his status as a fantasy. Despite the evident shock value of Depardieu in a dress (played on by the poster), the film concludes with the image of Michel Blanc as 'Antoinette' in a miniskirt and heels, sitting at the bar and putting on lipstick. With a 'lascivious pan' so characteristic of the representation of women in heterosexual cinema, the camera moves slowly up Antoinette's legs and body and then shows his (her) face in close-up as he (she) pouts and smiles directly at the spectator, in a supremely confident gaze which challenges the objectification of sexuality.

La Cage aux folles and La Cage aux folles II: the queens of camp cinema

In *Now You See It*, Richard Dyer observes that 'lesbian/gay film has used many of the images and structures of non-lesbian/gay film, [...] for instance in the practices of camp or the use of traditional romance and adventure narrative structures' (Dyer 1990: 2). Although *La Cage aux folles* (*Birds of a Feather*, 1978) and its sequels were made by a straight director, Edouard Molinaro, the films occupy precisely this site between gay and straight imagery: the realm of camp. Adapted from Jean Poiret's popular stage play, *La Cage aux folles* is a French-Italian co-production starring one male lead from each country. Albin (Michel Serrault) and Renato (Ugo Tognazzi) are a gay couple whose lives revolve around the nightclub which lends its name to the film. Renato runs the club while Albin is the star attraction, the glamorous drag queen 'Zaza'. The plot concerns the farcical lengths to which the couple have to go in order to present this gay milieu as an ideal, heterosexual family unit in order not to jeopardise the wedding plans of Renato's son Laurent.

From the very first scene, the film investigates the functioning of camp, and more generally, of both gay and straight sexuality, as spectacle. The opening credits roll over images of the stage show at the club, ostensibly performed by women. When the credits finish, the 'women' on stage bow and remove their wigs, revealing themselves as men. As the camera moves backstage and follows Renato upstairs, the spectator is implicitly promised a similar 'unveiling' of Albin/Zaza, who is due on stage. The impatience of Renato and of the audience in the club is shared by the spectator. But the revelation is deferred through a suspense which is twofold: Albin/Zaza is playing hard to get, and will not let Renato see 'her' – nor will Molinaro let the spectator see 'her' yet. Our first sight of Zaza is of a figure in bed hiding under a sheet. 'She' shouts in a high, feminised voice at Renato, and throws a pair of high heels at him, without revealing herself. This visual foreplay is extended until Renato agrees to call the doctor, who persuades Zaza to let him (us) see her. Even when Zaza is finally revealed as a balding middle-aged man (that is, as Albin), the play-acting continues, with a prolonged complaint identical to one that Renato has tape-recorded the previous evening. Albin/Zaza is hence constructed as a queen, a hysterical prima donna in both sound and image. And throughout the film he (she) is always walking on stage or into shot (the star) or exiting from shots/rooms (the unwanted sexual other). This is at once an act put on by a prima donna, and at a less explicit and comic level, a portrayal of the marginalisation of sexual identities (female and gay). Such is the drag queen's dual significance: to function as both a gay and a woman, to thereby embody 'the strategies of survival and resistance' against patriarchal sexual oppression (Dyer 1990: 83).

The plot of the film allows frequent cross-cutting between the theatrical, camp world of Renato and Albin (where the décor is kitsch and the 'maid' Jacob wears a wig and mules) and the austere, heterosexual patriarchy incarnated by Laurent's future father-in-law, Charrier (Michel Galabru). The Charrier household is an exaggeratedly repressive version of the heterosexual family, where Andrea (Laurent's fiancée), her mother and grandmother defer constantly to the authority of the *père de famille*. Images of this family tend to be gloomy and static, in contrast with the mobile, brightly-lit shots of Albin and Renato in their apartment, driving in cars, shopping for food. A farcical political edge is added to this portrait of the model family, since Charrier is the secretary of a reactionary party called 'L'Union pour l'ordre moral', whose leader has sensationally just been found dead in the arms of a black, underage prostitute. The threat of another marginalised element – camp homosexuality – to a man in Charrier's position will prove crucial to the plot. But the impending arrival of Charrier also requires that Renato and Albin normalise their appearance and behaviour. Their attempts to conform to a heterosexual masculine ideal which Renato takes from John Wayne movies prove highly comic as well as suggesting that straight identity is itself a culturally-constructed image. Renato does manage an approximation of virility, while in a motif from conventional farce, Albin cross-dresses as Laurent's 'mother'. With the apartment given a spartan new look, Albin and Renato are ready to entertain the Charriers, but of course their imitation of 'normal' family life collapses. Once Renato has acknowledged that Albin is really his transvestite lover, the camp spectacle that was temporarily banished returns as the cast of queens from the club burst into the apartment with a birthday cake. The film concludes with the comic reversal of accepted sexual images: the milieu of 'La Cage aux Folles' is more of a family than the disintegrating Charrier household, Charrier the arch-patriarch makes his escape from the press in drag (in a scene comparable to the ending of *Tenue de soirée*), and in the final image it is Renato and Albin, rather than the newly-weds Laurent and Andrea, who indulge in the affectionate bickering of the stereotypical married couple.

The film proved an enormous hit both in France and abroad, causing a sequel to be made by the same team. *La Cage aux folles II* (1980) was again popular, attracting nearly three million spectators to French cinemas. International distribution followed, as did a second sequel, and the three films have been shown together as a cycle at gay film festivals. What is notable about *La Cage aux folles II* is its cinematic status: although written by Jean Poiret, this is no stage play but an attempt to situate the original characters within a generic plot derived from the comedy thrillers so popular in France throughout the seventies and eighties (see chapter 5). Traditional narrative structures are employed in the original, namely farce (a theatrical model) and romance, but cinematic genres are largely absent. The sequel continues with the romance motif, which culminates in the reunion of Renato and Albin at the end, but has been criticised for its less successful appropriation of the espionage thriller. Although the resultant plot is much more laboured, and the mood more uneven, than in the first film, *La Cage aux folles II* does gain from the thriller genre in one area – images of sexuality. The thriller form imparts swift editing, tense music and car chases; it also brings a distinctly macho image of masculinity, similar to the John Wayne ideal mimicked by Renato in *La Cage aux folles*. And it is to this virile image that Albin has to conform, in order to avoid being tracked down and killed by a gang of spies. Hence the scene in which Albin reinvents himself, not as Zaza but as 'Maurice' the macho window-cleaner, complete with deep voice and homophobic comments. When the action switches to Italy, in a pastoral sequence derived from thrillers such as Jacques Deray's *Borsalino* (1970, see chapter 5), it is female roles which are questioned as Albin, disguised as a peasant woman, has to slave for 'her husband' Renato. Although cultural/racial stereotypes are in play here, none the less the film manages to explore through comedy the subordination of other sexualities by straight patriarchy. As a queen, Albin may represent 'the feminine principle' (Dyer 1990: 83), but as a gay man he is less valuable a commodity than women or children: consequently he has no exchange value as a hostage. However, it is this marginalised, ironically invisible status which allows the usually ultra visible Albin to escape from the siege at the close and reaffirm his relationship with Renato. The distinct pleasures of the film thus lie not so much in the uneasy juxtaposition of camp farce and comedy thriller, but in the interrogation of the sexual typing within these genres.

Gay cinema in France

Neither Blier nor Molinaro is a gay director. Films made by gays and lesbians about their own sexuality have traditionally been kept at the margins of French mainstream cinema (see also chapter 4). Gay film in France has at times been reliant on the more established field of gay literature, as in Jean Cocteau's film of his own play, *Orphée* (1950), or the various adaptations and derivations from the writings of Jean Genet, the most prominent of which is Fassbinder's Franco-German co-production *Querelle* (1982). After May 1968 however (see chapter 2), the creation of avant-garde gay film independent of mainstream cinema began to grow rapidly. Alongside the establishment of the Front Homosexual d'Action Révolutionnaire (FHAR) in 1971 and the Groupe de Libération Homosexuelle (GLH) in 1974, the development of the 'home-movie' as a viable artistic medium enabled gay film-makers to express themselves in both personal and political terms (Dyer 1990: 223–4). According to Dyer, this new 'confrontational cinema' typi-cally used montage in order to juxtapose erotic, comic and political images centring on the importance of drag, pornography and peder-asty in homosexual desire. Drag, celebrated later in *La Cage aux folles*, was 'accepted as part of the revolutionary gay repertoire right across Southern Europe' in the 1970s, and featured in films such as Adolfo Arrieta's *Les Intrigues de Sylvia Couski* (1974) and Michel Nedjar's *La Tasse* (1977) (Dyer 1990: 224–5). Gay activism and 'cinéma différent' informed each other in the film festivals organised in 1977 and 1978 by the FHAR, and particularly in the work of Lionel Soukaz, a director associated with the revolutionary faction within the GLH. In addition to avant-garde confrontational cinema, a number of documentaries championing gay liberation were made in France in the late seventies, including Norbert Terry's *Homo-actualités* (1977) and Soukaz's own *Race d'ep!* (1979) and *La Marche gay* (1980). None the less, the films of Soukaz *et al.* 'remained highly marginal' (Dyer 1990: 227), and it was not until over a decade later that gay (or more precisely, bisexual) film finally became part of French mainstream cinema with Cyril Collard, whose work and whose death also brought the reality of Aids belat-edly into the realm of French film (see below).

Stereotypes and sexuality: from *Sitcom* to *Swimming Pool*

Despite his sexuality, and his initial breakthrough with a series of short films exploring gay sex, the very successful *auteur* François Ozon has resisted definition as a queer film-maker. His prolific and varied filmography engages with sexual bodies that are gay and straight, male and female, young and old. In his early work, before *Sous le sable* (*Under the Sand*, 2000) and *8 femmes* (*8 Women*, 2001) – the first of which has a middle-aged female protagonist, the second a cast of eight star actresses – Ozon tends to celebrate and idealise the young, sexually active male body while the female body is usually abject, associated with suffering, ageing, decay or death. The early short films such as *La petite mort* and *Une robe d'été* explore gay male desire, relating it to filial identity and death in the former, and to performance and costume in the latter. The medium- and feature-length films begin to address female characters more, and to consider heterosexual relationships and the bourgeois family. This is achieved brilliantly in the horrific thriller *Regarde la mer* (1997), but less successfully in the farce *Sitcom* (1998). The virtuosity and diversity of Ozon's film style is illustrated by the fact that his subsequent three films are again in entirely different registers: *Les Amants criminels* (*Criminal Lovers*, 1999) mixes thriller with fairytale, *Gouttes d'eau sur pierres brûlantes* (*Water Drops on Burning Rocks*, 1999) is a camp yet tragic adaptation of a play by Fassbinder, and *Sous le sable* is close to the classical *cinéma d'auteur*, while none the less dealing with the taboo subject of female sexual desire in middle age.

It is against learned, culturally-constructed gender roles that Ozon's characters most often rebel. The mother and baby daughter in *Regarde la mer* are subtly positioned to repeat each other when putting on swimsuits or sunbathing on the beach, a learned feminine behaviour that the dangerous intruder will destroy, along with the bourgeois family itself (see chapter 5). Both *Sitcom* and *Gouttes d'eau* make use of gender roles and sexual stereotyping in a more theatrical, camp register. *Sitcom* begins with a caricature of the normative bourgeois family (detached father, housewife mother, one son and one daughter) before gleefully exploding it from within in a series of supposedly shocking and outrageous sexual behaviours such as gay and interracial sex, sadomasochism and incest. The aim is broad comedy at the expense of conservative thinking and sexual taboos but the result is, as Ozon has acknowledged, rather juvenile (see Rouyer and Vassé 2002). *Gouttes d'eau* is much darker, its pessimistic exploration of how power operates within sexual relationships only lightened by brief musical interludes at the close of each Act and in the show-stopping finale. The film looks kitsch thanks to its 1970s German setting, crystallized in the sight of Frantz wearing lederhosen, but the roles being played here are not those of national stereotypes (in contrast to *Swimming Pool* or *Regarde la mer*). They are instead the roles of a bleak and claustrophobic sexual power game characteristic of Fassbinder, which can be summed up in terms of 'fucker' and 'fuckee' (see Dyer 1990). Leopold (Bertrand Giraudeau) is the only character in control, the only one to have the freedom to leave the flat, and the dominant macho male. Each of the others assumes a subservient position, feminised by gender, costume, or activity (hence Frantz cleaning the flat, washing

Leopold's socks, and making himself pretty for the latter's return home from work). The transsexual Vera has taken this a step further by undergoing a sex-change operation. Both Vera and Frantz describe themselves as Leopold's creatures: he made them what they are, and continues to control them because they desire him. The same pattern is about to be repeated at the end of the film, when Leopold proposes to Anna that she prostitute herself for him. Fantasies of escape from this dead-end amount to nothing: Frantz dreams of murdering Leopold, but ends up simply killing himself. In the final image, Vera attempts at least to open a window in the flat, but finds that she too is trapped. The window – which was originally meant to open, according to Ozon – is wedged tight. There is no escape from the sexual role-play in Leopold's theatre of cruelty.

Theatricality and the playing of roles – in particular gender roles – is a constant in most of Ozon's work (the restrained *Sous le sable* is the exception). Ozon has said that he loves to introduce theatre into the cinema, and both *Gouttes d'eau* and *8 femmes* are based on plays. What he seeks in the theatre is above all 'distanciation', the feeling that 'on est dans le film et tout d'un coup on est dans la représentation' [you're in the film, and then all of a sudden you're in the realm of representation] (Rouyer and Vassé 2002: 22). This happens most obviously when the characters in both films step outside the narrative to perform song and dance numbers directly to the audience, in an outrageous, kitsch, but – in the later film – telling commentary on the situation in which they find themselves. *8 femmes*, focused as it is on women, makes it clear that femininity is a performance, a construct, albeit one presented positively as fulfilling (hence the frumpy aunt's transformation into a glamorous beauty) and associated with visual pleasure for the audience. The opening credits identify a flower with each of the eight star actresses, and with the colour of their costume or the symbolism of their character (a red rose for scarlet woman Fanny Ardant, and so on). This strategy draws attention to the actresses' performances (and away from the psychological realism usually expected of characterization in French cinema), as do the songs they perform. The women also execute a number of roles around the absent male: mother, wife, sister, daughter, lover, maid, cook. This is facilitated to an extent by the fifties setting, which entails outmoded stereotypes of female identity, clothed in a series of fetishising costumes (high heels, wide skirts, fur coats) of which the maid's uniform is only the most obvious. A plethora of references in both *mise en scène* and dialogue to classic films and female stars only accentuates the sense that we are watching a celebration of performance. But the film concerns the characters' desires as well as our own to see and hear such an array of stars together. The farcically tangled affairs of the eight women include incest, lesbian desire, the eroticisation of power relations, and inter-racial desire. These are all against the normative expectations of the late fifties/early sixties – the period when the film is set, and when its source play was written. But the fifties taboos broken down in *8 femmes* (with the possible exception of the inter-racial lesbian romance) have become sexual stereotypes in contemporary French cinema, so that *Positif* could ask, nowadays, 'qui n'est pas lesbienne? qui n'est pas incestueuse?' [who isn't a lesbian? who isn't involved in incest?] (Masson 2002: 18).

Ozon's fascination with the body is often overlaid with questions of class and of nationality. In *8 femmes* the eroticisation of class tension is glimpsed in the play of looks between the maid (Emmanuelle Béart) and her mistress (Catherine Deneuve). These elements (added by Ozon to the original play) hint at the violent and troubling vectors of class and desire between maid and mistress in Jean Genet's celebrated play *Les Bonnes*. Ozon also uses national stereotyping to add a sense of repression regarding the sexual body to some of his bourgeois characters. In *Regarde la mer* the repressed and lonely bourgeois mother is English, while the psychotic drifter is French. The bourgeois codes of cleanliness and etiquette are hence strengthened by a certain English reserve as they are again in the character of Sarah (Charlotte Rampling) from *Swimming Pool* (2002). Both Englishwomen are moreover shown sunning themselves outside a cafe in a deliberately idealized stereotype of what France means to the British. The apparent idyll of bourgeois existence in France is shattered in both films by the arrival of the dirty French woman. In *Regarde la mer* the result is a horrific descent into the abject, beginning with the grotesque body (the toothbrush dipped in shit, the questions about rupture in childbirth) and ending with death. *Swimming Pool*, however, places similar themes in a much more positive light. Now the intruder manages to redeem the bourgeois Englishwoman by acting as a kind of surrogate Brigitte Bardot as well as a surrogate daughter, a freewheeling and liberating personification of carefree sexuality. It is through Julie (Ludivine Sagnier) that Sarah comes to a new understanding of her own middle-aged but still desiring body. To a certain extent, this theme reprises the age/sex taboo explored via Rampling's character in *Sous le sable*, but the tone here is much lighter, until a late lurch into melodrama. The pool of the title stands for female sexuality in general, and for Sarah's attitude to her own body in particular. At first the pool is abandoned, covered up (as is Sarah's body and her desire): she recoils from it, calling it 'a cesspool of living bacteria'. Julie – who swims naked in the pool – tells Sarah, 'You're just a frustrated Englishwoman who writes about dirty things but never does them'. Although initially disgusted by Julie's overt sexuality, Sarah slowly *thaws*, her creative *juices* are reawakened, she *takes the plunge*, and acknowledges the *hidden depths* of her own desires (as a potential lover for Franck and as a surrogate mother to Julie). If these terms seem stereotypical and hackneyed, then so does the water imagery in Ozon's film. What raises *Swimming Pool* above such clichés is the more subtle handling of the mother/daughter relationship at the close of the film, symbolized by the egg placed between Sarah and Julie when they part, and given a disorienting twist in the final image. But *Swimming Pool* remains much

Contemporary French cinema

more predictable than much of Ozon's work, tapping as it does into the long-running western tradition of representing 'woman as water [...] woman as the enchanting (or perilous) deep' (Theweleit 1987: 283) but without the ironic or kitsch distance that so often qualifies Ozon's images of the body.

Representing Aids

In 1986, Aids (known in French as 'le Sida') began to enter the cultural consciousness in France, and found its first forms of representation in French mainstream cinema. These forms were usually coded, metaphorical, even anonymous, and thus at one remove from lived experience.

Pseudonyms and metaphors: *Mauvais sang, Tenue de soirée, Merci la vie*

In its first manifestations, Aids in film appears almost as an afterthought, a topical allusion. This gratuitous status is exemplified in *Mauvais Sang* (1986, Carax), where the thriller element of the narrative consists of a plot to steal a virus called 'le STBO'. It is through his role in this theft that Alex (Denis Lavant) meets Anna (Juliette Binoche). The function of the virus here recalls Hitchcock's use of an arbitrary element, known as the 'McGuffin,' as the pretext for each of his films. The exact nature of the 'McGuffin' was of no importance whatsoever. As regards *Mauvais sang*, the virus adds a poignant tone to the doomed love between Alex and Anna. But although its effects are described as vomiting, blindness and eventually death, the meaning of the disease itself is romanticised: it only infects those who make love without feeling. The reality of Aids, and in particular the disturbing fact that its transmission transcends moral judgement, has no place in the romantic, highly stylised world of *Mauvais sang*.

Bertrand Blier's evocation of Aids in his film of the same year, *Tenue de soirée*, is also peripheral, but is more germane to both his subject – sexual identity, role-playing and transvestism – and to the style of the film, which is at least partially realistic. During the epilogue, which shows the three protagonists soliciting on the street, a cryptic mention is made of the 'new diseases' which constitute a threat to business. As in *Mauvais sang*, the topicality of the reference is highlighted by the allusion to the newspapers which are breaking the story. The shooting of *Tenue de soirée* (which Blier had written in the late 1970s) coincided with the rise of interest in Aids and thus in the general question of sexuality. Blier attributed the positive reception of the film in the United States, particularly by the gay community, in part to this topicality (Haustrate 1988: 81). But film-makers, like politicians, were still slow to actually name the disease. It is only in *Merci la vie* (1991) that Blier mentions – and engages with – 'le Sida'. If in *Tenue de soirée* there were hints that Aids was beginning to impinge upon the realities of daily existence, in *Merci la vie* it is Aids which has come to characterise contemporary life. Hence the desire of the infected Joëlle (Anouk Grinberg) to escape from the nineties and return to a time when sex was innocent and safe. The conflation of past and present in the film renders the German Occupation and Aids, both 'diseases' of their time, metaphors for each other (see chapter 2). And it is through the metaphor of Aids as a new Holocaust that Blier raises the implicit question of fascistic responses to the disease, such as the deportation and incarceration of victims as practised in certain countries. By adding elements of pathos and melodrama to his usual back comedy, Blier here achieves a desperate portrayal of how Aids has changed sex forever. But because he is also, uncharacteristically, engaging with history, he does not present in *Merci la vie* any sustained representation of Aids as an everyday reality. In contrast, *Mensonge* (*The Lie*, 1991) – the début feature by François Margolin – is a serious attempt to portray the impact of the disease on an 'ordinary' family. Distinguished from the more fantastical narratives of Carax or Blier by its deliberate realism, the film derives a note of authenticity from the collaboration of Denis Saada, a psychiatrist used to working with Aids victims. It nevertheless demonises the bisexuality of the male protagonist, Charles (Didier Sandre), and presents Aids as a threat to the 'normal' heterosexual family.

Les Nuits fauves: from reality to *cause célèbre*

The suggestion that Aids can provoke not just fear or despair, but also emotional growth, is controversially dramatised in Cyril Collard's *Les Nuits fauves* (*Savage Nights*, 1992). Collard had previously worked with Maurice Pialat and had written two novels, including the text adapted for the film. As well as directing *Les Nuits fauves*, Collard supplies some of the music and also plays the male lead, which had been turned down by Jean-Hugues Anglade, Hippolyte Girardot and others. Set in 1986, the film recounts how Jean, a bisexual cameraman (Collard), contracts the HIV virus after a trip to Morocco. His struggle to come to terms with being HIV positive is complicated by his relationships with Samy (Carlos Lopez), a butch young man with sado-masochistic obsessions, and Laura (Romane Bohringer), an eighteen-year-old he meets at an audition. Although Collard dynamises a range of reactions on the part of the three principal characters, and uses a variety of aggressive visual styles (handheld camera, jump-cuts), he in fact consistently asks the question implicit in the ending of Margolin's *Mensonge*: can Aids facilitate a form of emotional healing? A positive answer is given by both the Arab woman in Jean's Moroccan dream – 'Profite de l'épreuve de ta maladie' [Make the most of your illness] – and, towards the close, by his mother, who tells Jean that the virus can enable him to love. Between these two key scenes, the narrative veers from the clichés of heterosexual romance (the scenes between Jean and Laura, and her eventual descent into a hysteria reminiscent of the *récit* (see above)) to an anguished awareness of the imbrication of art and life, an interference which informs the film as a whole, since

Collard was HIV positive at the time and had made this known publicly. It is not just the figure of Jean/Collard, but the use of sound and image that explores the relation between reality and fiction: in her audition for Jean, Laura uses lines of dialogue that she will later reprise when her jealousy of him becomes 'real' and not just acted. And from the outset, Jean's persistent use of the video camera to dramatise himself and what he sees not only replicates Collard's project, but establishes a flux between the video image and the 'real' film image. The photogenic images of Jean's suffering – driving too fast, getting drunk, singing a raging lament (penned by Collard) – are further complicated by the presence of the real virus in Collard's blood, and of real, visible lesions on his body, even while these images are parodied by Samy's imitation of suffering, as he cuts his body while looking at it in the mirror.

The idiosyncratic nature of Les Nuits fauves, and in particular the absence of any collective or political gay consciousness, attracted a degree of criticism. Despite the allusion to Genet's death early in the film, both Jean and Samy deny that they are gay. Collard himself acknowledged in interview that he was not interested in 'la militance gay', and that he wanted to engage with the reality of Aids, not with ideology (Cahiers du cinéma 1992: 79). To this end, much of the film – including Samy's association with skinheads and fascists – was based on actual events or anecdotes. By contrast, the climactic scene, in which Jean prevents Samy and the skinheads from beating up an Arab by threatening them with his infected blood, was not in the original scenario and not based on fact. This is also the only scene which Collard acknowledged as symbolic: 'C'est un peu gros comme symbolisme, le sida contre le fascisme. Mais en même temps, pourquoi pas?' [The symbolism is a bit heavy: Aids against fascism. But then again, why not?] (Cahiers du cinéma 1992: 79). The naivety of this remark (in direct contrast with Blier's sinister conflation of Aids and fascism in Merci la vie) suggests that Collard was wise not to embrace an ideological approach throughout the film. It is precisely the lack of ideology, the vibrant individualism, which made Les Nuits fauves such a popular success and, ultimately, a social as much as an artistic phenomenon. Praised by Cahiers du cinéma for disrupting the 'comfortable lethargy' of French cinema epitomised by 'official films' like Un cœur en hiver and Tous les matins du monde, Collard's film was voted best film of 1992 by the Cahiers readership, and fifth best by the critics (Cahiers du cinéma 1992: 77, 12). Collard, in the meantime, was dying of Aids, a fact which may or may not have influenced the judging of the Césars (the French Oscars) in March 1993. In any event, three days after Collard's death on 5 March 1993, Les Nuits fauves won four Césars, including best film. The television ceremony, an emotional response to Collard's death as much as to his film, heralded a general media celebration of Collard's work. Flammarion published L'Ange sauvage, journals written between 1979 and 1992, while the televising of the Césars by Canal Plus in 1994 was followed by 'Une Nuit fauve' consisting of Collard's entire film output: Les Nuits fauves, Taggers, his short films and video 'clips' (see Strauss 1994: 20). The year 1994 also saw a major backlash against Collard, predicated on the revelation that a female sexual partner of his had died of Aids after unprotected sex. Described as a 'criminal' by Dominique Jamet in *Le Quotidien de Paris* and attacked by the right-wing press, Collard was also defended in some quarters, for example by *L'Evènement du jeudi* which pointed out that he was simply the latest in a long line of scapegoats blamed for the spread of Aids. The magazine reminded its readers that *Les Nuits fauves* had, according to surveys, increased Aids awareness in France and had saved lives by encouraging the use of protective measures on the part of its predominantly youthful audience (Garcin 1994: 26, 27).

As a footnote to the *furor* surrounding *Les Nuits fauves*, one might consider the way in which HIV/Aids is handled in a film made only seven years later, *Drôle de Félix* (Ducastel and Martineau, 1999). This leisurely and brightly-coloured travelogue traces the journey undertaken by a young man from Dieppe as he travels throughout France looking for his father, and in the process gaining a surrogate family. Where the evocation of sexual identity, HIV, romance and death tends towards the hysterical in Collard's film, here similar issues are handled with a lightness of touch. Félix is an HIV positive homosexual of North African descent, who is made redundant at the start of the film and who comes across violence and racism at various points on his journey. But these matters (with the exception of the murder Félix observes in Rouen) are treated in a relaxed and matter-of-fact way. Félix's HIV positive status generates an early comic scene followed by casual reiteration in the repeated glimpses of him taking his medication. This calm and everyday depiction of Félix's HIV stands in contrast to the representation of Aids in the early nineties, whether in *Les Nuits fauves* or in the ambivalent and cryptic treatment of Camille, the HIV positive protagonist of *J'ai pas sommeil* (Denis, 1991, see chapter 4). It seems to suggest that HIV has become normalized rather than demonized in French cinema.

Sex returns from the ghetto

In the late nineties both film and literature in France began to portray a sexually-saturated society characterized by sex and violence, pornography, rape and brutalism. According to the novelist Michel Houellebecq, modern life is structured by the perpetual arousal of desire: 'la société érotique-publicitaire où nous vivons s'attache à organiser le désir, à développer le désir dans des proportions inouïes [...]. Pour que la société fonctionne, pour que la compétition continue, il faut que le désir croisse, s'étende et dévore la vie des hommes' [the society we live in, full of advertising and eroticism, attempts to organize and encourage desire in vast proportions. For society to function, and for competition to continue, desire has to grow, to spread and devour people's lives] (Houellebecq 1998: 161). Within the film industry, this tendency became apparent in the return of hard-core pornography to French screens, first with the broadcasting of seventies porn films such as *Exhibition* by Canal Plus in the mid 1980s, and subsequently with the development throughout the nineties of a revitalised pornographic cinema sector, featuring increased production, hard-core stars such as Coralie or Rocco Siffredi, and a porn awards ceremony held at Cannes alongside the regular film festival. Siffredi subsequently starred in *Romance* (1998) and *Anatomie de l'enfer* (*Anatomy of Hell*, 2003), both directed by Catherine Breillat, sexually explicit films that despite his presence were received as examples of art cinema or *auteur* cinema rather than porn. By the year 2000, the French press were reporting that 'le porno sort du ghetto pour envahir les écrans' [porn is leaving the ghetto and invading the big screen] (Dutilleul 2000: 11). In June 2000 the controversy generated by the X-rating given to Virginie Despentes and Coralie Trinh Thi's brutal road movie *Baise-moi* saw *auteur* cinema and hard-core linked together more visibly than ever before (see Audé 2004: 19–20). Recent research has bracketed *Baise-moi*, *Romance* and Gaspar Noé's *Irréversible* (2002) together as 'postmodern porn', a form of sexual cinema that deconstructs hard-core norms to create unease rather than the certainties of sexual pleasure: 'Pornography displaced, fragmented, relativized, undermined is not pornography' (Downing 2004: 278). This trend can be seen as a tangent to the renewed interest in the body and in realism manifest in much recent French cinema (see chapter 9), or alternatively as an attempt by predominantly female directors to reclaim explicit sexual representation as a way of showing female rather than male desire (see Wilson 2001).

Breillat is the most prolific and arguably the most important of the film-makers just mentioned. Her earliest novels and films about sexuality date from the seventies, but *Romance* remains her most well known film, partly because of the casting of Siffredi but principally because of the graphic exploration of female desire (including masochism) enacted by the female protagonist Marie (Caroline Ducey). Despite the explicit sexual imagery and the inclusion of non-simulated sex acts, the effect of *Romance* is far from evoking the sexual pleasures of the traditional porn film, since 'Breillat uses a series of techniques that trouble the straightforwardly erotic apprehension of the sexual spectacle, including a constant voice-over [...] and slow camerawork' (Downing 2004: 269). Certain critics have attacked Breillat for making sexual desire too ponderous and itemized in her films, so that for François Audé, 'A chaque nouvel opus, le dégoût s'alourdit de modalités laborieuses' [in each new opus, disgust is weighed down with laborious practical details] (Audé 2004: 20). For her part, Breillat claims the right to address sex as a form of discourse which is not erotic or 'natural' but which must be taken seriously (see Rouyer and Vassé 2004: 38). The discourse that circulates around adolescent sexuality is the focus of one of her key films, *A ma sœur!*

A ma sœur!: dissecting the discourse of the sexual body

A ma sœur! (Fat Girl, 2001) represents a shift away from Romance, with its focus on explicit adult experience, to return to the subject of Breillat's earlier films Une vraie jeune fille (A Real Young Girl, 1976) and 36 fillette (Virgin, 1988), namely adolescent sexual desires and anxieties. The film follows two sisters on holiday with their distant and cold parents. The elder sister, fifteen-year-old Elena (Roxane Mesquida), is slim with pale skin and long dark hair: she is the epitome of conventional beauty. Twelve-year-old Anaïs (Anaïs Reboux) is obese, with a round face and pink blotchy skin. As Breillat puts it, 'L'une a la grâce aux yeux du monde; l'autre a la disgrace' [in the eyes of the world, one is graceful and the other disgraceful] (Goudet and Vassé 2001: 27). The girls' personalities are also contrasted: Elena is socially at ease, enjoys flirting with the opposite sex, and has had a series of sexual encounters whilst remaining a virgin. Anaïs meanwhile is socially and sexually awkward, an observer of behaviour rather than an active participant, an outsider who is repeatedly shown eating as a means of seeking comfort. However the sisters are also linked, initially by the clothes they wear in the opening scene: each is dressed in a short skirt and short coat, Elena in brown and black, Anaïs in black and brown. Moreover, although their experiences and opportunities are contrasted, both are fascinated by the sexual body. There is a degree of complicity between them, although this serves the elder sister best: Anaïs is placed in the role of chaperone by her parents but is relegated to watching and waiting while Elena begins a holiday romance with Fernando, an Italian student (Libero De Rienzo). When the girls' parents find out that Elena and Fernando have been in a sexual relationship, the father threatens a medical examination and a legal case (Elena is underage) while the mother drives both sisters back home. Resting at night by a motorway service station, they are attacked by a man who kills Elena and the mother, then drags Anaïs from the car and rapes her. The film ends with a freeze frame on her face as she tells the police she has not been raped.

Although the shock ending creates the most impact, Breillat's key achievement in A ma sœur! is the brilliant dissection of the language of sexual relationships. As she herself has stated, sex is a language (see Rouyer and Vassé 2004: 38). The close observation of this language in A ma sœur! is initially comic, but finally tragic. Thus we first see romantic discourse parodied by Anaïs in the pool, as she swims back and forth between a wooden jetty and a metal step, kissing each and murmuring stock phrases such as 'Tu es celui à qui je vais donner tout' [You're the one I will give myself to fully]. When the clichés of sexual discourse occur again in the film, they are in the mouth of Fernando as he bullies and begs Elena to allow him to penetrate her. The convention central to orthodox erotic cinema – the presentation of a sexual spectacle for male pleasure while absolving the male spectator of any responsibility or 'guilt' for what is shown – is here overturned (see

Breillat in Rouyer and Vassé 2004: 36). Fernando plays the male seducer but the results are painful and are filmed with an unwavering critical eye. Anaïs, pretending to be asleep on the other side of the bedroom, is a half disgusted, half fascinated spectator in the two seduction scenes. Both scenes are shot in long takes, with no music to alleviate the tension, and with frequent pauses and repetitions in the dialogue. Eventually, Elena reluctantly allows Fernando to sodomise her. At this point, Breillat cuts to Anaïs while Elena cries in pain. The direct and unmediated realism of these scenes and the simplicity of the narrative has seen Breillat compared to directors like Eric Rohmer in the French realist tradition (see Amiel 2001: 24). Certainly, the film is simply structured according to a series of subtle echoes and parallels. For instance, in the first seduction scene, as soon as Anaïs covers her face a cut reveals Elena lying with her sex *uncovered*. This same sequence uses a slow pan around the two lovers embracing in the foreground, to almost accidentally reveal Anaïs in bed in the background; in the second seduction scene, the shot is reversed so that the lovers' entwined legs are glimpsed in the background while Anaïs sobs in the foreground. But where Rohmer tends to privilege speech (or silence) as the expression of desire (see above), in *A ma sœur!* Breillat dissects sexual discourse in order to get at the body itself.

Each sister's relationship to the outside world is largely mediated through her body. Despite their contrasting appearances, Elena and Anaïs share adolescent anxieties about what others will think of them, and so persistently scrutinise their own bodies. Several scenes show first one sister then the other looking at herself in the mirror. Although Elena might seem to be empowered by her apparent beauty, she is manipulated by Fernando and humiliated when she has to return a ring he gave her to seal their romance. Anaïs meanwhile is an equally ambiguous character as far as her corporeality and sense of self are concerned. Despite the loneliness expressed in the despairing songs she murmurs to herself, and the images of her body as a massive, clumsy object (crouched shivering at the beach, or vomiting at the side of the road), there are also moments when her body is reclaimed by herself and by the gaze of another as a site of desire no less than her sister's. At the swimming pool Anaïs applies sun cream to her limbs with an almost joyous deliberation, smiling to herself. The scene is shot from a point of view that we can construe as belonging to Fernando since, in one of the few moments when he focuses on the younger sister, he has just been shown staring in her direction. This is the first hint in the film that Anaïs's body might exist sexually for another. The hint is of course followed up in a traumatic fashion in the final scene when Anaïs is raped. The ending is at once shocking and open. It functions in part to link the two sex acts (the rapist's and Fernando's) and to posit them both as rapes, with the only difference that one act is mediated by romantic discourse while the other is exaggeratedly brutal and sudden. The killing of her mother and sister, and indeed the rape itself, can also be interpreted as literalisations of Anaïs's fantasies as expressed earlier in the film. As Breillat remarks, the 'mythical' wishes of the child (that her family would die) are thus rendered horribly real (Goudet and Vassé 2001: 30). A further reading is also possible: criticised by Elena throughout the narrative for copying her, Anaïs here seems to be copying the earlier rape to the extent that she reclaims as consensual sex an act in which she was in effect powerless. In this respect the final line of the film represents Anaïs's victory over her sister at the same time as it signals her brutal entry into the sexual universe.

References

Amiel, V. (2001), *A ma sœur!* Ces corps au risque de tempêtes, Paris, *Positif*, 481, 24–5.

Audé, F. (2004), Cérémonies nocturnes pour belles d'aujourd'hui, Paris, *Positif*, 521/522, 17–21.

Austin, G. (2003), *Stars in Modern French Film*, London, Arnold.

Burch, N. (1979), *Correction Please, or How We Got Into Pictures*, notes to accompany the film.

Cahiers du cinéma (1992), Paris, numéro hors série.

Clover, C. J. (1992), *Men, Women and Chain Saws: Gender in the Modern Horror Film*, London, BFI.

Constellation Productions/Cargo Films (1993), *37°2 le Matin*, souvenir booklet with box-set video.

Daney, S. (1992), Falling out of love, London, *Sight and Sound*, July 1992, 14–16.

Downing, L. (2004), French cinema's new 'sexual revolution': postmodern porn and troubled genre, London, *French Cultural Studies* special issue: New Directions in French Cinema, 15:3, 265–80.

Dutilleul, G. (2000), Le porno sort du ghetto pour envahir les écrans, Paris, *L'Evénement du Jeudi*, 21–8 June, 11–15.

Dyer, R. (1990), *Now You See It: Studies on Lesbian and Gay Film*, London and New York, Routledge.

Forbes, J. (1992), *The Cinema in France After the New Wave*, London, Macmillan/BFI.

Garcin, J. (1994), Tous contre Collard?, Paris, *L'Evènement du jeudi*, 21–7 April, 26–7.

Godard, J.-L. (1980), Sauve qui peut ... Godard!, Norwich, *Framework*, 13, 10–13.

Goudet, S. and Vassé, C. (2001), Entretien – Catherine Breillat: Une âme et deux corps, Paris, *Positif*, 481, 26–30.

Haustrate, G. (1988), *Bertrand Blier*, Paris, Edilig.

Hayward, S. (1993), *French National Cinema*, London and New York, Routledge.

Houellebecq, M. (1998), *Les particules élémentaires*, Paris, Flammarion / J'ai Lu.

Irigaray, L. (1985), *Speculum of the Other Woman*, Ithaca, NY, Cornell University Press.

Klinger, B. (1988), In retrospect: film studies today, New Haven, CT, *Yale Journal of Criticism*, 2:1, 129–51.

Masson, A. (2002), *8 femmes*: Une comédie janséniste, *Positif*, 492, 16–18.

Mulvey, L. (1975), Visual pleasure and narrative cinema, originally published in *Screen*, Autumn 1975, reprinted in C. Penley (ed.), *Feminism and Film Theory*, London and New York, Routledge, 1988.

Norienko, S. (1991), Philippe Djian: the character of the writer and the writer as character, Chalfont St Giles, Bucks, *French Cultural Studies*, 2:2:5, 181–97.

Penley, C. (1982), Pornography, eroticism, originally published in *Camera Obscura*, Autumn 1982, reprinted in R. Bellour and M. Lea Bandy (eds), *Jean-Luc Godard: Son + Image 1974–1991*, New York, the Museum of Modern Art, New York, 1992.

Place, J. (1980), Women in film noir, in E. A. Kaplan (ed.), *Women in Film Noir*, London, BFI.

Prédal, R. (1991), *Le Cinéma français depuis 1945*, Paris, Nathan.

Prédal, R. (1995), Jacques Rivette ou le temps imaginare de l'amour fou, in C. W. Thompson (ed.), *L'Autre et le sacré: surréalisme, cinéma, ethnologie*, Paris, Editions L'Harmattan, 379–94.

Rohmer, E. (1980), *Six Moral Tales*, Lorrimer, Francombe.

Root, J. (1985), Céline and Julie, Susan and Susan, London, *Monthly Film Bulletin*, September 1985, 45.

Rouyer, P., and Vassé, C. (2002), Entretien – François Ozon: Se mettre en danger, *Positif*, 492, 19–24.

Rouyer, P., and Vassé, C. (2004), Entretien – Catherine Breillat: De l'évanescent qui n'est plus de l'ordre du charnel, Paris, *Positif*, 521/522, 36–40.

Sadoul, G. (1990), *Dictionnaire des films*, revised and expanded by E. Breton, Paris, Microcosme/Seuil.

Segal, N. (1988), *Narcissus and Echo: Women in the French récit*, Manchester, Manchester University Press.

Stacey, J. (1987), Desperately seeking difference, Glasgow, *Screen*, 28:1, 48–61.

Stacey, J. (1994), *Star Gazing: Hollywood Cinema and Female Spectatorship*, London and New York, Routledge.

Strauss, F. (1994), Cyril Collard dans la nuit, Paris, *Cahiers du cinéma*, 476, 20.

Theweleit, K. (1987), *Male Fantasies, I: Women, Floods, Bodies, History*, Cambridge, Polity Press.

Williams, L. (1990), *Hard Core: Power, Pleasure and the 'Frenzy of the Visible'*, London, Pandora.

Williams, L. (1991), Film bodies: gender, genre, and excess, Berkeley, California, *Film Quarterly*, 44:4, 2–13.

Williams, L. (1999), *Hard Core: Power, Pleasure and the 'Frenzy of the Visible'*, expanded edition, Berkeley, California, and London, University of California Press.

Wilson, E. (2001), Deforming femininity: Catherine Breillat's *Romance*, in L. Mazdon (ed.), *France on Film: Reflections on Popular French Cinema*, London, Wallflower, 145–57.

4 Women film-makers in France

Feminism and film in France

Although film-making remains male-dominated in France as else-where, 'more women have taken an active part in French cinema than in any other national film industry' (Kuhn and Radstone 1990: 163). France claims not only the first woman film director – Alice Guy, whose career began in 1900 – but also the first feminist film-maker, Germaine Dulac, a pioneer of 'impressionist' cinema or 'the first avant-garde' in the 1920s (see chapter 1). Dulac, however, was the exception, and women were generally on the other side of the camera in classical French cinema. In the immediate post-war years, women – now granted the vote – were largely restricted to filming documentaries and shorts, although Jacqueline Audry specialised in literary adaptations during the forties and fifties, and Agnès Varda initiated the *nouvelle vague* with *La Pointe courte* in 1954 (see chapter 1). The year 1968 was a watershed for French feminism and conse-quently for women making films in France: 'The Events of May 1968 [see chapter 2] are usually considered to have provided the impetus for the development of the women's movement, [...] the creation of women's organisations and an upsurge in women's publications' (Forbes 1992: 77). Subsequently, in 1972, the French women's move-ment – the MLF – was launched, and in 1974 a women's film festival (in later years held at Créteil) was established. Many first features were made by women in this climate, such as Yannick Bellon's *Quelque part, quelqu'un* (1972) and Coline Serreau's *Mais qu'est-ce qu'elles veulent?* (1976), as well as militant documentaries on feminist issues, the most celebrated of which is Marielle Issartel and Charles Belmont's film on abortion rights, *Histoires d'A* (1973). But while the rise of feminism was reflected positively in Agnès Varda's *L'Une chante, l'autre pas* (*One Sings, The Other Doesn't*, 1977), the response to the women's move-ment from male directors varied from a lucid account of male fears in Jean Eustache's *La Maman et la putain* (*The Mother and the Whore,*

1973) to hysterical fantasies about the war of the sexes in Bertrand Blier's *Calmos* and Louis Malle's *Black Moon* (both 1976), and about lesbian vampires in Jean Rollin's sex/horror cycle of the early seventies (see Weiss 1992: 85–90).

Although the 1970s generation of women directors included feminist themes in their work – the reversal of gender roles in Serreau's *Pourquoi pas!*, a denunciation of rape in Bellon's *L'Amour violé* (both 1977), a portrayal of lesbian desire in Diane Kurys's *Coup de foudre* (1983) – they tended to move towards less politicised, more popular genres in the 1980s. This move led to the comedy for Serreau, the thriller for Bellon and the heterosexual romance for Kurys (see below). By 1987 the Belgian film-maker Chantal Akerman was declaring that the idea of women's cinema was 'outdated'. The principal reason for this was that there was no longer any ideological difference in France between cinema made by men and by women, as 'feminism as a debate has vanished from the French cultural scene since the early 80s' (Vincendeau 1987: 4). Unlike the United States or Britain, France has not generated much feminist film theory, and has never shared in Anglophone feminist concerns with apparatus theory, the positing of a 'male' gaze and a 'female' object – a tendency which was subsequently challenged by other Anglophone critics such as Linda Williams and Carol Clover (see Williams 1994). Several key female directors, including the most successful woman film-maker in France in the 1980s, Coline Serreau, have distanced themselves from feminism and questioned the significance of their gender in determining their work: 'Serreau: "*je ne suis pas une femme qui fait du cinéma*" [I am not a woman who makes films]; Diane Kurys: "*ça m'exaspère qu'on parle de films de femmes*" [it exasperates me that people should talk about women's films]; Issermann: "we resist any collective image or any attempt to make us into a school" ' (Hayward 1993: 258). These women embrace a sense of diversity and individualism born not of feminism but of the *auteur* tradition in French cinema, 'a romantic tradition of humanist individualism which constitutes the bedrock of French critical approaches to film' (Vincendeau 1987: 7).

Avant-garde *auteurs*: Marguerite Duras and Agnès Varda

Two of the principal *auteurs* in French film since the 1960s, women whose idiosyncratic styles epitomise avant-garde *auteur* cinema, are Marguerite Duras and Agnès Varda.

India Song and 'the vanity of cinema'

For Marguerite Duras, literature and cinema are inseparable. The *auteurist* conception of film as a form of writing is taken to an extreme in her career – which spans thirty years and features novels, plays, and over a dozen films – and in her statements on cinema: each of her films is 'un livre sur de la pellicule' [a book recorded on film], while film-makers are described as writers whose work is read and

Delphine Seyrig in *India Song*

reread by the public (Duras 1989: 62). The two fields inform each other most dynamically in what has been termed her 'Indian cycle' of three novels – *Le Ravissement de Lol V. Stein, Le Vice-Consul, L'Amour* – and three films – *La Femme du Gange* (1974), *India Song* (1975), *Son nom de Venise dans Calcutta désert* (1976) – which offer variations on a basic narrative and a single group of characters. In all of her films, Duras lays unusual emphasis on the function of sound, above all as an expression of women's experience: hence the 'resistant' silence in *Nathalie Granger* (1972) and the productive power of the woman's voice (her own) in the 1977 film *Le Camion* (see Forbes 1992: 99–101). The general austerity of her work, which is almost devoid of the visual pleasures traditionally offered by cinema, has led the French feminist critic Françoise Audé to argue that 'if Marguerite Duras' characters are too intent on being engulfed in "submissiveness" for feminists to adopt them wholeheartedly ... they painfully endorse the destitution which is at the heart of the feminist protest' (Kuhn and Radstone 1990: 128).

India Song is set in Calcutta in the 1930s. It concerns the experiences of Anne-Marie Stretter (Delphine Seyrig), the wife of the French ambassador to India, principally in relation to three other characters: her lover Michael Richardson (Mathieu Carrière), the disgraced Vice-Consul (Michel Lonsdale) who is obsessed with her, and an unseen beggarwoman whose life in some ways runs parallel to her own. The film has a clear tripartite structure, consisting of a half-hour prologue, a central section of one hour, and a twenty-three minute epilogue. Both the prologue and the epilogue are obliquely narrated by anonymous voices which discuss the characters and the settings: in the former evoking the heat, leprosy and death associated with Calcutta, in the latter the historical events of 1937 as the characters gather at a hotel prior to Anne-Marie's suicide. Duras, whose voice is one of those narrating the film, has called them 'the authors ... the motors of the story' (Lyon 1988: 266). They are absent only from the central section, the reception given by Anne-Marie, and even here, the principle that all voices in the film are off-screen is maintained. The guests' dialogue is heard, but when they appear on screen, they are never seen to speak, so that their words, 'spoken by unmoving lips, unsettle the distinction between on-screen and off-screen' (Ropars-Wuilleumier 1980: 252).

As this summary indicates, Duras's textual conception of cinema here results in an unusual privileging of sound (the voices, the spoken word) over image. There is moreover a fundamental and sustained disjuncture between sound and image tracks. The two do not illustrate each other, but are autonomous, allowing Duras to use the same sound-track with a completely new image track for her subsequent film, Son nom de Venise dans Calcutta désert (1976), where the Indian heat evoked by the voices contrasts with shots of wintry landscapes. Duras has even suggested that the two films should be seen one after the other, so that one could witness in Son nom de Venise the destruction of India Song (Duras 1989: 64). The annihilation of visual pleasure in India Song – Duras was attempting to film 'the vanity of cinema' (Duras 1989: 65) – is achieved through the reduction of camera movement to a minimum, and the reliance on fixed tableaux which can last for minutes at a time. While most films comprise hundreds of shots, India Song has seventy-four in all, including repeated images such as the close-up of Anne-Marie's breast. The deathly stillness of these images, and their repetition, reinforces the thematic and structural importance of death in the film: the narrative returns compulsively to Anne-Marie's suicide, spoken of by the voices at the beginning and the end of the film, symbolised in the image of her photograph and possessions, and prefigured by the disturbing off-screen cries of the beggar-woman and of the Vice-Consul. The association between Anne-Marie and the beggarwoman is reaffirmed in the film's conclusion. Both, the voices in the prologue reveal, left Savannakhet in their teens to travel eastwards to Calcutta. After Anne-Marie leaves the frame (the implication is that she drowns herself) in the closing sequence, a slow pan across a map of Asia retraces the journeys of the two women from west to east, ending on Savannakhet: 'The trajectories of Anne-Marie Stretter and the beggarwoman, told in the present tense by the voices at the beginning of the film, are then retraced in reverse as history at its end' (Lyon 1988: 268). In the same way, conjured up by the anonymous voices in the prologue before she appeared on the screen, Anne-Marie now makes the reverse journey, leaving the on-screen space occupied by the living to enter the off-screen space where her death has long been evoked by the voices which control her story.

Tracking towards death: *Sans toit ni loi*

Agnès Varda has declared: 'I make *auteur* films ... I am always very precisely implicated in my films, not out of narcissism, but out of honesty' (Kuhn and Radstone 1990: 411). Like Duras, she speaks of her work in literary terms, calling it *cinécriture*, a writing of films in which editing, camera angles, and the rhythm of the shoot are equated with the choice of words, sentences and chapters in the work of a writer (Murat 1994: 35). She also shares with Duras a concern for death as a central theme. Varda inaugurated the *nouvelle vague* with *La Pointe courte* in 1954 (see chapter 1), and cemented her reputation with *Cléo de 5 à 7* (1961). But the commercial failure of *Les Créatures* (1966) resulted in a ten-year gap before she made another feature film in France. She continued to work in the documentary field, however, and has combined fiction and documentary throughout her career. An avowed feminist, Varda's work reflects upon the women's movement, at times obliquely but nowhere more explicitly than in the feminist buddy movie *L'Une chante, l'autre pas* (*One Sings, The Other Doesn't*, 1977). Consistently undervalued by American critics and feminists (Hayward 1987: 285), Varda was attacked in the American media for making a lyrically optimistic film about feminism: Pauline Kael found that in *L'Une chante, l'autre pas* 'Varda brings a Disney touch to women's liberation' (Heck-Rabi 1984: 349). Like her colleagues from the *nouvelle vague* – Jean-Luc Godard, Claude Chabrol and Eric Rohmer – Varda enjoyed a resurgence in the 1980s, although she continued to suffer more problems than her male counterparts in financing her films. *Sans toit ni loi* (*Vagabonde*, 1985), her major critical and popular success of the decade, was initially refused the government funding known as the *avance sur recettes*, before being granted direct aid from the Ministry of Culture. When released, the film was greeted with critical acclaim as a rejuvenation of *auteur* cinema, which had been perceived as flagging in the mid-eighties (Varda 1994: 271). It also signals Varda's interest in the excluded and the marginalized within French society, a theme she returned to in 2000 with her influential documentary *Les Glaneurs et la glaneuse* (see chapter 9).

Varda's own voice introduces the episodic narrative of *Sans toit ni loi*. Over the image of a woman's corpse found in a ditch in the middle of winter, she remarks: 'She had died a natural death without leaving a trace. [...] But people she had met recently remembered her. Those witnesses helped me tell the last weeks of her last winter.' But during the course of the film this woman proves to be an enigma. Mona (Sandrine Bonnaire) is a hitch-hiker who has been passing through the Midi region. In a complex series of flashbacks, the film records her journey, largely through the eyes of eighteen people she meets on the way. As these characters reflect on what they thought of Mona, they reveal as much about themselves – they come from various walks of life, and according to Varda represent 'la France profonde' (Varda 1994: 269) – as they do about the taciturn hitcher. Although there are long sequences concerning Mona's relations with Madame Landier (Macha Méril), a biologist, and Assoun (Yahiaoui Assouna), a Tunisian vineyard worker, she remains an enigmatic figure, resistant to easy interpretation. At the end of the film, exhausted and starving, she is caught up in an aggressive folk ritual before falling, dazed, into the ditch where she dies.

The synthesis of realism and mythical symbolism which characterises Varda's work is evident throughout *Sans toit ni loi*. The primary myth alluded to is that of the goddess of love, Venus/Aphrodite, when Varda's voice-over – 'I know little about her myself, but it seems to me she came from the sea' – introduces an image of Mona emerging from a swim in the Mediterranean. The pictorial reference here is to Botticelli's painting of *The Birth of Venus*, an icon of classical female beauty. But, ironically, we soon learn that Mona is 'the opposite of the female [...] icon: she is dirty, unkempt, overweight, repulsive in her personal habits and her moral practices' (Forbes 1992: 93). The Venus/Aphrodite myth ties in with the folk ritual at the close of the film, in which Mona is attacked and daubed with wine dregs, since in legend 'the goddess [...] yields to Dionysus the god of the vine' (Hayward 1987: 290). Thus a mythical narrative underlies Varda's realistic depiction of the Midi region in winter, and her documentary-style observation of life on the road. The other major mythical structure underlying *Sans toit ni loi* is that of the road movie. The narrative traces Mona's journey from her emergence out of the waves until her death. But Varda subverts the genre, since the road movie is a traditionally male form, and a variant on the buddy movie – as in Bertrand Blier's 1974 film *Les Valseuses* (see chapter 3) – while Mona is a woman, and alone. Viewed from the outside by those she meets, Mona makes no self-discovery, undergoes no rites of passage, and is unfathomable in terms of psychology. Even the temporary couple of Mona and David (Patrick Lepczynski) subverts generic expectations. Whereas the lovers on the run in Arthur Penn's *Bonnie and Clyde* (1967) or Terence Malick's *Badlands* (1973) are self-mythologising, Mona and David are self-effacing: when Mona writes their names in the dust David rubs them out, wanting to leave 'no trace' of their passage. Of course *Sans toit ni loi* does rely heavily on the imagery of the road movie, and principally on the tracking shot. There are in fact fourteen tracking shots in *Sans toit ni loi*, most of them accompanied by Joanna Bruzdowicz's bleak string music. But contrary to convention, 'in all these tracking shots [Mona] and the camera [...] move from right to left', so that her journey 'is filmed going backwards down the road' while providing a recurrent visual 'metaphor for both the flashback, and, even more significantly, death' (Hayward 1987: 290). The contrast with the left-to-right tracking shot – which usually denotes progression from the past to the future – is emphasised by the relation between the beginning of *Sans toit ni loi* and the ending of François Truffaut's *Les 400 Coups* (*The 400 Blows*, 1959). In that film, the young protagonist Antoine Doinel (Jean-Pierre Léaud) escapes from a detention centre and, in a famous and lengthy left-to-right tracking shot, runs to the sea. The direction of the movement in this sequence signals that Antoine is embarking on a journey of self-discovery, and that further adventures await him (the story is continued in four more films about the same character, the 'Doinel cycle' (see chapter 3)). The first tracking shot in *Sans toit ni loi* reverses this pattern, with Mona emerging from the sea and heading right to left towards no other destination than her own death (which has already been shown in the opening sequence of the film). Varda thus inverts the inherent optimism of the road-movie form, and of Truffaut's *nouvelle vague* vivacity.

Whereas the image and sound tracks in Marguerite Duras's films tend to be disparate (see above), in much of Varda's work sound and image are directly illustrative of each other. In particular, Varda's use of authorial voice-over tends to be 'pleonastic' (Forbes 1992: 95); in other words, what she says and what is shown on the screen are one and the same. Hence in *Jane B. par Agnès V.* (1987), a complex portrait of the singer and actress Jane Birkin, bizarre images are conjured up and authorised by Varda's voice-over. Her remark to Birkin 'I can see you as Ariadne' is immediately followed by a shot of the actress in classical costume in a labyrinth with a ball of thread. This self-consciousness, attacked in the *Cahiers du cinéma* review of the film (Philippon 1988), also entails a slow tracking shot from a cockerel to a donkey to illustrate Varda's use in voice-over of the idiomatic expression 'passer du coq-à-l'âne' [to jump from one subject to another]. *Jane B. par Agnès V.* is also notable for the filming of Birkin in several compositions derived from classical paintings, including one slow pan across her naked body which 'produces the woman's body as landscape, that field across which play multiple possible reflections about women's representation' (Flitterman-Lewis 1993: 315). Similarly in *Jacquot de Nantes* (1991), a portrait of her dying husband the film-maker Jacques Demy, Varda employs slow pans across the human body, here in extreme close-ups of his face, hands, hair, and eyes, 'comme s'il était un énorme paysage et qu'on s'y promène' [as if he were a huge landscape one was walking across] (Varda 1994: 279).

Popular cinema: Diane Kurys and Coline Serreau

Less radical, both ideologically and aesthetically, than Duras or Varda, Diane Kurys and Coline Serreau took women's film-making into the popular mainstream during the mid-1980s. In part because of their commercial success, both directors have been denied by critics the high cultural status of the *auteur*, while their declarations that they are merely film-makers who happen to be women have seen them often neglected by feminist criticism. Yet Kurys and Serreau have managed to explore personal concerns with issues of gender and sexuality within popular genres, while at the same time addressing millions of spectators.

Lesbian desire in *Coup de foudre*

Perhaps even more so than gay film (see chapter 3), lesbian film-making has occupied the margins of French cinema, from Germaine Dulac's avant-garde critique of marriage in *La Souriante Madame Beudet* (1923) onwards. The portrayal of lesbian desire did at times enter mainstream classical cinema in the form of the 'community of women' genre, exemplified by Jacques Deval's *Club de femmes* (1936) and Jacqueline Audry's *Olivia* (1951). Although made by a male director, the former was one of the first films to treat lesbianism in what the American lesbian journal *Vice Versa* called 'a sane, intelligent manner, rather than furnishing the usual subject for harmful propaganda or mere sensationalism' (Weiss 1992: 13). With the rise of the women's movement in the early 1970s, male-authored representations of lesbianism included the pathologising fantasies of Jean Rollin's vampire films, but this period also saw lesbian directors such as the Belgian Chantal Akerman beginning their careers. The major Francophone lesbian film-maker currently working, Akerman remains, for all the commercial success of *Golden Eighties* (1987), outside the mainstream. None the less many of the female *auteurs* who, since the 1970s, have become increasingly active in French cinema, 'although speaking from a heterosexual (or unclear) position, provide very affirmative images of lesbianism, often seen as an enviable alternative to relations between the sexes' (Dyer 1990: 272). One of the most prominent and popular examples of this is Diane Kurys's *Coup de foudre* (*Entre nous*, 1983).

Coup de foudre has clear *auteurist* origins, based as it is on Kurys's account – co-authored with Olivier Cohen – of her mother's life. The narrative centres on the friendship – which implicitly develops into a lesbian relationship – between Lena (Isabelle Huppert) and Madeleine (Miou-Miou). After a prologue set during the Occupation, the action switches to Lyon in 1952, where the two meet for the first time. The intensity of this meeting, evoked in a silent shot/reverse-shot of the faces of the two women, immediately suggests an emotional undercurrent which will run counter to the rather dull married lives that Lena and Madeleine have at this point. That undercurrent is, however, buried very deep, while Kurys's nostalgic attention to fifties costume and popular music, and above all her avoidance of the strident excesses of melodrama, ensure that *Coup de foudre* is for the most part merely a tasteful period piece. As Andréa Weiss has commented, 'the film's formal qualities – so dependent are they on the codes of art cinema – restrain the women's relationship as the narrative seeks to extend it', although as a consequence 'the shroud of ambiguity surrounding the exact nature of the women's relationship leaves space for the lesbian imagination' (Weiss 1992: 125). Once Madeleine has left her husband and moved to Paris to await Lena, the narrative pace quickens, with

Lena first visiting her friend secretly and then attempting to secure the financial independence needed to join her by setting up a boutique. Fearing that she has been abandoned by Lena, Madeleine has a breakdown, and it is in the emotional reunion of the two friends that the 'excessive' code of melodrama – signalled by tears (Williams 1991) – is first mobilised by Kurys. Although the tone becomes more measured again once Lena and Madeleine begin living together, their escape from Lena's jealous husband Michel is again signalled by tears, this time those of Michel himself, who finally accepts the situation with an appropriate 'feminine' response (weeping) rather than his previous inappropriate macho violence (destroying Lena's shop). As it has done throughout, however, the period music – here Perry Como – maintains a wistful and nostalgic note which characterises the film as a whole, and keeps the excesses of melodrama at arm's length, just as the image track assiduously avoids any direct representation of lesbian desire.

Kurys's subsequent film, *Un homme amoureux* (*A Man in Love*, 1987), was a lush heterosexual romance filmed at Rome's Cinecittà studios with an international cast (Peter Coyote, Greta Scacchi, Claudia Cardinale, Jamie Lee Curtis and Vincent Lindon). The result is a largely predictable array of stereotypes, including the angst-ridden film star (Coyote) and the nagging wife (Curtis). *Un homme amoureux* is mediated, like *Coup de foudre* and *Après l'amour* (1992), by a female *auteur* figure, in this case Jane (Scacchi). Whereas the mother–daughter relationship underpinning *Coup de foudre* is only suggested in the final dedication, in *Un homme amoureux* it is Jane's mother (Cardinale) who bestows on her daughter the narrative powers which result, in the closing scene, in her writing the story we have just watched as one long flashback. This framing device, although a cinematic staple, is usually associated with a male narrator (see chapter 3), and to that extent, its function in *Un homme amoureux* is emblematic of Kurys's cinema in general: stylistically orthodox, but from a woman's point of view.

Maternal men in *Trois hommes et un couffin*

Coline Serreau's *Trois hommes et un couffin* (*Three Men and a Cradle*, 1985) is one of the greatest domestic box-office hits of recent French cinema. Over ten million people saw the film in the year of release, rising to twelve and a half million within three years, making it by far the most popular French film of the 1980s, and the most successful home product since Gérard Oury's *La Grande Vadrouille* in 1966. Moreover, the budget – recouped ten times over – was only 9.7 million francs, and the three leads – Roland Giraud, Michel Boujenah and André Dussolier – relatively unknown. Serreau was subsequently asked to direct the Hollywood remake but pulled out, leaving Leonard Nimoy to direct *Three Men and a Baby* in 1989. In Serreau's film, three bachelor buddies – Pierre (Giraud), Michel (Boujenah) and Jacques (Dussolier) – live together in Paris. While Jacques is out of the country

10   Michel Boujenah and Roland Giraud in *Trois hommes et un couffin*

– he works as an airline pilot – Sylvia, an ex-girlfriend, sends him baby
Marie to look after. Although Jacques is Marie's father, he is unaware
of her existence. It therefore falls upon Pierre and Michel to act as
surrogate fathers and, more pertinently, surrogate mothers too. Their
attempts to care for Marie are complicated by a sub-plot involving
stolen drugs which, like the baby, are thrust upon them. Jacques's
arrival is followed by Sylvia's reclaiming of Marie but she proves a less
able mother than the three men, and the baby is returned to Jacques,
Pierre and Michel.

Serreau had considered the cultural difficulties fatherhood raised
for men ten years previously in her first film script, *On s'est trompé
d'amour*, which she summarised as follows: 'On écrase les hommes
sous leur propre phallus et on leur inculque qu'il est au-dessous de
leur dignité de partager avec leurs femmes les préparatifs de la venue
du bébé' [Men are crushed under their own phallus, and taught that
it is beneath their dignity to share with their wives in preparing for a
new baby] (Trémois 1993: 21). But by contrasting the caring male
trio of *Trois hommes et un couffin* with female examples of 'bad' motherhood, she gave rise to accusations from American feminist critics
that the film was misogynistic, and subverted French feminist theory's emphasis on the importance of biological motherhood (Durham
1992). *Trois hommes et un couffin* may not be a feminist film, but it does
present – like much of Serreau's work – an optimistic response to a
genuine social question (the role of men in bringing up children). The
film also presents a fairly realistic picture of domestic routine – via the
shots of nappy-changing, washing feeding bottles, and so on – which

Women film-makers

recalls the importance of representations of domesticity in feminist cinema, most famously in Chantal Akerman's real-time study of a house-wife's existence, *Jeanne Dielman, 23 Quai du Commerce, 1080, Bruxelles* (1976). Not only do Pierre, Michel and (eventually) Jacques thus inhabit a 'female' domestic space, and carry out 'female' domestic chores, they are feminised by their love for baby Marie which, as François Audé has observed, is maternal rather than paternal (Audé 1985: 70). This is most evident when Marie is temporarily taken away by Sylvia: in a drunken maternal fantasy, Jacques puts a cushion up his jumper, claiming that he is pregnant, and bemoans the sterility of men compared to the life-giving creativity of women. The question of gender roles also informs Serreau's manipulation of genre in the film, with the two plots deriving from genres traditionally encoded in gender terms: the drugs plot belongs to the 'male' thriller genre, the baby plot to 'female' domestic realism. The confusion between the two packages – the baby and the heroin – 'introduces narrative rivalry between a male story of [...] opposition to law and order, and a female plot of [...] compliance with societal norms and values' (Durham 1992: 775). The two plots are integrated when the baby herself (her nappy) is used by Pierre and Michel as a hiding-place for the drugs, and in a parody of the macho thriller genre, the archetypal set-piece in which bags containing drugs are switched involves not two brief-cases (serious, 'male', business-like), but two nappies. As in Serreau's subsequent films, *Romuald et Juliette* (1989) and *La Crise* (1992), the apparently banal narrative of *Trois hommes et un couffin* thus mobilises an examination of conventional roles and contemporary social problems. If in the latter it is gender typing which is addressed, in *Romuald et Juliette* it is racism and class snobbery, and in *La Crise* a crisis of masculinity in the face of divorce, unemployment and loneliness, while all three films are characterised by Serreau's use of parallelism in plotting and montage, and of frenzied, repetitious dialogue.

The films of Claire Denis

While Kurys and Serreau were prolific and popular throughout the 1980s, other female directors found it harder to attract funding. Catherine Breillat, now a key figure in the recent 'sexual revolution' in French cinema (see chapter 3), did not follow up *Tapage nocturne* (1979) for nearly ten years, until *36 fillette* (*Virgin*, 1988). Caroline Roboh, whose *Clémentine Tango* (1982) was an early example of the *cinéma du look* style (see chapter 6), made no more films that decade. More successful was Aline Issermann, whose début *Le Destin de Juliette* was well received in 1982, and whose subsequent work includes *L'Amant magnifique* (1986) and *L'Ombre du doute* (*A Shadow of Doubt*, 1992). The early 1990s saw a wave of well-received début films by women directors, which was represented in foreign distribution – at the 1994 Sarasota French Film Festival in Florida, 'seven of the twenty new features were directed by women' (Corliss 1994: 97)

– as well as in the domestic market: the magazine *Télérama* claimed in late 1994 that half of the thirty young *auteurs* working in French cinema were women (Trémois 1995: 18). Moreover, the number of popular female-authored productions was seen as ending the historical marginalisation of women film-makers: 'Fini, le temps des "films de femmes!" ' [The time of 'women's films' is over!] (Trémois 1995: 18). Among the major successes of 1994 were Marion Vernoux's *Personne ne m'aime*, Pascale Ferran's *Petits arrangements avec les morts* and Tonie Marshall's *Pas très catholique (A Dubious Business)*. That year also saw female directors well represented in the influential series of television films commissioned by Arte, *Tous les garçons et les filles de leur âge* (see chapter 9). Of the nine films screened on TV, five were made by women: Chantal Ackerman's *Portrait d'une jeune fille...*, Laurence Ferreira Barbosa's *Paix et amour*, Patricia Mazuy's *Travolta et moi*, Emilie Deleuze's *L'Incruste*, and Claire Denis's *U.S. Go Home*. Denis in particular has since become one of the most important film-makers working in France today.

Chocolat and women's experience of the colonies

Whereas during the 1970s, films set in the French colonies tended to dwell on the military or the political (see chapter 2), it was only in the 1980s that 'the personal experience or semi-autobiographical recollection of an ex-colonial' became a common theme (Hayward 1993: 252). Many of these 'ex-colonial' films have been made by women, among them Claire Denis's *Chocolat* (1988) set in Senegal, Marie-France Pisier's *Le Bal du gouverneur* (1990) set in Nouméa, and Brigitte Rouan's *Outremer* (1990) set in Algeria. A singular precursor of these films is Marguerite Duras's oblique treatment of the female colonial experience in *India Song* (1975, see above). Accused at the time of belonging to the wave of nostalgia for the thirties and forties known as *la mode rétro* (see chapter 2), *India Song* transcended the empty stylisation of colonial history by evoking leprosy, madness, passion and death (see Bonitzer 1975). Euzhan Palcy's altogether more conventional and popular representation of Martinique in 1930, *Rue cases nègres (Black Shack Alley*, 1983), considers the experience of the African work force rather than the European colonisers. What seems to characterise women's representations of colonialism is a critical perspective, but on a personal or domestic rather than a historical or epic scale. Frédéric Strauss has rather schematically contrasted the 'soft' films by Denis, Pisier and Rouan with 'hard' military accounts of colonialism by male directors such as Pierre Schoendoerffer, Régis Warnier and Jean-Claude Brisseau (Strauss 1990: 30). Certainly the marginal position of women in the colonies symbolises their marginality in society as a whole. Claire Denis has said of colonial wives and daughters that they represented France, but lived an empty and futile existence while their husbands and fathers lived a romanticised adventure closer to the world of Tintin (Strauss 1990: 32). She has also declared that her own decision to make a film about Africa was a moral one, and this moral concern with issues of race, identity and territory has run throughout her work.

Denis spent her early childhood in Senegal, and on her return as an adult found herself accused of being a mere tourist (Strauss 1990: 31). The question of identity raised by that experience is dramatised in the frame narrative of *Chocolat*, which presents a white adult narrator (Mireille Perrier), rather predictably called France, whose Senegalese childhood forms, in one long flashback, the main body of the film. As France drives (left to right) through the African landscape, the past is suddenly evoked in a tracking shot which reverses her direction, and leads us (right to left) into the past. France's point of view is thus no longer that of a French tourist but of a young girl who is part of colonial West Africa. The narrative now centres on France's parents (Giula Boschi and François Cluzet), and in particular on her mother's unfulfilled desire for the black houseboy, Protée. The thematics of female desire, insufferable heat, and stifling convention are reminiscent of Duras's *India Song*, but *Chocolat* is far more conventional in form, and the constraints of the female colonial experience are tempered with an evident nostalgia for the period, the setting, and for childhood. Nevertheless this impression is qualified in the epilogue, in which the adult France is told by a black American soldier that he has both an Afrocentric past and a future, while she, as an ex-colonial, has neither. Denis has stated that she was determined not to restrict herself to the story of her childhood, but intended in this conclusion to give a glimpse of Africa after colonisation (Strauss 1990: 31). Her subsequent films continue this interest in post-colonial society and its effects on the body of the individual.

Genre and the body in Denis's cinema

Unusually for a film-maker so readily identified as an *auteur*, Denis has a very productive relation to genre. Much of her work makes use of generic conventions to some degree, although they are often submerged, qualified, or inflected in some way. One might therefore say that Denis fulfils perfectly a dominant idea in current French film criticism: that genre is deemed acceptable as long as the film-maker subverts its codes (see Goudet and Vassé 1999). But Denis is clearly interested in genre on its own terms as well, as is evident from *Trouble Every Day* (2001), a gorily orthodox horror film which as a result seems to have been her least critically-acclaimed work. In this film and others, from *J'ai pas sommeil* (1993) via *Beau travail* (2000) to *Vendredi soir* (2002), genre allows Denis to explore the human body in states of violence, desire, and performance, and this concern – along with attention to issues of gender and race – is consistent throughout her varied and fascinating filmography. Nonetheless, her characteristic film style with its long silences, oblique narratives and disorienting use of extreme close-ups, is aesthetically far removed from popular cinema. As Martine Beugnet has observed in her recent study of Denis, 'Even as they portray the most ordinary places and situations, her films draw on the effect of defamiliarisation that cinema can create so powerfully' (Beugnet 2004: 4–5). One thinks of the mysterious shots of nocturnal windows and glowing neon signs in *Vendredi soir*, or banal tasks like shaving and ironing made strange when performed by groups of legionnaires in the desert setting of *Beau travail*. Montage in Denis's films can also create unfamiliar and quasi-surrealist visual associations, linking shots not according to narrative or character but through formal patterning, as in *Beau travail* where the thin branches of a tree are juxtaposed with the wires of an obstacle-course, and then in turn with lines of washing. This lyrical editing, along with careful attention to framing and lighting (sickly artificial light for *J'ai pas sommeil*, sulphurous reds and oranges for *Trouble Every Day*) means that Denis's films are more overtly stylized than many of the offerings of her contemporaries in the so-called *jeune cinéma* or 'new realism' of the nineties (see chapter 9).

J'ai pas sommeil tells the story of a real-life serial killer of elderly women in Paris, but keeps the police inquiry incidental to the narrative while avoiding psychological explanation for the characters' actions. It is thus a kind of submerged thriller, with the daily struggles of the protagonists taking centre stage while the murders run through the film like an underground river, only rarely coming to the surface. One could say that the central concerns of the thriller narrative have become marginal, while the lives of the socially marginalized characters – nearly all immigrants – have become central. Daïga (Katherine Golubeva), a young woman from Lithuania, arrives in Paris where she is eventually employed cleaning in the hotel where gay black nightclub performer Camille (Richard Courcet) lives. Meanwhile, Camille's brother Théo (Alex Descas) is attempting to leave Paris for Martinique, taking with him his little son. *J'ai pas sommeil* has many strands which run parallel but do not always cross: Daïga never encounters Théo, for instance, and only meets Camille for a fleeting moment at the close of the film. Ultimately, Camille is revealed as the serial killer, and Daïga steals the money he has taken from his victims before leaving Paris again. Several police procedural scenes punctuate the narrative, but these are often very brief and low key, and concern police harassment of Daïga as much as the murder hunt. Longer and more dynamic are the rhythmic or musical sequences that serve to express the desires of their performers, and which herald the focus on the body in performance that is evident in *Beau travail*. The first of these is a self-defence class run by Daïga's employer Ninon (Line Renaud) and which underlines the fear of violence circulating in the city while also presenting a partly comic, partly empowering view of older women preparing to fight back against their potential assailants. Although there is no musical backing, Ninon's chanting of 'Couilles! Tempe!' [balls! head!], and the synchronized movements of the identically-dressed stick-wielding women give this scene a bizarrely entertaining choreography and rhythm. The sense of community evoked here through a performance of anxiety and aggression is given a warmer tone at the birthday party for Théo and Camille's mother. Both sons dance in turn with their mother, but even here tension remains, as the brothers pointedly refuse to form a trio, as if they are unable to communicate through dance any sense of understanding or closeness with each other. The mother's unspoken desire for unity through family is evaded by her sons, and will be destroyed when she learns that Camille is the serial killer.

The most theatrical performance in *J'ai pas sommeil* is Camille's drag act. This is the one occasion when we get close to some understanding of the charisma of this otherwise taciturn and morose killer. Cross-dressed in a black dress, headband and long gloves, Camille lip-syncs to a moody ballad. He is presented as an object of fascination and desire for the audience in the gay club, and the camera celebrates his body with long close-ups on his muscular back. The sequence recalls music video, all the more so since Camille is obviously miming to the music track. In the context of the film's thriller narrative, this is a daring celebration of Camille as a kind of star. But it may also be interpreted as a display of inauthenticity, since Camille is lip-synching and hence is removed from the music in a way that Théo, in his own musical performance, is not. In the final music sequence, Théo's desire to return to Martinique is expressed in his melancholy violin playing at a concert by his group. The music here is full of longing for the homeland, but it also relates to the potential for communication between the two brothers: Camille is in the crowd, and a silent look is exchanged between himself and Théo. Once Camille leaves the club the music continues, sound-tracking the glorious tracking shot of him being tailed by the police prior to his arrest. The poignancy of Théo's violin thus expresses a lost or impossible bond between the brothers, the music of one matching the alienation and downfall of the other. The murders themselves are not performances, however: there is no music, and no dramatization of these low-key but brutal events. The fact that the murders are committed by a gay, HIV-positive black man caused controversy when the film was screened in the United States (see Marker 1999: 138), but while we are offered no psychological explanation for Camille's actions, he is never demonized. *J'ai pas sommeil* explores the opacity and ambivalence of the ethnic other, and above all a resistance to easy categorization, in a way that is taken up in an even more paranoid vein in Michael Haneke's *Caché* (2005, see chapter 2). Denis's film is also about the places of individual bodies in a modern capitalist society, be they the neglected and discarded bodies of the elderly women, the working bodies of Daïga and Théo (both operating on the margins of the economy), or the body of Camille himself, who is sleepwalking into murder and theft as a dysfunctional means of social integration, thereby fulfilling Frantz Fanon's dictum that 'In Europe the black man is the symbol of Evil. [...] The black Antillean is a slave to this function' (see Beugnet 2004: 96).

The theme of the body in performance is taken up again in *Beau travail*. Much has been written about this most academically-scrutinised of Denis's films, in particular regarding masculinity and colonialism (see Hayward 2001, Sillars and Beugnet 2001, Beugnet 2004). In terms of genre, *Beau travail* can be also read as a musical. Since the musical idealises community (Feuer 1993: 3), it is an apt choice of vehicle for Denis's project about a mythologised body of men, the Foreign Legion. The musical can seem obsolete in contemporary cinema, since 'Because of [the] realist imperative, most musicals appear ridiculous today, their imaginative worlds implausible and naive' (Hallam with Marshment 2000: 7). But among her achievements in *Beau travail*, Denis succeeds in giving the musical a contemporary resonance. She does so by combining a realist setting (the desert and coastal landscapes of Djibouti) with the symbolism of a masculine colonial ideal embodied above all by the legionnaires themselves. Trained as a group of soldiers by their sergeant, Galoup (Denis Lavant), the men are also organised as a group of dancers by the choreographer Bernard Montet. The plot of *Beau travail* is loosely based on Melville's story *Billy Budd*, but its structure, like that of a musical, is built around a series of 'numbers' or dances. These are traditionally 'self-contained "show-stopping" elements [that] emphasise exhibition rather than narrative progression, bodily display rather than character psychology' (Hallam with Marshment 2000: 72). There are nearly twenty sequences in *Beau travail* that function like dance numbers, from the nightclub scenes to the soldiers' various choreographed exercises and even the underwater training sequence, which is close to the coordinated movements of synchronized swimming. Two worlds and two types of body are on display in these sequences: the athletic, masculine world of the Legion and the exotic, 'foreign' and feminine world of Djibouti. The film begins by establishing these two groupings, represented both visually and musically: the first by a painting of the Legion and a chorus from the legionnaires, the second by the sight and sound of North African women dancing in a nightclub. One world defines itself via a heroic myth and collective singing (Legion songs and Britten's opera *Billy Budd*) while the other is the modern but still – for these men – exotic reality of Djibouti. The sexual charge between the two (as well as the homoerotic charge between legionnaires) underlies the story of Galoup's dismissal from the Legion. The two worlds compete and cross throughout the film, the swelling choruses of *Billy Budd* juxtaposed with the exhilarating dance music of the nightclub scenes, until the ending when the two worlds are brought together by Lavant's stunning dance performance. Like the African women, Galoup expresses his identity bodily on the dance-floor rather than in a group exercise like the soldiers. But he also carries in his body the memory of those exercises. His expulsion from the Legion is initially expressed by the anthem of the Legion, sung by his former comrades, from which he is excluded, and then by the final sequence where Galoup dances alone in a nightclub to the house anthem *Rhythm of the Night*. Loneliness and despair combine with a thrilling physical prowess, the legacy of his military training, to form a danced lament for his lost identity and a frenzied exit from 'the rhythm of my life', as well as a celebration of the athletic male body.

If *Beau travail* and *J'ai pas sommeil* engage with genre in an indirect fashion, *Trouble Every Day* (2001) does so wholeheartedly. A graphic horror film, it stars Béatrice Dalle as the cannibalistic Coré, and Vincent Gallo as Shane, an American on honeymoon in Paris who is succumbing to the same predatory passions. Both, we learn, are suffering the monstrous consequences of experimental scientific research. Denis positions the film very deliberately in the genre by referring to key horror narratives: Dracula (vampires with sexualized adolescent victims), Frankenstein (a monster made by science but uncontrollable by the same), and Jekyll and Hyde (the rogue scientist lives with the monster, establishing a dichotomy between deadly nocturnal behaviour and outwardly calm diurnal 'normality'). These horror archetypes function within the realm of Denis's own characteristic passions: desiring bodies and defamiliarised spaces. *Trouble Every Day* begins with a classic generic gesture, a kind of initiation into the adult world of horror and desire, with young lovers kissing in a parked car at night. This scene immediately establishes a link between sexual desire and the threat of terror, and it is followed by Coré's seduction and devouring of a lorry-driver in a vacant lot, where the grasses are soon dripping with blood. By entering such everyday but mysterious spaces, the curious risk giving up their bodies to monsters. Even though this is a willing action in the case of Coré's young neighbour, and partially so in the case of the maid cornered by Shane, the result in both cases is bloody and grotesque. The two sex/cannibalism sequences that follow are among the most shocking in mainstream French cinema, and bear comparison with the 'new brutalism' of Catherine Breillat and Gaspar Noé (see chapter 3). The victims' bodies are not just assaulted, but are literally consumed. In the film's central and most notorious scene, Coré is seen devouring the young man's face, rubbing her fingers in his gaping wounds and tearing out his throat. The focus on Coré's devouring mouth here and throughout the film plays on Dalle's star iconography as 'La Grande Bouche' (see Austin 2003: 117) as well as evoking the monsters in the *Alien* series or in Francis Bacon's nightmare paintings.

Denis's regular cinematographer, Agnès Godard, made regular use during shooting of the Minicam, a tiny camera which allows bodies to be filmed in extreme close-up. The results, particularly in a valedictory inventory of the young man's body before he is devoured by Coré, recall Varda's portrayal of the body as landscape in *Jacquot de Nantes*, on which Godard herself had worked (see above). *Trouble Every Day* also explores how banal and seemingly neutral spaces – the aeroplane, the hotel – become monstrous bodies too, the first a kind of hive full of sleeping people where Shane imagines his young wife drenched in blood, the second a network of uterine corridors, with in its bowels the changing-room where the young maid is raped and consumed. In her director's commentary on the film, Denis has stated that the basement of the hotel is like the stomach of 'un grand corps' [a huge body], linked by a series of vessels (pipes, corridors, the smells and sounds of the maids' bodies) to Shane's predatory senses. Like its horror antecedents, *Trouble Every Day* is about how human bodies are possessed by bestial desires, but it is also about how its Parisian settings are in turn possessed by the monstrous bodies that inhabit them. There is also, in the sequence where Coré's husband sponges the blood off her, and in the aborted love scene between Shane and his young wife, a hint at the tenderness of bodily contact that is always foreclosed in the horror film but which remains central to the romance and hence to Denis's subsequent film, *Vendredi soir* (2002).

Denis has compared *Vendredi soir* to the fairy-tale of Cinderella and Prince Charming. It is also possible to place the film within Janice Radway's 'narrative logic of the romance', according to which a series of misunderstandings and reconciliations begins when 'The heroine's social identity is thrown into question', to include disagreement, separation and tenderness between hero and heroine before 'The heroine responds sexually and emotionally to the hero' and finds her identity 'restored' (Radway 1987: 150). We can follow a very similar pattern through *Vendredi soir*, from start to finish. The film concerns a one-night stand between Laure (Valerie Lemercier) and Jean (Vincent Lindon), a stranger she picks up during a huge traffic jam. Laure's social identity is clearly at stake here since the film concerns her last night of 'freedom' before she moves in with her long-term boyfriend. Masculinity is first introduced in the film as either threatening or indifferent: one man knocks aggressively on her windscreen and then follows her; another refuses her offer of a lift. On first appearance, Jean also seems to be potentially threatening: he is taciturn and monosyllabic, and the camerawork emphasises his physicality with repeated close-ups on his hands. He proves his worth in normative masculine terms as an action man, by taking the wheel and reversing her car out of trouble. But Laure is still unsure of Jean until he shows consideration by getting out when she appears panicked by his presence. The romance values the film employs are thus traditional and unashamedly generic: the heroine is confronted by male physicality but must be reassured by the presence of tenderness and insight before she can commit to the hero. Beyond the narrative, *Vendredi soir* also evokes fairy-tales by taking a banal setting and showing it to be magical. Paris at night is lit up like a stage set at the start of the film, and playful fairy bells are heard, signalling the fantasy romance to follow, while the lack of dialogue and the speeded-up motion of traffic and pedestrians recalls silent cinema. Set during a transport strike, the film acquires an ephemeral, miraculous atmosphere: Paris not only looks unusual on this particular night, it will be the setting for once-in-a-lifetime happenings. This sense of entering a different world is dramatized by Denis's brilliant use of the traffic jam, which serves as the portal to a fantasy world, a world of romance. Traversing the traffic is like going through the looking-glass, but in a romantic context. The film is a fantasy of the female body and the male body in happy union with no consequences. It is a fairy-tale made flesh, with recurrent reminders of corporeality in the extreme close-ups during sex, the sound effects, and the intimate gestures, as when Jean slips his hand inside the glove Laure is wearing, or she pushes her hand up the sleeve of his shirt. The film, the night, the affair, ends with a feeling of exhilaration for Laure and also for the spectator. The final scene of *Vendredi soir* – like that of *Beau travail* – conveys a sense of energy and joie de vivre incarnated by the actor's body in motion (Lemercier running down the street, Denis Lavant on the dancefloor) that is characteristic of Denis's cinema as a whole and which refutes the accusations of formalism and pessimism sometimes aimed at her work.

Denis is nonetheless a serious and ethically-motivated director who chooses to represent issues of race and identity, declaring that 'All my films function as a movement toward an unknown Other and toward the unknown in relation to other people' (cited in Beugnet 2004: 4). Her cinema also engages with social exclusion, most notably in the fragmented Paris of *J'ai pas sommeil* but even in the hotel from *Trouble Every Day* which segregates workers and guests, granting different levels to each like a version of the body politic. Denis's fascination with (foreign) bodies is celebratory as well as socially-rooted, however. Her lyrical attention to both sounds and images, together with an acute awareness of how genre conventions can facilitate explorations of the body in action, makes Denis the most exciting, unpredictable and gifted film-maker of her generation in France.

References

Audé, F. (1985), *Trois Hommes et un couffin*: Hommes d'intérieur, Paris, *Positif*, 297, 70–1.

Austin, G. (2003), *Stars in Modern French Film*, London, Arnold.

Beugnet, M. (2004), *Claire Denis*, Manchester, Manchester University Press.

Bonitzer, P. (1975), D'une Inde l'autre (*India Song*), Paris, *Cahiers du cinéma*, 258/9, 49–51.

Corliss, R. (1994), Toujours les femmes, New York, *Time*, 28 November, 97–8.

Duras, M. (1989), J'ai toujours désespérément filmé ..., Paris, *Cahiers du cinéma*, 426, 62–5.

Durham, C. (1992), Taking the baby out of the basket and/or robbing the cradle: 'remaking' gender and culture in Franco-American film, *The French Review*, 65:5, 774–84.

Dyer, R. (1990), *Now You See It: Studies on Lesbian and Gay Film*, London and New York, Routledge.

Feuer, J. (1993), *The Hollywood Musical*, 2nd edn, London, BFI/Macmillan.

Flitterman-Lewis, S. (1993), Magic and wisdom in two portraits by Agnès Varda: *Kung-Fu Master* and *Jane B. by Agnès V.*, Glasgow, *Screen*, 34:4, 302–20.

Forbes, J. (1992), *The Cinema in France After the New Wave*, London, BFI/Macmillan.

Goudet, S. and Vassé, C. (1999), Ces idées qui tuent le cinema: L'abécédaire de *Positif*, *L'Evénement* 760, 11–12.

Hallam, J., with Marshment, N. (2000), *Realism and Popular Cinema*, Manchester, Manchester University Press.

Hayward, S. (1987), Beyond the gaze and into *femme-filmécriture*: Agnès Varda's *Sans Toit ni loi*, in S. Hayward and G. Vincendeau (eds), *French Film: Texts and Contexts*, London and New York, Routledge, 285–96.

Hayward, S. (1993), *French National Cinema*, London and New York, Routledge.

Hayward, S. (2001), Claire Denis's films and the post-colonial body, *Studies in French Cinema* 1:3, 159–65.

Heck-Rabi, L. (1984), *Women Film-makers: A Critical Reception*, Metuchen, NJ, and London, The Scarecrow Press.

Kuhn, A., and Radstone, S. (1990) (eds), *The Women's Companion to International Film*, Berkeley, University of California Press.

Lyon, E. (1988), The cinema of Lol V. Stein, in C. Penley (ed.), *Feminism and Film Theory*, New York, Routledge/BFI, 244–69.

Marker, C. (1999), Sleepless in Paris: *J'ai pas sommeil*, in P. Powrie (ed.), *French Cinema in the 1990s: Continuity and Difference*, Oxford, 137–47.

Murat, P. (1994), Le Temps des copains, Paris, *Télérama*, 2305, 34–6.

Philippon, A. (1988), Les Coquetteries d'Agnès, Paris, *Cahiers du cinéma*, 405, 12.

Radway, J. (1987), *Reading the Romance: Women, Patriarchy and Popular Literature*, London, Verso.

Ropars-Wuilleumier, M.-C. (1980), The disembodied voice: *India Song*, New Haven, CT, *Yale French Studies*, 60, 241–68.

Sillars, J., and Beugnet, M. (2001), *Beau Travail*: time, space, and myths of identity, *Studies in French Cinema* 1:3, 166–73.

Strauss, F. (1990), Féminin colonial, Paris, *Cahiers du cinéma*, 434, 28–33.

Trémois, C.-M. (1993), Vive les crises!, Paris, *Télérama*, 2243, 20–2.

Trémois, C.-M. (1995), Femmes de tête, Paris, *Télérama*, 2346, 18–19.

Varda, A. (1994), *Varda par Agnès*, Paris, Cahiers du cinéma/Ciné-Tamaris.

Vincendeau, G. (1987), Women's cinema, film theory and feminism in France, Glasgow, *Screen*, 28:4, 4–18.

Weiss, A. (1992), *Vampires and Violets: Lesbians in the Cinema*, London, Jonathan Cape.

Williams, L. (1991), Film bodies: gender, genre, and excess, Berkeley, California, *Film Quarterly*, 44:4, 2–13.

Williams, L. (1994) (ed.), *Viewing Positions: Ways of Seeing Film*, New Brunswick, Rutgers University Press.

5

The *polar*

The popularity of the *polar*

The first French thrillers date from the silent era, with Louis Feuillade's popular *Fantômas* and *Judex* series (between 1913 and 1918). Since World War Two, however, the form has often been associated with the American genres of the *film noir* and the gangster film (see below). The end of the war saw an influx of American crime novels published in France as the *série noire*, while a glut of Hollywood thrillers appeared on French screens, influencing the young critics of *Cahiers du cinéma* who went on to form *la nouvelle vague* (see chapter 1). For this reason the French thriller, also known as the *polar* or *film policier*, has been cited as 'the principal means by which the French cinema's relationship to Hollywood has been articulated' (Forbes 1992: 48). But the *polar* has also functioned in a variety of other ways, particularly in the years after *la nouvelle vague*. By the 1970s, 'the *polar* was naturalised as French' (Forbes 1992: 53), and proved a staple of the national cinema, diverse in format but always in demand. There remained a tradition of adapting American crime novels to the screen, from François Truffaut's *Tirez sur le pianiste* (*Shoot the Pianist*, 1960) to Jean-Jacques Beineix's *La Lune dans le caniveau* (*The Moon in the Gutter*, 1983). But the *polar* also functioned as a means of commenting on French society, whether it be urban decay in Alain Corneau's *Série noire* (1979), colonialism in Bertrand Tavernier's *Coup de torchon* (*Clean Slate*, 1981), or drug dealing in Maurice Pialat's *Police* (1985). The popular revolt of May 1968 (see chapter 2) led to a vogue for political thrillers, such as Costa-Gavras's trilogy – Z (1969), *L'Aveu* (1970) and *État de siège* (1973) – starring the left-wing icon Yves Montand. The same period saw Jean-Pierre Melville's apolitical and heavily stylised trilogy with Alain Delon (see below). The breadth of the genre thus contributed to its popularity in the subsequent decade: a quarter of all French films made in 1981 were *polars* (Marshall 1992: 33), and many of those were box-office successes.

At the most commercial end of the market, two kinds of *polar* dominated in the 1970s and 1980s: the action-packed comedy-thriller and the stylised gangster format. These sub-genres were incarnated by the leading stars of the time, Jean-Paul Belmondo and Alain Delon respectively, so that Melville could declare, 'There are only two formats here: Delon and Belmondo' (Forbes 1992: 53–4). Co-stars in 1970 for Jacques Deray's *Borsalino* (see below), the two embodied the popular thriller in films by Deray, Henri Verneuil and Gérard Oury. Belmondo's action movies in particular attracted a large audience: four million spectators watched him in Georges Lautner's *Le Professionnel* (1981), five million in Oury's *L'As des as* (1982), and four and a half million in Deray's *Le Marginal* (1983). In the subsequent years Claude Zidi scored at the box office with his cop comedies *Les Ripoux* (1984) and *Ripoux contre ripoux* (1990), each attracting over two million spectators. But by the turn of the decade, in terms of domestic film, the *polar* was being out-performed by the *cinéma du look* – a genre none the less often reliant on the thriller for plot and characterisation – and by the heritage film (see chapters 6 and 7).

Voyeurism and the Hitchcockian thriller

In 1957 Eric Rohmer and Claude Chabrol, journalists on *Cahiers du cinéma*, wrote *Hitchcock*, the first serious critical work on this seminal director to be published. The primary importance of Hitchcock to the thriller genre, and indeed to cinema in general, derives from his obsession with voyeurism. As Rohmer and Chabrol noted of *Rear Window* (1954): 'let us merely say that the theme concerns the very essence of cinema, which is *seeing, spectacle*' (Rohmer and Chabrol 1992: 124). By positioning his protagonists as voyeurs, and filming what they see through recurrent point-of-view shots, Hitchcock encourages an identification between the cinema spectator and the voyeur. This is most explicitly the case in *Rear Window*, where a chair-bound photographer, played by James Stewart, is analogous with the spectator in the auditorium. As he watches the suspicious or banal actions carried out in the building across the yard, 'We wait, hoping along with him', and when it becomes apparent that a murder may have been committed, 'the crime is desired' both by the protagonist and 'by us, the spectators' (Rohmer and Chabrol 1992: 125). Rohmer and Chabrol conclude that what the photographer sees are 'the projections of his thoughts – or desires' (Rohmer and Chabrol 1992: 126). This model of the voyeur controlling what he sees – a model which Hitchcock uses to suggest in *Rear Window* the photographer's pleasure in watching his girlfriend in danger of being killed – is subverted in the complex plot twists of Chabrol's *Le Cri du hibou* (1987) and Patrice Leconte's *Monsieur Hire* (1989). Hitchcock's second major exploration of voyeurism, *Vertigo* (1958), released after the publication of Rohmer and Chabrol's study, was based on a French novel written by Boileau and Narcejac with the director in mind. It proved Hitchcock's most influential work in France, and not least on the film-makers of *la nouvelle vague*. The sequences of detective James Stewart following mysterious woman Kim Novak are echoed in numerous films, including Rohmer's own *Ma nuit chez Maud* (*My Night at Maud's*, 1969) and *La Femme de l'aviateur* (*The Aviator's Wife*, 1981), while the crucial clock-tower murder is reprised by Truffaut in *Une belle fille comme moi* (*Such a Gorgeous Kid Like Me*, 1972). But the French director whose cinematic voyeurism owes the greatest debt to Hitchcock is undoubtedly Claude Chabrol.

Framing the voyeur: *Le Cri du hibou* and *Monsieur Hire*

Of the various film-makers who initiated *la nouvelle vague* (see chapter 1), Chabrol is the one most closely associated with the *polar*. From very early in his career, he has combined a realist depiction of everyday locations with thriller narratives. *Les bonnes femmes* (*The Girls*, 1960), his fourth film and early masterpiece, is permeated with a general air of unease rather than any Hitchcockian suspense. The thriller plot – one of four shop assistants is followed and then murdered – is submerged under the neo-realist observation of Paris, and is shot from the point of view of the victim, not the voyeur. It thus contrasts with the voyeurism of *Rear Window*, *Vertigo* and many of Chabrol's own later films. In part because of the commercial failure of *Les bonnes femmes*, for much of the sixties Chabrol had to work on formula thrillers, and his subsequent work is dependent on the Hitchcockian models of voyeurism, tight plotting and suspense, commercial generic elements which were absent from *Les bonnes femmes*. The 'Hélène cycle' of the late sixties, featuring Chabrol's wife Stéphane Audran, included in 1969 his most famous film *Le Boucher* (see chapter 2). For the next decade, he specialised in psychological thrillers in which an apparent bourgeois harmony tends to be disturbed by an outsider or a voyeur figure. His eighties police thrillers *Poulet au vinaigre* (*Cop au vin*, 1984) and *Inspecteur Lavardin* (1986) were sufficiently popular to spawn a television series based on the Lavardin character.

Le Cri du hibou (*The Cry of the Owl*, 1987) is based on a novel by Patricia Highsmith, whose *Strangers on a Train* had been adapted by Hitchcock in 1951. Typically for Chabrol, the setting is provincial. In this case it is Vichy, a town with a guilty past, as Chabrol was to demonstrate in his Occupation documentary *L'Œil de Vichy* (1993, see chapter 2). The provincial setting derives from a tradition which includes Henri-Georges Clouzot's poison-pen thriller *Le Corbeau* (1943, see chapter 1). Hitchcock too shared 'this European perception of what may lurk beneath the surface of provincial respectability' (Buss 1994: 87). The disjuncture between a polished surface and the cruel depths beneath is essential to the action and *mise en scène* of *Le Cri du hibou*. The themes of surface gloss and inherent violence are embodied in the motif of the eagle's eye which recurs throughout the film, both in the protagonist's drawings and in Chabrol's use of lighting, whereby the characters' eyes glint yellow in the dark. The glossy photography and plush décors seem anomalous given the increasing violence and melodrama of the plot, but in fact this seemingly reassuring aestheticism simply mirrors the deceptive public image of Chabrol's usual target, the bourgeoisie.

Le Cri du hibou stars Christophe Malavoy – previously the amateur detective in Michel Deville's playful and voyeuristic *Péril en la demeure* (*Death in a French Garden*, 1985) – as Robert Forestier, a divorced draughtsman. In this case, however, the urbane Malavoy is not long in control, but soon has to prove his innocence against a rising tide of coincidence and suspicion – again a theme favoured by Hitchcock. Forestier is a habitual voyeur, and at the start of the film has been spying on a young woman, Juliette (Mathilda May), for three months. Confronted by Juliette, he tells her that he was fascinated by the beautiful and reassuring image that she presented when knitting, watching television, or moving about the house. This reassuring picture, like Chabrol's rich *mise en scène*, is undermined by the cynicism and violence of what follows. As Forestier and Juliette rapidly become close friends, her fiancé Patrick spies on them in turn, proceeding to attack Forestier one night. After the struggle, Patrick disappears, and the police begin to suspect Forestier of his murder. Patrick has in fact fled to Paris, where he and Forestier's ex-wife Véronique plan to persecute the voyeur. The melodramatic last reel sees Juliette's suicide and the murder of a police doctor, deaths which again seem to point to Forestier. Ultimately, Patrick and Véronique decide to visit Forestier's house; here a brawl develops, in which both Patrick and Véronique are accidentally killed, leaving Forestier implicated in two more murders. The film thus concludes with the voyeur not only victimised by his enemies, but trapped by circumstance. Moreover, during the course of the narrative Chabrol reveals that the 'normal' bourgeois citizens apparently threatened by Forestier's behaviour in fact pay him back with violence and malice. This is true not only of Véronique and Patrick but of the entire community apart from Juliette, and is realised in the image of Forestier's neighbours pressing their faces against his window, staring at him as he lies wounded, shot by Patrick. This image, and indeed the film as a whole, enacts a reversal of the opening sequence in which Forestier is the prowler looking in. Earlier, he had plaintively informed the police that 'one has the right to look at people'. For exercising that right, the voyeur is punished by the hostile gaze of the community and the implacable gaze of Chabrol's camera.

A similar transformation from voyeur to victim is achieved in Patrice Leconte's *Monsieur Hire* (1989). Better known for his rather misogynistic sex comedies (see chapter 3), Leconte based this *polar* on a psychological novel by Georges Simenon, but again Hitchcock is a dominant reference. If *Rear Window* informs the exposition, *Vertigo* is echoed in the denouement. Monsieur Hire (Michel Blanc) is a fastidious tailor who lives alone and spies on his neighbour Alice (Sandrine Bonnaire) every night as she undresses. When a young girl called Pierrette is murdered in the vicinity, the investigating detective immediately suspects Hire. Meanwhile Alice apparently befriends Hire and

11   Michel Blanc in *Monsieur Hire*

he begins to entertain thoughts of a relationship with her. It transpires that the voyeur saw Alice's boyfriend kill Pierrette. When he promises silence on this matter if she will run away with him, Alice betrays Hire to the police, effectively framing him for the murder. Escaping across the rooftops, he slips and falls to his death.

The parallels with *Le Cri du hibou* are clear: demonised by 'normal' society for his solitary behaviour and strange, effeminate appearance, Hire – like Forestier – goes from being a peeping Tom to the object of a hostile collective gaze. In the reconstruction of the murder, he is forced to run the gauntlet under the eyes of a suspicious crowd; this public spectacle is repeated when he trips at the ice rink, and again at the moment of his death, when a crowd gathers waiting for him to fall. The Chabrolian disjuncture between soothing imagery and cruel actions is here too, Leconte filming this narrative of deceit and betrayal with a sedate, measured camerawork matched by Michael Nyman's baroque score. But unlike Chabrol, Leconte creates a mood of overwhelming pathos, derived in part from Nyman's music but also from the central relationship between the voyeur and the woman he watches. *Monsieur Hire* maintains an intimacy that *Le Cri du hibou*

Sandrine Bonnaire in *Monsieur Hire*

loses with Juliette's suicide, and most of Leconte's film concerns the shifting power relations between Hire and Alice. At first it was he who framed her with his gaze, staring at her through the window; by the film's close, she has asserted control by framing him for the murder. This question of framing remains in the foreground throughout the film through the iterative point-of-view shots and compositions using window frames, and culminates in the play of looks exchanged at the film's climax. As Hire falls to his death, the camera gives his point of view in a slow-motion pan down the side of the building, briefly capturing Alice standing at the window of his own apartment. Finally occupying the powerful position of the voyeur, Alice looks down on her victim even as the subjective camera allows him one last look at his betrayer.

Seeing and believing in *L'Enfer*

Chabrol's *L'Enfer* (*Torment*, 1994) is based on a scenario written then abandoned thirty years earlier by Henri-Georges Clouzot, the director of *polars* such as *Le Corbeau* (1943) and *Les Diaboliques* (1954). Clouzot is of course one of Chabrol's major influences, and *Les Innocents aux mains sales* (*Innocents with Dirty Hands*, 1975) in particular refers to *Les Diaboliques*, both in terms of plot – a murder victim's body mysteriously disappears – and *mise en scène*, with Romy Schneider made up throughout the film to resemble Simone Signoret in the Clouzot thriller. *L'Enfer* considers the growing jealousy of Paul (François Cluzet), a hotelier, regarding his wife Nelly (Emmanuelle Béart). When she lies about the cost of a new handbag, he begins to wonder what else she is keeping from him. As Paul's jealousy develops he begins to follow his wife to town, and suspects her of sleeping with the local garage owner, Martineau (Marc Lavoine). Nelly denies the accusations and persuades Paul to forget them, but a home movie shown to the guests acts as a spur to Paul's jealousy. Eventually he accuses Nelly of sleeping with everyone in the hotel and proceeds to rape her. Nelly takes refuge with the local doctor but is persuaded to go back to her husband. In the final sequence, Paul locks her in the bedroom and appears to murder her. Or perhaps just fantasies that he does. While the plot is straightforward, its realisation is far from simple. This is because Chabrol questions the status of the sounds and images we are presented with during the course of the film. Despite the scenes of Paul trailing Nelly – a reprise of Chabrol's own *L'Œil du malin* (1961) and Hitchcock's *Vertigo* (1958) – *L'Enfer* is not concerned with one man's voyeurism so much as with the destruction of a married couple who projected 'une trop belle image du bonheur' [a too beautiful image of happiness] (Taboulay 1994: 35). As in *Le Cri du hibou*, beautiful and reassuring images prove illusory. But here the process of shattering illusions is so violent as to destroy not only the family group – Paul, Nelly, their young son, Vincent – established in the idyllic early scenes and parodied in the wedding and the family picnic glimpsed later, but also the spectator's faith in the realist illusion itself.

At first Paul's jealousy is a controlled spectacle, viewed by the spectator from the outside. Even when Paul follows Nelly, Chabrol rarely uses the point-of-view shots favoured by Hitchcock, and does not therefore encourage an identification between the spectator and the jealous husband. What we see and what Paul sees are not at this point one and the same. Sounds, not images, are in fact the first subjective elements of Paul's delirium which the audience is offered, beginning with the slightly amplified cry of baby Vincent, and including the insistent roar of passing jets, the buzzing of flies and Paul's own interior monologue, the voice of his paranoid delusion. As the jealousy increases, Chabrol uses the subjective camera to give Paul's perspective, not in 'reality' but in the first of half a dozen fantasy sequences that punctuate the film: driving home from town with Nelly, Paul imagines her meeting Martineau. From this point on, Paul begins to create a 'film' about Nelly which is increasingly hard to tell apart from the 'reality' of Chabrol's film. Thus at a given point we see Nelly apparently kissing Martineau or vamping with the guests: 'Paul *se fait* littéralement *un film* qui déboussole tout. C'est le film d'un homme qui confine et change le monde par son regard' [Paul literally *makes a film for himself* which disorients everything. It is the film of a man who confines and changes the world with his gaze] (Taboulay 1994: 35–6.) This is made explicit in the references to photography, slides and filming: Paul first disturbs Nelly and Martineau together as they watch slides in the dark, and when a guest shows his innocent home movie in the hotel, Chabrol intercuts it with lurid scenes from Paul's imagination. Since no dissolves or obvious visual devices are used to encode such sequences as fantastical, it is largely their narrative contextualisation – usually via close-ups of Paul in a fit of rage – which signals that they are subjective. Chabrol does provide some aural clues, however, – amplified buzzing and roaring noises, or snatches of the song 'L'Enfer de mes nuits' – which suggest that certain scenes are wholly imaginary. Luis Buñuel had made a similar use of sound as an indicator of fantasy in the dream-like ending of *Belle de jour* (1967). But in the startlingly ambiguous final sequence of *L'Enfer*, Chabrol provides no hint as to whether Nelly's murder is fantasy or reality. In the first of what are in effect two alternative endings, Paul cuts his wife's throat; in the second, he seems to wake from a fantasy to find that Nelly is still alive. Ironically, in the former, Paul claims that he has changed, and is no longer jealous: 'ça se voit pas?' [can't you tell?]. In truth, it is impossible to tell. The principle that one can believe what one sees – the foundation of the spectator/voyeur identification – no longer holds.

American archetypes and the stylised thriller

The thriller genres of the gangster film and the *film noir* were initiated in Hollywood in the decades either side of World War Two. Both portrayed an urban nightmare, the down side of the American dream. The gangster film offered 'resonant myths of defeat' (Shadoian 1977: 59), in which organised crime confronted the forces of authority and lost, the charismatic gangster dying a tragic or melodramatic death. In *film noir*, in a sense, defeat has already happened: 'Frontierism has turned to paranoia and claustrophobia. The small-time gangster has made it big and sits in the mayor's chair. The private eye has quit the police force in disgust' (Schrader 1971: 86). The emphasis is no longer on violent action so much as a pervading tension, the hero's endeavour is solitary, not organised, and the morality is even more ambiguous. Both genres had some claims to realism – the gangster film began as a record of actual criminals like Al Capone and events like the Saint Valentine's Day Massacre of 1929, while the *film noir* consistently portrayed the alienation of life in the big city – but they were also heavily stylised, the gangster film in its choreographed shootouts, the *film noir* in its shadowy, expressionist *mise en scène*. This stylisation allowed French film-makers to exploit the iconography of both the gangster film – in the work of Jean-Pierre Melville and Jacques Deray – and the *film noir* – from Jean-Luc Godard's *A bout de souffle* (*Breathless*, 1959) to the work of Jacques Audiard (see below).

The gangster thriller was established almost single-handedly in France by Jean-Pierre Melville, who filmed impassive loners caught in a cold *mise en scène*. Although *Le Doulous* (*The Finger Man*, 1962) starred Jean-Paul Belmondo, it was Alain Delon who went on to incarnate Melville's taciturn, solitary and increasingly abstract protagonists in *Le Samourai* (*The Samurai*, 1967), *Le Cercle rouge* (*The Red Circle*, 1970) and *Un flic* (*Dirty Money*, 1972). This stylised trilogy sees 'the transformation of the actor's performance into a pure display of physical characteristics and metonymic objects such as the trench-coat and the hat' (Forbes 1992: 55). The short *Borsalino* series of the early seventies, produced by Delon and directed by Jacques Deray, knowingly combined the iconography of Delon's persona in these films with a nostalgia for the American gangster genre of the thirties.

Borsalino and the iconography of the gangster

Borsalino (1970) is set in Marseilles in the 1930s. Two crooks – Capello (Jean-Paul Belmondo) and Siffredi (Alain Delon) – rise to power in the underworld by controlling the meat market. This power struggle is complemented by the romantic tensions traditional to the heterosexual buddy film (see chapter 3), with each man's infatuation for a dangerous or unattainable woman threatening the original friendship. Eventually, with the escalation of gang warfare and personal rivalry, the town is no longer big enough for both of them. At this point the light-hearted tone becomes melodramatic. The two gangsters decide to part before one of them kills the other, but after a false ending Capello is shot and dies in his friend's arms. Following Capello's death and Siffredi's disappearance 'never to be heard from again', the closing sequence presents still photographs of the two in a series of poses from the film.

Besides functioning as a straightforward buddy narrative, *Borsalino* pays a nostalgic and at times comic homage to the American gangster movies of the 1930s. It does so through the iconography of the genre – the urban setting, the sharp suits and hats, the cars – and also through Claude Bolling's score, which consists of thirties-style ragtime music. The film thus prefigures George Roy Hill's ragtime comedy *The Sting* (1973), as well as the films of *la mode rétro*, such as Francis Girod's *René la Canne* (1977, see chapter 2). While several sequences in *Borsalino*, like the brawl between Capello and Siffredi when they first meet, are played for laughs, generic set pieces are also played straight, as with the pastoral interlude – a feature of arguably the last classical gangster movie, Raoul Walsh's *High Sierra* (1941) – when Capello hides out in the country. But as the final sequence suggests, Deray's film celebrates above all the iconic status of its stars. The characters played by Belmondo and Delon are images to themselves as well as to the spectator, and are regularly framed looking at themselves in mirrors. Delon in particular, via reference to his persona in Melville's *Le Samourai* (1967), is a self-conscious figure throughout the film: hence the recurrence in *Borsalino* of his trademark gesture, running his hand along the brim of his hat, and of the piano motif. Siffredi, like Costello – Delon's cold but vulnerable hitman in *Le Samourai* – is fascinated with the piano, and even plays the *Borsalino* theme just before Capello's death. And unlike Belmondo/Capello, Delon returns as star and producer of the sequel, *Borsalino et Compagnie* (*Blood on the Streets*, 1974): 'Delon as producer clearly set out to establish a series which, had it continued, might have stood comparison with the serials of the silent period such as *Judex* or *Fantômas'* (Forbes 1992: 58). Like those earlier heroes, Delon's gangster is 'more recognisable in his accoutrements than in his person' (Forbes 1992: 58), an objectified collection of symbols rather than a psychologically realistic character.

Starsky and Hutch in Belleville: *La Balance*

The American Bob Swaim's *La Balance* (1982) takes its inspiration from television rather than from cinema. As *Cahiers du cinéma* noted at the time, the film is in the mould of the American television series *Starsky and Hutch*. This influence is apparent in the characterisation of Paluzzi and Tintin, two wise-cracking police buddies, in the racial stereotyping and in Roland Bocquet's funky score. On a broader level it informs the thriller plot, which centres around the role of the police informer (a comic character in *Starsky and Hutch*, here a tragic one). After the murder of their usual informer, the Belleville *Brigade territoriale* need to find a new grass in order to catch underworld boss Roger Massina (Maurice Ronet). Detective Paluzzi (Richard Berry) decides upon Dédé (Phillipe Léotard), a former member of Massina's gang whose prostitute girlfriend Nicole (Nathalie Baye) once slept with Massina. The police harass Nicole and brutalise Dédé until the latter agrees to turn informer. Dédé sets up an art theft with Massina, but when the plan is changed at the last minute, the police ambush goes wrong. Amidst a chaotic shoot-out, Massina escapes to confront his betrayer. Dédé kills him and considers going on the run himself, before Nicole betrays him to Paluzzi for his own protection.

Despite the reliance on generic elements such as car chases and shoot-outs, and the frequent intertextual references to Hollywood thrillers – the *Dirty Harry* poster on the wall of the *brigade* headquarters, Dédé's allusions to Steve McQueen in *Bullitt* – the seedy Belleville locations lend the film a certain realism. And although the characterisation is largely dependent on the American archetype of the cynical cop, Dédé and Massina are coded as specifically French (via their obsession with cuisine), as are the Arab drug-dealers, albeit in a negative, racist sense. The tension in *La Balance* is generated by the clash between the violent police narrative and the romantic sub-plot involving Dédé and Nicole, which recalls the *film noir* as well as French poetic realism (see chapter 1), with its 'conventional underworld characters (sympathetic crook, affectionate prostitute) caught up in a story of doomed love' (Buss 1994: 145). This tension informs the film's imagery as well as its plot, and is notable in Swaim's use of slow-motion photography. In the opening sequence, the killing of the informer Paolo is realised in slow motion, a convention of the thriller (and the Western) which dates back to the films of Sam Peckinpah, and is also evident in Luc Besson's *Nikita* (1990) and *Léon* (1994). The penultimate sequence of *La Balance* redirects this technique by presenting a sexual image in slow motion. Dédé and Nicole's love-making, however violent, is also a privileged, extended moment salvaged from the scheming around them, an escape from the thriller into the romance.

La Balance was an enormous success in France, winning Césars for best film, actor (Léotard) and actress (Baye), and attracting over four million spectators in the year of release. The result was a spate of imitations, often with derivative titles, including Christine Pascal's *La Garce* – starring Richard Berry again – and Yannick Bellon's *La Triche* (both 1984). This was also a period of growing French interest in American television series. The 1980s in general was a decade of unprecedented expansion in French television, with a doubling in the number of channels and an increasing reliance on advertising revenues. As a consequence, rather than investing in expensive home-made drama the stations bought popular American imports, including police series such as *Starsky and Hutch* and *Chips*. The number of American series on French screens rocketed: in 1985, 73 million francs were spent by French channels on US television series; by 1987 the figure had grown to 613 million francs (Prédal 1991: 390). Hence *La Balance* can be seen to herald the popular demand for American drama series which the French television channels were to fulfil over the course of the decade.

Film noir and fantasy in *Poussière d'ange*

Edouard Niermans made his directorial debut in 1980 with *Anthracite*, a drama set in a Jesuit college in the early fifties. For the next six years he worked in television, before returning to the big screen with *Poussière d'ange* (*Angel Dust*, 1987), a seedy *film noir* mixing psychology, fantasy and realism. Inspector Simon Blount (Bernard Giraudeau) has been left by his wife Martine (Fanny Cottençon) in favour of a hotelier called Igor. Alcoholic, bitter and occasionally violent, Simon begins to look for his wife at night, while struggling with police work during the day. Asked to investigate thefts from a supermarket, he meets a mysterious young woman, Violetta (Fanny Bastien), who befriends him. While photographing Martine and Igor together in a hotel room, Simon inadvertently witnesses Igor's murder. From this point on, his investigation of the murder and his fascination with Violetta become increasingly interdependent. Despite the attempts of his boss Florimont (Michel Aumont) to have him transferred, Simon discovers that Violetta and her surrogate brother Gabriel are embarked on a series of murders to avenge the death of her prostitute mother, in which both Igor and Florimont were implicated. When Simon learns that Florimont is in fact Violetta's father, he confronts him and elicits a confession. Florimont is arrested, but in the violent conclusion Gabriel is killed escaping from the police. Simon helps Violetta to cross the border to safety before an epilogue shows him reunited with his wife and daughter.

Film noir archetypes are evident throughout *Poussière d'ange*, in the *mise en scène*, narrative voice-over and characterisation as much as in the generic plot (rogue detective with morals uncovers corruption in high places). The consistently underlit or nocturnal *mise en scène*, the ubiquitous rain, and the seedy urban locations are all reminiscent of

13   Bernard Giraudeau in *Poussière d'ange*

14   Fanny Bastien and Bernard Giraudeau in *Poussière d'ange*

classic Hollywood *film noir*. But it is above all in the knowing characterisation of the detective hero that the genre is most evident. In both actions and appearance, Simon is a hyperbolic version of the crumpled private eye. He narrates his own story with the laconic humour typical of the genre. The traditional ambiguity of the *film noir* hero – is he a criminal or a lawman? – is epitomised in the scene where he wakes up in the drunk-tank in his own police station. His exaggeratedly dishevelled appearance – unshaven, clutching a bottle of whisky, wearing an overcoat and practically living in his beat-up car – identifies him with 'the earlier iconography of, say, Sam Spade or Philip Marlowe' (Hayward 1993: 289). In contrast with Godard's homage to the genre in *A bout de souffle* (*Breathless*, 1959), where Michel (Jean-Paul Belmondo) is presented ironically as modelling himself on Humphrey Bogart, in *Poussière d'ange* there is no apparent critical distance between the director and the protagonist.

Deceit – a thematic preoccupation of *film noir*, where it is often personified by female protagonists – is fundamental to the characterisation of Violetta. But she is no *femme fatale*, rather a child of fantasy who encourages Simon to 'tell his life differently'. Violetta pretends to have a job at the museum and to have spent her childhood in Africa; she even hires actors to play her parents when Simon comes to dinner. Her central fantasy, however, is of vengeance for her mother's death. While this desire leads her to send Florimont taped death threats about a heavenly judgement on the whore of Babylon, Simon's equally violent revenge fantasy is enacted in terms of images, not sounds: his voracious photographing of Martine and Igor when together inspires a desire to kill them both, a desire enacted in part by Gabriel as his proxy. The recurrent fantasy motif in *Poussière d'ange* even contaminates the solution of the mystery at the film's close: Simon's showdown with Florimont takes place in the same empty house that Violetta populated with her artificial family, amid Florimont's accusations that the detective's theory is just another fantasy. To this extent, Niermans appears to qualify the formulaic ease with which Simon traps his corrupt boss. The rather perfunctory nature of this *film noir* ending is also challenged by the action sequence which follows. The violence and the driving score of the scene in which Gabriel kills Igor's lawyer before dying in a burning car at a police roadblock is far from the moody atmospherics of the rest of the film, and closer to the gangster movie or to Luc Besson's spectacular *Nikita* (1990) than to *film noir*. The influence of the *cinéma du look* is also apparent as regards plot and *mise en scène*, with the cassette implicating a police chief and the setting of an abandoned warehouse (where Violetta and Gabriel meet) recalling Jean-Jacques Beineix's *Diva* (1980, see chapter 6). But there remains in *Poussière d'ange* a realistic portrayal of bleak Parisian locations, including a red-light district under the *boulevard périphérique*, which derives from a different tradition, that of the naturalistic *polar*.

The naturalistic *polar*

While the films of Henri-Georges Clouzot, like those of Claude Chabrol some years later, explored the underside of provincial communities, most *polars* in the 1950s tended to be set in an unspecified place and an approximate present, 'le contemporain vague' (Marshall 1992: 41). The *nouvelle vague* thrillers of the 1960s – notably Jean-Luc Godard's *Made in USA* (1966) – and the political *polars* of Costa-Gavras and Yves Boisset began to situate crime narratives in precise socio-political contexts, often as a critique of the French (or American) governments. It is to this tradition that the work of Alain Corneau and Bertrand Tavernier is related. Their careers have run in parallel – both made their first film in 1974 – and both are associated with the period drama (see chapter 7) as well as the *polar*. Their similarity of outlook extends to adapting the work of the same American crime novelist, Jim Thompson, and even to working on screen versions of the same novel, Thompson's *Pop. 1280* (Tavernier successfully, Corneau without result).

Thompson transposed: *Série noire* and *Coup de torchon*

Rediscovered by Hollywood in the nineties – witness Maggie Greenwald's *The Kill-Off* (1989), Stephen Frears's *The Grifters* (1990) and Roger Donaldson's remake of *The Getaway* (1994) – Jim Thompson's bleak and brutal crime novels were part of the post-war American fare offered up to French readers in Gallimard's *série noire* range. Thompson had worked in Hollywood on Stanley Kubrick's *The Killing* (1956) and *Paths of Glory* (1957), and his novel *The Getaway* had first been filmed by Sam Peckinpah in 1972, but he died alcoholic and ignored. His rehabilitation after his death was in part sparked by his reputation in France, and by two French adaptations: Alain Corneau's *Série noire* (1979) and Bertrand Tavernier's *Coup de torchon* (*Clean Slate*, 1981).

Corneau worked with Costa-Gavras in the sixties, and his first two thrillers – *Police python 357* (1976) and *La Menace* (1977) – starred Costa-Gavras regular, and icon of the political *polar*, Yves Montand. *Série noire*, an adaptation of Thompson's *A Hell of a Woman*, is not a political thriller, but Corneau does achieve a naturalistic portrayal of alienation and poverty by transposing the action from Kentucky to *la zone*, the suburban wasteland surrounding Paris. Franck Poupard (Patrick Dewaere) is a door-to-door salesman making very little money. While looking for a client called Tikides, he meets an old woman who offers him her young niece Mona (Marie Trintignant) as payment for a dressing-gown, an offer Franck refuses. Having found Tikides and recovered the debt, Franck is none the less thrown in the cells when his boss, Staplin (Bernard Blier), accuses him of stealing on the sly. Franck is bailed out by Mona with some of her aunt's hidden savings. Franck begins to dream of stealing the money and escaping with Mona, particularly since his wife Jeanne has walked out. Having persuaded Tikides to accompany him, Franck returns to the old

15   Marie Trintingant and Patrick Dewaere in *Série noire*

woman's house, kills her, and steals the money, shooting Tikides and framing him for the crime. When Jeanne reappears and discovers the stolen money, Franck kills her too. Staplin, suspecting that Franck is the murderer, blackmails him and takes the money. In the final scene Franck, clutching an empty suitcase, meets Mona: they are finally ready to run away together.

The setting of *Série noire* is bleak and wintry: vacant lots and blocks of flats, deserted except for the central characters. Much of the film is shot in shabby interiors or in Franck's car, itself a restricted space from which he cannot seem to escape. The sound-track adds to the sense of realism, comprising the rumble of thunder and traffic, and incessant pop music from the radios which are found in almost every scene. In the wretched world of *la zone*, pop songs offer a fantasy of escape which is at once cheerfully appealing and pathetically sad: when Mona strips for Franck in her dingy room, Boney M's 'Rivers of Babylon' blares from her radio. Music expresses above all Franck's futile hopes, as when he and Tikides achieve a drunken camaraderie while recalling their favourite songs. In the crucial scene of Tikides's murder, Franck pauses to remind him of the closing words of Gilbert Bécaud's 'Le jour où la pluie viendra' – 'Nous serons toi et moi les plus heureux du monde, les plus riches du monde' [You and I shall be the happiest, the richest men in the world] – before shooting him dead. The fantasy expressed in the lyric belongs to Franck and Mona, no longer to Tikides, and remains their guiding obsession at the end of the film. While the pop music, from Sacha Distel to Sheila B. Devotion, also acts – like the setting – to situate the action in a precise everyday

16　　　Marie Trintingant and Patrick Dewaere in *Série noire*

reality, there is one fantastical element in *Série noire* which qualifies the pervading naturalism: Georges Perec's script. Perec has Franck speak a mixture of French backslang (*le verlan*) and street slang, combined with Anglicisms and spoonerisms. As Corneau remarked: 'The challenge was to give an appearance of naturalism, but at all costs to avoid succumbing to it: we had to do something totally unrealistic.' Consequently, when Franck tries to express himself, he is at odds with reality, and in his mouth even the most banal language 'is turned around and used obliquely' (Corneau cited in Buss 1994: 122). Franck's monologues, uttered in despair or frenzy while imprisoned in his car, are his own attempt to talk himself away from *la zone*.

Bertrand Tavernier had used a specific socio-political context for his first film, *L'Horloger de Saint-Paul* (*The Watchmaker of Saint-Paul*, 1974), a thriller adapted from Georges Simenon and featuring an analysis of the generation formed by May 1968 (see chapter 2), coupled with a naturalistic portrayal of the city of Lyons. In *Coup de torchon* (*Clean Slate*, 1981), Tavernier again enlisted screenwriter Jean Aurenche and actor Philippe Noiret to interpret a crime novel, but this time the transposition was more radical. Jim Thompson's *Pop.1280* is set in a small community in the deep south of the United States. Tavernier switched the action not to mainland France, as Corneau had done in *Série noire*, but to French West Africa at the end of the 1930s. The corrupt and murderous colonials embody the casual brutality of the French Empire, doomed by the imminence of World War Two, while the film's central metaphor – an eclipse of the sun – is an ironic reversal of the colonial symbol, a torch lighting up the dark continent of Africa. The violent narrative concerns the experiences of the local police chief Lucien Cordier (Noiret), who turns from a lazy do-nothing to a cynical murderer. Lucien is in fact the only policeman in the village of Boussarka; he has never arrested anyone, and turns a blind eye to racism and violence. Regularly abused by the local pimps, Léonelli and Le Péron, Léon finally snaps and shoots both men, dumping the bodies in the river. From this point on, he acts as a self-appointed vigilante: having killed the wife-beater Marcaillou, he embarks on an affair with the dead man's widow, Rose (Isabelle Huppert). When Vendredi, a black servant, learns of Marcaillou's murder, Léon shoots him too. Léon manages to deflect enquiries about the murders from Le Péron's brother and from the local colonel, until the declaration of war between France and Germany distracts the attention of the entire community. With the colonial way of life thus threatened forever, Léon confesses the murders to the schoolteacher, Anne, declaring that he himself has been dead inside for along time.

Léon is in fact present in practically every scene of the film, and operates as a guide to the colonial setting as well as a personification of corrupt imperialism. His wanderings around Boussarka allow Tavernier to introduce the seedy milieu, from the stinking privies to the corpse-ridden river. Moreover, by using a handheld camera to shoot these sequences, Tavernier lends them a documentary authenticity. While the images in *Coup de torchon* situate the film geographically, the sound-track of thirties jazz situates it temporally. A third form of contextualisation is provided by the official discourse of colonialism against which the narrative works. This is most evident in two sequences in which the African villagers constitute an audience for an imperialist spectacle: the film show and the classroom scene. In the former, the villagers gather to watch *Alerte en Méditerranée*, a French naval adventure which has to be translated to the audience by a bilingual African. A celebration of French imperial power, this black-and-white film is challenged by the lurid events around it in Tavernier's violent, naturalistic version of the colonial experience. A similar contrast between colonial myth and brutal reality is achieved when Léon writes his confession to the murders on the school blackboard. Realising that none of her African pupils can understand the written French, Anne tells them it is the words of 'La Marseillaise'. She then declaims the national anthem, which champions the glorious struggle against tyranny, while the text, visible behind her, ironically reveals the murderous consequences of French imperialism.

The naturalistic *polar* tends to illustrate Raymond Chandler's assertion that the ideal crime story would have no revelatory ending, but would concentrate instead on a series of discoveries about the nature of the society in which a murder is committed. Thus Corneau's *Série noire* is open ended – Thompson's novel ended with Mona's accidental death and the narrator's suicide – while in *L'Horloger de Saint-Paul* the motives for the central murder are never explained. *Coup de torchon* is similarly more concerned with an investigation into a particular community than with a psychological explanation for a series of killings. This tendency to privilege social observation over narrative closure is again evident in two naturalistic accounts of police procedures, Maurice Pialat's *Police* (1985) and Tavernier's *L.627* (1992).

Docu-drama in *Police* and *L.627*

In the 1980s, a new element was added to the urban setting characteristic of the *polar*: 'What does get introduced into this landscape as a signifier of Frenchness is the drug underworld almost always associated with an Arab "community"' (Hayward 1993: 291). This is true of Swaim's *La Balance* (1982) as well as the less overtly racist portrayal of an Arab drugs ring in Pialat's *Police* (1985) and of African drug users in Tavernier's *L.627* (1992). Both films use exactly the same setting as *La Balance* – the streets of Belleville – but are shot in a resolutely naturalistic manner.

Maurice Pialat trained as a painter, and began making films in 1960. Much of his work, including *Passe ton Bac d'abord* (1979) and *Loulou* (1980), is strongly influenced by documentary cinema, rejecting the theatrical values of *mise en scène* for shaky, dull-toned photography shot in real locations. Pialat has said of this naturalist aesthetic that 'perhaps because of my early career as a painter, I refused for many years to try to make my films pictorially interesting' (Forbes 1992: 220), although this subsequently changed in *Sous le soleil de Satan* (*Under Satan's Sun*, 1987) and *Van Gogh* (1991, see chapter 7). *Police* is the last of Pialat's broadly naturalistic films: sound-track music is absent until the very end, there are no opening credits, the dialogue seems improvised, the camerawork is often handheld and the locations naturally lit. Mangin (Gérard Depardieu) is a detective investigating a Tunisian drugs ring in Belleville run by Simon Slimane and his brothers. Mangin arrests both Simon and his girlfriend Noria (Sophie Marceau), but thanks to the efforts of the lawyer Lambert (Richard Anconina), Noria is released. Although Noria now starts seeing Lambert, Mangin's best friend, the detective falls for her too. With the disruption of the drugs ring, Noria steals the gang's money and is only persuaded to give it back by Mangin, with whom she has begun an affair. Mangin returns the money, and Noria leaves him.

The supposedly realistic portrayal of police brutality, racism and chauvinism which typifies most of the film has attracted more critical attention than its relation to the thriller form. But clearly some elements in *Police* are generic, above all the relationship between Mangin and Noria. He, a widower, is the classic lone cop, while she is characterised misogynistically as a *femme fatale* who lies to get what she wants, seduces men, and breaks up the buddy relationship between Mangin and Lambert. The narrative is also analogous to the modern gangster film, particularly Martin Scorsese's *Mean Streets* (1973), in its thematic concern with redemption. Despite his betrayal of Lambert, Mangin ultimately returns the stolen money to the Slimane brothers (who were holding Lambert responsible), thus at once saving his friend and reaffirming his own position on the right side of the law. (The distinction between law and criminality is blurred throughout the film, with Mangin and Lambert accusing each other of 'crossing over to the other side'.) Mangin's action, and his acceptance of Noria's subsequent departure, is coded as an almost spiritual achievement by the burst of music – Górecki's Third Symphony – as he stands alone at the end of the film.

The title of Bertrand Tavernier's *L.627* refers to the legislation against dealing in narcotics. The film was co-written by Michel Alexandre, an investigating officer who had worked in a Parisian drugs squad for thirteen years. Alexandre is also the model for the protagonist, Lulu (Didier Bezace), a detective transferred to an underfunded and overworked drugs squad. What little plot there is concerns Lulu's relationship with Cécile, a prostitute and informer who is HIV positive, and his unfulfilled ambition to escape from Paris for a pastoral life in the Auvergne. But in the main the film is a docu-drama about police methods, and about attitudes to race, ranging from the relatively enlightened (Lulu) to the bigoted (Dodo). Although the action includes chases and arrests, there is also a degree of monotony and repetition, and the generic form of the crime narrative – the solving of a mystery – is absent: 'I needed a structure that did not seem "constructed", which would remain "accidental", raw' (Tavernier 1993: 253). Tavernier's aim was to integrate 'fictional elements and research materials, without recourse to a plot [. . .]. This approach gave rise to a whole series of reflections and questions about the relation between fiction and documentary, truth and realism' (Tavernier 1993: 253). Above all the film was to 'refuse all stylistic effects inherent in the thriller genre' and to subvert the audience's formal and ideological references, 'American references in particular: promotion of individualism, rejection of collective spirit, predominance of plot' (Tavernier 1993: 253, 254). To this end, Tavernier presents the police as a team working together; Lulu is not the traditional lone cop of *film noir* or of *polars* such as *Police*. A documentary atmosphere is achieved by the casting of little-known actors and the use of hand-held cameras to film in sometimes dangerous Parisian locations. The lighting is natural, and often gloomy. Unlike *Police*, however, *L.627* does feature a substantial amount of sound-track music, with Philippe Sarde's score mixing western and African instruments.

Situating *L.627* in the tradition of the political *polar*, Tavernier has claimed that the film was an attempt to define the state of French society (Sineux and Vachaud 1995: 25). The hostile reception it met with from the police authorities confirmed him in this belief. In September 1992 Interior Minister Paul Quilès ordered that Tavernier's co-writer Michel Alexandre be investigated, declared that the film was an 'unjust and false caricature' of policing, and cancelled a public discussion due to be held after a screening in Lille (Tavernier 1993: 372, 376). More than two years later, Quilès's successor as Minister of the Interior, Charles Pasqua, demanded that all material relating to *L.627* be removed from an exhibition about films on police work (Sineux and Vachaud 1995: 26). All of which, combined with the increased ferocity of police operations in the area where the film was shot, led Tavernier to conclude that his didacticism was lost on the authorities: 'The boys at the Ministry have become like Dodo [the racist detective] in the film. And I had hoped they might follow the example of Lulu' (Tavernier 1993: 378).

Antisocial elements: *La Cérémonie* and *Regarde la mer*

France in the mid-nineties felt to many like a society on the verge of collapse. The phrase *la fracture sociale* was coined to describe this sense of fragmentation, and the gulf between rich and poor. As class-based identities and a hierarchical or 'vertical' society began to disintegrate, it became crucial to assert 'horizontal' identities associated with culture, religion and ethnicity. The new post-industrial, post-Marxist France of the nineties was therefore 'characterized by the "dualization of society": "you are either *in* or *out*"' (Silverman 1999: 49, citing Michel Wievorka). In terms of cinema, the result was a focus on spatial exclusion as a metaphor for social exclusion, as in Claire Denis's *J'ai pas sommeil* (1993, see chapter 4) or Mathieu Kassovitz's *La Haine* (1995, see chapter 9), both of which show excluded individuals making abortive and dangerous journeys into the city of Paris. But some film-makers, almost defiantly, continued to portray vertical rather than horizontal identities, ignoring matters of ethnicity or immigration to concentrate on class struggle. This is most explicitly the case in *La Cérémonie* (*Judgement in Stone*, 1995), described by its director Claude Chabrol as 'the last Marxist film' (Guérin and Taboulay 1997: 68). Where *La Haine* predicts social explosion, *La Cérémonie* predicts social implosion, a society collapsing in on itself rather than spiraling into mass confrontations (see Berthomieu et al 1995: 9). But for all that, the violence in *La Cérémonie* is shocking and decisive, as a servant and her friend execute a bourgeois family in cold blood. The theme of class conflict ending in a bloody dénouement was echoed two years later in a less well-known but equally chilling thriller, François Ozon's mid-length film *Regarde la mer* (*See the Sea*, 1997).

In both *La Cérémonie* and *Regarde la mer* intruders from a lower social class enter the apparently idyllic home of a bourgeois family. The intruders proceed to gradually infiltrate, question, unsettle, desta-bilize and eventually terrorize their victims, who remain 'blameless' except insofar as they are representative of a complacent bourgeoisie which denies or exploits its social inferiors. In *La Cérémonie* the power relations are explicit since they are based on employment and servi-tude: Sophie (Sandrine Bonnaire) works as a maid for the Lelièvre family, and is taught how to literally *serve* them. She is also restricted to certain parts of the house such as the kitchen and the back stairs. When she turns against her masters, her revolt is represented spatially as an incursion upwards into forbidden parts of the house: the main stairs, the master bedroom, a gallery overlooking the living room.

Power here is vertical, and it is only by climbing the stairs and looking down on her employers that Sophie can topple them. If Chabrol is overtly Marxist, deeming that the Lelièvres have to die because of their class (see Guérin and Jousse 1995: 28), Ozon veers more towards the grotesque and the abject, the themes of the horror film. In *Regarde la mer* the threat of lower-class violence is represented less via a spatial continuum (rising from low to high) than via an assault on physical propriety and on the bourgeois body. It is also, in common with other films by Ozon, a categorical rejection of traditional gender roles (see chapter 3). The female camper in *Regarde la mer*, asked by the bourgeois mother if she is not vulnerable to (male) assault when travelling alone, declares revealingly, 'C'est plutôt moi qui agresse' [It's me that does the assualting]. Like Mona in Agnès Varda's *Sans toit ni loi* (1985, see chapter 4), she challenges conventional definitions of femininity through her unkempt appearance and taciturn manner. In the absence of male authority – the husband/father is working away from home – the figure of the intruder seems initially to be positive and liberating, as she prompts the mother towards an awareness of her own loneliness and sexual hunger. But the threat to the bourgeois family is also unnervingly hinted at, in the camper's taciturn and impassive behaviour, her unpredictable comings and goings, her malicious tricks (making the mother eat shit, literally), and finally the revelation that her own baby is dead. (This last is an echo of *La Cérémonie*, where Sophie's friend is suspected of killing her child.) The threat of violence, building throughout the film, explodes in the shocking colours of the final sequence, the bright red of the tent where the mother's body is discovered and the dazzling blue sea of the final shot. The ending of *Regarde la mer* – in which the camper assumes the identity of her victim, and also steals her baby – recalls the final scene of Chabrol's *Les Biches* (*The Does*, 1967) where one female character kills and then 'becomes' another (see Austin 1999: 44–9). In both *Les Biches* and *La Cérémonie* Chabrol renders murders political by presenting them as the attack by the lower classes against the bourgeoisie. He has even called the violence in *Les Biches* 'a revolution: the replacement of one class by another' (Yakir 1979: 9). In *Regarde la mer* the violence is antisocial but it is also more intimate, more corporeal. Chabrol's characteristic restraint when portraying the body is replaced by Ozon's macabre and sadistic fascination with the abject (shit, sex, the decaying corpse). If French society is disintegrating in the nineties thriller, then Ozon lets us smell the rot.

In whose hands?: identity in *De battre mon cœur s'est arrêté*

Having started his career writing films in the eighties – among them *Poussière d'ange* (see above) – Jacques Audiard has built a very strong reputation as a director of thrillers, most notably with *Sur mes lèvres* (*Read My Lips*, 2001) and *De battre mon cœur s'est arrêté* (*The Beat That My Heart Skipped*, 2005). The former combines the resentments of the office workplace, the logistics of hearing impairment, the skills of lip-reading, and an immersion into the world of organized crime. The latter is equally striking in bringing together apparently unrelated worlds: those of the concert pianist and the small-time gangster. And just as the thriller plot of *Sur mes lèvres* is ultimately subordinated to the emotional crux of the film – Audiard has said the key question is will the two leads ever kiss? – so in *De battre...*, the thriller plot is subordinated to the hopes and tensions arising from a piano audition. Both films therefore reveal that the thriller narrative, far from being a reductive and closed space, is open to infiltration by other concerns, be they romantic, familial, cultural or social.

De battre... swept the board at the 2006 César awards, except in the case of Romain Duris, who failed to secure best actor. Duris's performance is however absolutely central to the film, which is shot entirely from the perspective of his character, Tom, who is following in his father's violent footsteps through the black economy of the Parisian housing market. A chance meeting drives him to revive his ambition to become a classical pianist, a dream shared by his mother before her death. As played by Duris, Tom is a man burning with energy, rage and a tenuous hope for a new life. This edgy performance, like Tom's jacket, the nocturnal city scenes and even the poster for the film, recalls the iconic presence of Robert de Niro in *Taxi Driver* (Scorsese, 1976). The last image of *De battre...*'s pre-credit sequence, which shows a young girl glancing suddenly at something out of shot, also mimics the disturbing final image of *Taxi Driver*. Audiard's film is in fact a remake of an American thriller of the same period, *Fingers* (Toback, 1978). In each case the narrative centres on a young man caught between two worlds which are coded as masculine and feminine, not just through their traditional cultural status (violent crime as against musical creativity) but because one is represented by his father and one by his mother. He is thus wrestling with the legacy of his parents and with his own sense of identity. In *Fingers* the focus of this struggle is male sexuality, hence the gynecological sequences and the repeated anxieties about impotence. Audiard however removes most of these psychosexual elements and replaces them with a much more persuasive social milieu in which Tom's drama is played out. This involves not just the black economy, its perpetrators and victims, but also the world of the conservatoire and the concert hall. In both domains, without overstatement or dogma, Audiard makes it clear that immigration is central. Whether they are squatters being driven out by Tom and his colleague Sami, or music students whose expertise offers Tom a chance of self-actualisation, immigrants are an integral part of the identity of France presented in the film. One could equate Tom's ambivalent position with that of French society confronted by immigration: violent antipathy on one hand and yet also need and even gratitude on the other. The key character in this regard is Miao Lin (Linh Dan Pham), Tom's Vietnamese piano teacher, a role added to the original by Audiard. As a very recent arrival to Paris, Miao Lin learns to speak French with Tom's help while she prepares him for his audition, and by the end of the film she has integrated successfully into French society and the music industry, embarking on concert tours and recording contracts with Tom as her manager and partner.

The crux of the film is personal rather than national identity, however. This is why Tom appears in every scene: *De battre...* is the story of his own passage from childhood to adulthood (even though he is nearly thirty). Audiard has stated that the film's subject is the moment when the child has to begin looking after the parent, and this much is made clear in the raw pre-credit sequence in which Sami tells the story of his father's demise and death. This introductory scene predicts the shape of Tom's own narrative and it is onto this dynamic that the competing claims of crime and music are grafted. Beneath the semantics of the *film noir* (nocturnal sequences, urban setting, a troubled anti-hero) and of the sports film (training sequences, shots of Tom's naked torso as he prepares for his shot at glory), *De battre...* belongs, through its syntax, to the fairy-tale. It is essentially a story about how to find one's adult identity by moving beyond parental control. Bruno Bettelheim could easily be describing the film when he writes of fairy-tales, 'If we want to function well, we have to integrate the discordant tendencies which are inherent in our being. Isolating these tendencies and projecting them into separate figures [...] is one way fairy tales help us visualize and thus better grasp what goes on within us' (Bettelheim 1991: 97). The film's mobilizing of such universal concerns may in part explain its success with critics and audiences both in France and abroad.

The child's dilemma, caught between parents while seeking individuation, is crystallized in the two family photos that show Tom as a boy, positioned between his parents. This position still obtains at the start of the film, with Tom caught between a sense of loyalty to his corrupt father and a sense of vocation derived from his dead mother. The world of classical music provides Tom with a potential exit from criminality, and offers him idealized surrogate parents: the impresario Fox and the teacher Miao Lin. But it is above all Tom's dead mother who is figured as the source of his musical creativity. The identification of the child with the mother through music has been theorized by Julia Kristeva as the *chora*, a pre-linguistic and pre-Oedipal union which she describes as 'The loving discourse of the pregnant mother with the fruit, barely distinct from her, that she shelters in her womb [...] a loving discourse that is only gesture and voice – sound, cry, music' (Kristeva 1987: 81, 84). The connection between Tom and his mother is articulated by music, her legacy to him, and also by the 'loving discourse that is only gesture and voice'. This is represented in the film by two recordings: the gesture of the disembodied, ghostly hands playing the piano on the videotape and the voice of his mother caught on the audiotape. *De battre...* ends, however, with a brutal reassertion of machismo and of the thriller plot, which explodes ironically enough at the concert hall. At this point in the narrative Tom is playing a supporting role to Miao Lin, now a star pianist (the role he himself coveted). In a reversal of archetypal gender conventions, he now functions as her appendage and supporter, helping her achieve a successful career. Tom's rather subservient, feminised identity is however torn aside by the macho violence of the film's ending. Coming across Minskov – the man responsible for his father's murder – in the toilets under the concert hall, Tom attacks him in a combat that is both revenge for his father and a form of self-definition. He has to see if he is still a man, for 'Masculinity has nothing to prove yet somehow needs constantly to prove itself' (O'Shaugnessy 1994: 224). That Tom's sexual identity is at stake here is clear from the fact that he wins the fight by grabbing hold of his opponent's genitals. Although – in contrast to the ending of *Fingers* – Tom cannot manage to kill Minskov, he has in some way proven his point. His masculinity is reasserted, but nonetheless his identity remains unstable. This is signalled after the fight by Tom's sobbing and by repeated close-ups on his hands: battered and bloody, they bespeak macho violence and yet their involuntary twitching both parodies and repeats the creative energy of his own musicianship (throughout the film we have seen Tom repeatedly mime playing the pieces of music he is listening to). These close-ups also recall the moment when, discovering his father's corpse, Tom pushes his trembling hand into his mouth to stop himself from gagging. Finally, the bloody hands begin to mime once more the playing of a piano, in time to Miao Lin's performance. This closing image encapsulates the uneasy balance that Tom has achieved, incorporating the legacy of both his parents while occupying a tenuous position beyond them. If in the traditional fairy-tale 'The child not only survives the parents but surpasses them' (Bettelheim 1991: 99), this is in a sense true of *De battre...* But Tom's identity here seems as brittle and subject to collapse as his abortive audition performance. There is no fairy-tale ending.

References

Austin, G. (1999), *Claude Chabrol*, Manchester, Manchester University Press.

Berthomieu, P., Jeancolas, J-P., and Vassé, C. (1995), Entretien avec Claude Chabrol, *Positif*, 416, 8–14.

Bettelheim, B. (1991), *The Uses of Enchantment: The Meaning and Importance of Fairy Tales*, London, Penguin.

Buss, R. (1994), *French Film Noir*, London, Marion Boyars.

Forbes, J. (1992), *The Cinema in France After the New Wave*, London, BFI/Macmillan.

Guérin, M-A., and Jousse, T. (1995), Entretien avec Claude Chabrol, Paris, *Cahiers du cinema*, 494, 27–32.

Guérin, M-A., and Taboulay, C. (1997), La connivence: Entretien avec Isabelle Huppert, *Cahiers du cinéma*: Spécial Claude Chabrol, 66–71.

Hayward, S. (1993), *French National Cinema*, London and New York, Routledge.

Kristeva, J. (1987), *Tales of Love*, translated by L. S. Rodiez, New York, Columbia University Press.

Marshall, B. (1992), National identity and the *film policier*: the moment of 1981, Chalfont St Giles, Bucks, *French Cultural Studies*, 3:1:7, 31–42.

O'Shaugnessy, M. (1994), Jean-Paul Belmondo: masculinity, violence and the outsider, in R. Gunther and J. Windebank (eds), *Violence and Conflict in Modern French Culture*, Sheffield, Sheffield Academic Press, 215–38.

Prédal, R. (1991), *Le Cinéma français depuis 1945*, Paris, Nathan.

Rohmer, E. and Chabrol, C. (1992), *Hitchcock: the First Forty-Four Films*, Oxford, Roundhouse.

Schrader, P. (1971), Notes on *Film Noir*, in K. Jackson (ed.), *Schrader on Schrader and Other Writings*, London, Faber and Faber, 80–94.

Shadoian, J. (1977), *Dreams and Dead-Ends*, Cambridge, MA, MIT Press.

Silverman, M. (1999), *Facing Postmodernity: Contemporary French Thought on Culture and Society*, London, Routledge.

Sineux, M., and Vachaud, L. (1995), Entretien avec Bertrand Tavernier: 'Comment montrer la violence sans en devenir complice?', Paris, *Positif*, 409, 25–30.

Taboulay, C. (1994), L'Enfer me ment, Paris, *Cahiers du cinéma*, 476, 34–7.

Tavernier, B. (1993), I wake up, dreaming, London, *Projections*, 2, 252–378.

Yakir, D. (1979), The magical mystery world of Claude Chabrol: an interview, *Film Quarterly* (spring), 2–14.

Fantasy film

6

Fantasy cinema in France: from long neglect to new blood

The privileging of director over genre in French film criticism – most explicitly in the *politique des auteurs* (see chapter 1) – has mitigated against the habitually formulaic genres that make up fantasy film: horror, fairy-tale and science fiction. Moreover, despite the pioneering work of Georges Méliès, and later of surrealist cinema, the fantastic has been perceived as a principally Anglo-Saxon form, epitomised by German expressionism, Hollywood melodrama and Hammer horror. As Claude Chabrol observed in 1977, the year he made his solitary and long neglected fantasy film *Alice ou la dernière fugue*, 'there is no real tradition of fantasy cinema in France' (Overbey 1977: 81). French film-makers associated with the fantastic – notably Jean Cocteau and Georges Franju – were perceived as mavericks. Cocteau in particular, like the eighties perpetrators of the *cinéma du look*, faced constant attacks from critics schooled in psychological realism and narrative cinema, but was appreciated by an enthusiastic youth audience. It is ironic that at the end of his own career Cocteau should write of Franju's horror movie *Les Yeux sans visage* (1959) that it had been 'a long time since we last experienced the dark poetry and the hypnotic effect of the macabre' (Cocteau 1991: 121), for it was at this point that the French fantasy film began to fade from sight, to be represented only intermittently over the next two decades by New Wave interest in science fiction and the musical (see chapter 1), by Walerian Borowczyk's erotic fantasies and by Jean Rollin's low-budget vampire films. Yet French companies continued to finance co-productions, such as the Franco-Italian Jules Verne adaptations of the 1960s, while the French fantasy film lay dormant. This is partly because American imports have always been commercially successful, and partly because French fantasy has had a particular national outlet: the *bande dessinée*. The rise of BD – which comprises comic strips and cartoon books – as a repository of the fantastical for an adult audience began in 1959 with the launch of *Pilote* magazine (see Starkey 1990: 95), and paralleled the decline of fantasy in the French cinema during the sixties and seventies. Even the most celebrated live-action film of a French BD fantasy, *Barbarella* (1967), although a Franco-Italian production, was made in English with a Hollywood star, Jane Fonda, in the lead. Thus BD might be said to stand in place of a French fantasy cinema, rather than alongside it.

This state of affairs has recently changed, however. Since around 2000, a new generation of fantasy film-makers has sprung up in France. Their influences include the Italian horror films of Dario Argento but also the pages of French BD. The result has been a number of domestic BD adaptations, including the fantasy Western *Blueberry* (*Renegade*, Kounen, 2004). The horror film has also prospered in France of late, with the massively successful *Le Pacte des loups* (*Brotherhood of the Wolf*, Gans, 2001) followed by *Maléfique* (Valette, 2002), *Brocéliande* (Headline, 2002) and *Saint Ange* (Laugier, 2004). Elements of 'gore' have also been found – and welcomed by horror fans – in more *auteurist* films like *Seul contre tous* (*I Stand Alone*, Noé, 1998), *Trouble Every Day* (Denis, 2001), and *Dans ma peau* (*In My Skin*, de Van, 2002). As a result fan sites on the internet have begun to ask whether French horror films might finally be successful, after decades of marginalisation and indifference within the film industry. Clear reasons for the revival of French horror and fantasy are harder to find. One reason might be the economic and social malaise that France has been experiencing since the nineties. Writing on Hollywood, Roger Dadoun pointed out that the horror film has 'deep affinities with [...] economic crisis' and that 'the great period of the horror film in the United States comes immediately after the crash of 1929' (Dadoun 1989: 46). In terms of current cinema practices, the special effects allowed by digital technology and computer generated imagery (CGI) permit a convincingly graphic iconography of the fantastic, comparable to the nineteenth-century association between ghosts and photography. One might also speak of horror and fantasy as engaging fully with the body, and hence as conforming to French cinema's current interest in the corporeal. This is most explicit in the graphic representation of the sexual body in the films of Gaspar Noé and Catherine Breillat amongst others (see chapter 3). And finally there is the gradual privileging of fantasy over the traditional values of social and psychological realism, a trend that began in the eighties with the *cinéma du look* and has continued with the extremely popular blockbusters of directors like Luc Besson, Jean-Pierre Jeunet and Christophe Gans.

The *cinéma du look*: popularity and critical reception

The *cinéma du look* was a style of film-making which came to the fore in the 1980s and remains influential in French film. It is characterised not by any collective ideology but rather by an interest in fantasy rather than realism, a technical mastery of the medium, an intertextual tendency to cite from other films, and a spectacular visual style (*le look*). Beginning with Jean-Jacques Beineix's *Diva* (1980), the *cinéma du look* has had numerous popular successes, but has consistently been taken to task by the critical establishment in France, and even more so in Britain. The three main directors grouped together in this 'New New Wave' are Beineix, Luc Besson and Léos Carax. They have been bracketed as a movement because of a perceived similarity of visual style and, to a lesser extent, of subject matter (young lovers in urban or alienating surroundings). In France, populist cinema magazines like *Première* championed Beineix and Besson, who were notably more successful at the box office than Carax in the eighties and early nineties. The more intellectual and ideological *Cahiers du cinéma* tended to mount virulent attacks on Beineix and Besson while setting Carax apart as a film-maker closer to Jean-Luc Godard than to the *cinéma du look*. This is no surprise, since Carax – like Godard – once wrote for *Cahiers*. It is largely the *Cahiers* line that has been dominant in critiques of the *cinéma du look*: namely that it is superficial, and shows a complete absence of political and social concerns. Other common objections include attacks on the lack of plot and of psychological realism (the basis for the canon of 'great' French cinema from the thirties to the seventies). Comparisons to 'inferior' cultural forms like television, music video, advertising and the comic strip also abound. But it is the absence of ideology which is the central plank of attacks on Beineix, Besson and even Carax – an absence which is seen to stem from the fading of Marxism in France (and indeed Europe), the electoral triumph of the Socialists in May 1981, and the growth of centrist consensus politics in the decade that followed. Equating 'authentic cinema' with ideology, critics have tended to neglect the aesthetic importance of the *cinéma du look*. An important exception is Raphaël Bassan's essay, 'Trois néo-baroques français', which appeared in *La Revue du cinéma* in 1989. Bassan welcomed the *cinéma du look* as a break with the 'chronic naturalism' of French cinema, and valued its synthesis of 'high' and 'low' art as well as its engagement with the problems of alienated protagonists who are outside any cosy familial structures (see Bassan 1989).

Diva: 'the first French postmodernist film'

The eldest of the practitioners of the *cinéma du look*, Jean-Jacques Beineix worked as assistant to Claude Zidi, Claude Berri and René Clément in the 1970s. He also enjoyed a spell in advertising in the mid-eighties, his defence of which provides a fine summation of the debate surrounding the *cinéma du look*. Because it 'kidnapped colour', 'dispensed with stories' and 'captured youth', advertising ran counter to France's 'ageing' realistic, narrative cinema, while any film which privileged colour over narrative was attacked by the critics as being not cinema but advertising (Russell 1989: 45–6). Beineix made his film début, aged thirty-four, in 1980 with *Diva*. The 7.5 million franc

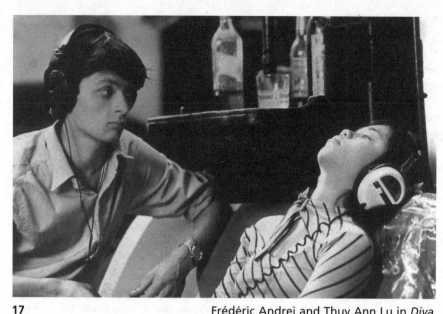

Frédéric Andrei and Thuy Ann Lu in *Diva*

budget was spent on producing the best possible image and sound rather than on stars, and gave the film highly visible production values. Initially distributed in only a few cinemas, and met by an ambivalent press reaction, *Diva* gradually became a cult hit, and in 1982 was a surprise winner of four Césars: for sound, music, photography and best first film. It was subsequently redistributed and became a landmark in eighties cinema. The *cinéma du look* had arrived.

The film's plot comes from a novel by Delacorta, and is notable only for the dual intrigue which allows Beineix to oscillate between the realms of obsessive love and urban thriller. Jules, a young postman (Frédéric Andrei), becomes involved in two narratives concerning tapes: he has made an invaluable bootleg of the opera singer Cynthia Hawkins (Wilhelminia Wiggins Fernandez) in concert, and has also come into possession of a message from a prostitute, Nadia, which incriminates police inspector Saporta in a vice ring. Pursued across Paris by villains in search of each of the cassettes, Jules is befriended by Alba (Thuy Ann Lu) and Gorodish (Richard Bohringer), thanks to whom Saporta is eventually killed. Finally, Jules returns the concert bootleg to Cynthia at the Opéra and is reconciled with her as they listen to the tape. The film thus has two plots from two different genres: the culturally 'low' thriller plot (Nadia's tape) meets the culturally 'high' opera film (Cynthia's tape). In between the two lies the romance, and Jules's infatuation with Cynthia, played out in the nocturnal Parisian streets. The cross-cultural address of the film is evident simply from the contrast between the classical sound-track (Wagner, Catalani, Satie) and an image track that many have compared to television advertising. Beineix's use of blue to create a calming mood (Gorodish's clothes and apartment) prefigures Besson's *Le Grand Bleu* (*The*

Big Blue, 1987), while stylised interiors feature throughout the film: Jules's flat, Gorodish's apartment, the lighthouse, the abandoned warehouse. *Diva* also suggests the importance that the *métro* was to assume as a key setting for the *cinéma du look* – in *Subway* (Besson, 1985), *Mauvais sang* (Carax, 1986), and *Les Amants du Pont-Neuf* (Carax, 1991). The importance of set design in the film, and in the *cinéma du look* in general, recalls the poetic realism of the thirties and forties (see chapter 1). On the other hand, the cartoon-strip villains who are comic as much as menacing derive from *la nouvelle vague*, especially François Truffaut's *Tirez sur le pianiste* (*Shoot the Pianist*, 1960). This juxtaposition of contradictory cinematic schools is characteristic not just of Beineix but also of Carax and Besson, who again fall between the influence of *la nouvelle vague* (mixing of genres and of high/low culture, symbolic use of colour, intertextuality) and that of forties production values (increasingly large budgets, sumptuous sets, studio rather than real locations, attention to *mise en scène*).

Press reaction to *Diva* was divided, with attention centring on its undoubted aesthetic appeal. Comparisons were drawn with Magritte and surrealism, as well as with comic strips. Ten years after the film's release, future fantasy director Christophe Gans offered a persuasive reading of its relation to advertising imagery and consumer society. Noting that Beineix achieves the advertising ideal of combining 'chic' culture with a young image, Gans found that the film as a whole replaced unique objects with manufactured reproductions: hence Cynthia's reluctant agreement to submit her voice to disc, and Gorodish's blowing up of his vintage Citroën only to produce an exact replica (Gans 1991: 3–4). Similarly, Fredric Jameson concluded that the fetish for technological reproduction in *Diva* is integrated successfully into the plot – in the form of Cynthia's attitude to recording and Nadia's recorded testimony – and is therefore not merely a superficial or self-conscious gloss (Jameson 1990: 62). Thus although the style of *Diva*, and in particular the knowing mixture of disparate cultural references, make it 'the first French postmodernist film' (Jameson 1990: 55), this quality is integrated into the narrative drive rather than detracting from it.

Les Amants du Pont-Neuf: neo-realism meets artifice

By some years the youngest film-maker of the *cinéma du look*, Léos Carax – real name Alex Dupont – has tended to be singled out for praise by a press generally antagonistic towards Besson and Beineix. Having studied cinema at Paris III university, Carax wrote a number of articles for *Cahiers du cinéma* in 1979–80 before releasing a short – *Strangulation Blues* – the same year, thus repeating the career pattern of the *nouvelle vague* critics-turned-directors (see chapter 1). This parallel also extends to his infatuation with silent cinema, which – like Godard, Rohmer and Truffaut before him – he first encountered at the Cinémathèque française. What distinguishes Carax from his peers is the eclectic and sometimes disruptive nature of his cinematic references and the autobiographical thread in his work. The latter tendency is enhanced by the presence of an alter ego called Alex – played by Denis Lavant – as the male protagonist in *Boy Meets Girl* (1984), *Mauvais sang* (*The Night is Young*, 1986) and *Les Amants du Pont-Neuf* (1991).

Originally a tight personal project like its two predecessors, *Les Amants du Pont-Neuf* mutated into the most expensive film (at that time) in French cinema history, taking three years to complete. Part way through, the crew had to cease shooting on the Pont-Neuf in Paris and a replica bridge and surrounding sets had to be built in the south of France. This change of location in fact simply enhances the interplay between realism and artifice which runs throughout the film. Carax integrates spectacular fantasy with a portrayal of the harsh realities experienced by the Parisian homeless, achieving an intermittent documentary quality far removed from the usual concerns of the *cinéma du look*.

The narrative centres on the romance between Alex (Denis Lavant) and Michèle (Juliette Binoche), she a painter who is slowly going blind, he a down-and-out who lives on the bridge. The two first meet in the brown-toned neo-realist section which opens the film, Michèle witnessing Alex being run over, and sketching what she supposes to be a dead man. The beatific close-ups of Binoche in *Mauvais sang* are here replaced by images of Lavant's battered and filthy face. Subsequently, we follow Alex to a shelter in Nanterre where he and a group of homeless people are filmed with a handheld camera and grainy film stock in a strikingly raw sequence. This is Paris by night as a bleak reality rather than as the throw-away spectacle provided by Beineix's *Diva* (1980) or Eric Rochant's *Un monde sans pitié* (*A World Without Pity*, 1989). And yet Carax's film also features a nocturnal Parisian fantasy so exaggerated as to at once parody and celebrate the most spectacular offerings of the *cinéma du look*, with Michèle and Alex water-skiing on the Seine as a waltz plays, fountains gush and fireworks explode. These two sequences – the neo-realist and the fantastical – illustrate the breadth of Carax's achievement in *Les Amants du Pont-Neuf*. That they can successfully co-exist is due to a consistent social concern with the dual function of Paris, the site of public spectacle and also of personal suffering. If the bicentennial celebrations are the embodiment of the one, Alex and Michèle's story exemplifies the other. Hence the juxtaposition of Alex's dangerous yet exhilarating fire-breathing with the tricolour vapour trails of the jets passing overhead, or the cross-cutting between parading soldiers and Michèle's flight after she has shot Julien. In this context, the water-skiing sequence is both an ironic exaggeration of the bicentennial fireworks (and of the *cinéma du look's* reliance on the spectacular) and a desperate escape fantasy on the part of the protagonists, who have already escaped Paris once for the lyrical interlude on the coast.

In terms of genre, the film moves between the poles of neo-realism and fantasy, encompassing the exaggerated perspectives of

18   Denis Lavant in *Les Amants du Pont-Neuf*

expressionism – the shot of Michèle and Alex lying drunk next to enormous wine bottles and fag ends – the photogenic imagery and cultural mix of the *cinéma du look* – the coast at sunset, a sound-track running from Public Enemy to Shostakovich – and the studio-bound lyricism of poetic realist film. Even the bicentenary imagery is in a sense intertextual, deriving from Godard's use of Eisenhower's visit to Paris as the backdrop for *A bout de souffle* (*Breathless*, 1959). Given the sustained nature of this cinephilia – including a borrowing from Bresson's *Pickpocket* (1959) for the prison sequence and an allusion to Truffaut's *Les 400 Coups* (*The 400 Blows*, 1959) in Alex's first sight of the sea – it is no surprise when Carax's protagonists themselves escape into cinema, namely into a scene from Jean Vigo's *L'Atalante* (1934), by jumping into the Seine and being rescued by a barge heading for Le Havre. As Keith Reader has noted, 'It is almost as though one filmic intertext of escape alone were not enough to free Alex from the attachment that is clearly destroying him' (Reader 1993: 414). And yet it is ultimately the romantic narrative, rather than the intertextuality, which carries the film. In terms of the elemental symbolism which runs throughout *Les Amants du Pont-Neuf*, the couple's escape from Paris by river is only the last example of how their romance depends on the agency of water. Where the Seine has already carried away all threats to that romance (in the form of Michèle's diary, the money that could restore her sight, and even the old tramp Hans), now it carries away the lovers themselves.

Subway: pastiche, celebration, pessimism

Luc Besson is the *look* filmmaker who has received the most sustained ridicule from the critics while proving a consistent hit with the public.

19   Christophe Lambert in *Subway*

His recent projects have seen him set up a global production company, Europacorp, and oversee popular blockbusters such as the *Taxi* series (see chapter 8). His days as a director may be numbered (he has said he will only shoot ten films) but his influence is such that the press in France speak of Besson as a 'planet' within the film industry.

At the age of twenty-five Besson directed *Le Dernier Combat* (1983), a black-and-white, low-budget post-nuclear piece short on dialogue but strong on atmosphere. The film won prizes at the Avoriaz festival for science fiction and fantasy film, but more significantly it opened Besson to the accusations of cinematic autism that were to dog his later work, *Le Grand Bleu* especially. On its release in 1985, *Subway* was attacked in *Positif* for its meagre scenario and lack of characterisation. Described as a three-minute 'clip' (music video) over-extended to feature film length, it was compared unfavourably to Besson's television advert for Dim tights (see Tobin 1985). Certainly, the plotting in *Subway* is both derivative and perfunctory: Fred (Christophe Lambert) steals some documents from a powerful crook whose wife, Helena (Isabelle Adjani), eventually finds him hiding in the depths of the Paris *métro*. Their mutual attraction is doomed by the closing-in of both the police and the crook's men, one of whom ultimately kills Fred. But setting has more importance here than plot, and Besson's excellent choice of milieu structures the claustrophobic narrative. Much of the film involves Fred discovering the service tunnels behind the *métro*, and then exploiting them to keep one step ahead of his pursuers. As with Beineix's *La Lune dans le caniveau* (*The Moon in the Gutter*, 1983), the sets recall poetic realism: *Subway's* set designer was in fact Alexandre Trauner, who had designed the *métro* station set for Marcel Carné's *Les Portes de la nuit* (*Gates of the Night*, 1946, see chapter 1). This underground environment is populated by a gallery of minor characters, drop-outs from Parisian society. In a rather lame sub-plot, Fred persuades some of them to form a rock band with himself as manager. This does allow Fred/Besson to stage a finale in which middle-aged 'high' culture – a Brahms recital – is replaced by the pop culture of the Anglophone rock band, whose audience of the young, marginal and trendy apparently mirrors Besson's own target audience.

The subplot concerning the rock band also overtly, one might say defiantly, aligns *Subway* with music video. Critics have tended to see both music video and the *cinéma du look* as postmodern, and hence as characterised by pastiche, that is, by uncritical imitation, what Fredric Jameson has called 'blank parody' (Jameson 1990). But this pessimistic diagnosis ignores 'the extent to which the phenomenon [of pastiche] is also one of *celebration*' (Goodwin 1987: 47). Where Goodwin writes 'music video' one can read the *cinéma du look* as a whole: 'Much music video "pastiche" is actually a celebration of popular culture that has nothing at all to do with parody' (Goodwin 1987: 47). By playing to the cine-literate nature of its target audience, *Subway* pays homage to previous films and generic models without wishing to launch any critique of them. The opening car chase initially places *Subway* within the thriller genre, but when the cars pass under the elevated *métro* line it pays specific homage to the celebrated chase scene in William Friedkin's Oscar-winning *The French Connection* (1971). There is a brief quotation from George Lucas's *Star Wars* (1977) when Fred, lost in the bowels of the *métro*, picks up a piece of fluorescent tubing to use as a torch and is momentarily recast as a Parisian Luke Skywalker. And Besson's ending is based on the shooting of Michel Poiccard at the conclusion of Godard's *A bout de souffle* (*Breathless*, 1959). Celebratory cinephilia is also emphasised by the lyrics sung (in English) by the band during this finale: 'Just one glance and love had hit me/ Just like being in a movie'. Meanwhile in melodramatic slow motion, Helena finds Fred in the concert crowd only for him to be shot dead as she reaches out to him. Besson qualifies any tragedy in Fred's death by emphasising the surrounding spectacle: *Subway* ends with the crowd cheering the band. There remains, however, a covert bleakness about the film, emphasised in Bassan's reading of *Subway* as a pessimistic view of eighties society. The apparently seductive elements of the film

– the neon lighting, the costumes, the hairstyles – are, he claims, signs of death rather than of well-being; although looking like an advert for youth and for 'Paris by night', *Subway* is in fact a desperate vision of stifled individuals (Bassan 1989: 48).

Perfect women: the Pygmalion myth in *Nikita* and *The Fifth Element*

Fantasy cinema is based on several established archetypes (see Fraisse 1999: 73). Among these we might include the male scientist and his often monstrous creations. Present in fantasy film from the earliest Frankenstein movies to *La Cité des enfants perdus* (1995, see below), the paradigm of the male creator and his (usually) female creation is in part derived from the classical myth of Pygmalion. An ancient king, dissatisfied with mortal women, carved a female statue and fell in love with it. He prayed to the goddess of love, Aphrodite, to make the statue come alive; it did, and the two were married. The myth has had a pervasive influence on fantasy narratives, in particular in combination with explorations of the way that technology and science might allow men to create their own offspring and thus bypass women. Lucy Fisher has memorably called this fantasy 'womb envy' (Fischer 1996: 39). It is a fantasy which is explicit in Besson's *Nikita* (1990) and *The Fifth Element* (1997).

Nikita is an urban thriller which combines fantasy, romance and action in a very successful modern version of *My Fair Lady* (Cukor, 1964). Like that famous musical version of Pygmalion, *Nikita* concerns the transformation, by a controlling male authoritarian, of a wild and aggressive woman into some kind of feminine ideal. The twist in Besson's film is that this ideal woman is also trained to become a killer. Nikita (Anne Parillaud, Besson's partner of the time) is the only woman in a gang of young junkies who becomes involved in a gun battle with police. When she shoots and kills an officer at point-blank range, she is condemned to death and then given a reprieve which furnishes the film with its basic plot: the state will let her live in order to train her as an assassin. The resultant narrative is divided almost exactly into two halves: the first relating Nikita's transformation during three years in a secure training centre; the second her life 'outside', her subsequent missions and eventual desertion.

In *Le Mensuel du cinéma*, John Badham's US remake *Point of No Return* a.k.a. *The Assassin* (1992) was preferred to the French original (see Verkindere 1993). Besson's already 'Americanised' film was seen as functioning only on a personal level while Badham explored the chaotic nature of American society, and its rejection by the heroine. This is doubly ironic, since the scenario for the remake was written by Besson himself, and since the original, like much of the *cinéma du look*, in fact concerns an alienated individual within a fragmented and threatening society. Besson has said of this strand in his films: 'Je suis guidé par une préoccupation: la société moderne crée un grand déséquilibre familial, un manque affectif chez les jeunes' [I am guided by a single preoccupation: that modern society creates a familial crisis, and

Contemporary French cinema

an emotional lack for young people] (Gandillot 1994: 53). Treated in a less epic and more politicised way, this theme became central to the critically-favoured new realism of the nineties (see chapter 9).

At the outset, *Nikita* is presented as belonging to the thriller form, a male-dominated genre derived in part from American gangster movies and *film noir* (see chapter 5). The opening shoot-out includes an allusion to Mervyn Le Roy's seminal gangster movie *Little Caesar* (1930), while Besson's manipulation of lighting – blue, green and infra-red – recalls Godard's more overtly symbolic use of colour filters in *Le Mépris* (1963) and *Pierrot le fou* (1965). When Nikita is shot and wounded by her mentor, Bob (Tcheky Karyo), the slow-motion photography is also generic, reminiscent of thriller/Western director Sam Peckinpah and many others since. In these early sequences, Nikita herself is coded as male, through her androgynous name and appearance and her monosyllabic, abusive, and violent behaviour. Subsequently, she is trained not only in computing, martial arts and target practice, but also in the construction of a new and 'feminine' identity. No longer dressed in her leather jacket, trousers and Doctor Marten's, Nikita is provided with a wig, lipstick, and a little black dress. After she dances outlandishly to the Mozart sound-track, Bob pins a poster of a Degas ballerina on her graffiti-covered wall: Besson seems to be presenting the autocratic State as a purveyor of both gender stereotyping and of 'high' culture. The State also supplies an artificial familial structure: the surrogate mother Armande (Jeanne Moreau, herself a cinematic icon of femininity) teaches Nikita to use make-up, while Bob, the substitute father, normalises Nikita's origins by pretending to be her uncle and inventing stories of an idealised girlhood. The feminising process is concluded by her renaming (as 'Josephine', and also 'Marie'), and is realised visually in a series of facial close-ups and mirrored compositions. Nikita no longer spills out of the frame, she fits the screen as an amenable spectacle. Thus reconstituted as a 'feminine' ideal, a beautiful nurse – and also, in the supermarket sequence, a parodic housewife – Nikita gains a perfect cover (who would suspect a nurse of being a killer?) and a new generic role, no longer as a 'male' outlaw but as the predatory *femme fatale* of *film noir*. Hence the rather perfunctory love interest with Marco (Jean-Hugues Anglade), which recalls *Le Grand Bleu* (*The Big Blue*, 1988): in each film, the romance serves as a norm against which the extraordinary destinies of the protagonists are measured. In *Nikita*, this means that sex is deferred – most explicitly in the Venice hotel room – by the demands of Nikita's role as assassin. If the film combines the macho thriller with 'feminised' romance, it is always the former which wins out.

The narrative also functions at a mythical level, retelling the Pygmalion story and the plot of Jean Cocteau's *La Belle et la bête* (1946), which informs Nikita's transformation from beast to beauty. So too does *My Fair Lady*, with Bob as Professor Higgins and Nikita as Eliza. This debt is apparent not just in the narrative structure and the characterisation, but even in the costume: at one point Nikita wears an outrageous hat to a meeting with Bob, in a deliberate reference to Audrey Hepburn's outfit from the Ascot sequence of the musical. In the final reel, however, Besson changes tone and unleashes the violence of the thriller genre with farcical brutality. In response to the absurd machismo of Victor the 'cleaner' (Jean Reno), Nikita assumes a submissive position, first foetal and then hysterical. The reassertion of orthodox gender roles here – Nikita is no longer the cool assassin, she is merely Victor's sidekick – is brought centre stage, with Victor a ludicrous parody of the macho hit man of convention. Serge Daney has associated Victor with advertising's obsession for images of cleaning (Daney 1993: 237), but 'le nettoyeur' also has a cinematic resonance, as the American director Quentin Tarantino has realised: Harvey Keitel, the cleaner in Badham's remake, reprises the role for laughs in Tarantino's *Pulp Fiction* (1994), alongside more established stereotypes like the *femme fatale*. Besson himself subsequently based *Léon* (1994) entirely around the character of the cleaner, who was again played by Jean Reno.

If *Léon* has one or two similarities with *Nikita*, then *The Fifth Element* (1997) looks in many ways like a science fiction remake of it. Again, Besson's partner of the time – in this case, Milla Jovovich – plays the role of an initially unstable and aggressive woman who is (re)born into a government facility and revealed as some kind of ideal being. As Leeloo, Jovovich plays an alien in humanoid form, genetically recreated from a fragment of DNA recovered in outer space. Various central agencies such as government scientists, the police and the military (all male) attempt to control her, but she resists their interference. The romantic subplot involving Marco in *Nikita* is here much expanded, so that the world is saved not just by Leeloo or by the action hero Dallas (Bruce Willis) but by the couple that they form together. Even more insistently than in *Nikita*, the female protagonist in *The Fifth Element* is described as 'perfect' – at least half a dozen times, by virtually every male character she encounters. The science fiction narrative allows Leeloo to assume a mystical as well as technological or aesthetic importance: she is the fifth element of the title, a weapon that can be used to protect life against threat from the dark planet that is menacing earth. In terms of gender, Leeloo is like Nikita an androgynous figure, combining masculine traits such as athleticism and aggression with a maternal function: she is described as 'The supreme being, the ultimate warrior, created to protect life'. Leelo is also reminiscent of another androgynous alien super being, David Bowie as Newton in *The Man Who Fell to Earth* (Roeg, 1976). Like Newton she has orange hair, pale skin and is often dressed in white. Numerous references to other fantasy films also punctuate *The Fifth Element*, including the dystopian future world of *Blade Runner* (Scott, 1982) and the operatic finale of *Diva* (Beineix, 1980).

What sets Besson's fantasy apart, as Susan Hayward has shown, is its approach to gender, and especially masculinity, as a performative function. The film seems more fascinated by masculinity as performance than by Leeloo's androgynous mixture of physical prowess and maternal instinct. The key character here is Ruby Rhod (Chris Tucker), the transvestite black DJ who hosts the spectacle of the film's finale. If the characterisation of Leeloo 'challenges nothing', transgression is embodied instead by Ruby, who 'performs all the sexes, in dress and implicitly in action' (Hayward 1999: 254–5). After Dallas has shot his way out of trouble, accompanied by Ruby's screams, the latter concludes, 'That was the best show I ever did'. Both men are in fact performers in a show and their simultaneous actions (shooting or screaming), while encoded as masculine or feminine respectively, are both excessive. This allows the film to do something other than just create an idealised if androgynous fantasy of womanhood (Leeloo). *The Fifth Element* also reveals masculinity as a fantasy (aided by Jean-Paul Gaultier's costume designs for Dallas and Ruby), and so manages to put on display 'excessive and transgressive bodies' in order to 'raise issues around race and male sexuality' (Hayward 1999: 256). The film thus signals a possible route out of Besson's Pygmalion complex by exploring not the ideal woman so much as the excessive man.

Fantasy outside the *look*

The Occupation as comic fantasy in *Delicatessen*

If Besson's career has exploded into global production since the end of the *cinéma du look* in the early nineties, the careers of Beineix and Carax seem to have imploded. The influence of the *look* is apparent, however, in the equally stylised but more engagingly comic fantasies of Jean-Pierre Jeunet and Marc Caro. *Delicatessen* (1991), the début feature by Jeunet and Caro, is a comic fantasy set in a decaying city of the future, where nothing grows and food is so scarce that the local butcher (Jean-Claude Dreyfus) has started to sell human meat. In order to keep his trade going, he employs young men and then murders them, but is also prepared to slaughter his neighbours in the crumbling apartment block. Stan Louison (Dominique Pinon), a vegetarian circus performer whose chimpanzee partner has recently been killed and eaten, arrives at the butcher's shop looking for work. As Stan goes about his odd jobs he meets Julie (Marie-Laure Dougnac), the butcher's short-sighted daughter, and they fall in love. When her pleas to her father to spare Stan are rejected, Julie stumbles upon an underground network of vegetarian terrorists, and enlists their help. Ultimately, after a climax involving fire, flood and mayhem, the butcher is killed, and Julie and Stan are rescued by the underground, allowing them to start a new life together.

As well as being an inventive and futuristic comedy, *Delicatessen* also functions as a fantasy version of the German Occupation of France during the Second World War (see Daney 1993: 295), a historical subject which French cinema continues to reinterpret (see chapter 2). The central figure in *Delicatessen* is the butcher, a grotesque character who is not only a monster derived from the horror genre, but also the embodiment of the term applied during the Occupation to war criminals such as Klaus Barbie, 'the Butcher of Lyons'. The narrative presents several further parallels with the war period in France: an underground resistance movement, clandestine radio messages, the collaboration of the neighbours with the tyrannical butcher, rationing, the black market, and general deprivation. The *mise en scène*, moreover, evokes the 1940s not only in the décors, the costumes, and the persistent brown tones, but also in the primordial role of poetic realism as an overall influence on the look of the film: hence the impressive set design, expressionist lighting, nocturnal effects and ubiquitous vapour clouds, as in Marcel Carné's *Quai des brumes* (*Port of Shadows*, 1938, see chapter 1). Unlike poetic realism however, *Delicatessen* has a purely fantastical aesthetic, partly derived from BD, featuring crazy camera angles, facial contortions and bulging eyes, and a cast of bizarre minor characters including a man who lives in a slime-filled room full of snails and Aurore, a woman who keeps failing spectacularly in her suicide attempts. Pinon as Stan is a softer and more charismatic version of the acrobat played by Denis Lavant in Carax's *Mauvais sang* (*The Night is Young*, 1986), and his circus tricks are a source of visual humour in the film, as are the slapstick gags involving the myopic Julie and the unfortunate Aurore. There is also a superbly orchestrated sequence of sound gags in which the bed springs squeaking under the butcher and his wife set off an orgasmic crescendo of noises throughout the building, including mat-beating, cello-playing and tyre-pumping. Even in the furious action of the finale, however, there are moments of lyricism, such as the underwater embrace between Stan and Julie and the tender final scene on the rooftop (both scenes incidentally recalling films by Jean Vigo, one of the idols of the *cinéma du look*).

Fantasies of belonging in *La Cité des enfants perdus* and *Amélie*

Whether positing utopian or dystopian visions, fantasy narratives repeatedly explore anxieties and desires concerning the social context in which they are made: 'Les sociétés hypothétiques [...] sont construites sur l'allégorie des craintes et des espoirs propres à leur époque de production' [Hypothetical societies are built on the allegory of the hopes and fears belonging to the period in which they are produced] (Haver and Gyger 2002: 7). French fantasy films during the eighties and nineties, both within the *cinéma du look* style and beyond it, have tended to address the breakdown of familial and social ties, presenting worlds 'libres de toute autorité parentale directe' [free from any direct parental authority] (Beugnet 2000: 63). Orphaned, isolated protagonists struggle to form new family groupings and to find surrogate parents, like Nikita flanked by Armande and Bob, or the various orphans and parental avatars in Jeunet and Caro's *La Cité des enfants perdus* (*City of Lost Children*, 1995). It is also possible to see in such films as *Nikita*, *Les Amants du Pont Neuf* and *La Cité des enfants perdus* a focus on dispossessed characters living at the margins of society –

a focus that seems to predict the more realistic concerns of the late nineties film style known as *jeune cinéma* (see chapter 9). Beugnet for one has critiqued French fantasy cinema for presenting apparently anti-conformist rebels who actually aspire to 'trouver leur place dans le système – économique, social, politique – *tel qu'il existe*' [find a place in the economic, social and political system *as it is*] (Beugnet 2000: 47). The pessimism that is apparent in certain films of the *jeune cinéma* could be said to derive from exactly the same source: the protagonists of realist dramas such as *Y aura-t-il de la neige à Noël?* (*Will It Snow For Christmas?*, Veysset, 1997) and *Rosetta* (Dardenne brothers, 1999) are largely unwilling or unable to change the system in which they find themselves. The difference lies in the tone: for the 'new realism', the need to conform to existing structures is felt as tragic; the accommodation with social or economic necessity felt as a defeat – even when, as in *Rosetta*, it is also a hard-won victory (see chapter 9). In the fantasy genre the re-establishment of structures that remain relatively conservative is often presented as an ideal, a source of identity and belonging. That much is certainly true of *La Cité des enfants perdus* and of Jeunet's hugely popular solo triumph *Le fabuleux destin d'Amélie Poulain* (*Amélie*, 2001).

Where *Amélie* is a utopian fantasy based on the values of neighbourliness, family, and romance, *La Cité des enfants perdus* is a largely dystopian fantasy of reproduction in diverse forms, often monstrous and/or technological, but culminating in the re-establishment of the family. The film concerns Miette (Judith Vittet), an orphaned girl who joins circus strong-man One (Ron Perlman) in a quest for his little brother. The city of the title is terrorised by an evil collective called the Cyclops, who steal children and sell them to be experimented upon by the vampire-like Krank (Daniel Emilfork) and his dysfunctional family, which features six narcoleptic clones, a brain in a jar, a dwarf mother and a missing amnesiac father. Jeunet and Caro conjure up a beautifully realized fantasy environment of rusting docks and green seas, with cinephile references to the pioneer of French fantasy cinema, Georges Méliès, whose own short *L'Homme orchestre* (1900) had also featured six clones. Rather like much of Méliès's work, which has been described as 'attribut[ing] a masculine authority to the reproductive power of the camera' (Abel 1994: 81), *La Cité des enfants perdus* displays a fascination with reproduction and technology. More pessimistic than Méliès, Jeunet and Caro represent technology and indeed any scientific intervention into the biological process of reproduction as nightmarish, a dystopian repetition which results either in the ridiculous and comic (Krank, the six clones) or the threatening and nightmarish (the opening and closing dream sequences, the Cyclops who are violent cyborgs). It is not just the interventions of (male) science which are rendered monstrous however. One of the most threatening creatures in the film's bizarre menagerie is Le Poulpe (the Octopus sisters), Siamese twins who play the role of the sadistic 'bad mother' to the orphans of the city, whom they threaten with incarceration in the dark and spider-ridden space of 'le trou' [the hole], a demonised version of the maternal body. It is only by escaping from this bad mother that Miette can rescue the missing children and also form a new family group with One and his little brother, in which she herself is placed as the idealised 'good mother'. The film thus activates long-standing archetypes from the horror film – Krank as vampire, Le Pouple as 'the monstrous feminine' (see Creed 1989) – and also from fairy-tales, with their traditional emphasis on narratives of individuation, of growing to adulthood and of parental functions split between good and evil parents (see Bettelheim 1991). *La Cité des enfants perdus* also displays a fascination with uncanny uterine spaces that is recurrent in Jeunet and Caro's work (from the plumbing in *Delicatessen* to the trenches in *Un long dimanche de fiançailles*) and indeed in that of Luc Besson. The comic birthing scene towards the end of *La Cité des enfants perdus* – when the clones are thrown one after another down various chutes – recalls similar scenes in *Nikita* and *The Fifth Element* (see above) while reminding us that fantasies of partition are a staple of both Méliès's pioneering cinema (see Fischer 1996) and the horror film in general (see Clover 1992).

La Cité des enfants perdus does however add something very new to these variations on ancient fantasy figures. This is the use of digital special effects and computer-generated imagery (CGI). Although in the mid nineties CGI was in its infancy in French and indeed global cinema, Jeunet and Caro included seventeen minutes of digital effects in their film, raising its cost to a huge 85 million francs. The use of CGI is however dark and unsettling, and at times the film seems to offer a commentary on its own recourse to technological replication. In *La Cité des enfants perdus* repetition is ubiquitous but also fearful, with the narrative exploring in particular anxieties about biotechnology and cloning. The digital form of the film is matched to this theme when CGI is exploited to create the vast meeting of the terrible Cyclops, or for the distorted opening dream sequence where dozens of Father Christmases come down the chimney (there is meant to be only one Santa Claus!), as well as in the more light-hearted sequences presenting the six clones. Such frightening proliferation is contrasted with a celebration of individual identity in the shape of One (a freakishly strong and solitary figure) and Miette (the only girl in the gang of orphans). The discourse of authenticity and individuation that this implies is also sent up by the film in the ridiculing of the six clones' claims to be 'the Original' (the scientist who created them) and in the comic failure of Krank's Father Christmas routine, when the record he is miming to jumps and he is condemned to copy its repeated phrase over and over again to the growing distress of the listening orphans.

Jeunet's solo project *Amélie* initially appears to be far removed from the concerns of *La Cité des enfants perdus*. But although *Amélie* is a romantic comedy set in Paris during 1997, it has a lot in common with the earlier film. The premise for each is the collapse of the traditional family and the creation of new familial or community groups.

Both narratives are driven by a lonely female protagonist who ends up forming a heterosexual couple, hence promising the continuation of the family. But the similarity goes beyond these syntactical elements. Even the semantics of *Amélie* – the green lighting, the uterine passage-ways of the *métro*, the use of whip pans, ominous zooms, and CGI – are reminiscent of *La Cité des enfants perdus*. The difference is one of tone, since the world of *Amélie* is never menacing or nightmarish. When Amélie rides a ghost train, for instance, the horror genre is parodied and re-imagined as romantic: while Nino, dressed as a skeleton, groans in her ear, Amélie experiences not terror but delight. Played by Audrey Tautou, in a star-making turn, Amélie is an only child who grows up in a dysfunctional family with a distant father and a nervous mother who dies early on. Amélie works as a waitress in Montmartre, a heavily over-determined district of Paris associated with past painters, and whose touristic value is emphasised repeatedly. Throughout the narrative Amélie acts out her childlike fantasies of omnipotence and of belonging: she manipulates the lives of her neighbours and colleagues, whose idiosyncrasies are detailed in the persistent and rather cloying voice-over. Intrigued by Nino (Mathieu Kassovitz), a young man who seems as shy and solitary as herself, she prepares a laborious treasure hunt for him to follow before they finally fall into each other's arms. The romantic pleasures of the film, its evocation of a lost Paris of the imagination (established by the sepia filter, accordion music and cobbled streets of the opening scene) and its cast of eccentric characters proved extremely successful at the box office: over eight million spectators watched it in the year of release, helping to make 2001 the best season for the French consumption of domestic films since 1984.

The central metaphor in the film is that of the treasure trove or 'boîte à souvenirs' [box of memories] that Amélie discovers behind the tiles of her bathroom. This collection of memories enables her to reintroduce its middle-aged owner to the world of his childhood, and subsequently to his daughter and grandson. It also acts as a very effective summary of the film itself, which presents a fantasy based on a treasure trove of memories and nostalgia: the frequent black and white film clips and newsreels, the portrayal of Montmartre as a quaint village rather than as part of a modern, multicultural city, and the bringing to life of characters and scenes from well-loved French sources (the songs of Serge Gainsbourg, the paintings of Auguste Renoir). The nostalgic fantasy that the film inhabits is explicitly phrased when the voice-over declares 'Le temps n'a rien changé' [Time hasn't changed a thing]. If Nino and Amélie are at first lonely individuals whose families are absent, they successfully create surrogate families of their own before becoming a couple themselves: the passport photos collected by Nino in two huge albums, the colleagues and neighbours that Amélie gathers round her by intervening in their lives. Amélie's communitarian tendency has, moreover, apparently become a trend in French cities such as Paris and Lyons. According to a feature in *Biba* magazine in 2004, this so-called 'microsociality' is visible in the establishment of residents' associations and in the resurgence of small-scale local commerce. *Biba* explicitly relates these developments to the popular success of *Amélie* by calling them 'améli-poulanisés' and by comparing the two central factors proposed by local commerce – emotional warmth and vintage 'tradi-village' décor – to the film (Le Bellego 2004: 66). A vituperative feature in the daily *Libération* has gone further, damning *Amélie* as a whitewashed and reactionary version of Paris, both aesthetically and ethnically cleansed, with the streets as empty of dog shit as they are of sexual or ethnic minorities (Kagdanski 2001: 7). But Parisian fantasies are not always so squeaky clean and reassuring. They can prove just as dystopian as *Amélie* is utopian, as is the case in the futuristic thriller *Banlieue 13*.

The state versus the 'scum' in *Banlieue 13*

Directed by Pierre Morel but produced and co-written by Luc Besson, *Banlieue 13* (*District 13*, 2004), is an action movie set in Paris in 2010. If fantasy cinema is 'a history of popular fears' (Donald 1989: 235) then *Banlieue 13* is a very pertinent index of French fears about lawlessness in the urban ghetto. This otherwise conventional urban fantasy seems to have predicted the events of November 2005, namely the violent discontent of the urban ghettos (the *banlieues*) and the French state's contemptuous response to the unrest. In particular, the government minister who is the villain of the piece – with his dismissal of the inhabitants of the *banlieues* as 'scum' – predicts the very words of the controversial interior minister Nicolas Sarkozy in 2005. The film unites athletic *banlieusard* Leito (David Belle) and super-cop Damien (Cyril Raffaelli) against a secret government plot to destroy all two million people living in the ghetto at one fell swoop. Walled off and abandoned by the state, district 13 is run by the drug baron Taha and his private army, of whom one character remarks that they could easily invade Paris – a literalised version of the perceived threat from the *banlieues* to French security and order. When Taha kidnaps Leito's younger sister Lola and the government claim to have 'lost' a primed neutron bomb somewhere in the ghetto, the stage is set for the buddy pairing to embark on a double rescue mission. They manage to save Lola, defuse the bomb, and expose the minister responsible. The film ends with the wall coming down and the *banlieue* being reintegrated into the city of Paris.

Significantly, the weapon that threatens the *banlieue* is referred to as a 'clean bomb': its purpose is hence to clean up the ghetto, which is presented as decaying, drug-riddled and ultra-violent. The apparently sole law-abiding inhabitant of the ghetto, Leito, is referred to disparagingly as 'Monsieur Propre' [Mister Clean]. However the film twists these stereotypes so that by the end, the villain is revealed as the spotless but spineless politician, while the two heroes end up scarred, bloody and powdered with dust. Dirt, physical prowess, and the authentic masculinity of the ghetto are seen to triumph. At the close of the film, the government minister responsible for the plan declares that French voters are sick and tired of spending their taxes on the violent and terrifying 'racaille' [scum] that live in the *banlieue*. The use of the word 'racaille' predicts Sarkozy's controversial use of the same term to described the rioters of autumn 2005. A year after the film's release, on 27 October 2005, two teenagers of African origin were electrocuted while hiding from the police in Clichy-sous-Bois, a suburb north of Paris. Days of rioting and clashes with police followed, in Paris but also in Toulouse, Rouen and Lille. The riots were fanned by Sarkozy, who had days earlier described the youth of the *banlieues* as 'scum': 'Vous en avez assez de cette racaille. Eh bien je vais vous en débarasser' [You've had enough of this scum; well, I'm going to get rid of them for you]. Sarkozy's stance remained just as hard-line during the riots: 'Pas question de laisser transparaître le moindre signe de faiblesse vis-à-vis de ceux qu'il avait qualifié de "racaille"' [No question of showing the slightest sign of weakness regarding those he had called 'scum'] (Guiral 2005: 4).

As well as predicting in remarkable fashion this particular controversy, *Banlieue 13* also reflects the more general withdrawal of the French state from the ghettos over the previous twenty years or so. In the early 1990s sociologist Pierre Bourdieu had identified 'la démission de l'Etat' [the withdrawal of the state] from certain sectors of society (Bourdieu 1993: 219–28). For Bourdieu however there was still a front line of individuals such as police officers, postal staff or teachers struggling on to provide some kind of service despite underfunding and disinterest from the state (see Marlière 1997: 54–5). But in *Banlieue 13* this last line of provision has disappeared: we are told that there are no schools, no post offices, no police stations in the ghetto. This too seems like a reference to the policies of Sarkozy since he oversaw the dismantling of community policing initiatives in the *banlieues*. The film's futurist setting allows it to extrapolate slightly – but only slightly – from the Sarkozian position so that the 'scum' have now been entirely walled off and abandoned.

In some ways the film may seem entirely generic, with its Hollywood-derived plot structure (basically a revenge narrative combined with a ticking bomb à la James Bond), setting (reminiscent of John Carpenter's *Assault on Precinct 13* (1976) and *Escape from New York* (1981)) and characterisation (rogue cop teamed with good-hearted lad from the wrong side of the tracks). But as we have seen, *Banlieue 13* engages with French socio-political concerns. This is again evident when one character pauses to explain that there are six million unemployed in France. If the narrative presents a critique of one form of French ideology (embodied by Sarkozy), it celebrates another – the Republican universalist values of *liberté, égalité, fraternité*. At the end of the film Damien reiterates that he and Leito are fighting for the same values and that these apply to all French citizens, wherever they come from. *Banlieue 13* thus presents a very clear awareness of the social context, as well as of the mass appeal to be generated by car chases, explosions and martial-arts combat. In fact the two are combined throughout the narrative, since a politicised French space (the Parisian ghetto) is traversed by a spectacular French form of movement (*le parkour*).

Also known as urban running, le *parkour* is a way of crossing urban spaces and scaling buildings by means of great athleticism and gymnastic skill. David Belle, here in his first major film role, invented *le parkour*, and his character makes several stunning escapes from tight corners by leaping through windows and off balconies. His co-star Cyril Raffaelli is similarly adept, having worked in the circus and as a stuntman. Both men embody fantasies of authentic masculinity via their stunts, since 'stunt performances are expressly masculine' and are valorised as 'dangerous, hyper-masculine work' (Smith 2004: 36, 38). In the fantasy genre perhaps more than any other, 'computer generated imagery (CGI) threatens to erase the stunt performer in a radical new way' (Smith 2004: 50). This tendency is defiantly challenged in *Banlieue 13*, however, where Belle and Raffaelli perform all their own stunts. Far from relying on CGI, the athletic stunt work on the film actually recalls the early days of action cinema, especially the comedies of Buster Keaton, whose silent film work uses very similar stunts. In his early short *The Goat* (1921), for example, Keaton twice dives through a window as Belle does in *Banlieue 13*. Circus performance also informed Keaton's pratfalls as it does Raffaelli's stunts. Hence *Banlieue 13*, while engaging with the socio-political context of the new millennium, also refers back to the pleasures of very early cinema and the bodily prowess on display in the circus. In so doing, it presents two heroes who are identified with authentic masculinity through the ways that their bodies occupy and traverse the urban spaces of the setting. The two stars also embody republican values, and in a sense replace Bourdieu's ignorant and arrogant political elite with a spectacular version of public service. It is thanks to these superhero public servants that the bomb is defused, the wall removed, and the state reinvests in the *banlieue*, thus shifting the mood from the dsytopian to the hopeful. Compared with the problems that continue to dog the French *banlieues* at the time of writing, however, one might call this a fairy-tale ending.

Hybridity, horror, heritage: *Le Pacte des loups*

Christophe Gans's *Le Pacte des loups* (*Brotherhood of the Wolf*, 2001) is to date the most successful film from the new generation of French fantasy directors, among whom one can also include Pascal Laugier, a protégé of Gans who made the less well-received *Saint Ange* (2004). Where *Saint Ange* is a relatively straight gothic horror in the haunted house sub-genre, *Le Pacte des loups* is much more ambitious, a spectacular and dynamic example of cross-genre cinema that attracted a large home audience as well as earning nearly thirty million euros in foreign box-office receipts. Fans labelled Gans a 'messiah' for his role in resurrecting French fantasy cinema (see BaNDiNi 2004), while the film was welcomed by the press as a 'monster' (Blouin 2001: 82). Set in 1766, *Le Pacte des loups* concerns the gentleman naturalist De Fronsac (Samuel Le Bihan) and his blood-brother Mani (Mark Dacascos), a Mohawk Indian, who are sent to the remote region of Gévaudan in order to hunt down a huge beast that is slaughtering local women and children. Apparently based on a real-life mystery from French history, the film transcends its origins in a heterogeneous fantasy which combines multiple genres and allusions.

The generic hybridity of *Le Pacte des loups* is evident in both its syntax and its semantics. In terms of the former, the narrative mixes thriller elements (the central mystery to be investigated, revelations about motives and identities) with sub-plots from the romance, the action film, the buddy movie and the horror film. The semantic mixture is even more apparent: lighting and sound effects, the CGI monster and its bloody victims, and certain settings such as pits, caves and crypts, derive from the horror genre. (It is worth noting that Gans went on to film the American horror movie *Silent Hill* in 2005). The historical setting, aristocratic milieu and characters, period costumes and crowds of extras are taken from the heritage film (see chapter 7). Western elements include the use of landscape, certain musical themes, the characterisation of Mani and the reliance on horses and bows and arrows in several sequences. *Le Pacte des loups* can also be compared to the tradition of the cloak and dagger film (*le film de cape et d'épée*) in French cinema, where this genre functions as a marker of national identity (see De la Bretèque 2005: 177). The final and perhaps most innovative feature, borrowed from Hong Kong cinema, is the use of martial arts, shot in super slow motion, to contribute an exhilarating dynamism to the combat sequences. What unites these diverse generic features is a powerful sense of spectacle. This is most evident in the action scenes and the costumes, but is also inherent to the characterisation of certain figures, notably Mani and Sylvia, the Vatican spy played by Monica Bellucci. Both have their bodies introduced to the gaze of the camera and of onlookers within the film as an object of curiosity and desire. Both are associated with mysterious arts (Mani's communication with animal spirits, Sylvia's mastery of poisons), in contrast with the emphasis on reason and observation in the characterisation of De Fronsac, who personifies the Age of Enlightenment. De Fronsac in fact displays Mani to the amused or disapproving French aristocrats, rather as he displays the body of another exotic creature he has brought back from Canada, a fur-covered fish. Mani is an exotic object of spectacle because of his ethnic otherness. A similar orientalism operates in the representation of Sylvia who, although Italian (and played by an Italian star), is accompanied by a distinctly Arabian theme in the film's score. When Mani is killed by the beast's master, De Fronsac finally solves the mystery and defeats the murderer by 'going native', emulating his dead friend by wearing black war-paint and hunting down his enemies with a bow and arrows. Even in the romantic final scene, De Fronsac's last action is to scatter Mani's ashes on the sea. Hence the film is, amongst (many) other things, an exploration of the white male's 'opening up' to the world-view of the other. To this extent *Le Pacte des loups* bears comparison with the possession film, a horror sub-genre whose subject is 'the transformation [...] in the male psyche' when science and reason (coded as white and male) confront the occult or the supernatural: 'Only when rational men have accepted the reality of the irrational [...] can the supernatural menace be reined in and the community returned to a new state of calm' (Clover 1992: 98). Such is the hybridity of *Le Pacte des loups* that it manages to play on this theme while also revealing that the beast is an entirely man-made (and hence rational, not supernatural) monster. (A more focused and generic representation of possession and the occult is to be found in Laugier's *Saint Ange*, which was facilitated and produced by Gans (see Austin 2007).)

One of the major contributions that *Le Pacte des loups* makes to French fantasy cinema is to take the markers of national identity (the history, the landscape, the allusions to domestic genres such as the heritage film or the cloak and dagger film) and to open them up to global influences. By borrowing from the traditions of Anglo-American horror or Asian martial arts, *Le Pacte des loups* can be seen to occupy a universal space that seems removed from the geography and history of France itself (see De la Bretèque 2005: 186). A similar move away from national markers (including the French language) is evident in the work of Luc Besson, both as director (*The Fifth Element*, 1997) and as producer (*Kiss of the Dragon*, Nahon, 2001). It is notable that Besson's trademark tracking camera, as seen in the opening sequences of many of his films, is echoed at the beginning and the ending of Gans's film. But by using the French Revolution as its frame narrative, *Le Pacte des loups* alludes to a myth of national identity embedded in French history in a way that Besson's determinedly ahistorical films do not. Moreover, the scenario (by Stéphane Cabel, adapted by Gans) has its roots in national folklore and legend. In the final analysis, the character of Mani seems most emblematic of the synthesis of the universal and the national that Gans achieves. Mani is both a means of adding martial arts action to the film and a shorthand reference to the French historical presence in Canada. He functions as history and as spectacle. Where Besson's recent output has been termed 'nationally ambiguous', *Le Pacte des loups* remains at least partially anchored in French history and myth (see Michael 2005: 71). As such it is triumphant proof that the French fantasy film has finally come back to life.

References

Abel, R. (1994), *The Ciné Goes to Town: French Cinema 1896–1914*, Princeton, Princeton University Press.

Austin, G. (2007), 'In fear and pain': stardom and the body in two French ghost films, *Scope*, February 2007, at www.scope.nottingham.ac.uk

BaNDiNi [sic] (2004), fan comment at www.ecranlarge.com/forum/archive/index.php/t-217.html, posted 13 November 2004, accessed 18 November 2005.

Bassan, R. (1989), Trois néo-baroques français, *La Revue du cinéma*, 449, 45–53.

Bettelheim, B. (1991), *The Uses of Enchantment: The Meaning and Importance of Fairy Tales*, London, Penguin.

Beugnet, M. (2000), *Marginalité, sexualité, contrôle dans le cinéma français contemporain*, Paris, L'Harmattan.

Blouin, P. (2001), Egalité chérie, *Cahiers du cinéma*, 554, 82–3.

Bourdieu, P. (1993), *La Misère du monde*, Paris, Editions du Seuil.

Clover, C. J. (1992), *Men, Women, and Chain Saws: Gender in the Modern Horror Film*, London, BFI.

Cocteau, J. (1991), *The Art of Cinema*, compiled and edited by A. Bernard and C. Gauteur, London, Marion Boyars.

Creed, B. (1989), Horror and the Monstrous-feminine: an imaginary abjection, in J. Donald (ed.), *Fantasy and the Cinema*, London, BFI, 63–90.

Dadoun, R. (1989), Fetishism in the horror film, in James Donald (ed.), *Fantasy and the Cinema*, London: BFI, 39–62.

Daney, S. (1993), *L'Exercise a été profitable, Monsieur*, Paris, POL.

De la Bretèque, F. (2005), Du *Miracle des loups* au *Pacte des loups*: Comment une 'série' (les films d'action français en costumes) a pu parvenir finalement à se constituer en genre, in R. Moine (ed.), *Le Cinéma français face aux genres*, Paris, AFRHC, 175–87.

Donald, J. (1989), The fantastic, the sublime, and the popular, or what's at stake in vampire movies?, in J. Donald (ed.), *Fantasy and the Cinema*, London, BFI, 39–62.

Fischer, L. (1996), *Cinematernity: Film, Motherhood, Genre*, Princeton, Princeton University Press.

Fraisse, P. (1999), Entre science et fiction: Un certain cinéma fantastique, Paris, *Positif*, 466, 71–4.

Gandillot, T. (1994), Luc Besson le professionnel, *Le Nouvel Observateur*, 1558, 52–3.

Gans, G. (1991), *Diva*, dix ans après ..., *L'Avant-Scène Cinéma*, 407, 3–4.

Goodwin, A. (1987), Music video in the (post) modern world, Glasgow, *Screen*, 28:3, 36–55.

Guiral, A. (2005), 'L'image de Sarkozy craque de partout', *Libération*, 7618, 4.

Haver, G. and Gyger, P. (eds), (2002), *De beaux lendemains? Histoire, société et politique dans la science-fiction*, Lausanne, Editions Antipodes.

Hayward, S. (1999), Besson's 'Mission Elastoplast': *Le Cinquième élément*, in P. Powrie (ed.), *French Cinema in the 1990s: Continuity and Difference*, Oxford, Oxford University Press, 246–57.

Jameson, F. (1990), *Signatures of the Visible*, London and New York, Routledge.

Kagdanski, S. (2001), *Amélie* pas jolie, *Libération*, 31 May, 7.

Le Bellego, G. (2004), Mon quartier sinon rien, *Biba*, 295, September, 64–7.

Marlière, P. (1997), Social suffering 'in their own words': Pierre Bourdieu's sociology of poverty, in S. Perry and M. Cross (eds), *Voices of France: Social, Political and Cultural Identity*, London and Washington, Pinter, 46–58.

Michael, C. (2005), French national cinema and the martial arts blockbuster, *French Politics, Culture and Society*, 23:3, 55–75.

Overbey, D. (1977), Chabrol: game of mirrors, London, *Sight and Sound*, Spring, 78–81.

Reader, K. (1993), Cinematic representations of Paris: Vigo/Truffaut/Carax, *Modern and Contemporary France*, NS1:4, 409–15.

Russell, D. (1989), Two or three things we know about Beineix, London, *Sight and Sound*, 59:1, 42–7.

Smith, J. (2004), Seeing double: stunt performance and masculinity, *Journal of Film and Video*, 56:3, 35–53.

Starkey, H. (1990), Is the BD 'à bout de souffle?', Chalfont St Giles, Bucks, *French Cultural Studies*, 1:2, 95–110.

Tobin, Y. (1985), *Subway*, Paris, *Positif*, 292, 79.

Verkindere, S. (1993), Nom de code: Nina, *Le Mensuel du cinéma*, 9, 42–3.

The heritage film

Filming and funding the heritage genre

The quality costume drama of the 1980s and 1990s has been termed the 'heritage film' (Higson 1993). In France it is a genre closely related to la *tradition de qualité* (see chapter 1), although chronologically it parallels the British trend for nostalgia initiated by *Chariots of Fire* in 1981. Classical in form, historical or literary in inspiration, the heritage genre tends to place a premium on high production values, often relying on international co-productions and famous stars in order to ensure a large audience. Although spectacle is clearly fundamental to the heritage film, it is always a supposedly authenticated spectacle, legitimised by claims to historical accuracy or cultural sources; hence the number of literary adaptations, biopics of forgotten figures, and reappraisals of revolution and empire. If the form is classical, following a straightforward linear narrative, so is the music: the theme from Claude Berri's *Jean de Florette* (1986) is derived from Verdi, while baroque music provides both subject and score in Alain Corneau's *Tous les matins du monde* (1992) and Gérard Corbiau's biopic of a seventeenth-century castrato, *Farinelli* (1994). A measure of the dominance of visual pleasures over narrative ones in the heritage genre is the privileging of the visual arts as a subject. Moreover, the generic camera style is pictorialist: 'crane shots and high-angle shots divorced from character point of view, for instance, are used to display ostentatiously the seductive *mise-en-scène* of the films. [...] The effect is the creation of heritage space, rather than narrative space' (Higson 1993: 117). As regards framing, the genre demonstrates 'a preference for long takes and deep focus, and for long and medium shots, rather than for close-ups and rapid cutting' (Higson 1993: 117). François Truffaut made a similar point when he vowed that after the 'picturesque' period drama of *Les Deux Anglaises et le continent* (*Anne and Muriel*, 1971), he would never again film *une guinguette* (an open air café) or a carriage drawing up in front of thirty extras in costume, electing to cut the landscape, extras and sky out of the nineteenth-century narrative *L'Histoire d'Adèle H.* (*The Story of Adèle H.*, 1975), so that only cropped frames, claustrophobic interiors and the face of Adèle (Isabelle Adjani) should remain (Truffaut 1988: 331). This unusual attention to private suffering rather than public spectacle, via intimate framing of the protagonist's face, is echoed in Corneau's *Tous les matins du monde* (see below).

Historical and mythical subjects are of course susceptible to a treatment outside the heritage genre: witness Robert Bresson's *Lancelot du Lac* (*Lancelot of the Lake*, 1974) or Eric Rohmer's *Perceval le Gallois* (1978). The bare demythologising of Arthurian legend in Bresson's film is achieved largely via ground- and body-level camera angles and a general absence of sound-track music. In Rohmer's *Perceval le Gallois* the spare yet evident artifice is the antithesis of the supposedly authentic period realism of the heritage film. All of the music and sound effects are provided by visible musicians, with the film shot in a studio against flat metal backdrops. In contrast, Daniel Vigne's medieval heritage film *Le Retour de Martin Guerre* (*The Return of Martin Guerre*, 1982) features detailed and extensive exterior locations, numerous extras, rich photography and sound-track music. This drama, based on a sixteenth-century court case which passed into legend, declares its legitimacy from the outset by including in the opening credits the contribution of Natalie Zemon Davis as historical consultant. Moreover, the introductory voice-over of the investigating judge assures the spectator that this is no adventure or fantasy but 'a pure and true (hi)story'. In clear contrast with the fundamentally cinematic aims of Rohmer and Bresson, Vigne's film 'offers innumerable validations of its own authenticity, of its capacity to document' the period in question (Pauly 1993: 41).

While some seventies works – such as André Téchiné's *Les Sœurs Brontë* (1979), or the period dramas of Truffaut and of Bertrand Tavernier (see below) – prefigured the genre, the 1980s was clearly the decade of the heritage film, and 1982 the break-through year, featuring not only *Le Retour de Martin Guerre* but also the international co-productions *Danton* and *La Nuit de Varennes* (*That Night in Varennes*). François Mitterrand's presidential victory of the year before was fundamental to the development of the heritage film as a coherent and successful genre in the eighties, for two reasons. Firstly, the victory of the Socialists in May 1981 stimulated a nostalgia for the 1930s, a time of left-wing government by the Front Populaire and, in terms of French cinema, the golden age of poetic realism. As the greatest French film-maker of that era, and one moreover associated with the Front Populaire, Jean Renoir became an important touchstone for the heritage film; in particular, his evocation of impressionism in *Partie de campagne* (1936) exerted a direct influence on films by Tavernier and Pialat, and more recently on Jean-Pierre Jeunet (see below). Secondly and more significantly, the Socialists began to target for funding a particular brand of French film, prestigious but popular 'cultural' cinema. The result was 'la "nouvelle qualité française" ' (Sainderchin 1982: 18), the filming of France's historical and cultural past as a form of national education, aiming to provoke 'le retour du grand public au cinéma' [the return of the general public to the cinema] (Le Péron 1982: 20), and funded or promoted by Jack Lang as Minister of Culture and later of Education.

Set up in 1959, the system of *avances sur recettes* is an advance loan made by the French government to film-makers, to be repaid from subsequent takings at the box office. During the 1980s, Jack Lang refined this funding mechanism and used it to support work by young directors like Besson and Beineix as well as by established *auteurs* such as Duras, Varda, Resnais and Bresson. The culturally respectable heritage genre, however, was the major beneficiary. The first year of Lang's influence, 1982, saw funding granted for the international co-productions of Wajda's *Danton* (1982) and Schlöndorff's adaptation of Proust, *Un amour de Swann* (*Swann in Love*, 1983). This tendency to favour prestigious international projects characterised government subsidising of the cinema throughout the Lang years of the early and mid-eighties. After an unexpectedly populist funding round in 1984, Lang chose the publisher Christian Bourgois as head of the *avances sur recettes* for the next year, with a brief to target 'culture' once more (see Prédal 1991: 384). This tactic enabled Claude Berri to film his expensive yet hugely successful Pagnol diptych, *Jean de Florette* and *Manon des sources* (both 1986), which epitomised Lang's vision of a cultural/popular French cinema (see below). When in the late eighties the Socialists were briefly out of power, Lang's successor François Léotard pointedly suppressed aid for 'artistic' films, but on his return to office Lang continued as before, and introduced a supplementary form of direct aid for ten to fifteen 'high quality' films per year (Prédal 1991: 388). Again, it was largely – though not exclusively – the heritage film which profited. The 'Langist' conception of film as high culture for the masses ensured that cinema now belonged to the new arena of the heritage industry, or in Lang's phraseology, 'les industries culturelles' (Toubiana *et al.* 1986: 27).

Revolution and empire

In the months following his election victory in May 1981, President Mitterrand was faced with 'a declining franc, an escalating arms race, a crisis in the Middle East, and trouble everywhere on the home front'. But in the autumn of 1983 'the crisis that he placed at the top of his agenda was the inability of the electorate to sort out the themes of its past' (Darnton 1984: 19). Launching a reform of the French curriculum, Mitterrand implicitly attempted to take control of French history, and in particular the founding moment of republican France, the Revolution of 1789, since to control the image of the Revolution 'is to exert political power, to stake out a position as the authentic representative of the left' (Darnton 1984: 23). This might also be seen as an attempt to challenge the reading of the Revolution myth presented in Andrzej Wajda's *Danton* (see below). According to *Cahiers du cinéma* in an A to Z of Lang's years as Minister of Culture, far from constituting a new left-wing cinema, political films such as *Danton* were in fact supplanted over the course of the eighties by evocations of cynical self-interest reflecting Lang and Mitterrand's own opportunism and drift towards the centre (Toubiana *et al.* 1986: 27). As for representations of French history, over the decade the focus switched from revolution to imperialism and ultimately – with Socialist power declining and Mitterrand's presidency clearly doomed – to decolonisation and the end of the Empire: witness in 1991 *Indochine* (see below) and in 1992 *Dien Bien Phu* (see chapter 2).

Relating 1789 to 1981: *La Nuit de Varennes* and *Danton*

Two mythical periods for the French left, the Revolution of 1789 and the Front Populaire government of the 1930s, came together in Jean Renoir's film *La Marseillaise* (1938), an evocation of the Revolution made under the auspices of the Front Populaire. A similar attempt to relate republican history to the society of the day resulted, immediately after Mitterrand's victory, in Andrzej Wajda's *Danton* and to a lesser extent Ettore Scola's *La Nuit de Varennes* (both 1982). These prestigious international co-productions were viewed by *Cahiers* as 'official' left-wing projects underwritten by the Socialist government (see Daney 1982 and Toubiana 1983). *Danton* was indeed funded in part by the Ministry of Culture, although the subsequent interpretations of the film proved resistant to government control (see below).

Although *La Nuit de Varennes* is not overtly politicised, its director had over the previous decade made several militant films for the Italian Communist Party, thus strengthening the association between himself and Renoir, who had overseen the Front Populaire/Communist campaign film *La Vie est à nous* (*The People of France*, 1936). A joint production financed by French and Italian television companies, *La Nuit de Varennes* was attacked in *Cahiers* for being merely a sumptuous exercise in televisual history (Daney 1982). Set in June 1791, it concerns the attempted escape from France of Louis XVI and the royal family. In Scola's fantastical version of history, they are pursued across country by a coach containing not only the lady-in-waiting Comtesse Sophie de la Borde (Hanna Schygulla), but also the cultural celebrities of the period: the legendary lover Giacomo Casanova (Marcello Mastroianni), the English revolutionary Thomas Paine (Harvey Keitel), and the libertarian writer Restif de la Bretonne (Jean-Louis Barrault). *La Nuit de Varennes* is hence as much an anthology of eighteenth-century culture as it is a historical account of the Revolution. As *Cahiers* noted at the time, political history is presented as literary history through the eyes of idealised witnesses who – along with the spectator – remain at a safe distance from the proletariat (Daney 1982). In a gesture typical of the heritage genre, Scola privileges cultural references of all kinds, and in particular literary forms, whether through direct quotations from contemporary texts or through the emphasis on written communication – messages, maps, articles and decrees – which is the motor behind the plot. The central narrative – the king's flight from Paris – is moreover framed by the self-conscious device of the puppet show, which first enacts revolutionary events prior to the king's disappearance, and ultimately closes with his execution.

The theatrical theme is continued throughout by Scola's *mise en scène*, which stages the celebrities' coach and the inns at which they pause as dramatic spaces where the characters endlessly argue opposing cultural or ideological viewpoints (see Pauly 1993: 55). Because the spectator travels with the pursuers, the king and family are never seen. Even when they are finally caught at Varennes, their faces are not visible, and the image of the king's body with his head outside the frame predicts the result of his return to Paris. Finally, after the return to the puppet show, the camera follows Restif de la Bretonne as he climbs up to the streets of Paris in 1981, a sequence one critic has interpreted as 'suggesting that the revolutionary crea-ture beneath the surface can rise again any time from the *pavés* so often used as weapons by the people' (Pauly 1993: 60). On release, the reception of the film in France was however far more cynical, with Serge Daney concluding in *Cahiers* that the heavy-handed final sequence epitomised a didactic gimmickry prevalent in 'official' histor-ical dramas. He added that Restif should have emerged not in Paris but in Cannes as Scola's press agent for the film festival, since such a resolutely 'cultural' work was bound to win a prize (Daney 1982). As it turned out, *La Nuit de Varennes* won nothing.

After three decades of film-making in Poland, Andrzej Wajda left in 1980 when the Communist authorities declared a state of emergency in response to the growing support for the banned trade union Soli-darity. He came to France and filmed *Danton*, at once a dramatisation of the French Revolution and an urgent commentary on the political situation in Poland. The narrative follows the manœuvrings of the charismatic man of the people Danton (Gérard Depardieu) and the harsh ideologue Robespierre (Wojciech Pszoniak, dubbed) during the Reign of Terror, and concludes with Danton's trial and execution, on the orders of Robespierre, in April 1794. The film's power derives from a series of contrasts between Danton and Robespierre on the level of characterisation and staging as much as ideology. The conflict is most evident when the two men confront each other in claustrophobic and enclosed spaces, particularly during the aborted supper in Danton's private apartment. In such scenes the theatricality of the dialogue, rendered all the more artificial by the dubbing of Pszoniak, is at odds with Depardieu's more relaxed and gestural performance, which recalls the more enigmatic power of the silent cinema (Toubiana 1983: 55). The political conflict between the two is underlined not just by the contrast in styles of performance, but also by Wajda's *mise en scène*, so that Danton's clothes and rooms are red, Robespierre's blue. This simple colour scheme is complemented by the use of white, which both symbolises revolutionary purity and completes the republican tricolour. In the ironic final sequence which takes place after Danton's death, the deathly pale Robespierre, having concluded that the Revolution has mutated into a dictatorship, passively listens to a young boy reciting the revolutionary creed. A close-up of the boy's face dissolves into a blank white screen, suggestive of the revolutionary purity that has been lost in the Terror. The irony is underlined by Jean Prodromides's discordant, wailing music, the sound-track of the Terror, which drowns out the boy's idealistic words.

A Franco-Polish co-production, the film was based on the Polish play *The Danton Affair*, written in 1935 by Stanislawa Przybyszweka and staged by Wajda himself in the late seventies and early eighties. Abel Gance's *Napoléon* (1927) and Renoir's *La Marseillaise* (1938) were also points of reference, but the Polish resonances dominated the film's critical reception:

The film is a triple parable for its Polish audiences, of Tadeusz Kosciuszko's role in fighting the Russians in 1794, of conditions in Poland during the 1930s when the play appeared, and lastly of Poland's situation in 1981, when Lech Walesa and Solidarity were struggling to free the nation from dominance by a stale soviet bureaucracy and its secret police. (Pauly 1993: 93)

According to the latter reading, the most prevalent in the press despite Wajda's disavowals, Danton was identified with Lech Walesa and Robespierre became General Jaruzelski. Interpretation of *Danton* in relation to French politics was far more problematic, and entailed a struggle over the film's meaning which again concentrated on the portrayal of the two protagonists. Historically associated with the victory of 'republican France against the combined forces of feudal Europe', and hence with the birth and identity of the modern state, Robespierre remained an iconic figure for the French left (Darnton 1984: 20). Hence the delight of the Gaullist opposition and the dismay of both Communists and Socialists, including Mitterrand, at the characterisation of Robespierre as a tyrant and Danton as a sympathetic pragmatist: 'The persona of Danton created by the immensely popular Gérard Depardieu [...] elicited a conservative bourgeois image in France, was even labelled Gaullist. Thus the implications of the film in Poland and France were reversed' (Pauly 1993: 94). Faced with a 'Gaullist' Danton, Mitterrand and Lang, despite being 'the champions of socialism with a human face' (Darnton 1984: 19), were obliged to identify with Robespierre, and thus to fall foul of a revision of accepted republican history which they had in effect financed themselves.

Fort Saganne: handing down the imperialist adventure

The tendency to recreate a 'televisual' slice of history which certain critics had detected in *Danton* and *La Nuit de Varennes* was rendered explicit two years later in Alain Corneau's *Fort Saganne* (1984), a hybrid production which was sold as an international television mini-series before being released at the cinema (see Prédal 1991: 389). A director who had made his name in the thriller genre (see chapter 5), Corneau made the transition to the heritage film with great success, *Fort Saganne* attracting over two million spectators in France. This is unsurprising when one considers that the film united Gérard Depardieu and Catherine Deneuve, two of the most powerful and popular French stars of the day.

Beginning in 1911, *Fort Saganne* is essentially an epic adventure story following the career of Charles Saganne (Depardieu), an army officer stationed in the Sahara. In keeping with the heritage genre's claim to historical, cultural, or geographical authenticity, the opening credits reveal that the Saharan sequences 'were shot in and around the historic towns of Chinguetti and Ouadane'. The exotic locations, numerous extras and imperialist subject are all comparable to the sub-genre of the British heritage film which concerns the Raj – as in David Lean's *A Passage to India* (1985) or the eighties television series *The Jewel in the Crown* – while the precise setting and epic military narrative recall Lean's *Lawrence of Arabia* (1962). As in these British productions, social class is a crucial theme: Saganne, who is of peasant stock, falls in love with Madeleine (Sophie Marceau), a daughter of the *haute bourgeoisie* and cousin of the President. The narrative concerns Saganne's rites of passage in the Sahara – where, he discovers, a man is judged by his actions and not his social origins – first under the tutelage of Colonel Dubreuilh (Philippe Noiret), a paternalistic figure described at one point as 'a medieval lord', and then in confrontation with the war lords of the desert. It is only when Saganne has learned a kind of chivalric 'nobility' – and won the Legion of Honour – that he can marry Madeleine and accede to a powerful social status. During the course of this military and social education, Saganne faces a sexual interlude in Paris with Louise (Deneuve), a predatory journalist. As a cool seductress, Louise manipulates Saganne as only men (his superior officers) have managed to do thus far in the film, exercising an ambiguous sexual power which Depardieu identified when he said: 'Catherine Deneuve is the man I would have liked to be' (Vincendeau 1993: 47). Deneuve's presence in *Fort Saganne* is not however limited to the role of *femme fatale* or, later, of nurse to the troops. She also functions as an icon of France, the mother country which Saganne and the empire-builders are defending (she makes her first appearance as he gives a speech about the need to protect France in the Sahara). This symbolic function, reprised in 1991 in Régis Warnier's *Indochine* (see below), is accentuated by Deneuve's iconic power outside cinema, whether as 'a semi-official ambassador for French fashion' and indeed for French womanhood as constructed by the advertising industry or, in the mid eighties and the nineties, as the model for official images of Marianne, the personification of the French Republic (see Vincendeau 1993: 46, 41). But although France is embodied by a woman in *Fort Saganne*, ultimately it is in the masculine arena of war and through the male line of descent that the continuity of the empire is assured. Hence no sooner is the threat of World War One announced to the spectator (in the form of the subtitle 'July 1914') than it is obviated by a sex scene between Saganne and Madeleine, in which a son is conceived. Even as Saganne lies dying on the Western Front, Madeleine is pregnant, and the imperialist adventure is thus guaranteed for one more generation. This is confirmed in the final sequence, set in 1922: young Charles Saganne junior accompanies his mother at the ceremonial naming of Fort Saganne, and is initiated into the ways of the desert by his father's ally, a Saharan war lord. With Madeleine excluded, and World War One forgotten, the 'noble' rites of passage and the masculine tradition of empire can continue.

The aftermath of war: *La Vie et rien d'autre*

Like Corneau, Bertrand Tavernier is equally adept at the heritage film and the thriller (see chapter 5), and in both genres he is associated with a return to the narrative and psychological values of the postwar *tradition de qualité*. Hence his frequent literary adaptations, and his collaborations with Pierre Bost and Jean Aurenche, scriptwriters popular during the 1950s before their rejection by *la nouvelle vague* (see chapter 1). Along with François Truffaut, Tavernier represents the first stirrings of the heritage film in France after *la nouvelle vague*. His costume dramas of the seventies – *Que la fête commence* (*Let Joy Reign Supreme*, 1975) and *Le Juge et l'assassin* (1976) – were followed by *Un dimanche à la campagne* (*Sunday in the Country*, 1984), *La Passion Béatrice* (1987), and *La Vie et rien d'autre* (*Life And Nothing But*, 1989). A film critic before he turned director, Tavernier is deeply influenced by classical Hollywood cinema, and his medieval frontier story *La Passion Béatrice* has been credited with 'doing for French history what the Western did' for American history (Forbes 1992: 168). His painterly style, sweeping camera movements and humanist themes also owe a debt to Jean Renoir, and have rendered Tavernier probably the most consistent heritage film-maker in France, producing a popular yet bourgeois left-wing cinema, humanist in tone yet conservative in form, emblematic of the Mitterrand years (see Prédal 1991: 285).

Despite the director's previous successes, *La Vie et rien d'autre* proved difficult to finance because its subject was considered 'morbid, uninteresting and sinister' (Tavernier 1993: 266). Set in 1920, the film portrays the aftermath of the First World War and its attendant traumas, an area elided in *Fort Saganne* by the gap between Saganne's death and the inauguration of his monument. As with his other heritage films, Tavernier's evocation of period is detailed and his cinematography fluid, while the enormous sets and the hordes of extras prefigure Claude Berri's realisation of the coal mine in *Germinal* (1993, see below). The plot concerns the efforts of Major Dellaplane (Philippe Noiret) to identify the bodies of thousands of missing men, and also to choose those to be entombed under the Arc de Triomphe as France's 'unknown soldiers'. The wider question of unearthing the horrors of the war before they can be buried again links the film with Tavernier's subsequent project, the Algerian War documentary *La*

Guerre sans nom (*The Undeclared War*, 1992, see chapter 2), of which he said: 'I have a sense of continuing *La Vie et rien d'autre*, taking a historical fact and studying its effects and consequences' (Tavernier 1993: 267). Dellaplane specialises, moreover, in the art of photography and thus his activity throughout the film parallels that of Tavernier himself: excavating the past by means of a camera. Rather as in *Le Juge et l'assassin*, Tavernier combines costume drama with a detective narrative, in this case via a sub-plot concerning two women looking for the same man, a dead soldier who was the lover of one and the husband of the other. Dellaplane meets both women and falls for the widow, Irène de Courtil (Sabine Azéma). In a crucial speech which reflects not just on history but on its filmic representation – in *Fort Saganne* or in the war film generally (see chapter 2) – Irène attacks the masculine discourse of war and its perpetuation in all-male clubs and gatherings. She concludes that Dellaplane is afraid of women and hence of life. This is followed immediately by the ritual entombment of Dellaplane's unknown soldiers in a cold, patriarchal ceremony. Dellaplane seems to have chosen death over life. Characteristically, Tavernier concludes with an elegiac epilogue and a lyrical tracking shot reminiscent of Renoir. As Dellaplane walks alone through his vineyard, his letter to Irène is read in voice-over; just as he evokes the enormity of the loss of life in the war, the camera tracks from right to left to reveal rows of vines like so many war graves.

Indochine: Mother France and melodrama

In contrast with the patriarchal genealogy of imperialist power in *Fort Saganne*, Régis Warnier's Oscar-winning *Indochine* (1991) presents the decline of the French empire as a tragic, matriarchal narrative. In other words, *Indochine* is, unusually for a heritage film, a melodrama. Set in Indochina in the 1930s, Warnier's film conveys the loss of the colony not as military history – like Pierre Schoendoerffer's *Dien Bien Phu* a year later (see chapter 2) – but as a family history, in which the central relationship between a French mother and her adopted Indochinese daughter explicitly symbolises the colonial power structure. By choosing melodrama, Warnier also subordinates the heritage genre's inherent nostalgia for another period and an exotic setting to a more primal desire, traditionally addressed by melodrama: the spectator's desire for union with the mother. The spectator watching a melodrama wishes for 'the union of the couple' in order to satisfy 'a nostalgic fantasy of childhood characterised by union with the mother: a state of total love, satisfaction, and dyadic fusion' (Neale 1986: 17). What is notable about *Indochine* is that 'the couple' here includes not only various personal relationships between a mother and her daughter, her lover and her grandson, but also the political relationship between France and Indochina. To this end, the film casts Catherine Deneuve in the role of Éliane, the French mother. As Corneau did in *Fort Saganne*, Warnier plays on Deneuve's status as an icon of French womanhood, able to 'signify a constellation of traits –

career woman who remains feminine, determined but tragic mother, strong-willed but vulnerable lover – that allude to the changing roles of French women, but at the same time confine them to this precisely symbolic function' (Vincendeau 1993: 48). While the narrative of *Indochine* casts her in each of these roles at one point or another, it is her function as a tragic mother which combines with her extra-filmic role as Marianne, the personification of France, to portray the French empire as a mother who has to reconcile herself to the loss of her colonial child.

Like Jean-Jacques Annaud's *L'Amant* (1992, see chapter 3), the film is shot in authentic oriental locations and is conveyed by a female narrator, in this case Éliane. Her voice-over states the film's melodramatic premise early on, declaring that in her youth she believed that the world was made up of inseparable dyads, 'men and women, Indochina and France'. If as a colonial rubber plantation owner Éliane embodies France, her adopted daughter Camille (Lin Dan Pham), a teenager gradually finding a sense of her own identity, embodies Indochina. The two are doomed to separation by the rules of melodrama as much as by political history. A tender and tragic mother to Camille, Éliane is portrayed as a cruel maternal figure – a kind of imperialistic career woman – in relation to her Indochinese workers, and as a seductive yet maternal lover to the young officer Le Guen (Vincent Perez). It is when Camille and Le Guen embark on an affair that the mother-daughter dyad is broken and the narrative takes on an epic sweep: Éliane has Le Guen transferred to a remote northern outpost, only for Camille to leave in search of him. In sequences reminiscent of Bertolucci's epic heritage film, *The Last Emperor* (1987), Warnier presents a brief panorama of the poverty, hunger and social unrest which are generating rebellion against French colonial power. Melodrama is privileged over history however, as Camille, captured by slave traders, is rescued by Le Guen. The reunited lovers are separated again during the uprising, but not before Camille has given birth to a son, Étienne. At this point the narrative frame allows us to glimpse that it is to the adult Étienne that Éliane is telling the story of the film. With the death of Le Guen and the imprisonment of Camille, the child is brought up by Éliane, functioning once more in a maternal role. But the division of mother and daughter (and hence of France and Indochina) is ironically confirmed at the moment of their reunion: released from prison, Camille has become a communist rebel – 'the red princess' – and therefore rejects her mother and imperialist power simultaneously. Her words to Éliane here sum up the pattern of melodrama: 'C'est trop tard, maman; je ne peux pas revenir en arrière' [It's too late, mother; I can't go back]. In melodrama, 'pathos is the product of a realisation that comes too late' (Neale 1986: 10). But the pleasure of the genre derives from the possibility that the desired reunion may simply be postponed or modified: the fantasy of oneness with the mother 'can be re-engaged, re-articulated, perhaps finally fulfilled in the next film, the next melodrama (or the next episode of a soap opera)' (Neale 1986:

21). In *Indochine*, the reunion is achieved in the superb final sequence: having lost her lover and her daughter, and at the precise moment that Indochina's independence from France is declared, Éliane is finally granted the love she deserves and craves. The sequence takes place in Switzerland in 1954; Éliane has given Étienne the chance to be reconciled with his mother Camille, who is a member of the Indochinese delegation to the Geneva Conference on the future of the ex-colony. By refusing this reunion, Étienne enacts another, telling Éliane that she alone is his mother. Camille, belonging to the realm of politics, has lost her place in the melodrama. Warnier concludes *Indochine* with a shot of Éliane looking at her own motherland, France, in the distance beyond Lake Geneva. The image is held in a sepia freeze-frame, signalling that what was melodrama has become history, as confirmed by the closing text, which reveals that the French empire is over: 'On the following day, 21 July 1954, the Geneva Conference closed, putting an end to fifteen years of divisions and sealing the partition into two distinct states of what would henceforth be known as Vietnam.'

Filming the arts

The heritage film often takes its subject or source from the 'culturally respectable classicisms of literature, painting, music' (Higson 1993: 113). Painting is obviously the most important of the three in determining the imagery of the genre, usually by means of the static tableau shot. In Eric Rohmer's mannerist *La Marquise d'O* (1976) the *mise en scène* replicates Fuseli's painting 'The Nightmare', later imitated in Ken Russell's *Gothic* (1986). Outside the heritage format, Jean-Luc Godard and Agnès Varda deconstruct the tableaux of famous classical paintings in *Passion* (1982) and *Jane B. par Agnès V.* (1987) respectively. But the essential precursor for the painterly images of the genre is the cinema of Jean Renoir. Renoir's homage to impressionism began with the short, unfinished masterpiece *Partie de campagne* (1936), set in the 1880s, in which a Parisian family spend a day in the country. In this film – and later in *French Cancan* (1954) and, to a lesser extent, *Le déjeuner sur l'herbe* (*Lunch on the Grass*, 1959) – Renoir founds his imagery on the impressionist paintings of Monet, Manet, Degas and his own father, Auguste Renoir. Within the heritage genre of the eighties and nineties, impressionism is evoked in a similar manner in Bertrand Tavernier's *Un dimanche à la campagne* (*Sunday in the Country*, 1984) and Maurice Pialat's *Van Gogh* (1991).

Mobilising the tableau in *Un dimanche à la campagne* and *Van Gogh*

Based on a novel by Pierre Bost, *Un dimanche à la campagne* details a day in the life of an elderly painter at the turn of the century. But the film is clearly a homage to the cinema of Jean Renoir as much as to the paintings of Monet or Renoir *père*. The opening sequence, like the title, establishes an analogy with *Partie de campagne* which runs

20   Sabine Azéma and Louis Ducreux in *Un dimanche à la campagne*

throughout the film. Renoir had characteristically made use in *Une partie de campagne* of the depth of field and painterly frame afforded when a window is opened to reveal action in the background (in this case, the impressionist scene of two women on the swings in the café garden). Tavernier begins *Un dimanche à la campagne* with a similar composition, although mediated by a slow tracking shot (another device typical of Renoir). The camera moves slowly from a shadowy interior towards a sunlit garden, framed in a doorway. Crossing the frame, the camera reveals the garden bathed in the morning light, before the screen fades to black. This simple painterly sequence initiates the narrative as a story of changing light, from morning to nightfall (an impressionist concern) and of varying depths of field (a Renoirian concern). It is moreover repeated at the film's close, and thus acts as a frame for the narrative.

Monsieur Ladmiral (Louis Ducreux), a widower and painter who lives in the country, receives a visit from his son, daughter-in-law and grandchildren. They are joined later in the day by the old man's favourite, his daughter Irène (Sabine Azéma). During the course of the day, family conversations and arguments are punctuated with flashbacks as Monsieur Ladmiral and others recall idyllic family scenes from the past, to a sound-track which features elegiac music by Fauré as well as occasional passages from Bost's novel read in voice-over by Tavernier. After his visitors have gone, Monsieur Ladmiral's impending death is heralded by nightfall, and thus the opening (and closing) sequence functions as a microcosm of the film's narrative: the

Jacques Dutronc in *Van Gogh*

movement from morning to night, from life to death. Nostalgia, the basic emotion of the heritage genre, dictates the nature of the film in four ways: on a narrative level, as the family's nostalgia for the past (when Madame Ladmiral was alive), and also as Tavernier's three-fold nostalgia, historical (for the turn of the century), painterly (for impressionism), and filmic (for Renoir). During the course of the film, Tavernier repeats the camera movement that reveals the garden through a doorway or window frame, a composition suggestive of Matisse as well as of Jean Renoir. But the most explicit reference to impressionist art is made when Irène and her father dance at a riverside café – a *guinguette* – which recalls Auguste Renoir's paintings 'The Luncheon of the Boating Party' and 'Dance at Bougival'. Knowingly, Irène even tells her father that he should have painted the scene. The image of the dancers is, unusually for Tavernier, a fixed shot and one viewed from the front in a classic tableau format. (Maurice Pialat includes a very similar image in *Van Gogh*, but one mobilised by a camera which dances with the characters.) Typically in Tavernier, as in Renoir, the tableau is not static but explored by a moving camera. Most often in *Un dimanche à la campagne* this involves a slow tracking shot into the painterly image, be it the garden, a portrait of Madame Ladmiral, or the white tablecloth spread like a blank canvas on the grass. In *Van Gogh*, meanwhile, Pialat varies between fluid camera movements and lingering, still tableaux to reproduce almost exactly Van Gogh's last paintings.

Such a painterly concern marks a development in Pialat's work, which has been more notable for the use of improvised dialogue, handheld camera and seedy locations to create a documentary style, as in the urban love story *Loulou* (1980) and *Police* (1985), a naturalistic thriller (see chapter 5). The commercial success of the latter allowed Pialat to use bigger budgets and consequently to modify his style, paying more attention in his next two films to production values and establishing a stylised *mise en scène*. *Sous le soleil de Satan* (*Under Satan's Sun*, 1987), taken from a novel by Georges Bernanos and influenced by Robert Bresson's *Le Journal d'un curé de campagne* (*Diary of a Country Priest*, 1950), is a rather uneasy combination of naturalism and spectacle. The interior shots in the church, especially the image of Mouchette's body on the altar, are lit and framed like sumptuous tableaux. In *Van Gogh* (1991) the composition of tableaux at times detracts from a lengthy account of the final months of the artist's life. By far the most expensive film Pialat has made, it was perhaps fittingly (given the subject) a commercial disaster.

The subject of numerous biopics in the United States and Europe, Van Gogh also inspired Alain Resnais and Gaston Diehl's black-and-white documentary *Van Gogh* (1948), in which 'camera movements across the surfaces of canvases were increased in speed until the paintings became unreadable, focus was also pulled to create blurs, and montage was accelerated as the film neared its end', such distortions aiming to symbolise the artist's growing mental turmoil (Walker 1993: 181). Pialat's representation of the paintings is by contrast tame imitation, but he does integrate them with the circumstances of Van Gogh's life by including compositions in the course of the narrative, ostensibly by chance, and sometimes in the background. The film begins with the arrival of Van Gogh (Jacques Dutronc) in Auvers-sur-Oise in May 1890, and follows his deteriorating relations with his host, Doctor Gachet, Gachet's daughter Marguerite, and his own brother, Theo. Drinking heavily and in despair, the artist shoots himself in the chest and dies two days later. Photographed largely in melancholic blue tones, although at moments imitating the palette of Van Gogh's canvases, the film is reminiscent of Pialat's earlier work in the unsteady, restless camera movement and the absence of soundtrack music. Although the seemingly improvised dialogue and the harsh, unsentimental tone are far from the conventions of the heritage film, the composition of impressionist tableaux demonstrates a desire to reproduce the 'authentic' which is fundamental to the genre. Among the paintings by Van Gogh reproduced here are the portraits of Gachet and of Marguerite and the views of wheatfields and of boats on the Oise; Renoir *père* and Degas are also alluded to in the long Parisian cancan sequence and the scene at the riverside *guinguette*. And again, Jean Renoir's *Partie de campagne* and *French Cancan* are visible influences on this painterly enterprise.

Private space in *Camille Claudel* and *Tous les matins du monde*

Like *Van Gogh*, Bruno Nuytten's *Camille Claudel* (1988) is the lengthy biopic of a troubled artist, but a biopic watched by three million spectators. The popularity of the film is above all attributable to the presence of Isabelle Adjani and Gérard Depardieu as the leads. For Adjani this was a personal project, directed by her ex-partner Nuytten and co-produced by herself amid accusations that she had abused her position as president of the *commission d'avances sur recettes* (see Reader 1989). The film may also have benefited from the publicity surrounding Adjani at the time, whose public declaration that her father was Algerian and her mother German was followed by a rumour in the press that she was dying of Aids. As she noted later, the two events were not unconnected: 'the French have long regarded foreigners as an infectious body within the nation, and of course that's like Aids. So to the right-wingers like Le Pen, I became a good target' (Andrew 1995: 25).

Camille Claudel has been termed 'the climax of a long period of art-historical rehabilitation' inspired by feminist reassessments of cultural production (Walker 1993: 79). The sculptor had previously been known, not as an artist in her own right, but as pupil, assistant and mistress to Auguste Rodin in the 1880s and 1890s, and also as the sister of the poet Paul Claudel, who was in fact responsible for her incarceration in an asylum for the last thirty years of her life. Three biographies of Camille Claudel had been published in France in the early 1980s, initiating a revision of this reductive image. Anne Delbée, having written a play and a biography about Camille which were critical of her treatment by her family, planned to make a film too. This project was scuppered by the Claudels, who granted access to personal documents and letters to Nuytten and Adjani instead, since their version was based on a much more favourable biography by Camille's grandniece Reine-Marie Paris (Reader 1989). The resultant film relates how Camille (Adjani), an ambitious young sculptor aged nineteen, meets Rodin (Depardieu) in Paris and becomes his model and assistant, ultimately subordinating her own work to his so that he even signs what she has sculpted. Despite her family's disapproval, and the fact that Rodin has a long-term partner, Camille becomes his mistress. Later she leaves him and tries to establish an independent career, which is jeopardised by her drinking and an increasing paranoia about Rodin. After a disastrous exhibition at which she appears drunk, she destroys many of her sculptures, and on her father's death her mother and brother have her taken to an asylum.

Authentic in terms of setting – as in the shot of a half-built Eiffel tower – and costume, the film is less persuasive as an account of the creation of art, which is seen 'only in snatches, so the drawn-out sequence of steps from concept to finished work [...] is never fully documented' (Walker 1993: 87). This could be said of Pialat's *Van Gogh* and of the heritage genre's approach to art in general, and is in contrast with the extensive exploration of the creative process in Jacques Rivette's *La Belle Noiseuse* (*The Beautiful Troublemaker*, 1991). As one might expect from a cinematographer turned director, Nuytten shoots *Camille Claudel* effectively in brooding nocturnal colours and with intricate camerawork. But although Rodin's visit to the Claudels' house in the country is the cue for an impressionist-inspired

22   Jean-Pierre Marielle and Gérard Depardieu in *Tous les matins du monde*

mise en scène, the compositions are often intimate and gloomy, and thus unusual for a heritage film. The predominance of interiors over public spaces can be related to Paul Claudel's definition of his sister's art as an 'interior' sculpture, 'proscribed from public square and open air' (Walker 1993: 88), but also to François Truffaut's claustrophobic period drama *L'Histoire d'Adèle H.* (1975), a clear influence on *Camille Claudel*. Adjani received Oscar nominations for both performances, each time for her role as a troubled woman seeking independence from a dominant father figure only to end up in an asylum. Unlike *L'Histoire d'Adèle H.*, however, *Camille Claudel* does at times feature those clichés of the costume drama – such as carriages pulling up in front of houses – which Truffaut had excised from his film, making it altogether shorter, sparer and more psychologically convincing than Nuytten's.

If in *Camille Claudel* Nuytten fails to fully match his *mise en scène* to the 'interior sculpture' of his subject, in *Tous les matins du monde* (1992) Alain Corneau achieves a perfect integration of theme and form, of private music and private space. The film reunites the co-stars of Jean-Paul Rappeneau's *Cyrano de Bergerac* (1991), Gérard Depardieu and Anne Brochet, and like *Cyrano* a year before, won numerous awards at the Césars. Marin Marais (Depardieu) is a seventeenth-century court musician. It is he who narrates the action of the film proper, in which the young Marais (Guillaume Depardieu, Gérard's son) is schooled in the art of the viol by the brilliant but puritanical Sainte-Colombe (Jean-Pierre Marielle), who has retreated into solitude since his wife's death. Marais and his teacher's eldest daughter, Madeleine (Brochet) fall in love, but when Marais leaves her to marry an aristocrat and enter the court, and her child by him is still-born, Madeleine hangs herself. The

23 Gérard Depardieu in *Tous les matins du monde*

remorse-filled Marais is finally reconciled with Sainte-Colombe as the two men play music together in memory of Madeleine.

For all the apparent melodrama of such a plot, *Tous les matins du monde* is in fact a melancholic film which always privileges *mise en scène* over narrative. As impressive as the seventeenth-century music is the photography by Yves Angelo, who went on to direct his own heritage film, *Le Colonel Chabert*, in 1994 (see below). The use of colour filters, based around a simple red/blue opposition with pastoral green as a neutral tone, replaces the conventional naturalism of the historical drama with an emotional symbolism as effective in conveying passion and conflict as Godard's famous colour scheme in *Le Mépris* (1963). Throughout the film, warm red interiors, reminiscent of Rembrandt's paintings, contrast with cold blue nocturnal exteriors. The *mise en scène* – lighting, décors and costumes – is an index of the tension between spirituality and materialism, between Sainte-Colombe's suffering and creativity and the cold indifference of the wider world, Marais and the court. The luminous but narrow palette of the *mise en scène* is complemented by the austere framing – which makes great use of facial close-ups – and is only relieved in the rare court sequences where public space is represented by a wider frame and a diversity of colours typical of the heritage genre. The theme of austerity is invoked from the start of the film, when the aged Marais, in a red close-up, evokes the memory of Sainte-Colombe. After this spare opening sequence, the main body of the film comprises a flashback. Sainte-Colombe's withdrawal into his music on the death of his wife is realised in repeated facial close-ups, lit in red, as he plays

The heritage fim

183

or composes. When the young Marais asks to study under Sainte-Colombe, his red costume relates him both to the musician and to the dead wife. Corneau's *mise en scène* divides the screen when the two men meet, with the left-hand side, occupied by Marais, coloured red, and the right, where Sainte-Colombe sits resisting the appeal of human contact and of music-making, coloured blue. This painterly composition is reversed near the end of the film when the two men are reconciled: Marais, 'a man fleeing palaces in search of music', stands in the blue darkness outside the cabin where Sainte-Colombe, bathed in red light, grieves and plays his viol. In between these two crucial scenes the romance between Marais and Madeleine is played out, ending with the bleak, blue-toned scenes of her decline and suicide. Corneau's privileging of painterly images and beautiful music in *Tous les matins du monde* takes the heritage film's usual aesthetic concerns to their limit. But the result is resolutely austere rather than spectacular, and the music melancholic and repetitious, illustrating Sainte-Colmbe's comment to Marais that 'music is not for kings', but for the expression of private sorrow.

The Pagnol phenomenon

A successful film-maker and novelist whose career stretched from the 1930s to the 1950s, Marcel Pagnol was famous for his evocation of the Provence region of France. Filmed in Provence, his comedies and melodramas are notable for the poetic dialogue and genuine southern accents. But whereas Pagnol's representations of the south were sometimes of the moment – *Toni*, directed by Jean Renoir and produced by Pagnol in 1933, was based on the newspaper report of a crime – the heritage films derived from his work are doubly picturesque, 'doubly exotic, temporally as well as spatially' (de la Bretèque 1992: 61). Perhaps because of this potent nostalgia for another time and another place, the Pagnol adaptations of the eighties and nineties were extremely successful at the box office. In 1986 more than 6 million people saw Claude Berri's *Jean de Florette* and more than 4 million the sequel *Manon des sources*, while Robert's far inferior diptych cashed in on the Pagnol vogue in 1990, with *La Gloire de mon père* (*My Father's Glory*) attracting 5.8 million spectators and *Le Château de ma mère* (*My Mother's Castle*) 3.4 million.

Operatic tragedy in *Jean de Florette* and *Manon des sources*

Claude Berri's avowed ambition in filming his Pagnol adaptations, to make a French *Gone With the Wind* and launch a mythical 'cinéma populaire' (Ostria 1986: 62), coincided exactly with Jack Lang's vision of the medium. With financial aid from Lang, he shot both films simultaneously, on location, over a period of nine months and at an almost unprecedented cost of 110 million francs. The review of *Jean de Florette* in *Cahiers du cinéma* noted that Berri's experience producing Roman Polanski's *Tess* (1979) had given him a taste for expensive and

24   Daniel Auteuil and Gérard Depardieu in *Jean de Florette*

risky literary adaptation, far removed from his earlier films as director
(Toubiana 1986: 49). It was a taste which Berri was subsequently to
indulge as a producer and director of heritage films, in *La Reine Margot*
(1994) and *Germinal* (1993) respectively (see below).

In 1952 Pagnol had shot the film *Manon des sources*, developing
the narrative a decade later in written form, and adding to the saga
a tragic dénouement and a prequel concerning Jean de Florette. The
resultant two-part novel, *L'Eau des collines*, is the source for Berri's
two films. Although these were shot simultaneously, *Jean de Florette*
is generally the stronger, benefiting from a tight dramatic focus on
its three protagonists. Berri's achievement in both films, particularly
the first, is to eschew the public space of the heritage genre in favour
of a private tragedy concerning disputed heritage (the farm left to
Jean in part one and ultimately to his daughter Manon in part two).
Jean de Florette follows the inevitable demise of the urban interloper
of the title (Gérard Depardieu) after his peasant neighbours, César
and Ugolin Soubeyran (Yves Montand and Daniel Auteuil), block
his water supply in order to buy his land on the cheap. Although the
Provençal landscape shown is spectacular, high camera angles are
rare, while throughout the film Bressonian ground-level close-ups
of Ugolin's carnations or Jean's withering crops convey the central
importance to the narrative of earth, water, and cultivation. This
elemental factor structures the rhythm of the narrative as well, with
rainfall and drought prolonging and finally confirming Jean's fate. As
Cahiers suggested, Jean can be identified with the director since both
are outsiders entering Provence (Toubiana 1986: 49), but he also
appears to embody the heritage genre which this film at least plays

The heritage fim

against. Hence Jean's conception of Provence as a pastoral idyll, and his intention to 'cultiver l'authentique', a parody of the heritage film's characteristic claims to authenticity; moreover his naive ambition is interpreted as literary (like so many heritage projects) when Ugolin assumes that 'l'authentique' is an exotic plant Jean has read about in a text on horticulture. The character of Jean departs from a naturalistic portrayal of the Provençal peasant community in two other ways: first through Depardieu's appearance – he is a hunch back, recalling the archetype from popular literature, Victor Hugo's Quasimodo – and melodramatic acting style, and second through his association with music and above all with opera. His wife Aimée (Elisabeth Depardieu), an ex-opera singer, suggests that *Jean de Florette* is an ideal name for an opera, while an early scene shows him playing his harmonica as she sings the theme from Verdi's *The Force of Destiny*. The absurdity here stems from the gulf between an idealised, musical fantasy of rural living and the harsh reality to which the family are exposed through the Soubeyrans' plotting. Jean's illusions remain, however, encapsulated above all in the scenes in which he pauses to play the operatic theme on his harmonica. These musical interludes, as well as qualifying Berri's realism with a romanticised element, convey a touristic, facile picture of Provence which was uncritically reproduced not just in Yves Robert's Pagnol adaptations but, with the Verdi theme intact, in a long-running advertising campaign for Stella Artois beer.

If *Jean de Florette* is a sombre and at times melodramatic tragedy, *Manon des sources* is a simple revenge narrative. After Jean's death, Manon (Emmanuelle Béart) is avenged upon the Soubeyrans, and in the final twist César is revealed as Jean's father and thus the destroyer of his own son. Again, the score is dominated by the harmonica theme from Verdi, here played by Manon at several points in the film. Like her father, and again in part through the operatic association of the music, Manon is a mythical rather than naturalistic character. An elusive goatherd, she is already a legendary figure at the start of the film, associated with the Provençal landscapes she inhabits, and reminiscent of the folk archetype of the water nymph (de la Bretèque 1992: 65). As in *Jean de Florette*, the characterisation is balanced between realism and fantasy: while César and Ugolin function at one end of the scale, Manon belongs to the other, and the villagers, sketchy stereotypes akin to those presented by Yves Robert, fit uneasily between them. It is above all the evocation of village life – largely absent from the narrower frame of *Jean de Florette* – which links *Manon des sources* to Pagnol's own films and also to a touristic image of Provence: the tableaux of villagers working recall the supposedly ethnographic set pieces 'beloved alike by opera (Gounoud's *Mireille*), advertising agencies and the cinema', while the increasing importance of the village square in the film is analogous not only to conceptions of a public heritage space but also to the traditional symbolism of the square 'as a metonymy for the "territory" of Provence' (de la Bretèque 1992: 63, 67). Although envisioned as a simplification of Pagnol, avoiding picturesque images of folk ritual, of villagers drinking pastis and playing *pétanque* (Ostria 1986: 62), *Manon des sources*, unlike the prequel, falls back with increasing regularity on such scenes. Manon's revenge – the drying up of the fountain – and her denunciation of César and Ugolin both take place in the village before an audience, as do the public rituals which follow: the religious procession, the wedding, the Christmas service. Only in the revelation of César's relation to Jean, and in his decline and self-willed death does Berri return to the spare, private spaces so frequent in *Jean de Florette*. César's death scene also sees the Verdi theme return with a fresh status, narrative rather than decorative: playing over an image of César's body, Jean's theme finally unites father and son.

Sentimental tourism in *La Gloire de mon père* and *Le Château de ma mère*

Yves Robert's apparently cynical attempt to emulate the format and thus the popularity of Berri's Pagnol adaptations proved hugely successful, despite the marked difference in styles. Robert's two films seem to owe as much to Disney as to Pagnol, despite being based on the latter's memoirs, *Souvenirs d'enfance*. The first part introduces the young Marcel (Julien Ciamaca) and his family, including his school-teacher father Joseph (Philippe Caubère) and his mother Augustine (Nathalie Roussel). Beginning in 1900, the film evinces a nostalgia for childhood and for the early years of the century as well as a certain geographical exoticism. Like *Jean de Florette* and *Manon des sources*, *La Gloire de mon père* and *Le Château de ma mère* were shot largely on location in Provence, but tragic intrigue is replaced by domestic and sentimental comedy, while the peasant milieu of the Berri films here becomes a picturesque diversion for bourgeois tourists. As such, *La Gloire de mon père* and *Le Château de ma mère* reflect tellingly the spatial and temporal tourism fundamental to the heritage film, Berri included. The spectacular landscape, the rustic archetypes and the folk rituals of the genre are all here, while Robert's use of high camera angles to realise public places, whether the parks and avenues of Marseille or the Provençal mountains, epitomises the construction of 'heritage space' (see Higson 1993). The model of the heritage spectator as a kind of temporal, as well as spatial, daytripper is evoked – without a hint of irony or awareness – by the narrative of both films. If in *La Gloire de mon père* the family stay in a country villa for the school holidays, in *Le Château de ma mère* they travel to Provence, and to the château of the title, every Sunday. Naturally, they meet none of the hostility with which Jean de Florette is greeted, but are in fact fêted by the locals. The tone is consistently one of light comedy until the conclusion of the second part, which relates the deaths of Marcel's mother, his brother Paul and his peasant friend Lili. The coda which follows legitimises the narrative, not merely via the male voice-over – implicitly the voice of Pagnol's text, which punctuates both films – but also by representing the now adult Pagnol as a film-maker in the thirties, and by including a brief sequence from one of his films. Thus in a gesture characteristic of the heritage genre, Robert ultimately 'authorises' his work by reference to an original source, indeed to two, Pagnol's text *Souvenirs d'enfance* (the voice-over) and Pagnol's cinema (the black-and-white sequence).

Literary legitimacy

As a novelist and film-maker, Pagnol has occupied both sides in the relationship between film and literature, adapting the work of Alphonse Daudet, but adapted in turn by Claude Berri and Yves Robert. The heritage film as a genre relies heavily on a cultural legitimacy derived from 'the adaptation of literary and theatrical properties already recognised as classics within the accepted canon', and in each adaptation, 'the "original" text is as much on display as the past it seeks to reproduce' (Higson 1993: 114–15). These films sell themselves by invoking not only 'the familiarity and prestige of the particular novel or play, but also [...] the pleasures of other such quality literary adaptations and the status of a national intellectual tradition' (Higson 1993: 115). Thus Yves Robert's Pagnol adaptations invoke both Marcel Pagnol and Claude Berri, while less cynically, Claude Chabrol's *Madame Bovary* (1991) refers directly to the original novel by Flaubert and implicitly to Jean Renoir's film version of 1933. As regards 'a national intellectual tradition', literary adaptations in France during the eighties and nineties have consistently celebrated the nineteenth-century novel, a high point of French cultural history. Since the heritage genre 'can also invent new texts for the canon by treating otherwise marginal texts or properties to the same modes of representation and marketing' as the recognised classics (Higson 1993: 115), Pagnol – Berri's *Jean de Florette* (1986) – appears beside Proust – Volker Schlóndorff's *Un amour de Swann* (1983) – and Dumas – Patrice Chéreau's *La Reine Margot*, Bertrand Tavernier's *La Fille de Dartagnan* (both 1994) – beside Flaubert, Zola and Balzac (see below).

Beyond the illustration of the text in *Madame Bovary*

The most common way for a literary adaptation to display the original text is to use part of it as a narrative voice-over, often read by an anonymous voice which one is free to identify as that of the author. In Tavernier's *Un dimanche à la campagne* (1984) the director himself provides the voice-over, reading passages from Pierre Bost's novel. (Alternatively, adaptations of plays – such as Jean-Paul Rappeneau's highly popular version of Edmond Rostand's *Cyrano de Bergerac* (1990) – function simply as filmed theatre. The result is a collective spectacle which often presents a stage on which Cyrano performs to an audience who revel in his rhetoric and his swordplay, and which only opens up a wider perspective in the action-oriented battle sequences.) Giving the text a voice within the film is a crucial question when the literary source is idiosyncratic in its expression. This is perhaps a reason why realist novels are often adapted: the staple of literary realism, graphic description, is easily reproduced by a detailed *mise en scène*. But with a writer like Flaubert, renowned for his unusual style, the transposition of text to image may not seem sufficient. Hence Claude Chabrol's efforts, in *Madame Bovary* (1991), to find a suitable filmic vehicle for the original novel.

Chabrol's film follows the plot of Flaubert's novel scrupulously, although to simplify the narrative the opening chapter is cut and the epilogue narrated in a brief voice-over rather than shot in detail. Emma (Isabelle Huppert) marries a country doctor, Charles Bovary (Jean-François Balmer), but soon after the birth of their daughter, she tires of her dull husband and her constrained small-town life. She embarks on an affair with the local landowner, Rodolphe (Christophe Malavoy) and harbours illusions of an escape into a romantic idyll. When Rodolphe breaks with her and refuses to pay her secret debts, she commits suicide. In a gesture which epitomises the heritage genre's claims to authenticity, Chabrol declared that his aim was to make the film that Flaubert himself would have made of the story (de Biasi 1991: 106). In visual terms, this entails the detailed reconstruction of nineteenth-century Normandy, with three hundred extras in period dress. As for sound, Chabrol employs three or four passages of music, one of which is described in the novel, and of course the narrative voice-over. A male voice – which one might interpret as representing Flaubert or his narrator – reads five or six passages of text during the course of the film, passages chosen by Chabrol because he felt the sublimity of Flaubert's expression could not be transposed into cinema (de Biasi 1991: 50). Thus during Emma's drawn-out death (from swallowing arsenic), a pause in the dialogue between husband and wife allows the off-screen voice to read 'five of the most beautiful lines Flaubert ever wrote' (de Biasi 1991: 105). A concluding voice-over reaffirms the film's dependence on the text, as part of the last page of the novel is read over the final image. A similar strategy is employed at the end of Claude Berri's 1993 adaptation of Zola's *Germinal* (see below). This use of voice-overs taken from the original text can jeopardise what Chabrol identifies as the need for film-making to remain autonomous, rather than merely the 'illustration' of a literary work (de Biasi 1991: 56). In the latter case, images merely duplicate the sound-track, as in Yves Robert's Pagnol adaptations: 'Le narrateur nous dit d'une voix profonde: "Le ciel était bleu", et vlan, on nous sert à l'écran un grand ciel bleu avec la musique appropriée, non, ça, je n'en veux pas' [The narrator tells us in a deep voice: 'The sky was blue', and bang, we're given a big blue sky on the screen with the appropriate music. No, I don't want that] (de Biasi 1991: 62). In order to avoid this redundancy of the narrated image, Chabrol attempted to be faithful to Flaubert not merely in *mise en scène*, but in montage too, and to match his editing to the 'interior rhythm' of Flaubert's narrative (de Biasi 1991: 79). In the agricultural show sequence, for example, the cross-cutting between Rodolphe's declaration of love for Emma and the speeches from the square below follows precisely the alternation of voices given in the text (de Biasi 1991: 84).

Certain scenes in Chabrol's *Madame Bovary* are none the less represented in a manner at variance with the novel: Emma's hallucination just before her suicide is rendered not by any fantasy sequence but by the glimpse of a bright red backdrop behind her as she pleads with Rodolphe for money. Chabrol claims that this sudden burst of colour evokes a kind of vertigo which matches Emma's desperate state of mind (de Biasi 1991: 93). But it is much less powerful than François Truffaut's blood-red close-up at a crucial moment in *Les Deux Anglaises et le continent* (1971). More evocative in *Madame Bovary* are the virtuoso camera movements, which do not simply realise the events of the novel, but actually equate the heritage format with Emma's desires, so that she almost personifies the genre. In contrast with the generally static shots of cramped interiors which characterise much of the photography, the moments when Emma glimpses a romantic escape from her lifestyle are conveyed in self-consciously sumptuous sweeps of the camera, conveying her state of mind but also foregrounding the favoured techniques of the heritage film. This first happens at the ball she and Charles attend early in the film, during which the camera rises elegantly to give an aerial view of the dancers, before descending again to floor level. Emma's rising hopes – and the construction of heritage space – are again conveyed by fluid camerawork when she and Rodolphe have made love in the woods: the camera rises ecstatically into the trees, to the accompaniment of choral music. But again, as in the ball sequence, the camera motion also encapsulates the pattern of Emma's life, by returning to earth like her dreams which, we are told in a voice-over from the text, fall into the mud like wounded swallows.

Germinal 'is more than just a film'

Émile Zola's novel of 1885 explores the living and working conditions of miners in the north of France, and contrasts their suffering with the greed of the mine owners. Claude Berri's adaptation of 1993 tends to neglect the latter group, who are subject to sketchy characterisation in the film, and concentrates on the miners. Étienne Lantier (Renaud) comes to the Voreux coal mine looking for work. He is hired and works alongside the experienced Maheu (Gérard Depardieu). Étienne soon moves in with Maheu, his wife Maheude (Miou-Miou) and their family, falling for their daughter Catherine (Judith Henry). Prompted by his socialist convictions and the management's decision to reduce the miners' pay, Étienne organises a strike fund. When the strike begins, Catherine and her brutal lover Chaval (Jean-Roger Milo) work as 'scabs' at a nearby pit. Although the miners manage to close this pit, at Voreux they are fired on by the army, and Maheu is killed. The strike ends, and Étienne, Catherine and Chaval return to work, only to find themselves trapped underground when the mine is sabotaged. Étienne fights with Chaval and kills him; Catherine dies in Étienne's arms before he himself is rescued. On his return to the surface, he finds Maheude – the most committed striker – preparing to go down the mine to keep her family alive. It is at this closing moment that Berri – like Chabrol in *Madame Bovary* – falls back on the original text in the form of a voice-over. The last page of Zola's novel is read off-screen, heralding a future blossoming of the miners' struggle even as Étienne leaves the scene of the abortive strike. Ironically, Berri's *Germinal* was interpreted in *Cahiers du cinéma* in the opposite sense, as a closing down of the miners' struggle in much the same way as the French government had closed down the mines: 'La "gauche" qui a fermé les mines [...] a donc eu son film qui ferme la mémoire vive des mineurs et la voue, comme leurs mines, au musée' [The 'left wing' which has closed down the mines has thus got the film it wanted, which closes down the vivid memory of the miners and condemns it, like the mines, to the museum] (Scala 1993: 25).

At the time of release, *Germinal* was rated the most expensive French film ever made, with a budget of more than 160 million francs. It attracted 5.8 million spectators, coming third behind *Les Visiteurs* and *Jurassic Park* at the French box office in 1993. This fact led *Cahiers* to establish a distinction between the genuinely popular cinema of Jean-Marie Poiré's *Les Visiteurs* (see chapter 6) and the worthy, government-sponsored project that is *Germinal*. In an editorial entitled 'Vous avez dit populaire?', Thierry Jousse credited *Les Visiteurs* with a carnival-like power, while attacking *Germinal* for vulgarising and fossilising literature (Jousse 1993). This critique was elaborated by Andréa Scala, who remarked that the marketing of *Germinal* as an exemplar of national culture – a marketing carried out by the then Education Minister Jack Lang as well as by the film's producers and distributors – merely converted a cultural object into a commodity in a vain attempt to persuade the public to consume *Germinal* as avidly as they did *Les Visiteurs*. In short, the film was a theme-park version of the novel and of history, emptied of any attack on capitalism and populated by stereotypes (Scala 1993: 24–5). This criticism is at least partly justified. Berri's portrayal of the mine owners is perfunctory and close to caricature, while the marching strikers are rendered strangely theatrical and false by Jean-Louis Roques's jolly score. Both the music and the camerawork are more effective in conveying the conviviality of public rituals – the tavern, the fair – than the tension of the strike or the claustrophobia of the flooded pit. The generally bleak colour scheme is none the less impressive, the persistent brown tones suggesting realist paintings of the period. The prime contribution that *Germinal* makes to the heritage genre does not lie, however, in painterly allusions or period reconstruction, but in an attempt to go beyond cinema and to achieve a socio-cultural function typical of Jack Lang's conception of cinema. The didactic imperative of the project – to celebrate the working class and remember the days of French heavy industry – was emphasised at the government-sponsored première of the film in Lille. In the months that followed, Lang peddled the film – as Spielberg was to do in the United States and Britain with *Schindler's List* – as a form of national education by sending free videotapes to schools (Scala 1993: 24). This is the ultimate function of the heritage film in the Lang/Mitterrand years: to provide a facile public education about the literary and historical past. As Depardieu claims at the start of the French video: '*Germinal* is more than just a film'.

Reflecting the war in Bosnia: *La Reine Margot*

If, as the director of *Germinal*, Berri attempted to relate the heritage form to the social circumstances of the 1990s – namely the recession – as the producer of Patrice Chéreau's *La Reine Margot* (1994) he oversaw another adaptation of a nineteenth-century novel with claims to reflect the political realities of the moment. In Chéreau's film, based on a popular historical potboiler by Alexandre Dumas, the allusions are to the religious divisions and civil war in Bosnia. A major concern of French foreign policy in the nineties, the former Yugoslavia was, naturally enough, subject to documentary representation, as in Marcel Ophüls's *Veillée d'armes* and Bernard-Henri Lévy and Alain Ferrari's *Bosna!* (both 1994). To reflect on Bosnia through a literary period drama is altogether more unexpected, but in fact provides a means of reaching a wide audience while exploiting the potential of the heritage film, 'in the displaced form of costume drama', to create 'an important space for playing out contemporary anxieties and fantasies of national identity [...] and power' (Higson 1993: 118).

Patrice Chéreau, who made his first film in 1975, is noted for his subversions of realism and his attention to *mise en scène*. In fact, during the 1980s he worked more extensively in theatre – as director of the Théâtre des Amandiers in Paris – than in cinema, although in 1987 he did combine the two in simultaneous stage and screen versions of Chekov's *Platonov*. For *La Reine Margot* – previously filmed in 1954 – fidelity to the text was not stressed. Unlike Chabrol's *Madame Bovary*, Chéreau's project did not require the actors to read the original novel. Instead of an 'authentic' literary adaptation, 'Chéreau saw the film partly as a tale that would echo religious, political and social conflicts in the modern world: the highly effective score is by the Serbo-Croatian Goran Bregovic, while the carnage on view is unusually explicit for a historical drama' (Andrew 1995: 24). While Chéreau and the lead, Isabelle Adjani, stressed the Bosnian sub-text in their interviews, critics also linked *La Reine Margot* to the 'new violence' epitomised by the work of Quentin Tarantino. An editorial on screen violence in *Sight and Sound* suggested that the film showed 'it may be possible to fuse these two idioms, the costume drama and the revenge thriller, and use such a hybrid to address the whole European nightmare of ethnic cleansing' (Dodd 1995: 3).

The focus of the plot and the central metaphor of religious intolerance and 'ethnic cleansing' is provided by the Saint Bartholomew's Day Massacre of August 1572, in which six thousand Protestants were slaughtered throughout Paris. In the opening sequence, Chéreau portrays the arranged wedding between the Catholic Marguerite de Valois, known as Margot (Adjani) and the Protestant Henri de Navarre (Daniel Auteuil), a political device intended to keep the peace in France. This sequence also introduces the court and Margot's Machiavellian family, including her brother, the unstable King Charles IX (Jean-Hugues Anglade), and her mother, the sinister Catherine de Medici (Virna Lisi). Following a frantic order from Charles, all Protestants gathered in Paris for the wedding are massacred. Navarre, rejected by Margot, is kept under house arrest but gradually befriends the king and saves his life after a hunting accident. When Catherine attempts to dispose of Navarre by giving him a poisoned book to read, it is the king who inadvertently succumbs to the trap, licking his fingers to turn the pages. Charles dies sweating blood, in one of the gruesome images which typify the graphic violence of the film. After Charles's death, and partly reconciled with Navarre, Margot leaves Paris in secret to join the Protestants. On a more private scale, the narrative includes two sub-plots concerning La Môle (Vincent Perez), a Protestant who engages in an illicit romance with Margot and a buddy relationship with his Catholic adversary, Conconnas (Claudio Amendola).

As the plot outline suggests, *La Reine Margot* is a visceral experience, the blood, sweat and dirt far removed from the niceties of heritage convention. Bregovic's menacing score creates a brooding atmosphere heightened by the constant rumbling of thunder and ringing of unseen bells. Filmed often in red and bloody tones, the action is frequently confined to claustrophobic interiors. The conventional reliance on wide-angle shots and luscious *mise en scène* is restricted to the opening wedding sequence, which functions to situate the film in the heritage genre and to present the public façade behind which brutal, private acts are hidden. Moreover both of the key exterior sequences, the massacre and the hunting scene, subvert generic expectations. In the former, the painterly tableaux beloved of the genre present a horrific spectacle, that of the dead and dying in the streets of Paris, reminiscent of images from the Holocaust or from Bosnia. As in Yves Angelo's Balzac adaptation *Le Colonel Chabert* (1994), where the French dead are piled high after the battle of Eylau, the static poise of the tableau has been transformed into a pile of still or frozen bodies. The shock of such images breaches the normally assured, touristic distance between spectator and spectacle which is the usual premise of the heritage film. In the hunting sequence from *La Reine Margot*, the gaze of the Duke of Anjou (Pascal Greggory), aimed directly at the camera, also erodes this distance. In contrasting such chilling self-consciousness with the heat of brutal passions, in balancing the 'illustrative tableaux' and the 'Olympian' perspectives of the heritage film against the claustrophobic 'two-shots, close-ups and [...] interior spaces of the Mafia film', and above all in reflecting on the urgent realities of the moment through a literary period drama, *La Reine Margot* clearly stands as the 'powerful apotheosis of the French heritage film'

(Darke 1995: 5). As *Cahiers du cinéma* declared in an editorial, the film brings to the genre an impressive energy and brutality never seen before (Jousse 1995: 5).

Digital reconstruction and golden nostalgia: *Un long dimanche de fiançailles*

New developments in the heritage genre have centred less on narrative, *mise en scène* or camerawork than on the use of digital effects. Computer-generated imagery (CGI), so often associated with the fantasy film (see chapter 6), plays a more discreet but nonetheless important role in several recent French heritage films. The genre's defining gesture towards historical authenticity remains, however. In fact CGI is used primarily as a means of allowing digital reconstruction of the period and setting in question. Thus in *L'Anglaise et le duc* (*The Lady and the Duke*, 2001) and *Vidocq* (2001), historical Paris is carefully recreated using CGI. And a digital version of the Paris of the 1920s features heavily in Jean-Pierre's Jeunet's *Un long dimanche de fiançailles* (*A Very Long Engagement*, 2004). The follow-up to his massively popular romantic/comic fantasy *Amélie* (see chapter 6), the film cost 35 million euros and took three years to make. The result is a prime example of the way that new technology can exist very happily alongside the most nostalgic and orthodox tendencies of the heritage film.

Set mainly in 1920, the long and repetitive narrative follows Mathilde (Audrey Tatou) as she pieces together the events surrounding the disappearance of her sweetheart Manech (Gaspard Ulliel) during the bloody trench warfare of the First World War. Last seen at a trench called 'Bingo Crépscule' in 1917, and condemned to death with four others for self-mutilation in an attempt to escape the horrors of the front, Manech went missing in the middle of no man's land. Mathilde's investigations track back and forth across France, aided by technologies such as the telephone and the steam engine (both of which become recurrent symbols of the mechanical glories of the age) as well as by her uncle and aunt, a private detective, and a well-placed relative. If the narrative is characterised by numerous flashbacks and interviews with witnesses or survivors, strategies which seem closer to the thriller or the war film than to heritage cinema, the *mise en scène* and camerawork remain resolutely orthodox. The use of CGI presents the spectator with recreations of a lost Paris of the 1920s: the Trocadéro, the street market at Les Halles, the Gare d'Orsay when it was a train station not a museum (although Jeunet's version has steam trains rather than the electric trains actually used at Orsay). These settings are presented very deliberately as tableaux, mediated by smooth, gentle camera movements or fixed shots that allow us to take in the view. The camera tends to glide in left-to-right tracking shots that evoke Mathilde's steady journeying, and after the opening sequences there is little of the rapid editing that is apparent in Jeunet's early films in tandem with Marc Caro (see chapter 6). While the

Contemporary French cinema

narrative concerns the reconstruction of Manech's last movements and, metaphorically, of France after the Great War, *Un long dimanche de fiançailles* also includes the reconstruction not just of an imaginary lost Paris but also of certain archive documents, as with the simulation of an original film of execution by guillotine which is shown, in trembling black and white, to mark Tina's death. So effective was this act of reconstruction that spectators assumed the footage was genuine (see Lavoignat 2004: 127).

Most noticeable, however, is the use of colour throughout the film. For the sequences set in the trenches, bleak greys and blues dominate, evocative of misery and suffering. These sequences are in many ways at odds with heritage conventions, as was the case in the graphic battle scenes from *Le Colonel Chabert* (see above). Jeunet does indeed depict massacres, mutilations, body parts and blood. Much of this brutal nightmare is mediated however via Mathilde's enquiries and the survivors' testimony, and is presented as a series of flashbacks where the overriding concern is less with the horrors of the war than with the search for any clue to explain whether Manech is alive or dead. Even when potentially horrific scenes are glimpsed, Jeunet is careful to leave most of the violence off-screen, as when the five soldiers wound themselves in the hand. Jeunet has acknowledged that he had in mind a family audience for the film, including in particular a female demographic which he assumes (using his wife as indicative!) would be repulsed by explicit violence (Narbonne and Schaller 2004: 92). Hence the film is relatively restrained in its portrayal of the trenches. For the most part, *Un long dimanche de fiançailles* concerns itself with peacetime France, embodied by Mathilde and bathed in a relentlessly nostalgic and literally golden glow. Digital manipulation of the image ensures that every single scene set in the twenties glows with a soft golden light, not as brown as sepia but more radiant. The effect is to generate associations of innocence, beauty and peace. In terms of the film's historical setting one can interpret this as a return to peace after the end of the war. More generally, however, it creates a very sustained impression that the France of the past is a lost Eden, a prelapsarian time and place. The myth of *la France profonde* is celebrated here, particularly in the rural sequences on the Breton coast and in the wheat-fields of the Dordogne, or when Mathilde locates her final interviewee and the man who rescued Manech at a farm called 'Le bout du monde' (The world's end). The film is full of nostalgic imagery: a lighthouse, steam trains, golden cornfields, old-fashioned bathing costumes, the original Métro signs of the Paris underground. Across this Edenic landscape moves Mathilde or, when the terrain is too difficult for her (she has a limp), her proxy the detective, whom we see making investigations in Corsica.

Both temporally and spatially, then, the film takes us on a journey into a lost France which is resolutely utopian, despite the context of the war and its aftermath (hospitals, traumatised veterans and so on). Unlike *La Vie et rien d'autre* (see above), which tells a pessimistic version of a similar story, there is no poignant final evocation of the war dead. The narrative is one of healing and Mathilde is the personification of this process. Although not fulfilling the function of a nurse literally (as various minor characters do) she is in a figurative sense both a healer and a guide to the therapeutic power of the French landscape. She personifies, in Charles de Gaulle's words about another war, 'la vraie France, la seule France, la France éternelle' [the true, sole, eternal France]. In this context, the amnesiac and orphaned Manech, first missing and then eventually tracked down at the end of the film, rather obviously represents the trauma of the First World War. In Manech's absence, Mathilde is throughout the film contrasted with Tina Lombardi, the passionate and dangerous Corsican woman who is also on a quest to find out what happened to her lover during the war. Tina is both figuratively and literally darker than Mathilde, appearing as a dark avatar, Mathilde's repressed self, her pathologised and eroticised counterpart. When the two meet, Tina tells Mathilde 'on se ressemble' [we're alike]. Mathilde denies the similarity: it is formal but not symbolic. In other words their trajectories are similar but their meanings are opposed: Tina is the threatening and sexualised woman as other (Corsican not French, a murderess who uses her sexuality as a weapon) while Mathilde is the desexualised woman as a carer and as an embodiment of idealised feminine values such as devotion, persistence and faith. Richard Dyer has demonstrated how the white woman in western culture has often been represented as the personification of 'light and chastity', and how 'Glow remains a key quality in idealized representations of white women' (Dyer 1986: 44, 132). This is the glow that surrounds Mathilde and, more generally, the post-war sequences throughout Jeunet's film. If grey and blue are the bleak colours of the wartime scenes set in and around the trenches, most of *Un long dimanche de fiançailles* is bathed in yellow and gold.

Born in 1900, Mathilde is also an embodiment of the century itself. Her limp (a result of childhood polio) could be read as the trace of trauma on the body of the century, but it in no way holds her back from her purpose. Her quest ends in triumph and so the film presents a sense of progress and achievement which is personal and romantic, but also national and technological, given that Mathilde's quest is facilitated by such means as trains and telephones. *Un long dimanche de fiançailles* concludes with Mathilde and Manech meeting at last in a sunny garden. In a reference back to the gentle tracking shots and depth of field in Renoir's *Partie de campagne* and Tavernier's *Un dimanche à la campagne* (see above), Jeunet frames the garden through a doorway as Mathilde and the camera move slowly towards it, with Manech just about glimpsed in the distance, in the depths of the shot. Mathilde approaches the table where Manech is at work, sits down, and tearfully watches him. The final voice-over declares 'dans la lumière du jardin, Mathilde le regarde...' [in the light of the garden, Mathilde looks at him]. The concluding emphasis, then, in both the sound-track and the image, is on the light that surrounds the reconciled couple. It is the golden glow of an idealized past, idealized characters, and an idealized place (the rural depths of *la France profonde*). Above all it is the golden glow of nostalgia.

References

Andrew, G. (1995), Isabelle époque, London, *Time Out*, 1273, 22–6.

Daney, S. (1982), Le Cinéma explore le temps, Paris, *Cahiers du cinéma*, 338, 65.

Darke, C. (1995), La Reine Margot, London, *Sight and Sound*, January 1995, 55.

Darnton, R. (1984), Danton and double-entendre, New York, *New York Review of Books*, 16 February 1984, 19–24.

De Biasi, P.-M. (1991), Un Scénario sous influence: Entretien avec Claude Chabrol, in Boddaert, F., *et al.*, *Autour d'Emma: Madame Bovary, un film de Claude Chabrol*, Paris, Hatier, 23–109.

De la Bretèque, F. (1992), Images of 'Provence': ethnotypes and stereotypes of the south in French cinema, in R. Dyer and G. Vincendeau (eds), *Popular European Cinema*, London and New York, Routledge, 58–71.

Dodd, P. (1995), History nasties, London, *Sight and Sound*, February 1995, 3.

Dyer, R. (1986), *Heavenly Bodies: Film Stars and Society*, London, BFI.

Forbes, J. (1992), *The Cinema in France After the New Wave*, London, BFI/Macmillan.

Higson, A. (1993), Re-presenting the national past: nostalgia and pastiche in the heritage film, in L. Friedman (ed.), *British Cinema and Thatcherism: Fires were Started*, London, UCL Press.

Jousse, T. (1993), Vous avez dit populaire?, Paris, *Cahiers du cinéma*, 473, 5.

Jousse, T. (1995), La Reine et le fou, Paris, *Cahiers du cinéma*, 479:80, 5.

Lavoignat, J-P. (2004), Jeunet face aux lecteurs, *Studio*, Paris, November 2004, 124–9.

Le Péron, S. (1982), L'Affiche douze ou le retour du grand public, Paris, *Cahiers du cinéma*, 336, 19–20.

Narbonne. C. and Schaller, N. (2004), Les petits secrets de Jean-Pierre Jeunet [interview], Paris, *Première*, October 2004, 90–7.

Neale, S. (1986), Melodrama and tears, Glasgow, *Screen*, 27:6, 6–22.

Ostria, V. (1986), Les Saisons et les jours, Paris, *Cahiers du cinéma*, 380, 60–6.

Pauly, R. M. (1993), *The Transparent Illusion: Image and Ideology in French Text and Film*, New York, Peter Lang.

Prédal, R. (1991), *Le Cinema français depuis 1945*, Paris, Nathan.

Reader, K., (1989) 'L'Air du temps' – three recent popular French films, paper given at Warwick University Conference.

Sainderchin, G.-P. (1982), La Rupture, Paris, *Cahiers du cinéma*, 336, 18.

Scala, A. (1993), Le 18 Brumaire de Claude Berri, Paris, *Cahiers du cinéma*, 374, 24–5.

Tavernier, B. (1993), I wake up, dreaming: a journal for 1992, London, *Projections*, 2, 251–378.

Toubiana, S. (1983), L'Histoire en dolby, Paris, *Cahiers du cinéma*, 343, 54–5.

Toubiana, S. (1986), L'Opéra Pagnol, Paris, *Cahiers du cinéma*, 387, 49–51.

Toubiana, S., *et al.* (1986), L'Image a bougé: Abécédaire du cinéma français, *Cahiers du cinéma*, 381, 18–34.

The heritage fim

Truffaut, F. (1988), *Le Cinéma selon François Truffaut*, ed. A. Gillain, Paris, Flammarion.

Vincendeau, G. (1993), Catherine Deneuve and French womanhood, in P. Cook and P. Dodd (eds), *Women and Film: a Sight and Sound Reader*, London, Scarlet Press, 41–9.

Walker, J. A. (1993), *Art and Artists on Screen*, Manchester and New York, Manchester University Press.

Comedy

Since Aristotle, there has been 'a long history of criticism that has viewed comedy as inferior to other genres in Western culture' (Horton 1991: 2). Within the French film industry, the critical denigration of genre cinema, the dominance of a realist aesthetic and the lasting influence of *la politique des auteurs* (see chapter 1) have all contributed to the neglect of comedy. This is in spite of the fact that comedy remains the most popular genre in French cinema, accounting for the most successful French film of all time, *La Grande Vadrouille* (Oury, 1966), numerous other huge hits such as *Trois hommes et un couffin* (*Three Men and a Cradle*, Serreau, 1985, see chapter 4) and several recent series including the *Visiteurs, Astérix,* and *Taxi* films. Nonetheless comedies rarely win plaudits in France, and comic stars are often only granted prizes when they play straight roles in serious dramas: comic action man Jean-Paul Belmondo won his only César award for *Itinéraire d'un enfant gâté* (Lelouch, 1989), the clown Coluche his only César for *Tchao pantin* (Berri, 1983). Despite this critical neglect, comedy has a very strong tradition in France, one which plays above all on the grotesque gestures and functions of the unruly body.

French comic tradition and the grotesque body

The most important attempt to theorise the importance of comedy in Western culture is Mikhail Bakhtin's work on the sixteenth-century French writer Rabelais. In *The Art of Rabelais*, Bakhtin describes how a universal strand of comedy developed in the Middle Ages and continued into modern times in popular forms such as carnival and 'grotesque realism'. This he calls the 'one culture of folk carnival humour' (Bakhtin 1984: 4). It is characterised by a focus on the 'low' body, on bodily functions such as eating and excreting, on sex and childbirth, as well as on death and decay. It celebrates processes of renewal and finds humour in the fragility and mortality of the human body so that 'all that [is] frightening in ordinary life is turned into amusing or ludicrous monstrosities' (Bakhtin 1984: 47). According to Bakhtin, from the early nineteenth century onwards, 'Laughter was cut down to cold humour, irony, sarcasm. It ceased to be a joyful and triumphant hilarity. Its positive regenerating power was reduced to a minimum' (Bakhtin 1984: 38). However, 'the tradition of the grotesque is not entirely extinct: it continues to live [...] in the lower canonical genres (comedy, satire, fable) [...]. Humour also goes on living on the popular stage' (Bakhtin 1984: 101–2). Thus it is no surprise to find that the body comedy so prevalent at the critically-neglected 'lower' end of French cinema has its roots in the 'popular stage', as we shall see.

The importance of the comic body in French cinema can first be observed in a style of physical comedy derived from the cabarets of the late nineteenth century. Prior to and during the very early years of cinema, the loss of bodily control observed in newly discovered and celebrated conditions such as epilepsy and hysteria became associated in French sociology and psychology with criminality, sexual patholo-gies and alcoholism (see Gordon 2001: 4). But this was –and remains – a source of humour as well as unease, as Rae Beth Gordon explains: '"Epileptic performers" cause anxiety and hilarity, and the latter is in response to the former. This is why deformity, dismemberment, contor-tions, grimaces, tics and epileptic convulsions are so funny to so many spectators' (Gordon 2001: 14). By the 1890s and the beginnings of film comedy, 'grotesque dislocations of the body, weird exaggerations of motor capability [...] and the specific gestures and gaits observed in hysteria and somnambulism were a major part of the repertoire of mimes, clowns, acrobats, contortionists and singers' (Gordon 2001: 22). This, Gordon argues, is the reason for the positive French recep-tion of what one might call an unconscious, epileptic or anarchic style of body comedy, from the cabarets of the turn of the century to Charlie Chaplin in the silent era and Jerry Lewis in the fifties and sixties. One can also observe a similar tendency in the popular success of the French comic style known as *café-théâtre* in the years after 1968 (see below).

Comedy explores popular fears, as do fantasy genres such as horror (see chapter 6). These fears concern the body above all, and what might happen if one lost control over its functions. Both Bakhtin and Gordon contrast the 'low' body with higher faculties like reason and control (be it individual or social). Comedy around the body thus often celebrates the grotesque body as a disruptive force, overturning official codes of behaviour and creating offence as well as humour. Although present in other cultures – witness for example American 'gross-out' comedies from *Dumb and Dumber* (Farrelly brothers, 1994) onwards – this strand of physical humour is recurrent in French cinema, particularly in the films analysed below. It is a form of comedy which, although concerned with the 'universal' body (that is, both female and male bodies), is often mediated through a male double act. Sue Harris

Contemporary French cinema

has noted that French male comedy duos derive from the servants or *valets* in the popular theatre tradition of the *commedia dell'arte*: 'recurrent male comic characters [...] were often found in pairs, one led by the other, one handsome, one ugly [...], with a range of mutual defining characteristics such as egotism, stupidity, vulgarity, wickedness' (Harris 1997: 120). As Harris notes, this tradition is evoked by the teaming of Gérard Depardieu and Patrick Dewaere in Bertrand Blier's seventies comedies. It can also be traced in numerous other male duos throughout the history of French film comedy: Fernandel and Gino Cervi in the *Don Camillo* series of the 1940s, Bourvil and Louis de Funès in *La Grande Vadrouille*, Ugo Tognazzi and Michel Serrault in the *Cage aux folles* series of the late seventies (see chapter 3), and Gérard Depardieu and Pierre Richard in Francis Veber's eighties trilogy of *La Chèvre, Les Compères* and *Les Fugitifs* (see Jackel 2001: 43). To this one could add Christian Clavier and Jean Reno in *Les Visiteurs* (Poiré, 1993) or Depardieu and Clavier in *Les Anges gardiens* (Poiré, 1995) and the *Astérix* series. An important exception, however, is the collaborative work of the group of actors and writers known as Le Splendid, whose popular comedies from the late seventies onwards have provided the most prominent and durable example in contemporary France of the grotesque body moving from the popular stage to the cinema screen.

Café-théâtre from stage to screen

Café-théâtre has been defined as 'a form of improvised theatre that has its roots in [...] cabaret, music-hall and vaudeville' and which became aggressively satirical in the years following the social and political upheaval of May 1968: 'Its characteristic tone was one of iconoclastic irreverence, with expressions of contempt for authority – in the family, the workplace, and in the community' (Harris 1998: 89). The *café-théâtre* troupes to have the biggest impact on French comic cinema in the seventies and eighties were the Café de la Gare (comprising Patrick Dewaere, Miou-Miou, Coluche and for a certain time Gérard Depardieu) and Le Splendid (principally Thierry Lhermitte, Josiane Balasko, Christian Clavier, Gérard Jugnot, Marie-Anne Chazel and Michel Blanc). Both groups developed excessive, repetitious and frantic acting styles, with perhaps more emphasis on stylised gestures from the Café de la Gare and on verbal abuse from Le Splendid. Both groups also shared a perceptible lineage going back to the hysterical tics and contortions of the cabaret tradition, and a tendency to make comic use of their actors' physical appearance. The looks of nearly all the actors concerned appeared to disqualify them from becoming orthodox romantic leads: Clavier, Jugnot and Blanc were small, the latter also prematurely bald; Lhermitte tall and gangly, Balasko and Coluche broad and chubby-faced, Miou-Miou and Chazel skinny, Depardieu large and threatening with heavy features. Only Dewaere had movie-star looks, and he was to move rapidly away from comedy to more serious or romantic roles in dramas such as *Le Juge Fayard, dit le shériff* (*Le Sheriff*, Boisset, 1976). As Pierre (Thierry Lhermitte) says of Thérèse (Anémone) in *Le Père Noël est une ordure*, 'elle n'est pas moche; elle n'a pas un physique facile' [she isn't ugly, she just has an unusual face]. This physical difference (not exactly ugliness but certainly not good looks) is a key component which is acknowledged and exaggerated in *café-théâtre* performances, in tandem with rapid and vulgar speech and those very 'automatic, repeated gestures, tics, grimaces, and contractures [which] characterize the pathologized body at the center of performance style in cabaret and early film comedy' (Gordon 2001: 22).

The collective ethos of Le Splendid was perhaps stronger than that of the slightly earlier and more amateur Café de la Gare. Whereas Miou-Miou, Dewaere and Depardieu made a name for themselves in Bertrand Blier's hugely successful *Les Valseuses* (1974, see chapter 3), the Splendid team wrote their own plays and screen adaptations, only rarely using any outside help – for example, from director Patrice Leconte on *Les Bronzés* (1978), a film he described as being written by seven pairs of hands (see Leconte 2004). It was the popularity of this project and its sequel, *Les Bronzés font du ski* (Leconte, 1979), that saw Le Splendid transfer their talents from the stage to the screen at the same time as Depardieu and Dewaere were cementing their double act in their second comedy together for Blier, *Préparez vos mouchoirs*.

Préparez vos mouchoirs: ridiculing bourgeois dreams

Though less famous and less popular than his hit comedy *Les Valseuses* a few years before (see chapter 3), Bertrand Blier's *Préparez vos mouchoirs* (*Get Out Your Handkerchiefs*, 1978) won an Oscar for best foreign film and crystallised the comic partnership between Gérard Depardieu and Patrick Deweare established in the earlier film. Once again the pair play two very close buddies who are entangled in a *ménage à trois* but whose own relationship is the crux of the film. The violence and working-class threat of *Les Valseuses* is here replaced by a satire on bourgeois values and cultural pretension. Established bourgeois social rituals, like the Sunday lunch in a Parisian restaurant that starts the film, rapidly descend into absurdity. Yet the two protagonists, a driving instructor called Raoul (Depardieu) and a sports teacher called Stéphane (Deweare), insist on clinging to their aspirations. Together they epitomise the bourgeois ideal of a secure, tasteful and cultured domestic environment. Two central scenes show each man proudly displaying his apartment and the values enshrined therein: for Raoul, old-fashioned furnishings, all beams and fireplaces, with a placid wife quietly knitting, cooking and arranging flowers; for Stéphane, a shrine to cultural capital, with Mozart permanently on the record-player and the entire collection of five thousand Livre de Poche novels arranged round the walls in alphabetical order. The plot derives from the gender assumptions at the heart of these two scenes: Raoul's wife Solange (Carole Laure) is unhappy in the role assigned to her, so he persuades Stéphane to 'try her out' just as he tried out Raoul's armchair; Stéphane's own intellectual pretensions and assumption of cultural superiority over Solange are of course doomed to leave her just as unsatisfied with him as with her husband. In the end it is only a thirteen-year-old boy, Christian, who can make Solange happy. The film concludes with the bourgeois ideal family absurdly recast. The setting is thoroughly upper middle class: the large townhouse of a factory-owner, with antique furniture throughout and Schubert on the stereo. But within, all adult males are absent or emasculated (the owner has had a stroke, while Raoul and Stéphane are locked out in the street), the mother has lost her memory and disappeared, and Solange has been made pregnant not by either of the protagonists but by her thirteen-year-old lover.

As in *Les Valseuses*, the characters played by Depardieu and Dewaere begin as distinct but gradually become identified with each other, in particular via the use of matching costumes. In *Préparez vos mouchoirs* this results in Raoul and Stéphane (and eventually Christian) wearing identical jumpers knitted by Solange. We also see the two men joined by their neighbour, all dressed in black tie, attending a Mozart concert together. Other moments of visual comedy in which the central characters become indistinguishable from each other include the recurrent chase scenes throughout the film, and the use of disguise when Stéphane and Raoul kidnap Christian. As Sue Harris has pointed out, such techniques align Blier's comic style with the tradition of carnival, especially insofar as carnival 'expresses little sense of the individual, or of individual psychology, and concentrates instead on [...] the community experience' (Harris 1997: 118). A further technique employed by Blier in *Préparez vos mouchoirs* is a close attention to sound, be it the careful pacing of dialogue to create maximum comic tension (the 'Mozart back to life' scene), the use of ambient sound to generate realism in the setting (traffic noise in Béthune, background conversations in the restaurant sequence), or the graceful use of Mozart's music at idealised or pathetic moments throughout the narrative. Classical music is a similarly pervasive presence in Blier's *Trop belle pour toi!* (*Too Beautiful For You*, 1989), where Schubert dominates the sound-track to such an extent that the central character (again played by Depardieu) finally shouts directly at the camera, 'Il fait chier, votre Schubert!' [Your Schubert is a pain in the arse!]. Characteristically, Blier here makes a formal point about music entering the diegesis via the use of blunt language and direct address. His comedy does not mince words.

Twenty years after *Préparez vos mouchoirs*, Manuel Poirier's *Western* (1997) presented an attenuated, better-behaved version of Blier's seventies comedies, with less satirical edge, less sexual chauvinism, less explicit nudity and less exaggerated physical performances. An updating of *Les Valseuses* and *Préparez vos mouchoirs*, this buddy-movie also has echoes of Michel Blanc's *Marche à l'ombre* (see below) as a comic duo, big Paco (Sergi Lopez) and little Nino (Sacha Bourdo), crisscross Brittany in search of sexual adventures. There are several reminders of Blier and Blanc, including leg injuries, hitch-hiking sequences, bogus surveys, a potential *ménage à trois*, and chase scenes involving incongruous vehicles such as wheelbarrows or shopping trolleys. Blier's personal influence has had less impact on French screen comedy, however, than the massive and continuing success of the Café de la Gare's rival group, Le Splendid.

Le Père Noël est une ordure: 'joy and suicides' and a cake that farts

Le Père Noël est une ordure (Poiré, 1982), although not a huge hit at the box office, rapidly became a cult film in France largely thanks to television. Over the next twenty years it was shown almost annually on French TV, and when screened by France 2 in 2003 it attracted 30% of the available audience (see Topaloff 2004: 62). As with *Les Bronzés*, the film was based on a successful stage play written by the Splendid group and thus combines collective authorship with a range of diverse characters brought together in a delimited space with farcical results. The main thrust of the film is an attack on the cultural norms celebrated at Christmas. These include gift giving, charity, goodwill to all men, tolerance and community, as well as a focus on family rituals and on the pleasures of consumerism. While positing the Splendid group as a kind of proxy family in order to torpedo these ideals, the film also acknowledges the ambivalence of the modern Christmas by making reference to the darker themes of depression and anger that accompany the festival: 'We are used to thinking of Christmas as the time for both joy and suicides, [...] of family togetherness and family quarrelling' (Miller 1993: 26). In the words of Claude Lévi-Strauss, at Christmas 'society functions according to a rhythm of heightened solidarity and exaggerated antagonism' (Lévi-Strauss 1993: 47). By situating the action in a Samaritans-style charity, 'SOS détresse', the Splendid team raise audience expectations of 'heightened solidarity', only to systematically dismantle these expectations as chaos and 'exaggerated antagonism' ensue. This assault on cultural norms saw the film rejected by American distributors and retitled to avoid offence in Belgium and Switzerland, while in France the SNCF, Air France, and the Morris publicity group all refused to advertise or screen it (see Grenier 1994).

Le Père Noël est une ordure begins with glittering images of a Parisian Christmas, with shoppers returning home under shimmering festive lights, stars and mirror balls, as upbeat easy-listening jazz plays on the sound-track. This glamourised, magical prelude sets the context for a violent collision between a group of grotesque and dysfunctional people in the offices of 'SOS détresse' on Christmas Eve. Amongst them is Félix (Gérard Jugnot), a thieving, violent, ex-con 'bad Santa' who traduces every value conventionally incarnated by Father Christmas and whom we first see advertising a strip show and then hitting a small child. 'SOS détresse', a kind of inner sanctum where Félix and various other misfits end up, is the site of the idealised Christian values of charity and loving one's neighbour as oneself. However, once put under the slightest pressure these values, as personified by the two volunteers Pierre (Thierry Lhermitte) and Thérèse (Anémone), quickly collapse to reveal the superficiality of the values and the inadequacies of the good Samaritans themselves. Pierre in particular encapsulates this deterioration: repressed and arrogant, he becomes increasingly intolerant and foul-mouthed, rejecting the transvestite Katia (Christian Clavier) and the Bulgarian neighbour Preskouitch (Bruno Moynot) with ferocity and something close to terror. Pierre represents a fear of difference, be it sexual or cultural. The one constant in his characterisation is the catchphrase 'C'est c'la-a-a, oui-i-i' [ye-e-s, that's ri-i-ight], which he repeats like a mantra as the events around him move further and further out of his control.

Verbal humour is not limited to the catchphrases which punctuate *Le Père Noël* as they do *Les Visiteurs* (see below). Nearly all of the characters, Félix and Pierre especially, explode with furious swearing at regular intervals. There is a contrast here with the Café de la Gare style, in that the Splendid team tend to favour verbal vulgarity and aggressive violence over explicit nudity and sexual discourse, while in Blier's comedies the reverse is the case. In *Le Père Noël* there is a lot of play with insults (the abusive caller, Pierre's ranting) and also with absurd accents, such as Josette's piercing Parisian screech and Madame Musquin's bourgeois tones, both of which recur in *Les Visiteurs*. The only nudity in the film is in the bizarre painting of Thérèse cavorting with a pig that Pierre gives her as a present. The Splendid and the Café de la Gare share a reliance on visual humour in their films, involving slapstick (in this case, the many pratfalls as Thérèse, Katia and Félix are variously hit or kicked in the face) and costume (the ludicrous knitted cardigan that Thérèse gives Pierre recalls the jumpers Solange knits in *Préparez vos mouchoirs*). There are also gags that combine visual with verbal humour, as when Josette (Marie-Anne Chazel), heavily pregnant and with absurdly protruding teeth, describes herself as 'enceinte jusqu'aux dents' [pregnant up to the teeth]. Both groups also showcase the grotesque body, although the emphasis in *Le Père Noël* is on bodily functions rather than on sex, the staple of much of Blier's comedy. Trapped in the lift, Madame Musquin (Josiane Balasko) becomes increasingly desperate as she needs to relieve herself. After Félix swallows an overdose of pills, we are informed by Pierre with a mixture of shock and glee that he has vomited at least three times. The traditional Christmas food presented to the group by Preskouitch is *kloug*, 'the cake that farts', a stinking dark brown morass that tastes disgusting and which one character compares to excrement. If Christmas means ritualised eating and drinking (as when Pierre tucks into oysters and white wine while half-heartedly listening to a depressed caller on the line) in this film it also means acknowledging the claim on our bodies of the other end of the alimentary tract.

The grotesque body is at stake not just in the sequences about eating and excreting, but also in the stylised gestures of Christian Clavier as the transvestite Katia. Whereas the other performers are relatively naturalistic, Clavier calls to mind the 'hysterical gesture and gait' of cabaret and early film comedy (see Gordon 2001). Clavier's gait in particular is a source of comedy: having lost a heel from one boot, he undulates up and down as he walks across the apartment. Katia is subsequently shot in the foot and hobbles around even more theatrically. The role of the transvestite entails a host of camp gestures but it also allows a brief glimpse of moral and cultural awareness beneath the broad comedy. We are shown that masculinity is a cultural construct in the sequence where Katia limps pathetically into the night and passes a series of film posters displaying Charles Bronson's rugged and supposedly authentic masculine image. Pierre's rejection of Katia as 'abnormal' moreover reveals the extent to which his caring values are simply a facade hiding bigotry and fear of difference. Katia in turn responds by damning the whole idealised project of 'SOS détresse' as 'coincé dans votre univers moral de merde' [stuck in your shitty moral universe]. S/he, meanwhile, is 'simplement quelqu'un de seul, qui a besoin des autres' [simply alone and in need of other people]. If this suggests the narrative might slide towards sentimentality however, the reverse is the case: in the frantic finale, a group of kinds is formed, but one based on desperation to remove a corpse from the apartment, and one from which Katia is still excluded. When a repair-man arrives to mend the lift and is accidentally shot dead, his body is hastily cut up and wrapped in Christmas paper to be distributed to the meat-eating animals in the local zoo. While this plan unites Félix, Josette, Pierre and Thérèse, Katia's exclusion is comically signalled by the fact that s/he is unaware of the contents of these presents, and so happily throws the packages to herbivores like the giraffes. The film ends with continuation rather than reconciliation: although Félix and Josette return home together, Katia is left to limp after Pierre and Thérèse, still looking for a welcome into the crumbling moral universe of 'SOS détresse'.

Generic pleasures in *Marche à l'ombre*

While *Le Père Noël est une ordure* is disruptive and iconoclastic, Michel Blanc's solo project *Marche à l'ombre* (1984) is aspirational and reassuring. Directed, co-written by, and co-starring Blanc, the film was the number one French success of the year, attracting over six million spectators. Although it lacks the frantic energy of the group efforts made by the Splendid team, *Marche à l'ombre* maximises its audience appeal and covers all bases with a mixture of conventional elements from various genres, including comedy, buddy movie, romance and thriller. Handsome musician François (Gérard Lanvin) and his accident-prone hypochondriac friend Denis (Michel Blanc) arrive penniless in Paris and try to make money by busking. They end up selling stolen goods for a criminal gang and living in a squat established by black immigrants. François begins a 'will they, won't they' relationship with Mathilde (Sophie Duez), a beautiful dancer, and the two men eventually leave Paris to follow her to New York.

Despite a background of bleakly realist urban settings, and naturalistic performances from all the actors, the film is nonetheless very formulaic in its use of genre (on-off romance, criminal thugs, chase sequences) and in its characterisation. As in French comedy tradition, the focus is on a comic duo, in this case the muscled, tall and dark Lanvin teamed with the diminutive and balding Blanc. The physical contrast between the actors is exaggerated via the action. François's strength, athleticism and good looks are emphasised in fight sequences and romantic scenes. Denis's sexual exploits, meanwhile, are always interrupted, and his small size is underlined by visual comedy: he repeatedly struggles to climb over obstacles, and cannot keep up with François's pace. When we first see Denis, moreover, he is limping, his leg wound recalling the similar injuries sustained by emasculated characters such as Katia in *Le Père Noël* and Pierrot in *Les Valseuses* (see chapter 3). The difference in physique between the two buddies is matched by a difference in outlook, which facilitates verbal comedy in the form of bickering, with Denis always complaining while François remains optimistic. Despite the humour, *Marche à l'ombre* offers a potentially depressing representation of a modern Paris where poverty, racism and criminality abound. This is obviated, however, by the representation of conventional, indeed stereotyped, pleasures: the black squatters performing a joyful concert in their ruined building, the love scenes between François and Mathilde. The aspirational values which run through the narrative are symbolised most of all by New York: while Paris is a place to escape from, the American dream lures the buddies, and Mathilde, to try a new start. As François tells Denis, in America nothing is impossible. The film ends with the two men walking down Broadway as an American disco anthem by Lavelle declares that the time 'is now'. Rather like the archetypal US disco film *Saturday Night Fever* (John Badham, 1977), *Marche à l'ombre* shows glimpses of urban desperation, but offers the hope of a way out through personal performance and ambition. Despite the presence of the comic duo, then, this particular French comedy's values seem to belong less to the collective anarchy of *café-théâtre* than to the aspirational individualism of Hollywood.

Folk humour and fantasy in *Les Visiteurs*

In 1993 Hollywood released Steven Spielberg's *Jurassic Park*, a blockbuster which dominated cinema on a global scale, and was the number one film in nearly every country in the world. In France, however, it was beaten into second place at the box office by Jean-Marie Poiré's comedy *Les Visiteurs*, which attracted more than double the audience, with an astounding 13.6 million spectators. *Les Visiteurs* features Poiré regulars Christian Clavier (who also co-wrote the screenplay), Valérie Lemercier and Marie-Anne Chazel. While Poiré uses farce to

25

Jean Reno and Christian Clavier in *Les Visiteurs*

send up the bourgeoisie in a manner derived from *café-théâtre*, he also presents a time-travel fantasy which pits a medieval knight and his servant against the modern-day world.

Poiré claims to have written the basic scenario at the age of seventeen, intending to make a short science-fiction drama which ended when the two protagonists arrived in modern times (see Nevers and Strauss 1993: 85). This remains the crux of the film, which transports the chivalrous Godefroy de Montmirail (Jean Reno) and the oafish Jacquouille (Clavier) from 1123 to 1993. Having mistakenly killed the father of his betrothed, Frénégonde (Lemercier), Godefroy drinks a magic potion hoping to travel back in time and undo his deed. Instead, he and his servant Jacquouille find themselves in modern-day France, where they meet their respective descendants, the kind-hearted upper-class twit Béatrice (Lemercier again) and the pompous *nouveau-riche* snob Jacquart (Clavier again). Jacquart, having changed the family name from the vulgar-sounding Jacquouille (which contains the French word for 'balls'), is running Godefroy's former castle as an overpriced hotel, while Béatrice and her dentist husband live in a gentrified cottage. Finding an ancient spellbook in the castle dungeon, Godefroy drinks a second potion and returns to his own time. Jacquouille, however, wishing to stay in the 1990s with friendly bag-lady Ginette (Chazel), drugs Jacquart and sends him to the Middle Ages in his place. The film ends with Godefroy and Frénégonde reunited and their lineage assured.

The persistent misunderstandings arising from Godefroy and Jacquart's arrival in the twentieth century generate both slapstick humour (Jacquart washing his face in a toilet bowl, or attempting to roast a leg of lamb on a spit made from an umbrella) and a commentary on present-day France which is vaguely ecological (the two express revulsion at the ugliness, pollution and noise around them), and politically anti-Revolutionary (Godefroy is disgusted to learn that his lands have been shared out democratically and that his castle is now owned by a peasant). On a narrative level, these two concerns are integrated in the finale: Godefroy's return to the Middle Ages is dependent on the castle dungeons remaining intact, that is to say, neither dismantled by the Revolution nor modernised by developers. The culture clash between 1123 and 1993 is most succinctly expressed in a sequence which shows Godefroy on horseback competing vainly against first a motorway, then a train, then an aeroplane. As well as giving rise to physical violence, as when Godefroy and Jacquouille attack a post-van thinking it is the devil's chariot, this comic conflict is also linguistic. Godefroy's anachronistic vocabulary and Old French verbs clash with Béatrice's bourgeois tones and Ginette's coarser slang, which Jacquart learns in order to stay with her. The massive popularity of the film in fact saw 'Clavier's aping of Lemercier's clipped and snooty pronunciation of "OK" (Okkaayy!) or "c'est dinnngue!", and weird expressions such as "mais qu'est-ce qu c'est que ce Bin's" [...] become national catchphrases ' (Jackel 2001: 46).

The film's initial setting, the Middle Ages, serves to emphasise the gleeful celebration of Bakhtin's 'universal folk humour', with jokes about farting and belching, sexual prowess, ageing and death, and the transformation of human bodies into animals, or piles of vomit and dung. The medieval scenes in Les Visiteurs also tend to pastiche the historical settings of historical dramas like Jean-Jacques Annaud's Le Nom de la rose (The Name of the Rose, 1986). Praising the smelly and dirty Middle Ages of Les Visiteurs as a subversion of the ornamental portrayal of the medieval in Le Nom de la rose, a Cahiers du cinéma review even proposed that Godefroy's inadvertent killing of Frénégonde's father symbolises Poiré's overturning of Annaud, an interpretation apparently suggested by the fact that Godefroy sees his victim in the form of a bear, representing Annaud's 1989 film L'Ours (see Nevers 1993). More persuasively, Cahiers contrasted the film's vigorous but culturally low humour with the high culture of the expensive décors and the historical setting. High production values and the trappings of the prestigious heritage genre are presented in the opening sequences before being assaulted later when chaos and destruction tear through the castle (Nevers 1993: 83). The film in fact begins by conforming precisely to the conventions of the historical drama, with period costume, spectacular landscapes shot from high and wide angles, lush music and an authoritative voice-over which situates the action in 1123. First undermined by the loutish violence of the English soldiers in the credit sequence, the heritage code is placed under increasing strain by the burlesque energy of the subsequent scenes. Les Visiteurs thus engages in combat with the values of Claude Berri's Germinal (1993), its major French box-office competitor (see chapter 6), and with all those 'cultural' projects which Poiré and

Clavier protest are better supported by the State, easier to finance and easier to cast than popular comedy (Nevers and Strauss 1993: 86). The huge success of *Les Visiteurs* despite the official funding and publicising of *Germinal* (by the Ministry of Culture) testifies to the power of what Bakhtin calls the 'language of the marketplace'. As one gloss on Bakhtin has it, 'The art of the marketplace is the art that people choose by purchasing it, not that guardians of the state and culture impose on them' (Paul 1991: 110). A similar choice was made by the French public over the sequel, *Les Couloirs du temps* (Poiré, 1998), which attracted eight million spectators despite – or perhaps because – it was all about what *Télérama* magazine dismissed as 'eating, shitting and puking' (Murat 1998: 225).

Twisting the comic trio in *Gazon maudit*

During the eighties, Josiane Balasko performed in and co-wrote several of the Splendid projects as well as directing her own comedy *Sac de noueds* (1985) and starring in Blier's *Trop belle pour toi!* (1989). Her most successful venture to date came in 1995 with *Gazon maudit* (*French Twist*), which she wrote and directed, and which sold nearly four million tickets at the French box office. The film stars Balasko as Marijo, a lesbian who enters the lives of unhappily married couple Loli (Victoria Abril) and Laurent (Alain Chabat). Changing permutations within their *ménage à trois* ensue, with first Laurent, then Marijo, excluded and rejected until finally, once Marijo has had a baby by Laurent, all three live happily together. While *café-théâtre* has been described as a 'rejection of "safe" stereotypes' (Harris 1998: 93), *Gazon maudit* makes great use of them to relatively predictable effect. Hence we are presented with the butch lesbian who smokes cigars and dresses like a man, the passionate Spanish woman, and the philandering and deceitful husband. Their roles do change as the narrative develops, with Laurent for instance getting his comeuppance and learning to accept Marijo, but it is interesting to note that the happy ending is achieved by recourse to a traditional construction of femininity: motherhood. Marijo's place in Loli and Laurent's household is only fully assured once she has given birth to Laurent's child.

What does set the film apart from convention is its authorship by a female comedy director (see Rollet 1999), the use of a comic trio rather than a male comic duo, and the presence of two women rather than two men in the *ménage à trois* – contrast for example Blier's *Les Valseuses*, *Préparez vos mouchoirs*, and *Tenue de soirée* (*Evening Dress*, 1986). The brilliant pacing, surprise cuts, and sense of shock that characterise Blier's best work are however largely absent from Balasko's film, with the hint at male homosexuality when Laurent meets Diego at the end of the film carrying nothing like the charge of the final scene in *Tenue de soirée*, for example (see chapter 3). Similarly the comedy, both verbal and visual, is much more restrained than in the earlier Splendid vehicles like *Le Père Noël est une ordure*. The language is on the whole less vituperative and aggressive, although Laurent does indulge in some homophobic and chauvinist abuse aimed at Marijo and Loli. There is a certain twist in the references to sex, so that Laurent's rants are balanced by the playful scene where Marijo and Loli swap affectionate French and Spanish slang terms for the vagina. Similarly, all three slapstick sequences function to undercut Laurent's assumption of masculine power and authority. Twice he is bested in fights with women (first by Marijo, then by her lover) and once he drunkenly falls off his bike into a pigsty. The other strand of humour twisting gender conventions concerns Marijo, whose deep voice, 'male' clothing and broad physique fool Loli and Laurent's son into thinking she is a man when she first appears. Identified with sweat, dirt and hairiness in this introductory sequence, Marijo displays the traits conventionally associated with masculinity (see Dyer 1990: 92). If this is a pretty orthodox portrayal of lesbianism, the passion that Loli develops for Marijo is less predictable but, as we have seen, the film finds its narrative resolution in a reassertion of heterosexual sex and motherhood. In so doing, *Gazon maudit*, like *Marche à l'ombre* before it, displays the extent to which solo projects by members of the Splendid team have tended to dilute to some extent their *café-théâtre* origins, as that 'aggressively iconoclastic culture of comedy has [...] entered into the mainstream' (Harris 1998: 91).

Foreign bodies in the family: *La Vie est un long fleuve tranquille, Tatie Danielle, Un air de famille*

During the 1980s several directors were making popular comedies with little or no connection to *café-théâtre*. Among them were Coline Serreau with *Trois homes et un couffin* and *Romuald et Juliette* (see chapter 4) and Etienne Chatiliez with his first two films, *La Vie est un long fleuve tranquille* (*Life is a Long Quiet River*, 1988) and *Tatie Danielle* (1990). Chatiliez's début proved extremely successful, the third most popular French film of its year with four million spectators. The follow-up was however a disappointment. Lacking the energy and satirical thrust of *La Vie est un long fleuve tranquille, Tatie Danielle* is a slow-moving black comedy about the anxieties caused by ageing: ill health, poverty, loneliness and exclusion. The running joke in the film is that all these misfortunes are faked by Tatie, and that she plays upon them in order to manipulate others. Moving in with her nephew and his family, she makes their lives a misery until an assertive home help, Sandrine, catches her out and develops a friendship with her. Despite a few jibes at the aspirational lifestyle of the nephew and his wife, the film is little more than a vehicle for the veteran actress Tsilla Chelton as Tatie. And notwithstanding her association with the stars of Le Splendid, to whom she gave acting classes in the seventies (see Topaloff 2004), Chelton's performance style is classical and restrained, relying on naturalistic facial expression and on monologues rather than on any frantic or involuntary gestures. Similarly, slapstick is avoided: when Tatie's old servant Odile falls and dies trying to clean the chandelier, the accident is elided and only the outcome is shown. There is only one moment of violence in the film (when Sandrine slaps Tatie in the face) and only one shocking visual gag: a play on the grotesque body when Tatie deliberately wets herself in order to disrupt her hosts' dinner party.

While *Tatie Danielle* is as slow and ponderous as its protagonist, *La Vie est un long fleuve tranquille* is a much more dynamic assault on middle-class values and on the institution of the French bourgeois family. The film concerns two families from different ends of the social spectrum: the Le Quesnoys (rich, respectable and Catholic upper-class twits) and the Groseilles (impoverished and criminal working-class slobs). The plot hinges on the swapping of two babies born on the same day twelve years previously, Maurice Le Quesnoy and Bernadette Groseille. It is typical of Chatiliez's irony at the expense of religious and cultural values that this action, which will contribute to the disintegration of one of the families, takes place at Christmas and is described as 'a miracle' by the nurse who carries it out. Now on the brink of adolescence, the two children are informed of their true parentage. While Bernadette (Valérie Lalande) and her mother (Hélène Vincent) fail to cope, Momo (Benoît Magimel) functions happily in both worlds, moving in with his true parents while remaining a welcome visitor to the Groseilles on the other side of town. Ultimately the Le Quesnoys lose control of their other children as the Groseilles introduce them to the joys of swimming in dirty rivers, getting drunk, having sex in the bushes and sniffing glue.

La Vie est un long fleuve tranquille takes its targets in part from Luis Buñuel's surrealist satires of the bourgeoisie, especially *Le Journal d'une femme de chambre* (*Diary of a Chambermaid*, 1965), which concerns an upper-class household who make a fetish of cleanliness while feeling at once attracted and repelled by the sexuality and dirtiness that they perceive in their maid and in the class she represents. Even the figure of the smug and repressed priest (the happy-clappy Father Auberge in Chatiliez's film) recalls *Le Journal d'une femme de chambre*. The acting style is more expressive than in Buñuel, but far from the exaggerated gesticulations of *café-théâtre*. There is no violence in the film and no slapstick. And as in *Tatie Danielle*, only one character exhibits 'automatic, repeated gestures, tics, grimaces and contractures' (Gordon 2001: 22). In both films, moments of stress bring on a tic that is evident but that is nonetheless underplayed: the repeated coughing of Tatie's servant Odile, the nervous twitch of Monsieur Le Quesnoy. Both performances avoid the excesses of Chazel or Lhermitte in comparable roles for Le Splendid and the physical comedy, although focusing on the body, remains relatively subtle. For instance, when sufficiently liberated by the sexual openness brought about by the Groseilles to tell his wife that she gives him an erection, Monsieur Le Quesnoy simultaneously signals his own repression of this desire by twitching his head again and by clasping his hands defensively across his lap.

Early sequences of *La Vie est un long fleuve tranquille*, set in each household in turn, establish the fundamental contrast at work in the narrative by mobilising the discourse of cleanliness and dirt and also, less explicitly, by using colour in the *mise en scène*. The Groseilles are first seen smoking, drinking and gambling at cards while two toddlers kiss on the bed in the background in an exaggerated parody of fears about underage sex. The room is untidy and dirty but the colour scheme expresses warmth, since all the family members are wearing red tones (the exception is Hamed, their Arab neighbour, who is in blue). Red is moreover traditionally associated with the proletariat and with working-class struggle. In contrast, cold blues dominate lighting and costume in the Le Quesnoy household. The family are introduced at bath time, and this emphasis on cleanliness becomes excessive later in the film when Bernadette, discovering she is really a Groseille, tries to remove the perceived stain of her working-class origins by washing obsessively, wearing white and drinking only milk. Madame Le Quesnoy's reaction to the news is no less excessive: she is heard vomiting repeatedly. The control of bodily fluids and appetites that the Le Quesnoys have attempted to maintain in their family and inculcate in their children thus collapses. When Bernadette visits the Groseilles, she is confronted by her new mother and siblings spitting at the television. Each swapped child is in a sense a foreign body within its family, but while Madame Le Quesnoy and Bernadette try to evacuate the working-class body (scrubbing it out, vomiting it out), Momo appears to integrate successfully into the bourgeoisie. Gradually the children of the two families begin to mix, too, and the discoveries that ensue – adolescent sex, alcohol, and experiments with drugs – are gleefully celebrated by Chatiliez. These discoveries all release the body from taboos and controls, allowing the satisfaction of bodily desires and escaping the inhibitions maintained by the bourgeoisie and the church. The evacuation of dirt is replaced by its celebration: Roselyne Groseille tells Paul Le Quesnoy after their last date of the summer, 'Je ne me laverai pas pour garder ton odeur' [I won't wash, so I can keep your smell]. The film also celebrates inclusion and mixing within French society through the figure of Hamed, the immigrant grocer above whose shop the Groseilles live. In the opening sequence, a news report on a car explosion outside his shop, Hamed presents himself as 'not an Arab but a Frenchman', and he is accepted by the Groseilles (despite their bad taste references to the Algerian War) as a neighbour and partner in crime. The car bomb is eventually revealed as an insurance scam between Hamed and Momo rather than the racist attack it first seems to be. In place of the stifling values of the bourgeoisie *La Vie est un long fleuve tranquille* posits the integration of foreign bodies into the family and the nation.

In a more muted and sombre way, Cédric Klapisch's *Un air de famille* (*Family Resemblances*, 1996) also explores the collapse of the cherished ideals and illusions that hold together a family. Here the outsider figure is Denis (Jean-Pierre Darroussin), a lugubrious waiter who works at the bar owned by Henri (Jean-Pierre Bacri). Every Friday night Henri puts on his special Friday tank-top, and his family arrives for a ritual dinner in a nearby restaurant: his domineering mother, sarcastic sister Betty, successful brother Philippe and banal sister-in-law Yolande. The film balances nostalgia for the past, expressed in slow-motion flashbacks of the three young children playing on their parents' bed, with a dark and increasingly bitter present as the family members argue and reveal longstanding resentments. The bar setting serves as a metaphor for the claustrophobic space of the family itself, while many of the tensions that arise are predicated on the absence of the dead father – hence the name of the bar, 'Au Père tranquille' (The Sleepy Father). Denis's position outside the family but eventually finding a way in – when Betty (Agnès Jaoui) finally reveals that he is her mysterious boyfriend – is contrasted with Henri's sense of exclusion from a family within which, as the flashbacks show, he once felt integrated. Henri calls himself the family idiot, finds himself repeatedly ignored or ridiculed by his mother and his siblings, and identifies with his absent father – as when he listens to a Caruso record, symbolising the voice of his dead father, at the close of the film.

Un air de famille is an adaptation of Bacri and Jaoui's successful stage play, and the comedy derives largely from the script, which features old-fashioned proverbs and chauvinist observations from Henri, vituperative sarcasm from Betty, and a droll account of Caruso, the paralysed dog that used to sing, from Denis. There are also certain moments of visual humour, as when Yolande mistakes a diamond choker for a dog collar, or when Henri's isolated and reduced position within the family group sees him framed in the trap door to the cellar with the others looking down at him. The setting, lighting and acting are all very carefully judged and gloomily realistic, with the excellent performances largely far removed from caricature or stereotype. As the evening wears on, Yolande gets drunk, Philippe rages at his wife and sister, and the mother falls down the stairs. The only expression of joy is provided by the two characters most peripheral to the family group, Denis and Yolande, as they dance to celebrate her birthday. However, a sense of comic resolution is provided in the public acknowledgement of Denis and Betty's relationship, prompting Yolande to note, 'Il fait partie de la famille, maintenant' [He's part of the family now]. This final assertion of continuity within the family is reiterated when Henri's wife (who has threatened to leave him) rings to arrange her return. Hence despite the conflicts that have arisen within the group, and the gradual revelation that the idolised favourite son, Philippe, is an aggressive and cowardly bully, the family is represented as an enduring presence, capable of absorbing an outsider like Denis. They will all meet again at Henri's bar next Friday.

Popular series and national heroes

The perennial comic duos we have observed in French film comedy can be read as fundamental to the national self-image. According to producer Patrice Ledoux, Frenchness tends to be personified in the stock characters of 'le héros noble' [the noble hero] and 'le prolo débrouillard' [the crafty pleb] (Ferenczi 1998: 24). Witness Godefroy and Jacquouille in *Les Visiteurs*, or François and Denis in *Marche à l'ombre*. Certain popular comic icons in French culture conflate these two types, as is the case with the comic-book hero Astérix. Displaying the cunning resourcefulness of the underdog, Astérix is at the same time the incarnation of noble and heroic values such as loyalty, honesty, and sacrifice. Whether in comic books or film adaptations, however, Astérix is always part of a double act.

Fighting authority in the *Astérix* series

Nine million tickets were sold for *Astérix et Obélix contre César* (*Asterix and Obelix take on Caesar*, Zidi, 1999). The film mixes familiar elements (the characters from Goscinny and Uderzo's well-loved cartoon books, the comic duo of little Clavier and big Depardieu from *Les Anges gardiens*) with up-to-date CGI by Pitof to provide digital special effects and thus facilitate the first ever live action Astérix story. In a scenario written by Zidi and dedicated to Goscinny, Astérix and Obélix rescue their village druid from the Romans, defeating both Caesar (Claude Piéplu) and Détritus (Roberto Benigni) in the process. A romantic subplot concerns Obélix's unrequited love for Panacéa (Laetitia Casta). Alongside the puns which tend to punctuate the cartoon books, the film deploys several visual gags around feasting and fighting, including a slow-motion brawl using rotten fish as weapons, and speeded-up CGI scenes of the Romans being battered. There is also visual humour at the expense of Obélix's love-sickness: a stone medallion he carves in the shape of a love-heart is the size of a boulder and too heavy for anyone else to lift. While Depardieu's performance as Obélix makes effective use of the ambivalence in his star image between massive physique and tenderness, Clavier as Astérix is more restrained than usual, at least until the set-piece sequence where he has to run the gauntlet in a Roman arena. Confronted by snakes, lions, crocodiles and tarantulas but with no magic potion to help him, Astérix is finally vulnerable, as expressed by Clavier's rolling eyes, contorted face and comic gait. His resourcefulness is enough to see him through however, and the little hero, the *débrouillard*, manages to outwit the authority of the Roman Empire. Gallic identity is thus celebrated while defeating military power and legal authority.

Although it is primarily the bodies of Roman soldiers which are under assault in the film, a number of scenes present visual comedy aimed at the universal frailties of the human body: ageing is ridiculed in the character of Geriatrix as well as in the appearance of the druid's great-grandfather, whose face is covered in fungi and whose beard is metres long. The vulnerability of the body is a source of comedy in the torture sequence where first Astérix and then his dog are stretched improbably on the rack. CGI is used to multiply the comic body when the magic potion creates an army of Astérixes and Obélixes. The importance of potions and transformations recalls *Les Visiteurs*, where a lord is turned into a bear, a priest into a pig and an old crone into a sex bomb. As in *Marche à l'ombre* and *Western*, the temptation offered by a woman threatens to split the male duo, but after one brief kiss with a double of Panacéa, Obélix returns to his rightful place beside Astérix for the ritual banquet that always concludes an Astérix story. In the sequel, *Astérix et Obélix: Mission Cléopâtre* (2002), Clavier and Depardieu are again present, with the addition of Monica Belucci as Cleopatra, but it is the young comedian Jamel Debbouze who makes the biggest impact, playing the Egyptian architect Numérobis. Announcing his arrival in popular film comedy after working in other media first, Jamel is a fast and furious performer, parodying *Star Wars* and martial arts, and functioning not as part of a comic duo but as a one-man show.

The *Taxi* series: French tortoise versus foreign hares

Just like *Astérix*, the *Taxi* series has proved immensely popular by pitting a comic duo against figures of authority and power. (Six and a half million people saw *Taxi* (Gérard Pirès, 1998) and over ten million *Taxi 2* (Gérard Krawczyk, 2000).) In this case the context is not ancient history but criminal activity in Marseilles, and the template for the humour is provided by national stereotypes. France is again personified by a comic duo and above all by the figure of a roguish and cheeky outsider, Daniel (Samy Nacéri) the pizza delivery boy turned taxi-driver turned police auxiliary. While Daniel displays the customary traits of the little French hero, including local knowledge, working-class roots, a dislike of authority, and the resourcefulness known as *débrouillardise*, he also crosses boundaries between criminality and legality. Despite his contempt for authority and his repeated driving offences, he ends up helping the inept detective Emilien (Frédéric Diefenthal) track down foreign crooks, and is eventually fêted by the establishment: the first film ends with him being awarded a medal and chosen to represent France in formula one; the sequel with his taxi joining the Bastille Day parade in front of President Chirac.

Daniel is repeatedly identified with Frenchness and also, to a lesser extent, with the city of Marseilles. *Taxi* sees him competing for France in formula one, driving a racing car painted in the red white and blue of the national flag. His beloved taxi in both films is a French-made Peugeot, and he wears a French football shirt for the entirety of *Taxi 2*. This is significantly the number 10 shirt, with the name of Zidane on the back. There are associations here between national pride and France's World Cup victory of 1998 (referred to explicitly in *Taxi 2*) as well as regional and racial associations which would be most apparent to a French audience: Zidane, a star in his own right, played for Olympique de Marseille (OM) and – like Samy Nacéri – is of North African parentage (see chapter 2). Little is made of the latter parallel in the *Taxi* series, but more of the local connection. Although he does not have a local accent, Daniel is equated with Marseilles by means of costume (his OM football shirt in the first film, the Zidane shirt in the second) and through the association between himself and his taxi, which is both the means whereby he displays his possession of the city (Daniel is repeatedly asked to prove his prowess as a driver and often uses short cuts that display his local knowledge) and a visual substitute or extension of Daniel himself (flash, fast, marked with a Marseille badge like the OM football shirt). The theme of national identity is foregrounded by the characterisation of the villains as foreigners: the German 'Mercedes gang' in *Taxi*, Japanese ninjas in *Taxi 2*. Again the vehicles driven embody national pride: red Mercedes for the Germans, black Mitsubishis for the Japanese. Both Germany and Japan represent not only economic competitors for modern France but also military enemies from the past. The Marseilles police chief refers to his grandfather's death in the trenches and urges his team to repel the Germans' new attempt to 'invade our territory'. In *Taxi 2* he has pretensions to respect Japanese culture but ends up ridiculing by imitation Japanese expressions and rituals (for example in the farcical repeated bowing at the airport).

Although some humour is derived from Daniel's run-ins with the local police, most is targeted either at his useless police buddy Emilien (who has failed his driving test eight times and is thrown into a rubbish bin in each of the films) or at the foreign criminals, via crude national stereotyping. Hence Germans are portrayed as efficient, powerful and arrogant, Koreans as workaholics, and Japanese as practitioners of secretive black arts such as ninjitsu and brainwashing. In a key exchange during the frenetic car chase finale to *Taxi*, Daniel is dismissed as 'insolent' by the Mercedes gang, who declare that 'On a plus de puissance!' [we are more powerful]. It is precisely against this assertion of (economic and military) power that Daniel reacts – just like Astérix defying the might of Rome. Having 'lost' the race by tricking the Germans into a spectacular dead end, Daniel celebrates his victory by evoking the story of the tortoise and the hare – 'c'est toujours la tortue qui gagne!' [the tortoise always wins] – thus positing French national identity as the comic and unexpected overturning of odds against an ostensibly superior rival.

One further reference point for the humour in the *Taxi* series comes from the extremely popular comic thrillers and action movies that starred Jean-Paul Belmondo in the seventies and early eighties. Known affectionately by his public as 'Bébel', Belmondo was famous for performing his own stunts and for incarnating lovable rogues with a mixture of clowning and machismo. Most relevant here is his performance in *Flic ou voyou* (Georges Lautner, 1979), a comedy thriller which sees Belmondo tread a fine line between his function as a police officer and his playful bending of the rules, and which involves repeated car chases, a driving test sequence, and a stunt in which Belmondo drives his sports car through a french window and into the living room of a suspect. This gag resurfaces throughout the *Taxi* series, with Emilien crashing inadvertently into shops while taking his driving test and Daniel deliberately driving his taxi into

Paris police headquarters to provoke a chase. There is a sense in which the success of the *Taxi* series could be construed as the passing on of Bébel's mantle to Samy Nacéri: witness the mixture of comedy and action, the warm smile and confident resourcefulness of the protagonist, the subsequent pairing of Belmondo and Nacéri in a TV remake of one of the former's films (see Austin 2003: 136).

Another comedy star of North African origin, and one perhaps more likely to maintain his status as a national hero than the troubled Nacéri (who has been repeatedly arrested for various offences and has just been sent to prison for racist comments) is Jamel Debbouze. Present but underused in *Le Fabuleux destin d'Amélie Poulain* (*Amélie*, Jeunet, 2001, see chapter 6), Jamel was one of the major attractions in the *Astérix* sequel, stealing the show from Clavier and Depardieu. His comedy relies at once on rapid delivery and frantic gestures, and has proved extremely popular on radio and television and in stand-up as well as on the big screen. What Jamel and Nacéri both demonstrate is that *beur* actors can become stars in modern French cinema, and notably in the traditional and often formulaic genre of the comedy.

References

Austin, G. (2003), *Stars in Modern French Film*, London, Arnold.

Bakhtin, M. (1984), *The Age of Rabelais*, Bloomington, Indiana University Press.

Dyer, R. (1990), *Now You See It: Studies in Lesbian and Gay Film*, London, Routledge.

Ferenczi, A. (1998), Le business Jacquouille, *Télérama*, 2510 (18 February 1998), 24.

Grenier, A. (1994), *Génération Père Noël*, Paris, Belfond.

Gordon, R. B. (2001), *Why the French Love Jerry Lewis: From Cabaret to Early Cinema*, Stanford, Stanford University Press.

Harris, S. (1997), The people's filmmaker? *Théâtre populaire* and the films of Bertrand Blier, in S. Perry and M. Cross (eds), *Voices of France: Social, Political and Cultural Identity*, London, Pinter, 114–26.

Harris. S. (1998), 'Les Comiques font de la résistance': Dramatic Trends in Popular Film Comedy, *Australian Journal of French Studies*, XXXV: 1 (April 1998), 87–100.

Horton, A. (1991), Introduction, in A. Horton (ed.), *Comedy/Cinema/Theory*, Berkeley, University of California Press, 1–21.

Jackel, A. (2001), *Les Visiteurs*: a feelgood movie for uncertain times, in L. Mazdon (ed.), *France on Film: Reflections on Popular French Cinema*, London, Wallflower, 41–50.

Leconte, P. (2004), *Les Bronzés*, c'est unique dans l'histoire du cinéma, *Marianne*, 382 (14–20 August 2004), 63.

Lévi-Strauss, C. (1993), Father Christmas Executed, in D. Miller (ed.), *Unwrapping Christmas*, Oxford, Clarendon Press, 38–51.

Miller, D. (1993), A Theory of Christmas, in D. Miller (ed.), *Unwrapping Christmas*, Oxford, Clarendon Press, 3–37.

Murat, P. (1998), *Les Couloirs du temps, Les Visiteurs II*, Paris, *Télérama* , 2510, 225.

Nevers, C. (1993), Les Visiteurs font de la résistance, Paris, *Cahiers du cinéma*, 465, 83.

Nevers, C., and Strauss, F. (1993), Entretien avec Jean-Marie Poiré et Christian Clavier, Paris, *Cahiers du cinéma*, 465, 84–9.

Paul, W. (1991), Charles Chaplin and the Annals of Anality, in A. Horton (ed.), *Comedy/ Cinema/ Theory*, Berkeley, University of California Press, 109–30.

Rollet, B. (1999), Unruly Woman? Josiane Balasko, French Comedy, and *Gazon maudit*, in P. Powrie (ed.), *French Cinema in the 1990s: Continuity and Difference*, Oxford, Oxford University Press, 127–36.

Topaloff, A. (2004), La véritable épopée des *Bronzés*, *Marianne*, 382 (14–20 August 2004), 60–62.

9 *Le jeune cinéma* and the new realism

In the taxonomy of French social history, 1995 is a watershed to match May 1968 (see chapter 1). The year 1995 saw mass demonstrations against the policies and practices of the right-wing government in France, particularly those concerning immigration. The perception had become widespread that French society was divided by *la fracture sociale,* a split between the haves and the have-nots: the term was common currency in the nineties and was widely used by Jacques Chirac during his successful presidential campaign of 1995 (see Higbee 2005: 123). That year also saw a big rise in support for Jean-Marie Le Pen's far right party, the Front National, signalling the presence of anxieties around race, immigration, and *sécurité* in French politics. As a corollary to this came a wave of militant protest: 'it was the mass mobilizations of 1995 which signalled a change of the socio-political climate in France, and which created the conditions for the rebirth of a committed cinema and for subsequent mobilizations such as that around the *sans-papiers*' (O'Shaugnessy 2003: 189; see also below). Mobilisation however could not disguise the fact that the erosion of class identities and of Marxism during the nineties had left many of the dispossessed in France feeling voiceless. In 1993 Pierre Bourdieu's vast study into French poverty, *La Misère du monde,* had suggested that poverty and suffering were now 'politically inexpressible' (see Marlière 1997: 47). A similar shift had taken place in the way in which social exclusion was formulated, 'a shift from political concern to moral concern, [...] from which the actors and profiteers of a system which allows, encourages or provokes exclusion are evacuated, and in which they are replaced by spectators, witnesses of exclusion' (Marlière 1997: 57). One of the characteristics of *le jeune cinéma* has been to address this issue and to attempt to voice the exclusion and suffering of its protagonists in ways that might potentially go beyond 'simply' witnessing, to retrieve some element of the political. This gives a sense of struggle and anger to many of these films, and means that 'If there is one thing that can be consistently found in post-1995 French cinema, it is revolt' (O'Shaugnessy 2003: 192).

Defining a new genre

A second inspiration for *le jeune cinéma*, besides the political and social unrest of the mid nineties, was the lead given by a series of television films called *Tous les garçons et les filles de leur âge*. Commissioned by the Franco-German TV station Arte and screened in autumn 1994, the series featured work by nine relatively young directors (discounting the more established *auteurs* Chantal Ackerman and André Téchiné). Three of the nine films also received a theatrical release, including Olivier Assayas' excellent early example of *jeune cinéma* style, *L'Eau froide* (1994). Although the films were all set in the past (each depicts a formative period in the director's youth), the series was felt by several critics to have a clear relevance to ongoing issues in French society. *Positif* magazine remarked that by being screened on TV rather than at the cinema, the films had somehow acquired a 'sociological' importance (see Amiel 1994: 32). Others compared *Tous les garçons et les filles* to the impact of *la nouvelle vague* in the late fifties (see chapter 1), with the dynamism and freshness of the films attributed to the use of small budgets, light cameras and reduced crews (see Pascal 1994: 63). Moreover, the last film of the series, Olivier Dahan's *Frères*, was influential in the establishment of a sub-genre within *jeune cinéma*, the *banlieue* film (see below and Jousse 1995b).

One of the first French film critics to attempt a definition of the new genre, Claude-Marie Trémois, listed eight characteristics of *le jeune cinéma*: urgency, topicality, tight chronology, wandering characters/cameras, improvisation, long sequences, open endings, and a non-judgemental presentation of the protagonists (see Trémois 1997: 47–55). Several of these features are associated with art cinema in general, notably a sense of openness or ambivalence. But where art cinema is often characterised by stylisation and even formal experimentation, the films of *le jeune cinéma* are usually raw and naturalistic, with a documentary aesthetic that reflects their often bleak socio-political content. As a result, this new genre has also been termed 'new realism' or 'the return of the real' (see for example Powrie 1999). Possibly influenced by the ultra-naturalistic shooting practices laid down by Lars von Trier's *Dogme* manifesto in 1995, *jeune cinéma* has tended to rely on handheld cameras and ambient sound, while often avoiding sound-track music in order to maintain the realist illusion (as in the films of the Dardenne brothers). After ten years or so this style of filming has become widespread, and functions to present the moral choices and social struggles experienced by its characters without an ironic or critical distance. In François Dupeyron's *Inguélézi* (2004), for example, the whiplash pans and the perpetually shaky handheld camerawork mimic the unplanned, spontaneous and disorienting experiences of the two protagonists, a young French widow and a Turkish immigrant she smuggles to England. The film is shot by Yves Angelo whose work in the nineties heritage film was much more classical and controlled, whether as cinematographer (*Tous les matins du monde*, Corneau, 1992) or director (*Le Colonel Chabert*, Angelo, 1994). Filmed with a team of seven and a lightweight camera, *Inguélézi* is the polar opposite of the high production values and visual pleasures of the heritage genre (see chapter 7), and as such epitomises the stance of *le jeune cinéma* generally.

As the example of Dupeyron suggests – his début film was *Drôle d'endroit pour une rencontre* (*A Strange Place to Meet*) back in 1988 – despite its name *le jeune cinéma* is not strictly defined by the age of its practitioners. And although since the nineties, 'French cinema is basically a cinema made by young filmmakers', not all these young directors are making *auteur* films, realist films, or works that square with the concept of *le jeune cinéma* (see Jeancolas 2005: 158). Nonetheless the equation between youth, socio-political commentary, and realism has been made in the critical reception of these films, in much the same way as *la nouvelle vague* was perceived in the late fifties as belonging to the renewal of the French republic by de Gaulle's presidency (see Chabrol 1976: 135). If youth is not an essential factor in *le jeune cinéma* then perhaps an engagement with regional identity is. Filming in the regions is not always a factor of production practices, which are still mainly centralised in Paris, but often reflects the origins and sense of identity particular to directors, such as Robert Guédiguian in Marseilles, Sandrine Veysset in Avignon, or the Dardenne brothers in Belgium. And although feature-length fiction films in France remain largely dependent on Parisian production companies, there is more decentralisation in the financing of shorts and documentaries (see Grandena 2004: 115).

What defines the genre even more clearly than its semantics (regional settings, handheld cameras, lack of music, alienated characters) is its socially-conscious syntax. It has been said that *le jeune cinéma* focuses on 'the fragments left behind once globalization has passed through the social terrain' (O'Shaugnessy 2005b: 75). The films concerned tend to represent 'the local struggles of small groups or individuals, usually with no viable collective, political language to name the wrongs done to them' (O'Shaugnessy 2005b: 77). Pessimistic and despairing plotlines run throughout the genre, with suicide attempts figuring in *L'Eau froide*, *La Vie rêvée des anges*, *Y aura-t-il de la neige à Noël?* and *Rosetta*. The social exclusion that lies at the heart of the films is embodied in the illicit migrants of *La Promesse* (*The Promise*, Dardenne brothers, 1996) and *Inguélezi*, the spatial barriers evoked in *La Haine* (*Hate*, Kassovitz, 1995) and *Rosetta*, or the metaphor of the clandestine journey from *Y aura-t-il de la neige à Noël?* (see Thomas 2001: 83).

If *le jeune cinéma* was embryonic in 1994 with *Tous les garçons et les filles de leur âge*, and exploded onto the global stage a year later with the huge impact of *La Haine* (see below), the apogee of the new genre came in the late nineties. In 1998 over a million spectators watched *La Vie rêvée des anges* (*The Dream-Life of Angels*, Zonca, 1998) while its co-stars, Elodie Bouchez and Natacha Régnier, shared the best actress prize at the Cannes film festival. A year later at Cannes came perhaps the crowning moment, with the Dardenne brothers' *Rosetta* (1999) winning the Palme d'or while three non-professionals shared the actor prizes (see Austin 2004). Press reaction was divided. The main-stream press was generally unimpressed, but magazines like *Cahiers du cinéma* and *Les Inrockuptibles* championed what they viewed as a renewal of French cinema. Moreover, the political commitment of many of the film-makers concerned had already been made impres-sively apparent. In the spring of 1997 *jeune cinéma* directors had been at the forefront of what became known as the *sans-papiers* affair. Their successful mobilisation in favour of the dispossessed demonstrated that, even if the new realism risked telling local stories whose frag-mentary and isolated status could be 'politically disabling' or 'worse still, voyeuristic' (O'Shaugnessy 2005b: 86), the active engagement of these film-makers in the political realm was one way of ensuring a form of collective victory.

The *sans-papiers* affair

In February 1997 longstanding tensions in France surrounding issues of immigration, race, and national identity came to a head. In the preceding months and years, the right-wing government had introduced new measures to restrict the access of immigrants to French citizenship. Those who lived and worked in France but were denied the legal documentation allowing them to stay had become known as the *sans-papiers* ('without papers'). The previous summer had seen the hunger strike of three hundred *sans-papiers* at a church in Paris supported by a number of celebrities, including the French film star Emmanuelle Béart. The events of February 1997 were to see the film-makers of *le jeune cinéma* take the lead in militant protest on the same issue. The month began with the far right Front National winning an election victory in the southern town of Vitrolles, and with a woman from Lille named Jacqueline Deltombe being found guilty of sheltering a *sans-papiers*. A week later, *Le Monde* published a statement known as *l'appel des 59* in which various film directors declared that they too had committed the same crime and should hence be punished by the law. Organised by the *jeune cinéma* directors Pascale Ferran and Arnaud Desplechin, the declaration was signed by Claire Denis, Matthieu Kassovitz, Olivier Assayas and Sandrine Veysset, as well as older figures such as Bertrand Tavernier. Other statements on behalf of other professions swiftly followed, and on 22 February a demonstration in Paris against the current immigra-tion laws attracted 100,000 protestors. At the end of the month the newspaper *Libération* asserted that the film-makers' intervention had triumphed, by forcing the government to remove the article of the law calling for the denunciation of those responsible for sheltering sans-papiers. Although *Libération* had reservations about the wisdom of focusing on just one part of the immigration project, it concluded that the film-makers' 'off-screen' actions had shown that the Left was still alive in France, and able to challenge the political system. There is debate about the lasting impact of the film-makers' movement (which was dissolved after the protests of 22 February). Jean-Pierre Jeancolas, one of the first French film critics to write about the phenomenon of *le jeune cinéma*, has recently declared that the humanitarian commitment visible in the *sans-papiers* protests 'did not last more than a few months', and that therefore the concept of *le jeune cinéma* as a cohesive, politically-engaged grouping is only valid for the year 1997 (Jeancolas 2005: 159, 157). One might claim that its legacy is apparent, however, in the civil disobedience of summer and autumn 2006, when – in the latest variation on the *sans-papiers* affair – efforts have been made by various French citizens to hide the children of immigrants from the police in order to prevent their deportation. The engagement of *le jeune cinéma* with the suffering of the marginalised and dispossessed (*les exclus*) has also been apparent on screen over the last decade.

The uses of *La Haine*: from *la fracture sociale* to *la fracture coloniale*

La Haine (*Hate*, Kassovitz, 1995) tells the story of three marginalised characters from diverse ethnic backgrounds, living in the suburban ghetto or *banlieue* on the edge of Paris. The film has attained totemic status not just in France but far beyond, as the epitome of the *jeune cinéma* of the nineties. Kassovitz won the best director award at Cannes, while the film attracted an audience of two million in France and was even screened for the prime minister Alain Juppé. Over the decade since its release, a variety of readings of *La Haine* have been proposed, such that we can speak of the uses to which it has been put by various discourses and critical perspectives.

Inspired in part by the police killing of a young *Beur* (of North African origin) called Makoumé in 1993, *La Haine* follows three young men, Hubert (Hubert Kounde), Saïd (Saïd Taghmaoui) and Vinz (Vincent Cassell), as they react to the police wounding of Abdel, a *beur* friend of theirs. On its release in France *La Haine* was received as the standard-bearer for the *banlieue* film (see for example Jousse 1995b), a sub-genre which was defined (like the Western) by reference to its setting. *Positif* described *banlieue* films like *La Haine* as contemporary anti-Westerns, comparing their urban ghettos to the Indian reservations in the traditional Western (see Tobin 1995: 28). Both *Positif* and *Cahiers du cinéma* bracketed *La Haine* along with films such as *Etats des lieux* (Richet, 1995), *Raï* (Gilou, 1995) and *Bye-Bye* (Dridi, 1995), which were released during the same year and which employed similar characterisation, setting, music and language. It was the latter in particular that *Positif* and *Cahiers* singled out as the crucial factor in *La Haine*, since the mixture of *verlan* (back-slang) with idioms of Parisian, Arabic or American origin, anchored the film both temporally and spatially in the *banlieue* of the nineties (see Tobin 1995: 28 and Jousse 1995a: 34).

In retrospect *La Haine* can also be seen to encapsulate several of the characteristics of the new realism or *jeune cinéma*, including a sense of engagement with socio-political realities, a scenario dealing with everyday life embedded in a marginalised social milieu, a sense of topicality and urgency, and long sequences in which characters and camera wander through a deprived environment. Shot on location in Chanteloup-les-Vignes, a western suburb of Paris, the film includes documentary footage of a riot on that very estate in its opening sequence. As we have seen, Kassovitz's use of language, setting, and characterisation were all praised in the French press as realistic means of embedding the narrative in the *banlieue*. However *La Haine* is in many ways much more stylised than much of *le jeune cinéma*, and is far removed from the ultra-realist films of the Dardenne brothers, for example. It makes very deliberate use of sound-track music (albeit often attempting to place this within the narrative, as when Hubert listens to Isaac Hayes on his stereo, or in the DJ sequence). It makes spectacular use of camerawork and effects such as slow motion, overhead shots, zooms, and direct camera address. It borrows its countdown chronology from the thriller and its hip-hop sensibility from the American movies *Do The Right Thing* (Spike Lee, 1989) and *Boyz N the Hood* (John Singleton, 1991). And it is shot in black and white. *Cahiers* felt that the choice of monochrome allowed the film to appear more 'urban' and closer to the concrete world of the *banlieue* (see Jousse 1995a: 34). One could equally argue, however, that shooting in black and white results in a loss of realism, and the creation of 'a visually seductive, highly stylized representation of the *cité*' (Higbee 2005: 127).

For all its stylisation, *La Haine* does engage directly and thrillingly with key identity issues at stake in French society of the nineties, centred around class, place, and race. As in the Dardenne brothers' *Rosetta* (see below), the film presents socially and spatially marginalised characters who attempt (rather half-heartedly in *La Haine*, with a desperate hunger in *Rosetta*) to accede to the centre. Crucial to the use of space in *La Haine* is its imbrication with issues of social and racial identity, since '*la banlieue* has become the major euphemism for the racialization (and fragmentation) of city space' (Silverman 1999: 75). With the collapse of class identities in contemporary France, identity is defined more and more in terms of ethnic origins and the space one inhabits. And the two can become identified as one: ' "Je suis Arabe", dit un jeune habitant d'une cité parisienne. "Eh bien oui, je suis Arabe pace que j'habite avec les Arabes" ' ['I'm an Arab', says a youth from a suburb of Paris. 'Well, I'm an Arab because I live with Arabs'] (Lapeyronnie 2005: 211).

The presence of a central character from a Maghrebi background (Saïd), plus certain similarities between *La Haine* and the film most often cited as its French precursor, *Hexagone* (Chibane, 1993), have led to *La Haine* being loosely associated with *beur* cinema (see chapter 2). However, as Tarr makes clear, while expressing 'a healthy anger at the injustices and inequalities of contemporary French society', Kassovitz does little to 'highlight the specificity of [...] second- and third-generation immigrants of Maghrebi origin in France' (Tarr 2005: 78). If there is one ethnic specificity highlighted in *La Haine* above and beyond the situation of multicultural youth in the French *banlieue*, it is in fact Jewishness, as some of the film's most acute observers have noted. This may come as no surprise, since Kassovitz is Jewish himself, but has tended to be submerged by accounts of the film that stressed the so-called *black-blanc-beur* trio of protagonists. The question was perhaps first raised in 1996, in an essay noting the evocation of the Holocaust by Grunwalski, the old Jewish man the trio meet in the toilets, whose story 'anchors the young men's displacement in contemporary history' and reminds us that 'the presence of Vinz, Saïd and Hubert in the *banlieue* results from specific historical disruptions' (Reynaud 1996: 57). More recently, Loshitzky's sustained analysis of the film has viewed *La Haine* in a post-Holocaust and postcolonial context, where the meeting with Grunwalski and the young men's failure to understand its significance becomes an allegory of 'Europe's failure to understand the consequences of racism and to treat its postcolonial minorities justly, even in the light of the aftermath of the Holocaust' (Loshitzky 2005: 140).

La Haine has thus been seen as much more than an exhilarating and popular film, but as a yardstick which measures various divisions within French society, from the social schisms perceived in the nineties (see Higbee 2005) to the postcolonial issues of the current decade. As regards the latter, Lapeyronnie has written that social divisions in France (*la fracture sociale*) have been normalised by immigration policies and by the ghettoisation of non-white French communities (*la fracture coloniale*), so that the one informs and supports the other (Lapeyronnie 2005: 210). He adds that the *banlieue* is a quasi-colonial space where the divisions and power relations of the colonial period are still enacted in contemporary France: 'Comme des "colonisés", les habitants des "quartiers sensibles" ont d'abord le sentiment de ne pas avoir d'existence politique, [...] d'être des citoyens de seconde zone' [Like colonised peoples, the inhabitants of 'difficult areas' feel primarily that they have no political existence, that they are second-class citizens] (Lapeyronnie 2005: 210). This surely recalls the experience articulated in *La Haine* and confronted by Hubert, Saïd and Vinz throughout the film. Their journey can be compared to the dilemma in which colonised peoples find themselves, according to Fanon, caught between the desire to escape from 'hell' and the fear that the 'paradise' of the other is guarded by terrible beasts (Fanon 1961, cited in Lapeyronnie 2005: 212). In *La Haine* these beasts take the form of the skinheads and the brutal police encountered when the trio leave the *banlieue* and travel to central Paris. This 'disastrous journey' to France's 'social, cultural, and economic center [...] sends a message to the nation' (O'Shaugnessy 2005b: 84). That pessimistic but urgent message can also be traced in the recent conceptualising of *la fracture coloniale* or in the riots of November 2005 during the reporting of which *La Haine* was once again used by the media as shorthand for the anger of France's dispossessed multi-ethnic youth.

Hardship and fairytale in *Y aura-t-il de la neige à Noël?*

Where the most totemic films of *le jeune cinéma* – from *La Haine* to *La Vie rêvée des anges* – concern urban alienation, *Y aura-t-il de la neige à Noël?* (*Will It Snow For Christmas?*, Veysset, 1996) presents a raw and detailed account of rural poverty. Set on a farm near Avignon in the south of France, the film exemplifies an interest in the regions evident also Guédiguian's work (Marseilles), in *La Vie rêvée des anges* (Lille), and in the Dardenne brothers' relentless portrayal of southern Belgium. For Veysset, *Y aura-t-il de la neige à Noël?* was a deeply personal project, filmed in her home region and dedicated to her mother. It was also her first film and demonstrates that the *avances sur recettes* funding system can occasionally allow a complete outsider to enter the French film industry. Unlike the vast majority of new film-makers in France, Veysset did not study at a film school (of which IDHEC and FEMIS are the best known) and had very little experience in the industry – painting the décors for *Les Amants du Pont Neuf* (Carax, 1991), for example, and working as a driver for the director. *Y aura-t-il de la neige à Noël?* was none the less a critical and popular success, winning the 1997 César for best first film, and attracting over 800,000 spectators.

The narrative follows a family struggling to survive through summer, autumn and winter, with the climactic sequence falling on Christmas Eve. The unnamed mother (Dominique Reymond) is bringing up her seven illegitimate children on a farm where they are kept in poverty and forced to work by the absentee father (Daniel Duval). Gradually it transpires that the father has a legitimate family in a nearby town, but despite this and his persistent exploitation of his second family, the mother cannot bring herself to break from him. Finally, at Christmas, she submits to despair and attempts to gas herself and her children. In a deliberately ambiguous ending, which may be a fantasy or a miracle, she wakes to see snow falling and the family are saved. The brutal patriarchal control exercised by the father, the subsistence level poverty, the hard labour and the mother's increasing despair are to a degree alleviated by the sense of play and the bonds of love that hold the family together. These joyful emotions are placed in jeopardy by the father (he sexually harasses the eldest daughter; he denies the family fuel at Christmas; the children's toy farm is destroyed by his machinery) but they cannot be destroyed. Consequently there is throughout the film a persistent mingling of the everyday realities of impoverished labour (repeated shots of monotonous agricultural tasks) with playful activities, as when the younger children make boats out of marrows and sail them down an irrigation channel into the field where their older brother Bruno is working.

Despite its realist style, lack of music (apart from the opening and closing sequences), everyday setting and naturalistic performances, the film's realism is illuminated by fairy-tale elements, just as certain scenes are illuminated by an apparently natural but beautiful glow: the yellow sunlight on the bales of straw, the snow falling at the end. The mother and her seven children recall Snow White and the seven dwarves. She herself is an orphan, while the father is a threatening ogre. When two of the younger children travel to stay with (and work for) their father's legitimate family, their journey inside a lorry recalls Jonah in the belly of the whale. The final sequences also partake of the power of Christmas as a family ritual, and as 'the time for both joy and suicides' (Miller 1993: 26), an ambivalence captured in the film's open ending. The most powerful element of all within the narrative is the mother's love for her children, which she herself mythologises in the dream that she recounts for them towards the end of the film. Hence it has been suggested that 'par le seul miracle de l'amour, le réalisme devient féerique' [by the miracle of love, realism becomes fairytale] (Trémois 1997: 45). Moreover, by characterising the mother and the father as at once realistic and archetypal, and by avoiding any precise temporal references, any use of regional accents or any of the stereo-types associated with the Provence region, Veysset universalises her narrative so that it moves beyond the local in a way that not all *jeune cinéma* films can (see Grandena 2004).

La Vie rêvée des anges: no way out

One of the major popular and critical successes of the genre, *La Vie rêvée des anges* (*The Dream Life of Angels*, Zonca, 1998) is a sustained although at times slightly schematic exploration of capitalism, social exclusion, gender politics and personal relationships set in Lille in northern France. Its two leads, Elodie Bouchez and Natacha Régnier, shared the best actress prize at Cannes in 1998 and the film did well at the French box office. Initially at least a buddy movie, the film concerns Isa (Bouchez) and Marie (Régnier), two young women sharing someone else's flat and trying to make a living at a series of dead-end jobs. Isa is a dreamer, full of life and humour, whereas Marie is a cynic who, we learn, is damaged and vulnerable. While Isa becomes fascinated by Sandrine, the girl whose flat they occupy and who is in a coma, Marie gets embroiled in an abusive relationship with Chris, the young owner of a local nightclub. Sandrine appears to make a miraculous recovery, partly thanks to Isa's regular visits to her, but Marie commits suicide. The film ends with a bleak tracking shot past Isa and rows of other women working in an electronics factory.

As the powerful final image indicates, *La Vie rêvée des anges* considers social and economic issues (class relations, the struggle to find work) in tandem with an acute awareness of gender. Throughout the film, the fact that Isa and Marie are women as well as potentially homeless and in precarious employment means that they are doubly excluded. Marie's relationship with Chris is the simplest expression of the way that class politics and gender politics combine. But this is also apparent in the audition scene, where Isa and Marie are asked to mimic their favourite stars in order to land jobs as waitresses at the 'Hollywood' bar. To the performativity of gender apparent in this sequence is added a class dimension, according to which working-class women like Isa and Marie are asked to play the role of servant (*serveuse*) to middle-class (predominantly male) clients. There is also an allusion here to the audition scene in Jacques Rivette's seventies fantasy *Céline et Julie vont en bateau* (*Céline and Julie Go Boating*, 1974), but without the sense of rebellion, whereby Julie condemns her male audience as 'cosmic pimps' (see chapter 3). Isa shares the slightly hippified charm of Rivette's characters, but here the pressing economic necessities mean that there is no escape into the imagination and no overturning of the male bosses' power. To these economic pressures is added the sexual violence of Marie's relationship with Chris, with suicide providing the only exit. Before her death, Marie threatens to kill Isa. This confrontation, symbolic as it is of the aggressive individualism fostered by capitalism, predicts a similar moment in the Dardenne brothers' *Rosetta*. Both films could be said to represent the struggle of the marginalised to find a place in society.

Inside exclusion: *Rosetta*

Having begun their career filming documentaries, Belgium's Luc and Jean-Pierre Dardenne turned to fiction film in the nineties, and have won the Palme d'Or at Cannes twice, first for *Rosetta* in 1999 and again for *L'Enfant* (*The Child*) in 2005. The recognition granted *Rosetta* in particular – the first Belgian film to ever win at Cannes – signalled an acceptance that the new realism had a central place in Francophone cinema, although this was not without controversy, especially with the award for best actress going to the newcomer Émilie Dequenne rather than to a more established star (see Austin 2004).

Rosetta introduces what *Positif* magazine described as a new type of character, and what *Cahiers du cinéma* termed a female action hero (Audé 1999: 52; Burdeau 1999: 45). Living with her alcoholic mother on a caravan site outside a small Belgian town, Rosetta is desperate to find work and a place in mainstream society. Her physical battle to pull her mother and herself out of 'the hole' they are stuck in involves a series of repeated actions that we witness by means of the handheld camera that follows her daily routine: returning from looking for work in the town, entering the caravan site by a secret route, changing into her boots and checking her illicit fishing lines. As Rosetta, Dequenne gives a genuinely powerful performance characterised by downcast eyes and a brutal energy directed at securing paid work and a route out of poverty: hence the scenes in which she literally bites her predecessor's name tag off her new work apron, or clings relentlessly to the sack of flour which signifies her job and the security it brings. Her universe is almost atavistic in its focus on heating, food, water, and shelter: she has no experience of emotional contact, no time for

26

Émilie Dequenne in *Rosetta*

sentimentality, no knowledge of leisure. The physicality of this world is captured not only by the camerawork but by the almost incessant sounds of Rosetta's breathing, which comes in gasps as she fights with her bosses and her mother, or in sobs when she collapses in pain and despair. The intrusion of her co-worker Riquet into this world, meanwhile, is signalled by the threatening noise of his approaching mobylette. This close attention to sound also prepares for Rosetta's suicide attempt at the close of the film, when the primary clue to the meaning of her actions is the hissing of the gas, which gradually fades as the bottle runs empty.

Only rarely do we see Rosetta resting or at peace, initially when she refuels after losing her job at the factory, then when she is sharing a meal with Riquet, and finally when at her happiest, serving customers in the waffle stand. The price she is willing to pay for the job selling waffles, however, is the betrayal of Riquet, the only person we see offering her friendship and help: firstly by leaving him to drown in the river and then, having rescued him, by informing on him to her boss so that she can take his place. Rosetta's search for social inclusion thus reaches a moral crossroads in her relationship with Riquet. The conundrum concerns the lengths to which she will go to enter into what she calls 'normal life': according to Luc Dardenne, 'La question que nous voulions poser [...] c'est: "est-ce que je tue un autre pour avoir une place?"' [the question we wanted to ask was 'would I kill someone to get a place on the inside?'] (O'Shaugnessy 2005a: 94). The answer is no, not quite. Rosetta betrays Riquet but cannot bring herself to let him die in the river. Listening to his cries for help, she finally lifts her eyes from the ground in a gesture which is repeated at the end of the film when she seems to *see* for the first time Riquet's offer of friendship.

The film tries not to look at Rosetta from the outside, but to be *with* her, 'dans le cul des choses' [up the arse of things] as Jean-Pierre Dardenne has put it (Benoliel and Toubiana 1999: 51). Rosetta is represented without mediation in the form of sound-track music, voice-over commentary, or explicit socio-political or psychological explanations. The camera simply follows her in the relentless struggle for entry into 'normal life', as she strides from one shop or office to another looking for work, as she crosses the dual carriageway that separates her own territory from that of society at large, or in the bravura opening sequence as she storms through a factory to confront her boss, slamming doors in the spectator's face. Nonetheless, even within a realistic style that employs the shaky handheld camera, ambient sound, and everyday locations that recall documentary techniques or the purist cinema of the *Dogme* movement, the Dardenne brothers include a subtle form of symbolism which fits within their realist *mise en scène* but also hints at the moral meaning of certain gestures. At the end of *Le Fils* (*The Son*, 2002), for example, the lengths of wood wrapped by the woodwork teacher and his apprentice evoke the body of the former's son, killed by the latter; in working together to hold and bind the wood they are also burying the son and gesturing towards a future relationship in which his death can be understood and forgiven. Throughout *L'Enfant* (2005) Bruno struggles with physical burdens (the empty pram, the scooter) which express his growing sense of guilt. In *Rosetta*, the symbolism sees Rosetta literally hanging on to her work (the locker doors in the factory, the sack of flour), shutting herself away from emotional contact with Riquet (locking herself inside her waffle stand with a piece of wire), and struggling to carry the burden of her poverty and her responsibilities (the gas bottle which she carries like her own cross before dropping it in despair).

It has been observed that 'realism has a political dimension that overrides technique: the bringing of hitherto neglected groups onto the screen, the speaking of previously unheard truths and unexpressed attitudes' (Hallam and Marshment 2000: 47). This is certainly the case as regards *Rosetta*. It was received as a cinema of protest by *Positif*, which declared that the experience of watching the film was likely to give rise to 'une prise de conscience politique' [a new political awareness], and that the suffering of Rosetta and Riquet was 'datée, localisée, identifiable donc affrontable' [of a specific time and place, possible to identify and therefore possible to confront] (Audé 1999: 54). This was borne out by the subsequent actions of the Belgian government, which in 1999 introduced 'the Rosetta Plan', a measure to increase employment prospects for unskilled workers under twenty-five (see Morgan 2004: 534). While not explicitly intended to change the world they depict, the cinema of the Dardenne brothers has thus carried its raw energy off screen, into the realm of 'the real'.

Class war and family conflict in *Ressources humaines*

Laurent Cantet's *Ressources humaines* (*Human Resources*, 1999) refers back to the political counter-cinema of the late sixties and early seventies, and in particular to Godard's *Tout va bien* (1972, see chapter 2) in its focus on a factory occupation and on the issues of class identity and industrial relations. Unlike Godard, however, Cantet presents a realist narrative, avoiding Brechtian alienation techniques, and dynamising the industrial theme by presenting it as a painful and moving oedipal conflict between father and son. Franck (Jalil Lespert), a very promising business student, returns from Paris to take a placement in HR at the factory where his father (Jean-Claude Vallod) has worked for thirty years and where his sister and various friends and neighbours also work. Immediately, Franck finds himself caught between the working-class community-based identity of his family and his own role as part of the middle-class management, the 'other side'. Trying to apply his theoretical knowledge of business to a factory where industrial relations are bitter and recriminatory, Franck finds his own plan for a questionnaire to explore the workers' views of the new 35-hour-week legislation being used as a smokescreen behind which the management seek to close the welding section, making twelve workers redundant, including his father. With the help of a black worker named Alain, Franck steals the incriminating redundancy letter, and initiates a strike on the part of the unions. Thrown out of the factory by the boss, he finally has to confront his father's reluctance to join the strike.

Throughout *Ressources humaines*, realism is served not just by the mundane setting, but also by a complete lack of music, by naturalistic performances and by unobtrusive camerawork. Unlike the Dardennes brothers, Cantet keeps camera movement slow and simple, avoiding whip pans and shaky handheld camerawork. His use of symbolism, however, is comparable to the Dardennes', with apparently realistic gestures or images often serving as subtle metaphors. As in *Le Fils*, woodwork is presented as the only activity that allows father and son figures to coexist without tension or conflict: the quiet celebration of craftsmanship, of natural materials, of manual skills that might be passed on down the generations, generates a sense of potential continuity and shared identity that is in fact problematised throughout the narratives of both films. The impenetrability of the working class to Franck's eyes is symbolised by his baffled perusal of the machines in the factory, peering at them with no understanding of their function or significance. Another important metaphor in *Ressources humaines* is the act of bending down, especially as associated with manual labour. In Agnès Varda's documentary *Les Glaneurs et le glaneuse* (*The Gleaners and I*, 2000) the humble gesture of the agricultural labourer or the gleaner, bending over to pick up an object, is repeatedly celebrated (see below). The same gesture is represented in *Ressources humaines* as entirely submissive. It is seen first when the workers, initially locked out of the factory after Franck and Alain's break-in, crawl through a hole the boss smashes in the glass door in order to get back to work. It is repeated in the crucial confrontation between Franck and his father when the son kicks tool parts across the floor and watches his father gather them up in a gesture which symbolises his whole working life: stooping to pick up crumbs. This is the source of Franck's alienating sense of shame in his working-class origins and equally in his inability to accept those origins. Working-class identity is shouldered as a burden by his father rather than celebrated, and the 'sacrifices' Franck's parents have made place him outside the very community to which they still belong. As Francks puts it, shouting at his father during the factory occupation, what is at issue is 'La honte d'être fils d'un ouvrier, puis la honte aujourd'hui d'être un étudiant qui a honte d'être fils d'un ouvrier. La honte de sa classe' [the shame of being son of a worker, then the shame today of being a student who's ashamed to be the son of a worker; ashamed of his class].

The relationship between Franck and his father, across which the division between workers and management runs like a fault line, is constructed in the film by means of three deliberate but subtle looks, each using the shot/reverse shot which is the conventional cinematic shorthand for linking two characters. In the first of these looks, Franck's father glances towards him for guidance on how to fill out the questionnaire. Franck however has his back turned, and the gulf between them (a gulf created by their contrasting roles in the factory and hence in class relations) is further evoked by five seconds of blackness that separate the two images (the shot of the father and the reverse-shot of the son). The second example occurs once the father has been told by his son that he is being made redundant. While Franck speaks on the phone to the most militant of the union representatives, trying to arrange a strike, his father sits alone and despairing on the couch opposite. As the union rep tells Franck that he is risking his own future, the old man lifts his head and stares for a brief but intense moment at his son, before grabbing the phone and throwing him out of the house. This is the moment when the division between the two becomes deepest, doubled as it is by the strike action initiated by Franck but refused by his father, who will be the last worker to down tools despite the fact that his own job is being fought for. Finally, in the rather idealised holiday atmosphere of the strike, with the factory blockaded and the working-class community gathered outside, Franck's father (significantly positioned among his extended family and holding a grandchild on his knee) glances across at his son who is, as usual, sitting alone. For the first time there is a sense of communication, a shared glance, as they look at each other without the conflict or distance evoked in the previous examples. The film does not end, however, with this tentative optimism. Instead, in a stunning final exchange, Cantet opens up a new and equally fraught terrain by reintroducing the character of Alain and raising the question of racial (as well as class) identity. Having told Alain that he himself is leaving to go back to Paris, Franck then asks, 'Et toi, quand est-ce que tu pars? Elle est où ta place?' [And when are you going? where is your place?]. The conflicts and tensions that Franck has struggled with, even if partially resolved by the end of the film, are not the end of the story.

The documentary boom

Technology has played a part in the continuing success of *le jeune cinéma*, as it did with *la nouvelle vague* in the fifties. The cheap, portable and increasingly small DV cameras available from the late nineties onwards have allowed the shooting of films 'comme on écrit un roman ou son journal intime' [as you might write a novel or a diary] (Prédal 2002: 62). Astruc's *auteurist* ideal of 'la caméra-stylo' (see chapter 1) seems to have become a reality. This has contributed to a blurring of boundaries between the documentary, the first person narrative, and fiction: 'It becomes difficult to use the label "documentary" for a filmed journal, where the camera acts like a pen' (Jeancolas 2005: 160). Perhaps the most iconic documentary associated with the *jeune cinéma* – Agnès Varda's *Les Glaneurs et la glaneuse* (*The Gleaners and I*, 2000) – does indeed mix the intimate concerns of the diary with a broader testimony to the struggles of the dispossessed (see below).

Varda's film also coincides with a boom in the popularity of documentary in France around the years 2000–02. If the most popular French documentary of all time remains Jacques Cousteau's *Le Monde du silence* (*The Silent World*, 1955) with 4.6 million spectators, a number of recent documentaries have attracted audiences of well over a million, including *Microcosmos* (Nuridsany, 1996), *Le Peuple migrateur* (*Winged Migration*, Perrin, 2001) and *Être et avoir* (Philibert, 2002). The latter – a year in the life of a tiny primary school in the Auvergne region – became the first non-wildlife documentary to be seen by over a million people in France. As has become typical for documentary screenings, including those of *Les Glaneurs et la glaneuse*, the director took part in various tours to present the film to its audience – in Philibert's case, on sixty different occasions. Moreover, *Être et avoir* was also presented – alongside Michael Moore's *Bowling For Columbine* (2002) – at the Cannes film festival that year. Reporting on *Être et avoir*'s unexpected success, *Cahiers du cinéma* spoke of the documentary genre entering the realm of commercial art cinema for the first time (Cerf and Joyard 2002: 16). In 2003, following the triumph of *Être et avoir*, over twenty full-length documentaries were given a theatrical release in France. Just as the French television stations played a role in the production of *jeune cinéma* from Arte's *Tous les garçons et les filles de leur âge* series in 1994 onwards, they have also often produced (although not always distributed) recent documentaries. Again Arte was at the forefront, with its documentary strand 'La Vie en face' launched in 1995. In this influential TV strand, as in *jeune cinéma* as a whole, common topics were unemployment, marginalisation, exclusion, poverty, immigration, and the collapse of the family (see Marie 2005: 94). Arte also contributed to the production of various feature documentaries that were released in French cinemas, including *Être et avoir* in 2002.

Among the reasons *Cahiers du cinéma* gave for the popularity of *Être et avoir* were its communitarian spirit, its nostalgic depiction of childhood and of French rural life, and its refusal to engage with delicate 'youth' subjects such as drugs and violence (see Tesson 2002: 18). To this extent, the film can be seen as removed from the harsh realities so often portrayed in *le jeune cinéma*. But other less well-known documentaries certainly bear comparison with the fiction films of the new realism. Prime among them are the politically militant films that Laurent Marie has grouped together as the 'counterglobalization' sub-genre (see Marie 2005). The vast majority of documentaries in this sub-genre are opposed to globalisation and economic liberalism, and are didactic in their aims: 'As globalisation makes everything more complex, the documentarists become political educationalists' (Marie 2005: 93). A key example of this trend, released after Marie's study was written, is Hubert Sauper's unpicking of European intervention in Tanzania, *Le Cauchemar de Darwin* (*Darwin's Nightmare*, 2004, see below). A more playful but similarly engaged example is *Les Glaneurs et la glaneuse*, in which Varda demonstrates 'a more self-conscious form of documentary practice that favours [...] revealing the transparency of the constructed image' (Hallam and Marshment 2000: 241). It is a report on the self and on the other at the same time.

Bricolage of the self and the other: *Les Glaneurs et la glaneuse*

Positif magazine has noted that the recent documentary work of female film-makers such as Agnès Varda, Dominique Cabrera and Jacqueline Veuve tends to be expressed in the first person singular: 'L'engagement politique ou citoyen refait surface, mais la tendance est au glissement vers l'intime' [Political or social commitment reappears, but the tendency is for a slippage towards the personal] (Audé 2001: 95). In *Les Glaneurs et la glaneuse* Varda manages to hold together the personal and the political by means of *bricolage*, using her DV camera to create a DIY documentary about herself as an ageing gleaner of images, about the gleaners that still exist at the margins of French society, and about the construction of a film around both these topics which itself recycles and reuses 'waste' material such as the accidentally-filmed sequence she calls 'the dance of the lens cap'. Varda has called the film a 'road-documentary' and declared that it was born of her desire to film herself growing older, plus the wider questions 'Comment peut-on vivre des restes des autres? [...] Comment témoigner pour eux sans les gêner?' [How can one live on other people's leftovers? how can one bear witness for these people without disturbing them?] (Gauthier 2004: 202). The two apparently opposed topics are juxtaposed through Varda's ludic and self-conscious manipulation of documentary form, facilitated by the cheap, tiny, personalised technology offered by digital video (DV): 'C'est la petite caméra comme prolongement du geste (du peintre et de l'écrivain) mais [...] si elle favorise l'observation de soi-même (intimisme), elle facilite aussi les contacts, donc l'approche de l'autre' [This is the tiny camera as an extension of the gesture made by the painter or the writer, but if the DV camera favours intimate self-observation, it also allows one to make contact, hence reaching out to others] (Prédal 2002: 63).

The starting-point for the film's idiosyncratic journey around France is the entry in the Larousse dictionary under the verb *glaner* (to glean), and the famous painting by Millet that accompanies it. There follows a *bricolage*, a collection of interviews with modern-day gleaners and recyclers, with farmers, lawyers and artists, interspersed with Varda's journey from Paris to regions as diverse as Burgundy, Brittany and the Jura, glimpses of her ageing hands and greying hair, and intertextual references to paintings, literature, and early cinema. In one key sequence five minutes into the film, Varda establishes the titular analogy between herself and the gleaners by posing with a sheaf of wheat in front of Jules Breton's painting 'La Glaneuse', before replacing the wheat with her little digital camera and demonstrating the painterly effects it can achieve. She thus positions herself as an artist and painter of the digital age as well as someone who recuperates and recycles neglected images, including shots of mould, decay and rotting vegetables. As Mireille Rossello puts it, 'Varda plucks images from a reality where others had seen only banalities or ugliness' (Rosello 2001: 32). Critical accounts of the film have celebrated the image track while neglecting Varda's use of music, however. In keeping with the DIY spirit of the film, Varda includes two or three rap songs on the subject of recycling and waste. These raps are heard during the urban sequences showing markets, or abandoned furniture and white goods in the Parisian streets. The use of hip-hop is surely deliberate since it is a musical form that itself uses recycled materials, in the form of sampling.

The autobiographical strand within the film, anchored by reference to Rembrandt's self-portraits, centres on the signs of ageing in Varda's own body, especially her hands, which she films in extreme close-up. Discovering a clock without hands that has been thrown away, Varda takes it home and observes that 'On ne voit pas le temps qui passe' [You can't see time passing]. It is her own wrinkled hands, rather than the missing hands of the clock, that display the passing of time. The broader question of how waste is produced, rejected and re-consumed develops gradually alongside Varda's personal journey. Slowly a portrayal of French society appears, in which consumption is related to over-production, supermarket practices, and the perpetual transporting of produce over vast distances (symbolised by the repeated shots of lorries on the roads). At the margins of this 'society of over-consumption' as one interviewee calls it, are individuals who – whether from poverty, ethical choice, or artistic motivation – scavenge for waste products in the fields, the bins and the streets of France.

Certain scenes throughout *Les Glaneurs et la glaneuse* recall the celebration of 'la France profonde' and of old-fashioned ways which contributed to the popular appeal of *Être et avoir*. But Varda's film, despite glimpses of nostalgia and playful autobiography, makes a potentially radical socio-political intervention too. Varda herself intervenes in the narrative not just by drawing attention to her own practices as a film-maker, to chance events and coincidences (such as the painting of gleaners spotted in a bric-a-brac store) and to her own ageing body, but also by intentionally aiding the gleaners – for example telling the 'Restos du Cœur' that potatoes are being dumped in a particular location, or informing a group of gypsies that they do have the right to glean unwanted vegetables. The most potent statement on the value of the marginal within French society is made at the close of the film when Varda comes across a man called Alain at various Parisian markets. As well as feeding himself from the food left by street markets and shops, Alain works as a volunteer teaching French to immigrants from Africa. Significantly, he does so for free and outside of the state education system. He is thus, like the neglected or forgotten products whose value is reasserted throughout the film, outside the normalised system of production and consumption, yet extremely useful. His contribution to the potential success of French society is underlined when Varda focuses on him teaching his class the meaning of the words 'le succès' and 'la réussite'. (As with much of the film, the political point here is also a source of humour: hence Alain asks his students who is 'a success' and is given the normalised answer Céline Dion, when he himself might be another answer.) What is most striking about Alain's lesson is that France reappears at the end of the film as a *terre d'accueil* for immigrants thanks not to state-funded central systems but to the efforts of a marginalised gleaner.

Le Cauchemar de Darwin: globalised capitalism as trauma

In March 2005 *Positif* magazine ran a feature on political commitment in documentary cinema, focusing in particular on critiques of globalisation. Among the films highlighted was Hubert Sauper's *Le Cauchemar de Darwin* (*Darwin's Nightmare*, 2004), greeted with the exclamation 'Accablant!' [devastating!] (Gili 2005: 105). Sauper's powerful indictment of western capitalist intervention in Africa is set in Mwanza, a town on Lake Victoria in Tanzania. The introduction of the giant Nile perch into the lake has seen the local fishing industry hugely expanded and geared towards exports to Europe, with the support of the EU and the World Bank. As Sauper's wandering camera takes in a diverse collection of local people and stories, it becomes increasingly apparent that hell has been created on the shores of the lake. The water itself is deoxygenated and indigenous species of fish have been destroyed by the incomer. The same is also proving true of the local people. Just yards from the airstrip used by cargo planes, a tracking shot reveals an impoverished shanty-town with an incongruous giant Coke bottle in its midst and the bitterly ironic Coca Cola slogan 'Life tastes good'. It transpires that prostitution and HIV infection are rampant, and that many of the children of the fishermen are abandoned to sleep rough and sniff glue. While the perch flown to Europe represent Tanzania's prime export, the inhabitants of Mwanza are left to consume the heads left behind. Radio and television bulletins ask for humanitarian aid to alleviate a famine in central Tanzania, even while vast fish stocks are being flown out of the country. The implication of globalised capitalism in this situation is reiterated throughout the film, symbolised most tellingly by the fact that the street children make the glue they are addicted to by melting down the plastic boxes used to package the perch.

Sauper's digital camera, like Varda's in *Les Glaneurs et la glaneuese*, allows him to capture up close the faces and testimony of the people he comes across, as well as the landscapes which they inhabit. An almost biblical vision of a stormy wind blowing across the hills follows his interview with Richard the investigative journalist. A staggeringly bleak vista of black mud, fires, and heaps of rotting fish sets the scene for one local woman's account of how the blinding ammonia from fish carcases has cost her an eye. Another of Sauper's interviewees, the prostitute Eliza, is killed by a client during the shoot. Raphael, the night-watchman, acts as a guide to various locations and revelations. It is through his eyes and over his shoulder that we discover the central revelation in the film, as he reads the *East African* newspaper. Nonetheless Sauper scrupulously avoids the omniscient narrative voice-over which characterises traditional documentary. Nor does he intervene as Varda does in *Les Glaneurs et la glaneuse*. Instead Sauper lets the horror unfold gradually from the mouths of those whose lives are entangled in it. This includes the Russian pilots whose giant cargo planes carry the fish away, but who remain tight-lipped about what cargo they bring to Tanzania on arrival.

The representation of globalised capitalism as a brutal invasion, contributing to traumas such as the spread of HIV, the exploitation of the workforce, poverty, drug addiction, homelessness, and the destruction of the natural environment, is also a politically engaged call for (re)action. This type of militant and powerful documentary calls forth a painful witnessing from those caught up in the traumas but it also calls for a committed response from the viewer, since '"Witnessing involves not just empathy and motivation to help, but understanding the structure of injustice"' (Kaplan 2005: 22). It is the structural nature of the suffering portrayed in *Le Cauchemar de Darwin* that emerges most powerfully in the closing stages of the film, when the persistent question of what the planes carry to Africa is finally answered. Although initially the film appears formless, it is constructed as a puzzle, 'dont l'assemblage fait apparaître un tableau infernal' [which, when put together, creates a picture of hell] (Mangeot 2005: 35). The last piece of the puzzle involves an exposé in the *East African* newspaper, and subsequently an interview with its author, Richard, revealing that at least some of the cargo brought to the lake consists of illicit arms shipments which are facilitating warfare in neighbouring countries like the Congo.

Le Cauchemar de Darwin works to create what Kaplan has called in the context of trauma theory 'a deliberate ethical consciousness' and to ensure 'the public recognition of atrocities' (Kaplan 2005: 122). The film closes with a partial admission from one of the Russian pilots about the nature of the atrocity. Having previously described what the planes carry to Africa as either 'cargo' or 'equipment', he finally declares that in the past he has delivered weapons: 'children of Angola received guns [...] European children received grapes. This is business'. When he states that 'Africa brings life to Europe' the corollary, that Europe brings death to Africa, is left unspoken but chillingly clear. The film ends on this moment of silence, as the pilot concludes 'I have no more words'. As in Holocaust documentary, the representation of trauma has reached what Claude Lanzmann calls 'the border of the unspeakable' (see chapter 2).

Whether in fiction film or in documentary, or in a synthesis of the two, the realism central to *le jeune cinéma* is not simply a question of technique, of handheld cameras and ambient sound. The political relevance of realism lies elsewhere, in 'the bringing of hitherto neglected groups onto the screen, the speaking of previously unheard truths and unexpressed attitudes' (Hallam and Marshment 2000: 47). This is perhaps most evident in documentaries like *Les Glaneurs et la glaneuse* and *Le Cauchemar de Darwin*, both of which allow those on the margins of globalised capitalism to tell their own stories. But it is also manifest in the fictional narratives of *Rosetta*, *La Vie rêvée des anges* and even *La Haine*. The political importance of *le jeune cinéma* did not begin and end with the *sans-papiers* movement in 1997; it is also present in the films themselves, and it continues to resonate in the new millennium. In 2003 film-maker Vincent Dieutre called for a 'Third Cinema' where 'Going back to the individual, to the self, is not to leap-frog over the collective; on the contrary, it means to invent a new political language, in line with a radically new social order' (cited in Jeancolas 2005: 161). At its best, this is what the new realism of *le jeune cinéma* has achieved over the past ten or fifteen years.

References

Amiel, V. (1994), Tous les garçons et les filles de leur âge, *Positif*, 406, 32–5.

Audé, F. (1999), *Rosetta*: 1999, l'invention du réel: début, *Positif*, 465, 52–4.

Audé, F. (2001), L'au-delà documenté des réalisatrices, *Positif*, 481, 95–7.

Austin, G. (2004), The amateur actors of Cannes 1999: a shock to the (star) system, *French Cultural Studies*, 15:3, 251–63.

Benoliel, B., and Toubiana, S. (1999), 'Il faut être dans le cul des choses': Entretien avec Luc et Jean-Pierre Dardenne, *Cahiers du cinéma*, 539, 47–53.

Burdeau, E. (1999), La défricheuse, *Cahiers du cinéma*, 539, 45–6.

Cerf, J., and Joyard, O. (2002), Le réel est entré dans les salles, *Cahiers du cinéma*, November, 12–16.

Chabrol, C. (1976), *Et pourtant je tourne...*, Paris, Robert Laffont.

LIBRARY, UNIVERSITY OF C

Gauthier, G. (2004), *Un siècle du documentaire français*, Paris, Armand Colin.

Gili, J. A. (2005), *Le Cauchemar de Darwin*: L'emblème du prédateur, *Positif*, 529, 105.

Grandena, F. (2004), The provinces in contemporary French cinema: the case of *Y aura-t-il de la neige à Noël?*, *Studies in French Cinema*, 4:2, 13–120.

Hallam, J., and Marshment, M. (2000), *Realism and popular cinema*, Manchester, Manchester University Press.

Higbee, W. (2005), The return of the political, or designer visions of exclusion? The case for Mathieu Kassovitz's *fracture sociale* trilogy, *Studies in French Cinema*, 5:2, 123–35.

Jeancolas, J-P. (2005), The confused image of le jeune cinéma, *Studies in French Cinema*, 5:3, 157–61.

Jousse, T. (1995a), Prose combat, *Cahiers du cinéma*, 492, 32–5.

Jousse, T. (1995b), Le banlieue-film existe-t-il?, *Cahiers du cinéma*, 492, 36–9.

Kaplan, E. A. (2005), *Trauma Culture: The Politics of Terror and Loss in Media and Literature*, New Brunswick and London, Rutgers University Press.

Lapeyronnie, D. (2005), La banlieue comme théâtre colonial, ou la fracture coloniale dans les quartiers, in P. Blanchard, N. Bancel and S. Lemaire (eds), *La fracture coloniale: la société française au prisme de l'héritage colonial*, Paris, La Découverte, 209–17.

Loshitzky, Y. (2005), The post-Holocaust Jew in the age of postcolonialism: *La Haine* revisted, *Studies in French Cinema*, 5:2, 137–47.

Mangeot, P. (2005), Tombeau pour la Tanzanie, *Cahiers du cinéma*, 599, 34–5.

Marie, L. (2005), Le réel à l'attaque: French Documentary and Globalization, *French Politics, Culture and Society*, 23: 3, 88–105.

Marlière, P. (1997), Social suffering 'in their own words': Pierre Bourdieu's sociology of poverty, in S. Perry and M. Cross (eds), *Voices of France: Social, Political and Cultural Identity*, London, Pinter, 46–58.

Miller, D. (1993), A theory of Christmas, in D. Miller (ed.), *Unwrapping Christmas*, Oxford, Clarendon Press, 3–37.

Morgan, J. (2004), The social realism of body language in *Rosetta*, *The French Review*, 77:3, 526–35.

O'Shaugnessy, M. (2003), Post-1995 French cinema: return of the social, return of the political?, *Modern and Contemporary France*, 11:2, 189–204.

O'Shaugnessy, M. (2005a), *Reprise* et les nouvelles formes du cinéma politique, in G. Hayes and M. O'Shaugnessy (eds), *Cinéma et engagement*, Paris, L'harmattan, 83–98.

O'Shaugnessy, M. (2005b), Eloquent fragments: French fiction film and globalization, *French Politics, Culture and Society*, 23: 3, 75–88.

Pascal, M. (1994), Et si la télévision sauvait le cinéma de demain?, *Le Point*, 1163, 63–4.

Powrie, P. (1999), Heritage, history and 'new realism': French cinema in the 1990s, in P. Powrie (ed.), *French Cinema in the 1990s: Continuity and Difference*, Oxford, OUP, 1–21.

Prédal, R. (2002), *Le jeune cinéma français*, Paris, Nathan.

Reynaud, B. (1996), le 'hood: *Hate* and its neighbors, *Film Comment*, March–April, 53–8.

Rosello, M. (2001), Agnès Varda's *Les Glaneurs et la glaneuse*: portrait of the Artist as an old lady, *Studies in French Cinema*, 1:1, 29–36.

Silverman, M. (1999), *Facing Postmodernity: Contemporary French Thought on Culture and Society*, London, Routledge.

Tarr, C. (2005), *Reframing Difference:* Beur *and* Banlieue *Filmmaking in France,* Manchester and New York, Manchester University Press.

Tesson, C. (2002), Foi en l'école ou lois des armes, *Cahiers du cinéma,* November, 17–19.

Thomas, L. (2001), The representation of childhood in Sandrine Veysset's *Y aura-t-il de la neige à Noël?,* in L. Mazdon (ed.), *France on film: reflections on popular French culture,* London, Wallflower, 81–93.

Tobin, Y. (1995), Etat des (ban)lieues, *Positif,* September 1995, 28–30.

Trémois, C-M. (1997), *Les enfants de la liberté: le jeune cinéma français des années 90,* Paris, Seuil.

Filmography

4 aventures de Reinette et Mirabelle (Eric Rohmer, 1986)
8 femmes (*8 Women*, François Ozon, 2001)
37°2 le Matin (*Betty Blue*, Jean-Jacques Beineix, 1986)

A ma sœur! (*Fat Girl*, Catherine Breillat, 2001)
Une affaire de femmes (Claude Chabrol, 1988)
Un air de famille (*Family Resemblances*, Cédric Klapisch, 1996)
Alice ou la dernière fugue (*Alice*, Claude Chabrol, 1977)
L'Amant (Jean-Jacques Annaud, 1992)
Les Amants criminels (*Criminal Lovers*, François Ozon, 1999)
Les Amants du Pont-Neuf (Léos Carax, 1991)
L'Amour en fuite (*Love on the Run*, François Truffaut, 1979)
L'Anglaise et le duc (*The Lady and the Duke*, Eric Rohmer, 2001)
Après l'amour (Diane Kurys, 1992)
Astérix et Obélix contre César (*Asterix and Obelix take on Caesar*, Claude Zidi, 1999)
Au revoir les enfants (*Goodbye Children*, Louis Malle, 1987)
Baise-moi (Virginie Despentes, Coralie Trinh Thi, 2001)
La Balance (Bob Swaim, 1982)
Banlieue 13 (*District 13*, Pierre Morel, 2004)
Beau travail (Claire Denis, 1998)
Une belle fille comme moi (*Such a Gorgeous Kid Like Me*, François Truffaut, 1972)
Borsalino (Jacques Deray, 1970)
Borsalino et compagnie (*Blood on the Streets*, Jacques Deray, 1974)
Le Boucher (Claude Chabrol, 1969)
Les Bronzés (Patrice Leconte, 1978)
Les Bronzés font du ski (Patrice Leconte, 1979)
Buffet froid (Bertrand Blier, 1979)
Bye-Bye (Karim Dridi, 1995)
Caché (*Hidden*, Michael Haneke, 2005)
La Cage aux folles (*Birds of a Feather*, Edouard Molinaro, 1978)
La Cage aux folles II (Edouard Molinaro, 1980)
Camille Claudel (Bruno Nuytten, 1988)
Le Cauchemar de Darwin (*Darwin's Nightmare*, Hubert Sauper, 2004)
Céline et Julie vont en bateau (*Céline and Julie Go Boating*, Jacques Rivette, 1974)

La Cérémonie (*Judgement in Stone*, Claude Chabrol, 1995)
Cet obscur objet du désir (*That Obscure Object of Desire*, Luis Buñuel, 1977)
Le Chagrin et la pitié (*The Sorrow and the Pity*, Marcel Ophüls, 1971)
Le Château de ma mère (*My Mother's Castle*, Yves Robert, 1990)
Chocolat (Claire Denis, 1988)
Le Cinquième Élément (*The Fifth Element*, Luc Besson, 1997)
La Cité des enfants perdus (*City of Lost Children*, Jean-Pierre Jeunet, Marc Caro, 1995)
Le Colonel Chabert (Yves Angelo, 1994)
Coup de foudre (*Entre Nous*, Diane Kurys, 1983)
Coup de torchon (*Clean Slate*, Bertrand Tavernier, 1981)
Le Crabe-Tambour (Pierre Schoendoerffer, 1977)
Le Cri du hibou (*The Cry of the Owl*, Claude Chabrol, 1987)
La Crise (Coline Serreau, 1992)
Cyrano de Bergerac (Jean-Paul Rappeneau, 1990)
Danton (Andrzej Wajda, 1982)
De battre mon cœur s'est arrêté (*The Beat That My Heart Skipped*, Jacques Audiard, 2005)
Delicatessen (Jean-Pierre Jeunet, Marc Caro, 1991)
Le Dernier Combat (Luc Besson, 1983)
Le Dernier Métro (*The Last Metro*, François Truffaut, 1980)
Les Deux Anglaises et le continent (*Anne and Muriel*, François Truffaut, 1971)
Dien Bien Phu (Pierre Schoendoerffer, 1992)
Un dimanche à la campagne (*Sunday in the Country*, Bertrand Tavernier, 1984)
Diva (Jean-Jacques Beineix, 1980)
Docteur Petiot (Christian de Chalonge, 1990)
Domicile conjugal (*Bed and Board*, François Truffaut, 1970)
Drôle de Félix (Olivier Ducastel, Jacques Martineau, 1999)
L'Eau froide (*Cold Water*, Olivier Assayas, 1994)
Emmanuelle (Just Jaeckin, 1974)
L'Enfant (*The Child*, Dardenne brothers, 2005)
L'Enfer (*Torment*, Claude Chabrol, 1994)
L'Été meurtrier (*One Deadly Summer*, Jean Becker, 1983)
Être et avoir (Nicholas Philibert, 2002)
Le Fabuleux Destin d'Amélie Poulain (*Amélie*, Jean-Pierre Jeunet, 2001)
Fahrenheit 451 (François Truffaut, 1966)
La Femme d'à côté (*The Woman Next Door*, François Truffaut, 1981)
Le Fils (*The Son*, Dardenne brothers, 2002)
Une flamme dans mon cœur (*A Flame In My Heart*, Alain Tanner, 1987)
Flic ou voyou (Georges Lautner, 1979)
Fort Saganne (Alain Corneau, 1984)
Gazon maudit (*French Twist*, Josiane Balasko, 1995)
Le Genou de Claire (*Claire's Knee*, Eric Rohmer, 1970)
Germinal (Claude Berri, 1993)
Les Glaneurs et la glaneuse (*The Gleaners and I*, Agnès Varda, 2000)
La Gloire de mon père (*My Father's Glory*, Yves Robert, 1990)
Gouttes d'eau sur pierres brûlantes (*Water Drops on Burning Rocks*, François Ozon, 1999)
Le Grand Bleu (*The Big Blue*, Luc Besson, 1988)
La Grande Bouffe (*Blow-Out*, Marco Ferreri, 1973)
La Guerre sans nom (*The Undeclared War*, Bertrand Tavernier, 1992)
La Haine (*Hate*, Mathieu Kassovitz, 1995)
Un héros très discret (*A Self-Made Hero*, Jacques Audiard, 1996)
Hexagone (Malik Chibane, 1994)
L'Histoire d'Adèle H. (*The Story of Adèle H.*, François Truffaut, 1975)

Histoire de Marie et Julien (Jacques Rivette, 2003)
Un homme amoureux (*A Man in Love*, Diane Kurys, 1987)
L'Horloger de Saint-Paul (*The Watchmaker of Saint-Paul*, Bertrand Tavernier, 1974)
India Song (Marguerite Duras, 1975)
Indochine (Régis Warnier, 1992)
Inguélézi (François Dupeyron, 2004)
Les Innocents aux mains sales (*Innocents With Dirty Hands*, Claude Chabrol, 1975)
Irréversible (Gaspar Noé, 2002)
Jacquot de Nantes (Agnès Varda, 1991)
J'ai 8 ans (Yann Le Masson, Olga Poliakoff, 1961)
J'ai pas sommeil (Claire Denis, 1993)
Jane B. par Agnès V. (Agnès Varda, 1987)
Jean de Florette (Claude Berri, 1986)
Je vous salue Marie (*Hail, Mary*, Jean-Luc Godard, 1985)
L.627 (Bertrand Tavernier, 1992)
Lacombe, Lucien (Louis Malle, 1974)
Lancelot du Lac (*Lancelot of the Lake*, Robert Bresson, 1974)
La Lectrice (Michel Deville, 1988)
Léon (Luc Besson, 1994)
La Ligne de démarcation (Claude Chabrol, 1966)
Un long dimanche de fiançailles (*A Very Long Engagement*, Jean-Pierre Jeunet, 2004)
Lucie Aubrac (Claude Beri, 1997)
La Lune dans le caniveau (*The Moon in the Gutter*, Jean-Jacques Beineix, 1983)
Madame Bovary (Claude Chabrol, 1991)
Manon des sources (Claude Berri, 1986)
Marche à l'ombre (Michel Blanc, 1984)
Le Mari de la coiffeuse (*The Hairdresser's Husband*, Patrice Leconte, 1990)
La Marquise d'O (Eric Rohmer, 1976)
Mauvais sang (*The Night Is Young*, Léos Carax, 1986)
Mensonge (*The Lie*, François Margolin, 1991)
Merci la vie (*Thank You, Life*, Bertrand Blier, 1991)
Monsieur Hire (Patrice Leconte, 1989)
Monsieur Klein (Joseph Losey, 1976)
Muriel ou le temps d'un retour (*Muriel*, Alain Resnais, 1963)
Nikita (Luc Besson, 1990)
Le Nom de la rose (*The Name of the Rose*, Jean-Jacques Annaud, 1986)
La Nuit américaine (*Day for Night*, François Truffaut, 1973)
La Nuit de Varennes (*That Night in Varennes*, Ettore Scola, 1982)
Nuit et brouillard (*Night and Fog*, Alain Resnais, 1955)
Les Nuits fauves (*Savage Nights*, Cyril Collard, 1992)
L'Œil de Vichy (*The Eye of Vichy*, Claude Chabrol, 1993)
L'Ours (*The Bear*, Jean-Jacques Annaud, 1988)
Le Pacte des loups (*Brotherhood of the Wolf*, Christophe Gans, 2001)
Papy fait de la Résistance (Jean-Marie Poiré, 1983)
Le Parfum d'Yvonne (Patrice Leconte, 1994)
Passion (Jean-Luc Godard, 1982)
Perceval le Gallois (Eric Rohmer, 1978)
Le Père Noël est une ordure (Jean-Marie Poiré, 1982)
Péril en la demeure (*Death in a French Garden*, Michel Deville, 1985)
Police (Maurice Pialat, 1985)
Poussière d'ange (*Angel Dust*, Edouard Niermans, 1987)
Prénom Carmen (Jean-Luc Godard, 1983)

Préparez vos mouchoirs (*Get Out Your Handkerchiefs*, Bertrand Blier, 1978)
La Promesse (*The Promise*, Dardenne brothers, 1996)
Le Rayon vert (*The Green Ray*, Eric Rohmer, 1986)
Regarde la mer (*See the Sea*, François Ozon, 1997)
La Reine Margot (Patrice Chéreau, 1994)
René la canne (Francis Girod, 1977)
Ressources humaines (*Human Resources*, Laurent Cantet, 1999)
Le Retour de Martin Guerre (*The Return of Martin Guerre*, Daniel Vigne, 1982)
Romance (Catherine Breillat, 1998)
Romuald et Juliette (Coline Serreau, 1989)
Rosetta (Dardenne brothers, 1999)
Rue cases nègres (*Black Shack Alley*, Euzhan Palcy, 1983)
Saint Ange (Pascal Laugier, 2004)
Samia (Philippe Faucon, 2000)
Sans toit ni loi (*Vagabonde*, Agnès Varda, 1985)
Sauve qui peut (la vie) (*Slow Motion*, Jean-Luc Godard, 1979)
Série noire (Alain Corneau, 1979)
Seul contre tous (*I Stand Alone*, Gaspard Noé, 1998)
Shoah (Claude Lanzmann, 1985)
Sitcom (François Ozon, 1998)
Le Souffle au cœur (*Murmur of the Heart*, Louis Malle, 1971)
Sous le sable (*Under the Sand*, François Ozon, 2000)
Sous le soleil de Satan (*Under Satan's Sun*, Maurice Pialat, 1987)
Subway (Luc Besson, 1985)
Sur mes lèvres (*Read My Lips*, Jacques Audiard, 2001)
Swimming Pool (François Ozon, 2002)
Tango (Patrice Leconte, 1993)
Tatie Danielle (Etienne Chatiliez, 1990)
Taxi (Gérard Pirès, 1998)
Taxi 2 (Gérard Krawczyk, 2000)
Tenue de soirée (*Evening Dress*, Bertrand Blier, 1986)
Tous les matins du monde (Alain Corneau, 1992)
Tout va bien (Jean-Luc Godard, 1972)
Trois hommes et un couffin (*Three Men and a Cradle*, Coline Serreau, 1985)
Trop belle pour toi! (*Too Beautiful For You*, Bertrand Blier, 1989)
Trouble Every Day (Claire Denis, 2001)
Les Valseuses (Bertrand Blier, 1974)
Van Gogh (Maurice Pialat, 1991)
Vendredi soir (Claire Denis, 2002)
La Vie est un long fleuve tranquille (*Life is a Long Quiet River*, Etienne Chatiliez, 1988)
La Vie et rien d'autre (*Life and Nothing But*, Bertrand Tavernier, 1989)
La Vie rêvée des anges (*The Dream-Life of Angels*, Eric Zonca, 1998)
Les Visiteurs (Jean-Marie Poiré, 1993)
Y aura-t-il de la neige à Noël? (*Will It Snow For Christmas?*, Sandrine Veysset, 1997)
Zidane, un portrait du 21e siècle (Philippe Parreno, Douglas Gordon, 2006)

Index